Tson
Final Expos

Tsong-kha-pa's Final Exposition of Wisdom

By Jeffrey Hopkins

Edited by Kevin Vose

Snow Lion
Boulder

Snow Lion
An imprint of Shambhala Publications, Inc.
4720 Walnut Street
Boulder, Colorado 80301
www.shambhala.com

9 8 7 6 5 4 3

Printed in the United States of America

♾ This edition is printed on acid-free paper that meets the American National Standards Institute Z39.48 Standard.
♻ Shambhala Publications makes every effort to print on recycled paper. For more information please visit www.shambhala.com.
Snow Lion is distributed worldwide by Penguin Random House, Inc., and its subsidiaries.

Library of Congress Cataloging-in-Publication Data

Hopkins, Jeffrey.
Tsong-kha-pa's final exposition of wisdom / by Jeffrey Hopkins; edited by Kevin Vose.
p. cm.
Includes bibliographical references and index.
ISBN 978-1-55939-297-6 (alk. paper)
1. Tsoṅ-kha-pa Blo-bzaṅ-grags-pa, 1357–1419. Skyes bu gsum gyi ñams su blaṅ ba'i byaṅ chub lam gyi rim pa. 2. Tsoṅ-kha-pa Blo-bzaṅ-grags-pa, 1357–1419. Dbu ma la 'jug pa 'i rgya cher bśad pa dgoṅs pa rab tu gsal ba. 3. Śes-rab-rgyal-mtshan, Dol-po-pa, 1292–1361. 4. Candrakīrti. Madhyamakāvatāra. 5. Dge-lugs-pa (Sect)—Doctrines. 6. Lam-rim. 7. Wisdom—Religious aspects—Buddhism. I. Vose, Kevin, 1970– II. Title.
BQ7950.T754S55 2008
294.3'420423—dc22
2007049614

Contents

Preface

I first went to India in 1972 on a dissertation research Fulbright fellowship, where although advised by the Fulbright Commission in New Delhi not to go to Dharmsala because of possible political complications, I went after a brief trip to Banaras. There I found that the Dalai Lama was about to begin a sixteen-day series of four- to six-hour lectures on Tsong-kha-pa Lo-sang-drak-pa's *Medium-Length Exposition of the Stages of the Path to Enlightenment Practiced by Persons of Three Capacities.* Despite my cynicism that a governmentally appointed reincarnation could possibly have much to offer, I slowly became fascinated first with the strength and speed of his articulation and then, much more so, with the touching meanings that were conveyed.

Enthused by his commentary, I translated the section on special insight shortly thereafter, checking about half of it with Lati Rinpoche by orally retranslating the English back into Tibetan. Returning to it in 2002,[a] I could recognize from my intervening work (on another Fulbright) on Dol-po-pa Shay-rap-gyel-tsen's *Mountain Doctrine: Final Unique Quintessential Instructions*[b] what Tsong-kha-pa was often seeking to refute. Thus this book first provides Tsong-kha-pa's presentation of special insight, as well as the sections on the object of negation and on the two truths in his *Illumination of the Thought: Extensive Explanation of (Chandrakīrti's) "Supplement to (Nāgārjuna's) 'Treatise on the Middle,'"* and then details Dol-po-pa's views and Tsong-kha-pa's reactions to them.

The chapter titles in the translations have been added for the sake of accessibility.

Jeffrey Hopkins
Emeritus Professor of Tibetan Studies
University of Virginia

[a] In 2007, I checked the translation against that by my old friend Robert Thurman as "The Middle Transcendent Insight" in *Life and Teachings of Tsong Khapa*, 108-185 (Dharmsala, India: Library of Tibetan Works and Archives, 1982).

[b] *ri chos nges don rgya mtsho zhes bya ba mthar thug thun mong ma yin pa'i man ngag;* see Jeffrey Hopkins, *Mountain Doctrine: Tibet's Fundamental Treatise on Other-Emptiness and the Buddha Matrix* (Ithaca, N.Y.: Snow Lion Publications, 2006).

Technical Notes

Please notice that:

- Full bibliographical references are given in the footnotes at first citation.
- For translations and editions of texts, see the Bibliography.
- The names of Indian Buddhist schools are translated into English in an effort to increase accessibility for non-specialists.
- For the names of Indian scholars and systems cited in the body of the text, *ch, sh,* and *ṣh* are used instead of the more usual *c, ś,* and *ṣ* for the sake of easy pronunciation by non-specialists; however, *cch* is used for *cch,* not *chchh.* In parentheses the usual transliteration system for Sanskrit is used.
- Transliteration of Tibetan is done in accordance with a system devised by Turrell Wylie; see "A Standard System of Tibetan Transcription," *Harvard Journal of Asiatic Studies* 22 (1959): 261-267.
- The names of Tibetan authors and orders are given in "essay phonetics" for the sake of easy pronunciation.

Part One: *Three Translations of Tsong-kha-pa's Views*

Background

The yogi-scholar Tsong-kha-pa Lo-sang-drak-pa[a] (1357-1419), who founded the Ge-luk-pa order of Tibetan Buddhism, was the fourth in a family of six sons in the Tsong-kha region of the northeastern province of Tibet called Am-do.[b] He took layperson's vows at the age of three from the Fourth Karma-pa Röl-pay-dor-jay[c] and took novice monastic vows at seven. Studying and practicing in Am-do until age sixteen, he left for Central Tibet, never to return to Am-do. In Central Tibet, Chö-jay Don-drup-rin-chen[d] advised him to study the Five Great Books of Indian Buddhism:

1. the coming Buddha Maitreya's *Ornament for Clear Realization*,[e] a rendering of the hidden teaching on the path structure in the Perfection of Wisdom Sūtras
2. Dharmakīrti's *Commentary on (Dignāga's) "Compilation of Prime Cognition,"*[f] largely epistemological and logical studies
3. Chandrakīrti's *Supplement to (Nāgārjuna's) "Treatise on the Middle,"*[g] a

---

[a] *tsong kha pa blo bzang grags pa.*

[b] *a mdo.*

[c] *karma pa rol pa'i rdo rje;* 1340-1383.

[d] *chos rje don grub rin chen;* 1309-1385.

[e] *mngon rtogs rgyan, abhisamayālaṃkāra;* Peking 5184, vol. 88. A notable exception is the curriculum at the monastery of the Paṇ-chen Lama, Tra-shi-hlün-po Monastic University (*bkra shis lhun po*), where Dharmakīrti's *Pramāṇavārttika* is the topic of this initial long period of study.

[f] *tshad ma rnam 'grel, pramāṇavarttika;* Peking 5709, vol. 130.

[g] *dbu ma la 'jug pa, madhyamakāvatāra;* Peking 5261, Peking 5262, vol. 98. Since Chandrakīrti often refers to Nāgārjuna's *Treatise on the Middle* (*dbu ma'i bstan bcos, madhyamakaśāstra*) merely by the appellation *madhyamaka*, the *madhyamaka* of "*madhyamakāvatāra*" is held to refer to a text propounding the middle, specifically Nāgārjuna's *Treatise on the Middle.* My translation of *avatāra* (*'jug pa*) as "supplement" is controversial; others use "introduction" or "entrance," both of which are attested common translations in such a context. My translation is based on the explanation by Tsong-kha-pa that Chandrakīrti was filling in holes in Nāgārjuna's *Treatise on the Middle;* see Tsong-kha-pa, Kensur Lekden, and Jeffrey Hopkins, *Compassion in Tibetan Buddhism* (London: Rider, 1980; reprint, Ithaca, N.Y.: Snow Lion Publications, 1980), 96-99. Among the many meanings of the Tibetan term for *avatāra, 'jug pa* can mean "to affix" or "to add on." To summarize the oral teachings of the late Ken-sur Nga-wang-lek-den:

> *Avatāra* means "addition" in the sense that Chandrakīrti's text is a supplement historically necessary so as to clarify the meaning of Nāgārjuna's *Treatise on the Middle.* He wanted to make clear that the *Treatise* should not be interpreted according to the Mind-Only system or according to the Middle Way

presentation of the explicit teaching on the emptiness of inherent existence in the Perfection of Wisdom Sūtras

4. Vasubandhu's *Treasury of Manifest Knowledge,*[a] a compendium of the types and natures of afflicted phenomena and their causes as well as the pure phenomena that act as antidotes to them and the states of cessation brought about by these antidotes
5. Guṇaprabha's *Aphorisms on Discipline,*[b] the source text for formulated codes of discipline.

These five texts became the basic curriculum of sūtra study in the monasteries that Tsong-kha-pa and his followers established.

From childhood, Tsong-kha-pa's study and practice was interlaced with tantra, which became the focus of a majority of his writings. He studied a great deal with masters of the Ka-gyu[c] and Sa-kya[d] orders. As

---

Autonomy School (*dbu ma rang rgyud pa, svatantrikamādhyamika*), the founding of which is attributed to Bhāvaviveka. During Nāgārjuna's lifetime, Bhāvaviveka had not written his commentary on the *Treatise*, nor had he founded his system; therefore, it was necessary later to supplement Nāgārjuna's text to show why it should not be interpreted in such a way. Moreover, it is said that Chandrakīrti sought to show that a follower of Nāgārjuna should ascend the ten grounds by practicing the vast paths necessary to do so. This is because some interpret the Middle Way perspective as nihilistic. They see it as a means of refuting the general existence of phenomena rather than just their inherent existence and conclude that it is not necessary to engage in practices such as the cultivation of compassion. Therefore, in order to show that it is important to engage in three central practices—compassion, non-dual understanding, and the altruistic mind of enlightenment—and to ascend the ten Bodhisattva grounds, Chandrakīrti—in reliance on Nāgārjuna's *Precious Garland*—wrote this supplementary text.

See Jeffrey Hopkins, *Buddhist Advice for Living and Liberation: Nāgārjuna's Precious Garland* (Ithaca, N.Y.: Snow Lion Publications, 1998).

This Tibetanized reading of *'jug pa* as "supplement" accords with the Tibetan term *rtags 'jug* (*liṅgāvaṃtāra* [Sarat Chandra Das, *A Tibetan-English Dictionary* (Calcutta: 1902; reprint, Delhi: Motilal Banarsidass, 1969, 1970; compact reprint, Kyoto, Japan: Rinsen Book Company, 1981], 535), "the affixing of gender," referring to the usage of letters—identified by gender in Tibetan grammar—in various positions in a syllable. It also perhaps accords with the fifth meaning given in Vaman Shivaram Apte, *Sanskrit-English Dictionary* (Poona, India: Prasad Prakashan, 1957), 163, "Any new appearance, growth, rise," though it seems that not much of a case can be made from the Sanskrit. Of course, such a supplement also serves as an introduction, or means of entry, to Nāgārjuna's *Treatise.*

[a] *chos mngon pa'i mdzod, abhidharmakośa;* Peking 5590, vol. 115.

[b] *'dul ba'i mdo, vinayasūtra;* Peking 5619, vol. 123.

[c] *bka' brgyud.*

[d] *sa skya.*

Stephen Batchelor says in *The Tibet Guide:*[a]

> While still very young he was recognized as possessing unusual spiritual qualities and as a young man was sent to Central Tibet to further his understanding of Buddhism in the more cultured region of the country. The first monastery he visited was that of Drigung, where he studied medicine and the doctrines of the Kagyu lineage. From here he proceeded to Netang, Samye, Zhalu, and Sakya monasteries. He met his main teacher Rendawa at Tsechen Monastery just outside Gyantse. For many years he studied the full range of Buddhist philosophy, including the more esoteric tantric systems. He then retreated to Olka, north of the Brahmaputra downstream from Tsetang, and spent the next four years in intense retreat. Upon returning to society he found himself much in demand as a teacher. One place where he taught was the hill in Lhasa on which the Potala was eventually built. Together with Rendawa he stayed for some time at Reting, where he composed his most famous work, *The Great Exposition of the Stages on the Path to Enlightenment.* After another meditation and writing retreat at Chöding Hermitage (above where Sera monastery now is), he founded, in 1409, the famous annual Mönlam (prayer) festival in Lhasa, which, after a twenty-five year hiatus, was reinaugurated in 1986....
>
> During his lifetime Tsongkhapa was regarded as a remarkable spiritual figure whose genius and saintliness held him above the sectarian differences of his times. Although greatly inspired by the example of Atisha, to the point of attributing authorship of his own major written work to him, and by the spirit of the Kadampa tradition, Tsongkhapa nonetheless studied widely with representatives of all the major orders in Tibet and assimilated their lineages.

Though some question whether Tsong-kha-pa intended to found a new order, it strikes me that the construction of seventy buildings in one

[a] Stephen Batchelor, *The Tibet Guide: Central and Western Tibet* (Boston: Wisdom Publications, 1998), 129-131. For a short biography, see Geshe Ngawang Dhargey, "A Short Biography," in *Life and Teachings of Tsong Khapa*, ed. Robert A. F. Thurman, trans. mainly by Khamlung Tulku (Dharmsala, India: Library of Tibetan Works and Archives, 1982), 4-39. For an inspired and inspiring account, see Robert A. F. Thurman, *Tsong Khapa's Speech of Gold in the Essence of True Eloquence* (Princeton, N.J.: Princeton University Press, 1984), 65-89.

year at the monastery he founded, Gan-den,[a] and his later instruction to two students to build other monastic universities in the Hla-sa[b] Valley—Dre-pung[c] coming to have 2,000 monastic residents one year after commencement of construction[d]—suggest that he did indeed intend to form a new order. In any case, the writings of his immediate followers, such as Gyel-tsap,[e] Ke-drup,[f] and the latter's brother Ba-so-chö-kyi-gyel-tsen,[g] clearly indicate the raising of this seminal teacher to the status of saint and founder of a new religious order.

His followers eventually came to have great influence throughout a vast region stretching from Kalmyk Mongolian areas, where the Volga empties into the Caspian Sea (in Europe), to Outer and Inner Mongolia, and the Buriat Republic of Siberia, as well as to most parts of Tibet and Ladakh. They established a system of education centered in monastic universities of varying size that became some of the prime centers of religious education in the region.

Tsong-kha-pa composed five expositions on the view of emptiness:[h]

1. In 1402, at the age of forty-five, he wrote the *Great Exposition of the Stages of the Path*,[i] which has a long and complicated section on special insight[j] into emptiness.
2. Five years later, when he was fifty, he began writing a commentary

---

[a] *dga' ldan.*

[b] *lha sa.*

[c] *'bras spungs.*

[d] Stephen Batchelor, *The Tibet Guide* (London: Wisdom Publications, 1987), 145.

[e] *rgyal tshab dar ma rin chen,* 1364-1432.

[f] *mkhas grub dge legs dpal bzang,* 1385-1438, born in the western province of Tibet, *gtsang*, in *ldog gzhung*. See José Ignacio Cabezón, *A Dose of Emptiness: An Annotated Translation of the* stong thun chen mo *of mKhas grub dGe legs dpal bzang* (Albany, N.Y.: State University of New York Press, 1992), 14.

[g] *ba so chos kyi rgyal mtshan,* born 1402.

[h] See Jeffrey Hopkins, *Emptiness in the Mind-Only School of Buddhism* (Berkeley: University of California Press, 1999), 12. My brief rehearsal of his works is drawn from Elizabeth Napper, *Dependent-Arising and Emptiness* (London: Wisdom Publications, 1989), 6-7.

[i] *lam rim chen mo;* P6001, vol. 152. For a translation into English, see Tsong-kha-pa, *The Great Treatise on the Stages of the Path to Enlightenment*, vols. 1-3, trans. and ed. Joshua W. C. Cutler and Guy Newland (Ithaca, N.Y.: Snow Lion Publications, 2000-2004). I refer to page numbers of this translation throughout this work. For a translation of the part on the excessively broad object of negation, see Elizabeth Napper, *Dependent-Arising and Emptiness*, 153-215; for a translation of the part on the excessively narrow object of negation, see William Magee, *The Nature of Things: Emptiness and Essence in the Geluk World* (Ithaca, N.Y.: Snow Lion Publications, 1999), 179-192.

[j] *lhag mthong, vipaśyanā.*

on Nāgārjuna's *Treatise on the Middle,*[a] called *Ocean of Reasoning,*[b] at Chö-ding[c] Hermitage above what became Se-ra Monastic University on the northern outskirts of Hla-sa, but in the midst of explicating the first chapter, he foresaw that there would be interruptions if he stayed there. Thus, he left Chö-ding Hermitage for another hermitage at Se-ra, Ra-ka Precipice,[d] where he wrote the *Treatise Differentiating Interpretable and Definitive Meanings: The Essence of Eloquence.*[e] (I imagine that he felt the need to compose his own independent work on the view of emptiness in the Great Vehicle schools as background for his commentary on Nāgārjuna's treatise. If this is so, he wrote *The Essence* as an overarching structure in which that commentary could be understood.)

3. After completing *The Essence* in 1408,[f] he returned to commenting on Nāgārjuna's *Treatise on the Middle,* completing the *Ocean of Reasoning.*
4. At age fifty-eight in 1415, he wrote the *Medium-Length Exposition of the Stages of the Path,*[g] from which a translation of the section on special insight is included in this book.[h]
5. At age sixty-one, one year before his death, he wrote a commentary

---

[a] *dbu ma rtsa ba'i tshig le'ur byas pa shes rab ces bya ba, prajñānāmamūlamadhyamakakārikā;* P5224, vol. 95.

[b] *dbu ma rtsa ba'i tshig le'ur byas pa shes rab ces bya ba'i rnam bshad rigs pa'i rgya mtsho;* P6153, vol. 156. For a translation of the entire text, see Geshe Ngawang Samten and Jay L. Garfield, *Ocean of Reasoning: A Great Commentary on Nāgārjuna's* Mūlamadhyamakakārikā (Oxford: Oxford University Press, 2006).

For a translation of chapter 2, see Jeffrey Hopkins, *Ocean of Reasoning* (Dharmsala, India: Library of Tibetan Works and Archives, 1974).

[c] *chos sdings.*

[d] *rva kha brag;* perhaps the meaning of the name is Goat-Face Crag.

[e] *drang ba dang nges pa'i don rnam par phye ba'i bstan bcos legs bshad snying po;* P6142, vol. 153. The Prologue and Mind-Only section are translated in Jeffrey Hopkins, *Emptiness in the Mind-Only School of Buddhism* (Berkeley: University of California Press, 1999). For a translation of the entire text, see Thurman, *Tsong Khapa's Speech of Gold in the Essence of True Eloquence,* 185-385.

[f] For the date, see Leonard W. J. van der Kuijp, "Apropos of a Recent Contribution to the History of Central Way Philosophy in Tibet: *Tsong Khapa's Speech of Gold*" in *Berliner Indologische Studien* 1 (Reinbek, Germany: Verlag für Orientalistische Fachpublikationen, 1985), 68, n. 2.

[g] *skyes bu gsum gyi nyams su blang ba'i byang chub lam gyi rim pa;* P6002, vols. 152-153.

[h] His Holiness the Fourteenth Dalai Lama gave an expansive series of lectures on Tsong-kha-pa's *Medium-Length Exposition of the Stages of the Path to Enlightenment* in 1972 in Dharmsala, India. For a book largely based on those lectures, see His Holiness the Dalai Lama, *How to See Yourself As You Really Are,* trans. and ed. by Jeffrey Hopkins (New York: Atria Books, 2006).

on Chandrakīrti's *Supplement to (Nāgārjuna's) "Treatise on the Middle,"*[a] called *Illumination of the Thought,*[b] from which translations of the sections on the object of negation in the doctrine of emptiness and on the two truths are included in this book.

Thus, the three translations in this book are from his final two compositions on the view of emptiness.

The first translation is the section on special insight in his next-to-last exposition of the view of emptiness, the *Medium-Length Exposition of the Stages of the Path to Enlightenment.* Here Tsong-kha-pa presents the topic of wisdom in a far more accessible manner than he did sixteen years earlier in his *Great Treatise on the Stages of the Path.* In other sections of the *Medium-Length Exposition* he merely condenses the *Great Treatise,* but for the section on wisdom he structures a new composition with the exception that the beginning and the end (these being chapters one and eleven in the following translation) are condensations of the *Great Treatise.* The most striking addition is the long section on the two truths (chapters seven through nine in the translation below), for which there is no corresponding section in the *Great Treatise.*

Also, of one hundred and forty-six scriptural citations from Indian texts in the section on special insight in the *Medium-Length Exposition,* seventy-six are not found in the *Great Treatise.* Listed by author and text these are:

Special Insight Quotations in *Medium-Length Exposition* but not in *Great Treatise*

AUTHOR AND TEXT	QUOTATIONS
Āryadeva's *Four Hundred*	2
Chandrakīrti's *Clear Words*	3
Chandrakīrti's *Commentary on the "Supplement"*	14
Chandrakīrti's *Supplement to (Nāgārjuna's) "Treatise on the Middle"*	6
Dharmakīrti's *Commentary on (Dignāga's) "Compilation of Prime Cognition"*	1
Jñānagarbha's *Commentary on the "Differentiation of the Two Truths"*	5
Jñānagarbha's *Differentiation of the Two Truths*	5
Kamalashīla's *Illumination of the Middle*	3

[a] *dbu ma la 'jug pa, madhyamakāvatāra;* P5261, vol. 98 and P5262, vol. 98.

[b] *dbu ma la 'jug pa'i rgya cher bshad pa dgongs pa rab gsal;* P6143, vol. 154. For a translation of chapters 1-5, see Hopkins, *Compassion in Tibetan Buddhism,* 93-230; for a translation of chapter 6 stanzas 1-7, by Jeffrey Hopkins and Anne C. Klein, see Anne C. Klein, *Path to the Middle: Madhyamaka Philosophy in Tibet: The Oral Scholarship of Kensur Yeshay Tupden* (Albany, N.Y.: State University of New York Press, 1994), 147-183, 252-271.

AUTHOR AND TEXT	QUOTATIONS
Nāgārjuna's *Essay on the Mind of Enlightenment*	3
Nāgārjuna's *Fundamental Treatise on the Middle, Called "Wisdom"*	3
Nāgārjuna's *Praise of the Element of Attributes*	6
Nāgārjuna's *Praise of the Supramundane*	1
Nāgārjuna's *Precious Garland*	3
Nāgārjuna's *Seventy Stanzas on Emptiness*	2
Nāgārjuna's *Sixty Stanzas of Reasoning*	6
Shāntarakṣhita's *Ornament for the Middle*	1
Shāntideva's *Compendium of Instructions*	1
Vasubandhu's *Principles of Explanation*	1
Descent into Laṅkā Sūtra	1
Guhyasamāja Tantra	1
Introduction to the Two Truths Sūtra	1
Meeting of Father and Son Sūtra	1
One Hundred Thousand Stanza Perfection of Wisdom Sūtra	1
Questions of Sāgaramati Sūtra	1
Questions of Upāli Sūtra	1
Superior Sūtra of the Meditative Stabilization Definitely Revealing Suchness	1
Sūtra on the Secrecies of the Ones-Gone-Thus	1
Verse Summary of the Perfection of Wisdom	1
TOTAL	76

The medium-length exposition of special insight has seventy quotations that are found in the special insight section of the *Great Treatise* but in a radically different order, as the following table reveals by setting side by side the order of these seventy as they appear in the *Medium-Length Exposition* and in the *Great Treatise:*[a]

[a] In translating these seventy citations I have drawn bracketed additions from the detailed commentaries in *Four Interwoven Annotations on (Tsong-kha-pa's) "Great Exposition of the Stages of the Path"* for the sake of clarity. About this collection of commentaries Elizabeth Napper says:

> In the Delhi edition of the text the annotations are identified as having been written by:
>
> 1. Ba-so Chö-gyi-gyel-tsen (*ba so chos kyi rgyal mtshan,* 1402-1473)
> 2. De-druk-ken-chen Ka-rok Nga-wang-rap-den (*sde drug mkhan chen kha rog ngag dbang rab brtan,* seventeenth century)
> 3. Jam-yang-shay-ba Nga-wang-dzön-drü (*'jam dbyangs bzhad pa ngag dbang brtson 'grus,* 1648-1712)
> 4. Dra-di Ge-shay Rin-chen-dön-drub (*bra sti dge bshes rin chen don grub,* seventeenth century).

Special Insight Quotations in Both *Medium Exposition* and *Great Treatise*

Order in *Medium Exposition*	Order & Location in *Great Treatise,* vol. 3, English trans.	Location in *Four Annotations,* vol. 2	Location in Napper's *Dependent-Arising and Emptiness*
1.	2. p. 111	150.5	158-159 and 247-253
2.	22. p. 206	418.3	
3.	27. p. 213	438.6	
4.	28. p. 213	439.6	
5.	24. p. 208	422.6	
6.	25. p. 208	423.2	
7.	26. p. 209	426.5	
8. and 12.	5. pp. 122, 208, and 209	189.2	172 and 298-299
9.	23. p. 207	421.5	
10.	20. p. 197	392.4	
11.	21. p. 197	392.6	
13. and 16.	3. p. 120 (and last two lines p. 335)	180.6	169 and 290
14.	12. p. 183	359.5	
15.	55. p. 335	756.1	
17.	13. last two of eight lines, p. 187		
18.	54. p. 335	755.2	
19.	52. p. 321	715.2	
20.	47. p. 311	686.6	
21.	32. p. 278	594.6	
22.	33. p. 290	628.6	
23.	34. p. 290	629.4	
24.	35. p. 291	629.6	
25.	36. p. 294	638.5	
26.	37. p. 296	643.6	
27.	38. p. 296	645.5	
28.	39. p. 296	645.6	
29.	4. pp. 121 and 307	681.6	
30.	46. pp. 307-308 (and last two lines, 193)	681.6	
31.	45. p. 306	674.5	

See her *Dependent-Arising and Emptiness*, 219-227, for a discussion of the commentators including controversy over the identification of the first author. In *Dependent-Arising and Emptiness* Napper covers *Four Interwoven Annotations*, 138.4-275.

Order in *Medium Exposition*	Order & Location in *Great Treatise*, vol. 3, English trans.	Location in *Four Annotations*, vol. 2	Location in Napper's *Dependent-Arising and Emptiness*
32.	44. pp. 304-305	670.6	
33.	40. p. 301	659.2	
34.	41. p. 301 (and except first sentence, 159)	659.3 and 289.1	
35.	42. p. 302	660.4	
36.	43. p. 303	665.1	
38.	14. p. 188	368.2	
39.	15. p. 188	369.2	
40.	48. p. 316	702.5	
41.	51. pp. 186 and 320	712.6	
42.	49. p. 316	702.5	
43.	50. p. 317	704.6	
44.	6. p. 133	218.5	187 and 336-337
45.	7. p. 142	243.6	199 and 364-365
46.	8. pp. 146-147 and 191	258.2 and 377.5	206 and 380
47.	31. p. 247	520.1	
48.	30. p. 218	452.3	
49.	11. p. 182	356.5	
50.	53. p. 323 (except first sentence)	722.2	
51.	9. p. 167	314.5	
51.	62. p. 352	801.1	
52.	29. p. 217	451.3	
52.	57. p. 344	782.1	
53.	10. p. 178	343.1	
53.	58. pp. 344-345	782.4	
54.	17. last two of four lines, p. 193	381.5	
55.	16. p. 193	381.4	
56.	59. p. 345	785.4	
57.	19. p. 193	382.3	
58.	60. p. 346	787.2	
59.	1. pp. 23 and 108	21.5 and 142.1	
60.	18. p. 193	382.1	
61.	61. pp. 348-349	795.5	

Order in *Medium Exposition*	Order & Location in *Great Treatise*, vol. 3, English trans.	Location in *Four Annotations*, vol. 2	Location in Napper's *Dependent-Arising and Emptiness*
62.	56. pp. 342-343	776.6	
63.	63. p. 353	804.1	
64.	64. p. 353	805.5	
65.	65. p. 354	808.1	
66.	66. p. 354	809.5	
67.	67. p. 358	819.5	
68.	68. p. 358	821.3	
69.	69. p. 358	822.4	
70.	70. pp. 361-363	827.4ff	

That more than half of the quotations from Indian texts in the *Medium-Length Exposition* are not found in the *Great Treatise* and that those that are in the *Great Treatise* are in a fundamentally different order illustrate the uniqueness of Tsong-kha-pa's presentation of special insight in the *Medium-Length Exposition.*

In this new exposition he presents at length the two truths, obscurational truths and ultimate truth, from the viewpoint of Chandrakīrti's Middle Way Consequence School with particular emphasis on:

- the mode of difference between the two truths (105ff.)
- the multiple meanings of *saṃvṛti* and how obscurational truths are truths for ignorance but are not posited by ignorance (109ff.)
- how the two truths are not two ways of perceiving the same object (114ff.)
- how one can know an obscurational truth, such as a pot, but not know it as an obscurational truth (115)
- how real and unreal conventionalities are posited just in relation to conventional valid cognition (116ff.)
- how the ultimate truth is non-deceptive (121)
- how the ultimate truth is found, or realized, by wisdom but cannot bear analysis by wisdom and thus is not truly established (122)
- how nirvāṇa is an ultimate truth (125)
- how all phenomena, ultimate and conventional, exist only conventionally (125ff.)
- how what exists conventionally cannot be undermined by valid cognition (127ff.)
- how the ultimate is seen in the manner of non-seeing (129ff.)
- how a Buddha perceives pure and impure conventionalities (135)

- how to understand the meaning of actual ultimates and concordant ultimates so as to eliminate that pristine wisdom itself is an ultimate truth in the Middle Way School (138ff.)
- how there are only two truths based on the deceptive and the nondeceptive being a dichotomy (148ff.)

Tsong-kha-pa also cites passages from Nāgārjuna's *Sixty Stanzas of Reasoning* to show that emptiness is approached through the reasoning of dependent-arising (55), that nirvāṇa also is empty of inherent existence (100), and that Buddhas perceive conventional phenomena (137), and he explains passages in Nāgārjuna's *Praise of the Element of Attributes* and *Praise of the Supramundane* to show that his Collection of Praises is harmonious with his Collection of Reasonings in terms of the view of reality (98ff.).

The last two translations in Part One are drawn from Tsong-kha-pa's final exposition of the view of emptiness, the *Illumination of the Thought: Extensive Explanation of (Chandrakīrti's) "Supplement to (Nāgārjuna's) 'Treatise on the Middle.'"* The first treats the issue of the difference between the Autonomy School and the Consequence School concerning the object of negation in emptiness. Tsong-kha-pa explains the topic not from the viewpoint of the controversy between Bhāvaviveka on one side and Buddhapālita and Chandrakīrti on the other, as he did in the *Great Treatise,* but by way of contrasting Kamalashīla's *Illumination of the Middle* with Chandrakīrti's views. The last translation is Tsong-kha-pa's commentary on Chandrakīrti's presentation of the two truths, thereby fortifying and expanding on his treatment in the *Medium-Length Exposition.*

Throughout these translations quotations are cross-referenced so that Tsong-kha-pa's treatments of them can be compared—"*Insight*" referring to the special insight section of the *Medium-Length Exposition of the Stages of the Path to Enlightenment* and "*Illumination*" referring to *Illumination of the Thought: Extensive Explanation of (Chandrakīrti's) "Supplement to (Nāgārjuna's) 'Treatise on the Middle'".*

These three translations provide a vantage point from which to contrast the views of the Tibetan scholar whom Tsong-kha-pa took as his main opponent in his writings on the view of emptiness, Dol-po-pa Shay-rap-gyel-tsen. Part Two presents this controversy structured around how these two great authors treat specific Indian source quotations. My aim is to bring more clarity to both of their views in the mirror of contrast.

SUPRAMUNDANE SPECIAL INSIGHT

From Tsong-kha-pa Lo-sang-drak-pa's
Medium-Length Exposition of the Stages of the Path to Enlightenment Practiced by Persons of Three Capacities

1. The Source Tradition

The explanation of how to train in special insight has four parts: prerequisites for special insight, divisions of special insight, how to cultivate special insight, and the measure of having established special insight through meditative cultivation.

Prerequisites for special insight

This section has two parts: general exposition of the prerequisites for special insight and how to delineate the view in particular.

General exposition of the prerequisites for special insight

Kamalashīla's second [of three works[a] on the] *Stages of Meditation*[b] says that relying on an excellent being, seeking hearing of the doctrine from that person, and proper contemplation are the three prerequisites for special insight. The generation of the view realizing suchness by the wisdoms of hearing and thinking—upon having heard the stainless texts in dependence on scholars who unmistakenly know the essentials of the scriptures—is an indispensable prerequisite for special insight.[c] For, if you do not have a view decisive to the fullest extent with respect to the meaning of the mode of being[d] [of phenomena, that is, emptiness], it is impossible to generate realization of the special insight realizing the mode[e] [of being of phenomena].

Furthermore, such a view must be sought by one who is relying not on interpretable meanings but on the definitive meaning.[f] Hence, it is

[a] These are not three chapters or sections of one work; they are three separate works on the same topic. The last two, which are the same length, are approximately two thirds (63%) as long as the first.

[b] *sgom pa'i rim pa, bhāvanākrama*, Toh. 3916, *dbu ma*, vol. *ki*, 46a.3; the first and third of these three texts (Toh. 3915 and 3917) have been edited by Giuseppe Tucci in *Minor Buddhist Texts, II and III*, Serie Orientale Roma 9 (Rome: Istituto Italiano per il Medio ed Estremo Oriente, 1958 and 1971), 43. For a translation of the second text see Dalai Lama, *Stages of Meditation*, trans. by Ven. Geshe Lobsang Jordhen, Losang Choephel Ganchenpa, and Jeremy Russell (Ithaca, N.Y.: Snow Lion Publications, 2001). Similar statements are made in Tsong-kha-pa, *The Great Treatise on the Stages of the Path to Enlightenment* (henceforth referred to as *Great Treatise*), vol. 3, 111 and 327.

[c] This and the next two paragraphs are in the *Great Treatise*, vol. 3, 111-112; for detailed analysis see Napper, *Dependent-Arising and Emptiness*, 158-159 and 247-253.

[d] *yin lugs.*

[e] *ji lta ba.*

[f] The four reliances found in *Teachings of Akṣhayamati Sūtra* are:

necessary to understand the import of scriptures of definitive meaning upon having recognized the difference between what requires interpretation and what is definitive.[a] Concerning this, if you do not rely on a treatise by one of the great valid openers of a chariot-way who commented on [Buddha's] thought, you will be like a blind person without a guide going in a direction of fright. Consequently, you should rely on an unmistaken commentary [of Buddha's] thought.

On whom should you rely? He is the Superior Nāgārjuna, widely renowned in the three levels [below, above, and on the ground], whom the Supramundane Victor himself prophesied very clearly in many sūtras and tantras as unraveling the essence of his teaching—the profound meaning [of emptiness] devoid of all extremes of [inherent] existence and no [nominal] existence.[b] Therefore, you should seek the view realizing emptiness in dependence on his texts.

Since Āryadeva is taken to be as valid as the master [Nāgārjuna] even by great Proponents of the Middle such as the masters Buddhapālita, Bhāvaviveka, Chandrakīrti, Shāntarakṣhita, and so forth, both the father [Nāgārjuna] and his spiritual son [Āryadeva] are sources for the other Proponents of the Middle.[c] Hence, earlier [Tibetan scholars rightly] used the convention "Proponents of the Middle of the model texts" for those two and "partisan Proponents of the Middle" for the others.

Some earlier [Tibetan] spiritual guides [wrongly][d] said that from the viewpoint of how Proponents of the Middle posit conventionalities,

---

Rely on doctrine, but do not rely on persons.
Rely on meaning, but do not rely on words.
Rely on definitive meaning, but do not rely on interpretable meaning.
Rely on pristine wisdom, but do not rely on consciousness.

For Jam-yang-shay-pa's detailed explanation of these by way of persons, times, and four validities as well as for identifying the four to be relied upon, the four not to be relied upon, and the benefits of the four reliances, see Jeffrey Hopkins, *Maps of the Profound: Jam-yang-shay-ba's Great Exposition of Buddhist and Non-Buddhist Views on the Nature of Reality* (Ithaca, N.Y.: Snow Lion Publications, 2003), 316-318.

[a] For Tsong-kha-pa's exposition of this in the *Great Exposition of the Stages of the Path*, see Tsong-kha-pa, *Great Treatise*, vol. 3, 112-114, and Napper, *Dependent-Arising and Emptiness*, 159-163 and 247-267.

[b] For a detailed account of the prophecies of Nāgārjuna, see Hopkins, *Nāgārjuna's Precious Garland*, 9-21.

[c] The material in this paragraph through the remainder of this chapter is in *Great Treatise*, vol. 3, 115-117; for detailed analysis see Napper, *Dependent-Arising and Emptiness*, 164-167 and 268-283.

[d] Tsong-kha-pa, after quoting Ye-shay-day on this topic below, explains that Chandrakīrti does not fit either of these.

they are designated as two types:

- Sūtric Proponents of the Middle,[a] who assert that external objects exist in conventional terms[b]
- Yogic Proponents of the Middle[c] who assert that in conventional terms there are no external objects.

They also [wrongly] said that from the viewpoint of how they assert the ultimate, Proponents of the Middle are designated as of two types:[d]

- those propounding an establishment of illusion by a rational

---

[a] *mdo sde spyod pa'i dbu ma pa, sautrāntika-mādhyamika.*

[b] *tha snyad du.* I translate *kun rdzob tu* as "conventionally" and *tha snyad du* as "in conventional terms" not because of a difference in meaning but for the sake of being able to follow which term is being used.

[c] *rnal 'byor spyod pa'i dbu ma pa, yogācāra-mādhyamika.*

[d] For an exhaustive discussion of the usage of the term "Thoroughly Non-Abiding Proponents of the Middle Way School" for Consequentialists and "Reason-Established Illusionists" for Autonomists, see Appendix One in Napper, *Dependent-Arising and Emptiness,* 403-440. Tsong-kha-pa's expositions of these two positions in his *Great Exposition of the Stages of the Path* and his later *Medium-Length Exposition of the Stages of the Path* differ slightly. Let us cite these with the differences highlighted; first the *Great Exposition:*

> those propounding an establishment of illusion by a rational consciousness, who assert that a composite of **appearance and emptiness** is an ultimate truth, and those propounding thorough non-abiding, who assert that a **mere** exclusionary elimination of the proliferations with respect to appearances is the ultimate truth (***snang stong gnyis*** *tshogs don dam bden par 'dod pa sgyu ma rigs grub pa dang snang ba la spros pa rnam par bcad* ***pa tsam*** *don dam bden par 'dod pa rab tu mi gnas par smra ba'o*)

and the *Medium-Length Exposition:*

> those propounding an establishment of illusion by a rational consciousness, who assert that a composite of **the appearances of the subject, such as a sprout, and of its absence of true existence** is an ultimate truth and those propounding thorough non-abiding, who assert that **an inclusionary elimination**—an exclusionary elimination of the proliferations with respect to appearances—is the ultimate truth (***myu gu la sogs pa'i chos can dang bden med kyi snang ba*** *tshogs* ***pa*** *don dam bden par 'dod pa sgyu ma rigs grub pa dang snang ba la spros pa rnam par bcad* ***pa'i yongs gcod*** *don dam bden par 'dod pa rab tu mi gnas par smra ba'o*)

The additions to his earlier explanation of those propounding an establishment of illusion by a rational consciousness merely identify the composite more clearly, whereas his addition of "inclusionary elimination" to his explanation of those propounding thorough non-abiding is more dramatic in that it serves to exclude his own position that the actual ultimate is a non-affirming negative, or mere exclusionary elimination. For my speculation on what this inclusionary elimination might be, see footnote b, p. 144.

consciousness,[a] who assert that a composite of the appearances of the subject, such as a sprout, and of its absence of true existence is an ultimate truth,[b] and

- those propounding thorough non-abiding,[c] who assert that an inclusionary elimination[d]—an exclusionary elimination of the proliferations with respect to appearances—is the ultimate truth.[e]

They asserted those propounding an establishment of illusion by a rational consciousness to be the masters Shāntarakṣhita, Kamalashīla, and so forth.[f] Some Indians also accepted the designations "illusion-like" and "thoroughly non-abiding." The great translator [Lo-den-shay-rap[g] rightly] says [in his *Epistolary Essay, Drop of Ambrosia*],[h] "The positing of the two from the viewpoint of how the ultimate is asserted is an obscured presentation generating amazement."[i]

Concerning this, the master Ye-shay-day[j] explains that:

---

[a] *sgyu ma rigs grub pa*, or Reason-Established Illusionists.

[b] For Tsong-kha-pa's later consideration of this position, see 143.

[c] *rab tu mi gnas par smra ba*, or Proponents of Thorough Non-Abiding.

[d] *yongs gcod;* an elimination that includes something positive.

[e] Tsong-kha-pa mentions this position later (144).

[f] Tsong-kha-pa refutes this identification later (144).

[g] *blo ldan shes rab, rngog lo chen po;* 1059-1109.

[h] *spring yig bdud rtsi'i thigs pa;* see Napper, *Dependent-Arising and Emptiness*, 165, 271, 275-276, 405, 667 n. 75, and 740 n. 316.

[i] Since Tsong-kha-pa himself posits the Autonomy and Consequence schools as subdivisions of the Middle Way School by way of their assertions of the ultimate, his objection concerns this particular way of making the divisions.

There are two types of amazement, at the good and at the bad. The *Four Interwoven Annotations on (Tsong-kha-pa's) "Great Exposition of the Stages of the Path"* (vol. 2, 168.3) explains that this is "not a presentation pleasing excellent scholars but merely a presentation causing the obscured (*rmongs pa rnam*) to generate amazement," in which case it is the obscured's amazement at something they think is good, and thus should be translated as "The positing of the two from the viewpoint of how the ultimate is asserted is a presentation generating amazement [in] the obscured." However, I take "obscured" (*rmongs pa*) as modifying the presentation, in which case the amazement is Lo-den-shay-rap's amazement at something bad. The import is the same in either case.

[j] *ye shes sde;* fl. c. 800. The synopsis of his opinions on this subject is a paraphrase drawn from his *Distinctions of the Views* (*lta ba'i khyad par;* Toh. 4360, *sna tshogs*, volume *jo*, 213b.1-213b.4.):

> *phyi rol gyi don yod par smra ba la sogs pa'i lta ba'i bye brag dang / theg pa gsum dang sku gsum la sogs pa mkhan po dag las thos pa dang / gsung rab mdo sde dang / bstan bcos las byung ba'i don mdo tsam zhig brjed byang du byas pa / A tsArya nA gA rdzu nas dbu ma'i kA ri kA mdzad pa'i 'grel pa shes rab sgron ma zhes bya ba dang / dbu ma'i snying po zhes bya ba mdzad pa dang / bar gyi mkhan po shAnta rakShi ta zhes bya bas A tsArya a saṅ gas rnam par shes pa tsam du bshad pa'i bstan bcos rnal*

In the Middle Way treatises by the Superior father [Nāgārjuna] and his spiritual son [Āryadeva], whether external objects exist or not is not clear.[a] After them, the master Bhāvaviveka refuted

---

'byor spyod pa mdzad pa la brten te / kun rdzob tu de'i lugs dang mthun par rnam par shes pa tsam du bsgrubs la / don dam par rnam par shes pa yang rang bzhin med par bshad pa'i dbu ma'i bstan bcos dbu ma'i rgyan zhes bya ba zhig mdzad de / dbu ma'i bstan bcos lugs cung zad mi mthun pa gnyis byung bas / A tsArya bha byas mdzad pa la ni mdo sde ba'i dbu ma zhes btags / A tsArya shAnta rakShi tas mdzad pa la ni rnal 'byor spyod pa'i dbu ma zhes btags so /

See also Napper, *Dependent-Arising and Emptiness*, 165-166 and 277-279.

[a] Jam-yang-shay-pa (*Four Interwoven Annotations*, vol. 2, 171.2; also Napper, *Dependent-Arising and Emptiness*, 277-278) points out that Nāgārjuna in his *Precious Garland* (stanzas 394-396) indicates that mind-only is a lower doctrine:

> Just as a grammarian [first] has students
> Read a model of the alphabet,
> So Buddha taught trainees
> The doctrines that they could bear.
>
> To some he taught doctrines
> To turn them away from ill-deeds;
> To some, for the sake of achieving merit;
> To some, doctrines based on duality;
>
> To some, doctrines based on non-duality;
> To some what is profound and frightening to the fearful—
> Having an essence of emptiness and compassion—
> The means of achieving [unsurpassed] enlightenment.

As Gyel-tsap's (*rgyal tshab dar ma rin chen*, 1364-1432) *Illumination of the Essential Meanings of (Nāgārjuna's) "Precious Garland of the Middle Way"* (*dbu ma rin chen 'phreng ba'i snying po'i don gsal bar byed pa*, 64a.2) elaborates:

> Just as a grammarian first has students read a model of the alphabet, the Buddhas do not teach trainees from the very beginning doctrines that are difficult to realize. Rather, they teach the doctrines that they can bear as objects of their minds. The stages are as follows:
>
> - to some they teach doctrines to turn them away from ill-deeds such as killing; this is so that these trainees who have the thought-patterns of beings of small capacity may achieve the ranks of gods or humans as fruits of their merit
> - to some trainees who have the thought-patterns of beings of middle capacity they teach doctrines based on the duality of apprehended object and apprehending subject and that cyclic existence is one-pointedly to be abandoned and nirvana is one-pointedly to be adopted
> - to some trainees they teach ultimately established consciousness empty of a difference in substantial entity between apprehended object and apprehending subject, thereby teaching to them [doctrine that is] not based on duality
> - to some trainees of highest faculties, who will achieve the unsurpassed

> the system of Cognition-Only[a] [or Mind-Only] and presented a system in which external objects exist in conventional terms. Then, the master Shāntarakṣhita made a different Middle Way system, teaching—based on Yogic Practice [that is, Mind-Only] treatises—that external objects do not exist in conventional terms and that the mind ultimately is without inherent existence.[b] Thereby, the Middle Way School arose in two forms; the former is called the Sūtric Middle Way School and the latter, the Yogic Middle Way School.

The chronology of the clarification [of the model texts of Nāgārjuna and Āryadeva by those masters] through great treatises[c] is evident in accordance with that [explanation by Ye-shay-day].[d] However, although the master Chandrakīrti asserts that external objects exist in conventional terms, he does not do so in comparison with another tenet system. Consequently, it is not suitable to call him a Proponent of the Sūtric [Middle Way School]. That he asserts external objects in

---

> enlightenment, they teach [doctrine] that has an essence of emptiness—the profound mode of subsistence [of phenomena] frightening to the fearful who adhere to the true existence of things—and compassion.

Also, there is the statement in Nāgārjuna's *Essay on the Mind of Enlightenment:*

> The teaching by the Subduer
> That all these are mind-only
> Is in order to get rid of the fears
> Of the childish. It is not suchness.

For Jam-yang-shay-pa's extensive treatment of these points in his *Great Exposition of Tenets,* see Hopkins, *Maps of the Profound,* 500-505.

[a] *rnam rig tsam, vijñaptimātra.*

[b] According to Tsong-kha-pa's explanation of Shāntarakṣhita's views, the mind conventionally exists inherently but does not ultimately exist inherently.

[c] The phrase "of the clarification through great treatises" does not appear in the *Great Treatise.*

[d] Tsong-kha-pa accepts the *chronology,* namely, that Bhāvaviveka preceded Shāntarakṣhita in illuminating the works of Nāgārjuna and Āryadeva through great treatises that *founded* the systems of the Sūtric Middle Way School and the Yogic Middle Way School by setting these systems forth in contradistinction to other systems. However, Tsong-kha-pa does not take Ye-shay-day's statement as a mere chronology of great Mādhyamikas who asserted tenets in accordance with those systems because there were earlier great Proponents of the Middle who had assertions similar to Bhāvaviveka and Shāntarakṣhita. Namely, Shūra asserted external objects prior to Bhāvaviveka, and Āryavimuktasena—in accordance with Maitreya's *Ornament for Clear Realization* and Haribhadra's *Clear Meaning Commentary*—refuted external objects prior to Shāntarakṣhita. See *Four Interwoven Annotations* (vol. 2, 172.2); for more detail see Napper, *Dependent-Arising and Emptiness,* 279 and 797-798 n. 482, and Hopkins, *Maps of the Profound,* 500-505.

accordance with the Proponents of the Great Exposition is also not feasible.[a]

[a] In his *The Essence of Eloquence* Tsong-kha-pa clearly states the reasons for these opinions:

> [Chandrakīrti] describes his own system as not shared with the commentaries [on Nāgārjuna's thought]* by other Proponents of the Middle. His *Autocommentary on the "Supplement to (Nāgārjuna's) 'Treatise on the Middle'"* says (Louis de La Vallée Poussin, *Madhyamakāvatāra par Candrakīrti,* Bibliotheca Buddhica 9 [Osnabrück, Germany: Biblio Verlag, 1970], 406.9, commenting on stanzas XIII.1 and 2):
>
>> May scholars ascertain that just as, except for Nāgārjuna's *Treatise on the Middle,* this doctrine called "emptiness" is not expressed nonerroneously in other treatises, so the system that appears in this [treatise]—set out together with objections and answers to any [other] system—does not exist, in terms of the doctrine of emptiness, in other treatises. Therefore, it should be understood that a certain [scholar's] propounding that just what are propounded ultimately in the system of the Sūtra School are asserted conventionally by Proponents of the Middle Way School is a proposition only by one who does not know the suchness of Nāgārjuna's *Treatise on the Middle.*
>
> At the end of also saying such with respect to the system of the Great Exposition School (La Vallée Poussin, *Madhyamakāvatāra,* 407.1), [Chandrakīrti] says:
>
>> This is because a supramundane doctrine is not fit to be similar to a mundane doctrine. May scholars ascertain that this system is unshared.
>
> Through the reason of his own system's not being shared with other Proponents of the Middle Way School, [Chandrakīrti] posits that one who asserts that what are propounded ultimately by the two Proponents of [Truly Existent External] Objects [that is, the Great Exposition School and the Sūtra School] are propounded conventionally by Proponents of the Middle Way School does not know the Middle Way suchness. The reason is that, in the [Consequentialists'] own system, even conventionally, phenomena that are established by way of their own character are not asserted, whereas those [Proponents of True Existence] only posit [all phenomena] in the context of that [establishment of objects by way of their own character].
>
> If one falls from either of the two truths, one also falls from the other; therefore, it is not suitable that a supramundane doctrine that has not fallen from the mode of the two truths be similar in terms of either of the two truths with a mundane doctrine that has fallen from the two truths. Therefore, this system of the Superior [Nāgārjuna]—in terms not only of the ultimate but also of the conventional—is not shared with the schools of the Proponents of True Existence.

*The bracketed additions are mostly drawn from Ta-drin-rap-ten's *Annotations,* 270.5-272.6. Jam-yang-shay-pa (*Four Interwoven Annotations, on (Tsong-kha-pa's) "Great Exposition of the Stages of the Path,"* vol. 2, 172.6) points out that although Chandrakīrti, like the

The terminology of Autonomist[a] and Consequentialist[b] is used with respect to Proponents of the Middle by scholars of the later dissemination [of Buddhism] in the Land of Snowy Mountains [Tibet]; this accords with Chandrakīrti's *Clear Words*[c] [in which he refutes the usage of

---

Great Exposition School, asserts external objects and does not assert self-cognition, he, unlike the Great Exposition School, asserts that external objects do not substantially exist, and also his non-assertion of self-cognition derives from not asserting establishment by way of the object's own character.

[a] *rang rgyud pa, svātantrika.*

[b] *thal 'gyur pa, prāsaṅgika.*

[c] *dbu ma rtsa ba'i 'grel pa tshig gsal ba, mūlamadhyamakavṛttiprasannapadā,* Toh. 3860, *dbu ma,* vol. *'a;* Sanskrit text edited by Louis de La Vallée Poussin, *Mūlamadhyamakakārikās (Mādhyamikasūtras) de Nāgārjuna avec la Prasannapadā Commentaire de Candrakīrti* (Osnabrück, Germany: Biblio Verlag, 1970); Tibetan text partially edited by Jan Willem de Jong, *Cinq chapitres de la Prasannapadā.* Documents et travaux pour l'étude du Bouddhisme, Tome IX (Paris: Librairie Orientaliste Paul Geuthner, 1949). The reference here is to the first chapter of Chandrakīrti's *Clear Words;* see Jeffrey Hopkins, *Meditation on Emptiness* (London: Wisdom Publications, 1983; rev. ed., Boston, Ma.: Wisdom Publications, 1996), 469-530.

I prefer to translate the title *prasannapadā* as *Clear Words* though it would be just as suitable as *The Lucidly Worded,* or *The Clear Worded* as Stcherbatsky has in his *The Conception of Buddhist Nirvana* (rpt Delhi: Motilal Banarsidass, 1978), or *Lucid Exposition of the Middle Way* as Mervyn Sprung has in his condensation of the text (London: Routledge & Kegan Paul, 1979). It strikes me that Chandrakīrti gave his commentary on Nāgārjuna's *Treatise on the Middle* this title in contrast to Bhāvaviveka's commentary, *Lamp for (Nāgārjuna's) "Wisdom"* (*shes rab sgron me, prajñāpradīpa*) which, due to its brevity and lack of elaboration, is often difficult to fathom and thus unclear. As an example of such difficulty, see Bhāvaviveka's refutation of Buddhapālita's explanation of the refutation of production from self (Hopkins, *Meditation on Emptiness,* 461ff). Also, in the *Clear Words* Chandrakīrti gives a very clear picture of the movement of Nāgārjuna's refutations by citing the qualm that each step answers, such as in his brilliant commentary on the second chapter of the *Treatise.*

Stcherbatsky, in his *The Conception of Buddhist Nirvana,* however, indicates that at least for him Chandrakīrti's text is not clear and that the title seems ironic (75, n.1):

> Candrakīrti has given to his commentary the title of "The Clearworded" (*prasanna-padā*) probably not without some dose of irony, since, as Prof. Wassilieff attests, its extreme dialectical subtlety, especially in the first chapter, is equaled by no other work in the whole domain of Northern Buddhist literature.

In the same vein, Mervyn Sprung (xii) says about the first chapter, in defense of his abridgements of the text:

> ...[the excisions] are, without exception I believe, concerned with Candrakīrti's controversy with Bhāvaviveka, his rival commentator within the Mādhyamika school, or with his support of Buddhapālita, a commentator he attempts to follow, or else with traditional arguments of the Sāṃkhya school having to do with causation. These controversies are important, obviously. Yet to place them with all their meticulous, Indian love of syllogistic detail, in

autonomous syllogisms[a] and shows that using only consequences[b] is sufficient for generating the view of the middle way].

Therefore, Proponents of the Middle are limited to two types—those asserting and those not asserting external objects in conventional terms. Furthermore, when names are designated from the viewpoint of how the view ascertaining emptiness is generated in the mental continuum, they are limited to two types—Autonomists and Consequentialists.[c]

---

what is otherwise a finely targeted introduction to the entire *Prasannapadā*, however natural they were to Candrakīrti's contemporaries, is to make access to the work for contemporary readers difficult and discouraging.

In Ge-luk-pa scholastic centers of learning this very controversy between the three masters of the Middle Way School is used as the means for gaining access to the Middle Way School, as it is the first major topic of debate in the Middle Way class of ge-shay studies at the point of the sixth chapter of Chandrakīrti's *Supplement to (Nāgārjuna's) "Treatise on the Middle."* Chandrakīrti's *Clear Words* forms the basis of the study with commentaries, such as that by Jam-yang-shay-pa, used to unravel its meaning; it is because of the clarity that I found in using Jam-yang-shay-pa's commentary that this controversy could be included in Part Five of my *Meditation on Emptiness.* Thus, I am not making any claims that Chandrakīrti's words in that section were clear to me on their own; rather, I think that from his own point of view that section, like the rest of his text, was a good deal clearer than Bhāvaviveka's.

[a] *rang rgyud kyi rjes dpag, svatantra-anumāna;* literally, "autonomous inference" but here referring to autonomous syllogisms (*rang rgyud kyi sbyor ba, svatantra-prayoga*).

[b] *thal 'gyur, prasaṅga.*

[c] For discussion of the Tibetan origins of the names of the subdivisions of the Middle Way School, see:

- Katsumi Mimaki, *Blo gsal grub mtha'* (Kyoto: Université de Kyoto, 1982).
- Katsumi Mimaki, "The *Blo gsal grub mtha'*, and the Mādhyamika Classification in Tibetan *grub mtha'* Literature," in *Contributions on Tibetan and Buddhist Religion and Philosophy,* ed. Ernst Steinkellner and Helmut Tauscher (Vienna: Arbeitskreis für tibetische und buddhistische Studien, 1983), 161-167.
- Jeffrey Hopkins, *Meditation on Emptiness* (London: Wisdom Publications, 1983; rev. ed., Boston, Ma.: Wisdom Publications, 1996), 455-530.
- Peter della Santina, *Madhyamaka Schools in India* (Delhi: Motilal Banarsidass, 1986).
- Jeffrey Hopkins, "A Tibetan Delineation of Different Views of Emptiness in the Indian Middle Way School: Tsong-kha-pa's Two Interpretations of the *Locus Classicus* in Chandrakīrti's *Clear Words* Showing Bhāvaviveka's Assertion of Commonly Appearing Subjects and Inherent Existence," *Tibet Journal* 14, no. 1 (1989), 10-43; the printing contains egregious typographical errors.
- Tom J.F. Tillemans, "Tsong kha pa *et al.* on the Bhāvaviveka-Candrakīrti Debate" in *Tibetan Studies: Proceedings of the 5th Seminar of the International Association for Tibetan Studies,* Monograph Series of Naritasan Institute for Buddhist Studies: Occasional Papers 2 (Narita: Narita-san Shinshō-ji, 1992).
- Kodo Yotsuya, *The Critique of Svatantra Reasoning by Candrakīrti and Tsong-kha-pa: A Study of Philosophical Proof According to Two Prāsaṅgika Madhyamaka Traditions of India*

Question: Following whom did those [Ka-dam-pa] masters seek the thought of the father, the Superior [Nāgārjuna], and his spiritual son [Āryadeva]?

Answer: Following the Great Elder [Atisha] who took the master Chandrakīrti's system to be chief,[a] the earlier great lamas of this guiding-advice also held that system to be chief.

The master Chandrakīrti, having seen that among the commentators on Nāgārjuna's *Treatise on the Middle*[b] the master Buddhapālita commented in a complete way on the Superior's thought, set Buddhapālita's system as his basis. He took many good explanations also from Bhāvaviveka and refuted those [within Bhāvaviveka's works] that appeared to be a little incorrect. In this way he commented on the Superior's thought.

Because the commentaries by these two masters [Buddhapālita and Chandrakīrti] are seen to be very highly developed with regard to explaining the texts of the Superior—the father—and his spiritual son, here their thought will be delineated following the masters Buddhapālita and Chandrakīrti.

and Tibet, Tibetan and Indo-Tibetan Studies 8 (Stuttgart: Franz Steiner Verlag, 1999).

- Georges B.J. Dreyfus and Sara L. McClintock, eds., *The Svātantrika-Prāsaṅgika Distinction* (Boston: Wisdom Publications, 2003).

[a] For Atisha' statement of this in his *Introduction to the Two Truths,* see below, 169.

[b] *dbu ma rtsa ba'i tshig le'ur byas pa shes rab ces bya ba, prajñānāmamūlamadhyamakakārikā,* Toh. 3824, *dbu ma,* vol. *tsa;* Sanskrit text edited by Jan Willem de Jong, *Mūlamadhyamakakārikāḥ* (Adyar, Madras: The Adyar Library and Research Centre, 1977).

2. Root of Cyclic Existence

How to delineate the view in particular

This section has three parts: identifying afflictive ignorance, showing that it is the root of revolving in cyclic existence, and showing that one wishing to abandon the apprehension[a] of self should seek the view of selflessness.

Identifying afflictive ignorance

The antidotes to the other afflictive emotions, desire and so on, set forth by the Conqueror are partial ones, but the antidote to ignorance that he describes serves as an antidote to all [afflictive emotions]. Hence, ignorance is the basis of all faults and defects. Chandrakīrti's *Clear Words* says:[b]

> Among the extensive teachings in nine forms[c]—the sets of

[a] "Apprehension" (*'dzin pa*) means a consciousness apprehending or holding, in this case, inherent existence.

[b] Toh. 3860, *dbu ma*, vol. *'a*, 198b.5-199a.1; these are the first two stanzas of the fourteen-stanza colophon. Brackets are from *Four Interwoven Annotations*, vol. 2, 418.3. Cited in *Great Treatise*, vol. 3, 206. The Sanskrit and Tibetan texts are edited by Jan Willem de Jong, "La Madhyamakaśāstrastuti de Candrakīrti," *Oriens Extremus* 9 (1962): 49, 51-52. Sanskrit: *yad buddhair iha śāsanaṃ navavidhaṃ sūtrādi saṃkīrtitaṃ lokānāṃ caritānurodhanipuṇaṃ satyadvayāpāśrayaṃ / tasmin rāganirākṛtau na hi kathā doṣakṣaye jāyate dveṣasyāpi nirākṛtau na hi kathā rāgakṣaye jāyate // mānāder api yat kṣayāya vacanaṃ nānyaṃ malaṃ hanti tat tasmād vyāpitaraṃ na tatra ca punas tās tā 'mahārthāḥ kathāḥ / yā mohasya parikṣayāya tu kathā kleśān aśeṣān asau hanyān mohasamāśritā hi sakalāḥ kleśā jinair bhāṣitāḥ //.*

[c] The *Four Interwoven Annotations* (vol. 2, 418.3) explains how the twelve branches of scripture are treated as nine. It lists the twelve classes as:

1. discourses (*mdo'i sde, sūtra*)
2. songs (*dbyangs kyis bsnyad pa'i sde, geya*)
3. prophecies (*lung bstan pa'i sde, vyākaraṇa*)
4. verses (*tshigs su bcad pa'i sde, gāthā*)
5. intentional aphorisms (*mched du brjod pa'i sde, udāna*)
6. biographical narratives (*rtogs pa brjod pa'i sde, avadāna*)
7. parables (*de lta bu byung ba'i sde, itivṛttaka*)
8. framing stories (*gleng gzhi'i sde, nidāna*)
9. extensive sayings (*shin tu rgyas pa'i sde, vaipulya*)
10. succession of former lives (*skyes pa'i rabs kyi sde, jātaka*)
11. delineations (*gtan la dbab pa'i sde, upadeśa*)
12. marvels (*rmad du byung ba'i chos kyi sde, adbhūtadharma*)

By counting the sixth, seventh, eighth, and tenth as one, the twelve become nine.

sūtras and so forth—rightly proclaimed by the Buddha[a]
Based on the two truths and corresponding to the forms of behavior of worldly beings,
Those spoken for the sake of removing desire do not remove hatred;
Also, those spoken for the sake of removing hatred do not remove desire;

Moreover, those spoken for the sake of removing pride and so forth do not overcome other defilements.
Therefore, they are not very pervasive, and those teachings are not of great import.
But those spoken for the sake of removing bewilderment overcome all afflictive emotions [from the root],
For the Conqueror said all afflictive emotions thoroughly depend on bewilderment.

Thus, you must meditate on suchness as an antidote to ignorance. Moreover, if ignorance is not identified, you will not know how to cultivate its antidote; therefore, identification of ignorance is extremely important.

Ignorance is the opposite of knowledge, but knowledge should not be taken as just any knowledge; rather, it is wisdom knowing suchness—selflessness. Its opposite is not suitable to be just the nonexistence of it or just other than it; hence, its opposite is its contradictory equivalent. This is a superimposition of self [that is, inherent existence]; furthermore, it is the two superimpositions of a self of phenomena and of persons. Hence, both a consciousness apprehending a self of phenomena and a consciousness apprehending a self of persons are ignorance.

The manner of superimposition by ignorance is to conceive that phenomena exist established by way of their own nature, by way of their own character, or inherently. Moreover, the *Questions of Upāli Sūtra* says that phenomena are posited through the power of conceptuality (see also *Illumination*, 201):[b]

[a] *sangs rgyas rnams kyis, buddhair;* as per George Hartt's remark in Sanskrit class, the Sanskrit plural is sometimes used as an honorific, which I take it to be in this case and also with respect to "Conqueror" (*rgyal ba rnams kyis, jinair*) in the final line.

[b] *nye bar 'khor gyis zhus pa, upālipariprcchā,* stanzas 69-70a; Toh. 68, vol. *ca* (*dkon brtsegs*); Tibetan and Chinese texts and Sanskrit fragments edited by Pierre Python, *Vinaya-Viniścaya-Upāli-Pariprcchā,* Collection Jean Przyluski, Tome V (Paris: Adrien-Maisonneuve, 1973), 59-60: *citramanorama sajjitapuṣpāḥ svarṇavimāna jalanti manojñāḥ / teṣvapi kāraku nāst'iha kaści te 'pi ca sthāpita kalpavaśena // kalpavaśena vikalpitu lokaḥ.*

Here even the various mind-pleasing blossoming flowers
And attractive shining supreme golden houses
Have no [inherently existent] maker at all.
They are posited through the power of conceptuality.
Through the power of conceptuality the world is imputed.

and Nāgārjuna's *Sixty Stanzas of Reasoning* says (see also *Illumination,* 201):[a]

The perfect Buddha stated that the world
Has the condition of ignorance.
Therefore, how could it not be feasible
That this world is [imputed by] conceptuality?

In commentary on the meaning of this, Chandrakīrti[b] explains that the worlds [that is, beings and environments] are not established by way of their own nature and are only imputed by conceptuality. Moreover, Āryadeva's *Four Hundred* says (see also *Illumination,* 202):[c]

Since desire and so forth
Do not exist without conceptuality,
Who with intelligence would hold
That these are real objects and are [also] conceptual?[d]

---

[a] *rigs pa drug cu pa'i tshig le'ur byas pa, yuktiṣaṣṭikākārikā,* stanza 37; Toh. 3825, *dbu ma,* vol. *tsa,* 21b.6; Tibetan edited by Christian Lindtner, *Master of Wisdom: Writings of the Buddhist Master Nāgārjuna* (Oakland: Dharma Publishing, 1986), 84.

[b] *rigs pa drug cu pa'i 'grel pa, yuktiṣaṣṭikāvṛtti;* Toh. 3864, *dbu ma,* vol. *ya,* 23a.2-23a.4; Cristina Anna Scherrer-Schaub, *Yuktiṣaṣṭikāvṛtti. Commentaire à la soixantaine sur le raisonnement ou Du vrai enseignement de la causalité par le Maitre indien Candrakīrti,* Mélanges chinois et bouddhiques, 25 (Brussels: Institut belge des hautes études chinoises, 1991), 77.

[c] *bstan bcos bzhi brgya pa zhes bya ba'i tshig le'ur byas pa, catuḥśatakaśāstrakārikā,* VIII.3; P5246, vol. 95, 136.2.1; Tibetan text and Sanskrit fragments edited by Karen Lang, *Āryadeva's Catuḥśataka: On the Bodhisattva's Cultivation of Merit and Knowledge,* Indiske Studier 7 (Copenhagen: Akademisk Forlag, 1986), 78: *vinā kalpanayāstitvaṃ rāgādīnāṃ na vidyate / bhūtārthaḥ kalpanā ceti ko grahīṣyati buddhimān //.* See *Yogic Deeds of Bodhisattvas: Gyel-tsap on Āryadeva's Four Hundred,* commentary by Geshe Sonam Rinchen, translated and edited by Ruth Sonam (Ithaca, N.Y.: Snow Lion Publications, 1994), 186.

[d] With material added in brackets from Chandrakīrti's commentary (*byang chub sems dpa'i rnal 'byor spyod pa bzhi brgya pa'i rgya cher 'grel pa, bodhisattvayogacaryācatuḥśatakaṭīkā;* P5266, vol. 98, 229.5.3), the passage reads:

> Without [imputation by] conceptuality [like the imputation of a snake to a rope] there is no [finding of] the existence of desire and so forth. If so, who with intelligence would maintain that a real object is [produced dependent on] conceptuality? [For, being imputed by conceptuality and existing as its own reality are contradictory.]

Also, Chandrakīrti's commentary on this says (see also *Illumination,* 202):[a]

> Those which exist only when the conceptuality [apprehending them] exists and do not exist when conceptuality does not are without question definite as not established by way of their own nature, like a snake imputed to a coiled rope.

He explains that desire and so forth are like a snake imputed to a rope from the viewpoint of being imputed to be established by way of their own nature whereas they are not. A rope-snake and desire and so forth are not similar in terms of whether they do or do not exist in conventional terms [since a rope-snake does not exist in conventional terms whereas desire and so forth do].

For those reasons, the mode of apprehending true existence—the object of negation—is to conceive [that objects] are not posited through the force of beginningless conceptuality but are established objectively by way of their own entity.[b] The conceived object of that apprehension is called "self," or "inherent existence." The non-existence of that with a person as the substratum is called a selflessness of a person, and the non-existence of that with [other] phenomena such as an eye, ear, and so forth as the substratum is called a selflessness of phenomena. Hence, it is implicitly understood that consciousnesses apprehending inherent existence with respect to persons and [other] phenomena are consciousnesses apprehending a self of persons and a self of phenomena.

Chandrakīrti's *Commentary on (Āryadeva's) "Four Hundred"* says (see also *Illumination,* 208):[c]

Gyel-tsap (*rgyal tshab dar ma rin chen,* 1364-1432) quotes both passages in his *Illumination of the Essential Meanings of (Nāgārjuna's) "Precious Garland of Madhyamaka"* (*dbu ma rin chen 'phreng ba'i snying po'i don gsal bar byed pa;* edition of 78 folios in library of H.H. Dalai Lama), 20b.6-21a.2. See also *Yogic Deeds of Bodhisattvas: Gyel-tsap on Āryadeva's Four Hundred,* commentary by Geshe Sonam Rinchen, translated and edited by Ruth Sonam (Ithaca, N.Y.: Snow Lion Publications, 1994), 186-187.

[a] *byang chub sems dpa'i rnal 'byor spyod pa bzhi brgya pa'i rgya cher 'grel pa, bodhisattvayogacaryācatuḥśatakaṭīkā,* commenting on VIII.3; P5266, vol. 98, 229.5.3. For the Sanskrit see Khangkar and Yorihito, 180 n. 34. Brackets are from *Four Interwoven Annotations,* vol. 2, 438.6. Cited in *Great Treatise,* vol. 3, 213.

[b] *rang gi ngo bo'i sgo nas yul steng du grub par 'dzin pa.* For an extensive discussion of the object of negation in the Autonomy School and the Consequence School, see below, 181ff.; see also Napper, *Dependent-Arising and Emptiness,* and Magee, *The Nature of Things: Emptiness and Essence in the Geluk World.*

[c] P5266, vol. 98, 103.4.4, chapter 12. This is quoted in Tsong-kha-pa's *Ocean of Reasoning, Explanation of (Nāgārjuna's) "Treatise on the Middle,"* P6153, vol. 156, 66.1.4. Brackets are from *Four Interwoven Annotations,* vol. 2, 439.6. Cited in *Great Treatise,* vol. 3, 213. For the

> Concerning that, "self" is inherent existence, an entity of things that does not rely on [being posited by] others [that is, conceptuality]. The non-existence of that [inherent existence] is selflessness. Through the division of [its substrata,] phenomena and persons, it is understood as twofold, "selflessness of phenomena and selflessness of persons."

With respect to the object of observation of a consciousness apprehending a self of persons:

- Chandrakīrti's *Supplement to (Nāgārjuna's) "Treatise on the Middle"*[a] explains that one Saṃmitīya sect asserts that all five aggregates are the object of observation of a view of self, whereas another Saṃmitīya sect asserts that just the mind is the basis, or object of observation, of a view of self.
- Also with respect to the mind, some Proponents of Mind-Only and Proponents of the Middle who assert a mind-basis-of-all[b] assert that the mind-basis-of-all is the object of observation, whereas other Proponents of the Middle such as Bhāvaviveka who do not assert a mind-basis-of-all and many Hearer Schools assert that the mental consciousness is the object of observation.[c]

Concerning the meaning—even in these systems—of the usage of conventions for person, as in the cultivator of a path and the revolver in cyclic existence, and so forth, you need to know the two modes of:

- [the Consequentialists'] positing the mere "I"
- [the other schools'] positing the mind-basis-of-all, and so forth, as

---

Sanskrit see Khangkar and Yorihito, 181 n. 39.

[a] Chandrakīrti (VI.126cd) says:

> Some assert all five aggregates as the base
> Of the view of self; some assert a mind.

See also La Vallée Poussin, *Madhyamakāvatāra,* 244.10-244.11; La Vallée Poussin, "*Madhyamakāvatāra. Introduction au traité du milieu* de l'ācārya Candrakīrti avec le commentaire de l'auteur," *Muséon* 12 (1911): 291.

[b] *kun gzhi rnam shes, ālayavijñāna.* Later Ge-luk-pa scholars uniformly say that even the Yogic Autonomy Middle Way School does not assert a mind-basis-of-all but instead asserts a subtle form of the mental consciousness; hence Tsong-kha-pa's reference here to Proponents of the Middle who assert a mind-basis-of-all is unclear, unless it is to just such a mental consciousness.

[c] Bhāvaviveka says in his *Blaze of Reasoning,* "we also actually impute the term "self" to [the mental] consciousness conventionally (P5256, vol. 96, 36.4.5)," and "Because [the mental] consciousness takes rebirth, it is said that it is the self." See Hopkins, *Maps of the Profound,* 890.

the illustration of that "I" [that is to say, as what is the person].[a]

With respect to the innate view of the transitory[b] that is a consciousness apprehending self, Chandrakīrti's *Supplement to (Nāgārjuna's) "Treatise on the Middle"*[c] refutes that the aggregates are the object of observation, and in his commentary he says[d] that the dependently imputed self is the object of observation. Since he says that even just the collection of the aggregates is not the conventional self,[e] neither the collection at one time, nor the collection that is the continuum of the aggregates over time are the object of observation. Rather, the mere "I" that is the object observed in generating the mere thought "I," that is to say, the mere person, is taken as the object of observation. Neither one from among the aggregates nor the collection of the aggregates is posited as an illustration of that "I" [that is, none of these is the "I"]. I

[a] For Tak-tsang Shay-rap-rin-chen's (*stag tshang lo tsā ba shes rab rin chen,* born 1405) criticism of Tsong-kha-pa's statement that some Buddhist schools posit that the mind-basis-of-all and so forth are the "I" and Jam-yang-shay-pa's response, see Hopkins, *Maps of the Profound,* 552-553 and 889-891.

[b] *'jig tshogs la lta ba, satkāyadṛṣṭi.*

[c] Chandrakīrti (VI.133) says:

> Other sūtras say that forms and feelings are not the self,
> Discriminations also are not, compositional factors are not,
> And also consciousnesses are not.
> Hence, in brief that "the aggregates are the self" is not asserted.

[d] Chandrakīrti, commenting on VI.133, says:

> It is to be known that those [sūtras] in which even forms and so forth are refuted as being the self refute [an inherently established] possessor of the appropriation of the aggregates, the dependently imputed self which is the object of the view of the transitory.

The bracketed material is from Tsong-kha-pa's *Illumination of the Thought* (Khangkar and Yorihito, 182-183 n. 45). Also, Chandrakīrti, commenting on VI.120, says:

> The object of observation of [a consciousness viewing the transitory collection as an inherently existent self] is the [nominally existent] self. For, that which apprehends an [inherently existent] "I" has as its object [an inherently existent] self.

P5263, vol. 98, 141.2.7; La Vallée Poussin, *Madhyamakāvatāra,* 234.13; La Vallée Poussin, "*Madhyamakāvatāra. Introduction au traité du milieu,*" *Muséon* 12 (1911): 283. Bracketed material is from Tsong-kha-pa's *Illumination,* P6143, vol. 154, 82.2.8.

[e] Chandrakīrti's *Supplement* (VI.135cd) says:

> Sūtra says that it is in dependence on the aggregates.
> Therefore the mere aggregation of the aggregates is not the self.

Toh 3861, *sde dge, dbu ma,* vol. *'a,* 210b.7; La Vallée Poussin, *Madhyamakāvatāra,* 258.8-258.9.

have explained at length elsewhere[a] that this is an unsurpassed distinguishing feature of this Middle Way Consequentialist system.

The object of observation of an innate view of the transitory must be something that naturally generates an awareness thinking "I." Therefore, although an innate consciousness apprehending [the inherent existence] of a person whose continuum is other [than one's own continuum] is an innate consciousness apprehending a self of persons; it is not an innate view of the transitory of that person.

With regard to the object of observation of an innate view of the transitory that apprehends [inherently existent] "mine," the object of observation of an innate awareness thinking "mine" is that very "mine"; it should not be held that your own eyes and so forth are the object of observation.[b] The subjective aspect [of such an innate misapprehension] is that, within observing the "mine," it apprehends the "mine" to be established by way of its own character.

The objects of observation of an innate consciousness apprehending a self of phenomena are the form aggregate and so forth, the eyes, ears, and so forth in your own and others' continuums, and the environments and so forth not included within the [personal] continuum. The subjective aspect [of such a misapprehension] is as explained before [to apprehend them to exist by way of their own character].

Chandrakīrti's *Commentary on the "Supplement to (Nāgārjuna's) 'Treatise on the Middle'"* says:[c]

> [Because this apprehension of true existence is mistaken and obscures viewing how the nature of things is, it is called] bewilderment. This ignorance—having a nature of obstructing perception of the nature [of all things] by superimposing an inherent existence of things [even though such] does not exist—is an obscurer (*kun rdzob, saṃvṛti*).[d]

and:[e]

---

[a] That is, in his *Great Exposition of the Stages of the Path* (see *Great Treatise,* vol. 3, 214-215) and *The Essence of Eloquence* in the section titled "explaining the meaning of the two selflessnesses being set out in dependence on the scriptural collections of the Hearers."

[b] For various opinions by Ge-luk-pa scholars about the meaning of "mine," see Hopkins, *Maps of the Profound,* 865-875.

[c] Commenting on VI.28; *dbu ma la 'jug pa'i bshad pa, madhyamakāvatārabhāṣya;* Toh. 3862, *dbu ma,* vol. *'a,* 254b.5; La Vallée Poussin, *Madhyamakāvatāra,* 107.6-107.8; La Vallée Poussin, "*Introduction au traité du milieu,*" *Muséon* 11 (1910): 303-304. Brackets are from *Four Interwoven Annotations,* vol. 2, 422.6. Cited in *Great Treatise,* vol. 3, 208.

[d] *kun rdzob, saṃvṛti.* For discussion of this term, see below, 109ff.

[e] Commenting on VI.28; Toh. 3862, *dbu ma,* vol. *'a,* 255a.1; La Vallée Poussin,

> Thus, [obscurational truths are posited] through the force [of being true in the face] of the afflictive ignorance included [as the initial link] within the [twelve] links [of the dependent-arising] of cyclic existence.

Hence, he asserts that:

- [a consciousness] apprehending an object as truly existent is an ignorance
- and this itself is afflictive ignorance.

Therefore, between the two modes of positing the apprehension of a self of phenomena as an afflictive emotion or as an obstruction to omniscience, here [in the Consequence School] it is the former.

This is also set forth by the Superior, the father [Nāgārjuna], and his spiritual son [Āryadeva]. Nāgārjuna's *Seventy Stanzas on Emptiness* says (see also *Illumination*, 210):[a]

> That [consciousness] which apprehends things produced
> From causes and conditions to be real [that is, to be established by way of their own entities]
> Was said by the Teacher to be ignorance.
> From it the twelve links arise.
>
> If through seeing reality one knows well
> That things are empty [of inherent existence], the ignorance [mistaking inherent existence] does not arise.
> That is the cessation of ignorance,
> Whereby the twelve links [of the dependent-arising of cyclic existence] cease.

To conceive things to be real [means] to apprehend them as established as [their own] reality, or as true [that is, truly established]. This is similar in meaning to the statement in Nāgārjuna's *Precious Garland* that until apprehension of the aggregates as truly existent is overcome, the

---

Madhyamakāvatāra, 107.17-107.18; La Vallée Poussin, "*Introduction au traité du milieu,*" *Muséon* 11 (1910): 304. Brackets are from *Four Interwoven Annotations*, vol. 2, 423.2. Cited in *Great Treatise*, vol. 3, 208.

[a] *stong pa nyid bdun cu pa'i tshig le'ur byas pa, śunyatāsaptatikārikā*, stanzas 64-65; Toh. 3827, *dbu ma*, vol. *tsa*, 26b.3-26b.4; Tibetan text edited by Lindtner, *Master of Wisdom*, 114; Tibetan text, English translation, and contemporary commentary in David Ross Komito, *Nāgārjuna's "Seventy Stanzas"* (Ithaca, N.Y.: Snow Lion Publications, 1987), 175-176. Brackets are from *Four Interwoven Annotations*, vol. 2, 426.5. Cited in *Great Treatise*, vol. 3, 209.

view of the transitory cannot be overcome:[a]

> As long as the aggregates are apprehended [as inherently established],
> So long thereby does the apprehension of "I" [as inherently established] exist.

Also, Āryadeva's *Four Hundred* (see also *Insight,* 51; *Illumination,* 212 and 246) says:[b]

> Just as the body sense power [pervades] the body,
> Bewilderment abides in all [afflictive emotions as their basis].
> Therefore, all afflictive emotions are overcome
> Through overcoming bewilderment.
>
> When dependent-arising is seen,
> Bewilderment does not arise.
> Therefore, with all endeavor here
> I will set forth just discourse on this.[c]

Concerning the bewilderment so described, since this is at a point of identifying the bewilderment that is one of the three poisons [desire, hatred, and bewilderment], it is *afflictive* ignorance. Also, [Āryadeva] says that, in order to overcome this ignorance, it is necessary to realize the meaning of the profound dependent-arising such that the meaning of emptiness appears as the meaning of dependent-arising. Therefore, afflictive bewilderment must be taken in accordance with the explanation of it—in Chandrakīrti's commentary on that passage (see also *Insight,* 51, and *Illumination,* 246)—as a consciousness superimposing true existence upon things. The honorable Chandrakīrti, following Buddhapālita's commentary on the Superior [Nāgārjuna's] thought, clearly

[a] *rgyal po la gtam bya ba rin po che'i phreng ba, rājaparikathāratnāvalī,* stanza 35ab; Hopkins, *Nāgārjuna's Precious Garland,* 98 and corresponding Tibetan text in Part 3. Sanskrit in Michael Hahn, *Nāgārjuna's Ratnāvalī* (Bonn: Indica et Tibetica Verlag, 1982), 14: *skandhagrāho yāvad asti tāvad evāham ity api /.* Brackets are from *Four Interwoven Annotations,* vol. 2, 189.2. Cited in *Great Treatise,* vol. 3, 122, 208, and 209; Napper, *Dependent-Arising and Emptiness,* 172 and 298-299.

[b] Stanzas VI.10-11; Toh. 3846, *dbu ma,* vol. *tsha,* 7b.2-7b.3; Lang, *Āryadeva's Catuḥśataka,* 66; Sonam Rinchen and Ruth Sonam, *Yogic Deeds of Bodhisattvas,* 156-157. Brackets are from *Four Interwoven Annotations,* vol. 2, 421.5. The first stanza is cited in *Great Treatise,* vol. 3, 207.

[c] That the verb is in the first person is confirmed by Chandrakīrti's commentary, Toh. 3865, vol. *ya,* 113b.2; Ren-da-wa Shön-nu-lo-drö's (*red mda' ba gzhon nu blo gros,* 1349-1412) commentary, 172.12-13 (Sarnath: Sakya Students' Union, 1974); and Gyel-tsap Dar-ma-rin-chen's (*rgyal tshab dar ma rin chen,* 1364-1432) commentary, chap. 6, 8.2-8.4 (Sarnath, India: Pleasure of Elegant Sayings Printing Press, 1971).

speaks to this point.

Showing that afflictive ignorance is the root of revolving in cyclic existence

Moreover, the ignorance explained above, which apprehends the two selves in that way, is not an artificial apprehension of a self of persons or an artificial apprehension of a self of phenomena, as in the assertions of the truth of:

- a person that is permanent, unitary, and under its own power
- external objects of apprehension that are minute particles which are partless in terms of directions—east and so forth—or that are gross objects which are composites of directionally partless minute particles
- internal apprehending consciousnesses that are partless moments of consciousness which are temporarily partless—there being no earlier or later portions, and so forth—or a continuum of consciousness which is a series [of temporally partless moments]
- self-consciousness which is non-dualistic in the sense of being empty of such apprehended object and apprehending subject

these being imputed by the uncommon assertions of the non-Buddhist and [non-Consequentialist] Buddhist systems of tenets. Rather, [the ignorance described above refers to] the two innate apprehensions of self, which all those whose minds are and are not affected by tenets have in common and which have operated beginninglessly without depending on the mind's being affected by tenets.

Just that [innate ignorance] is here held to be the root of cyclic existence:

- because through the reasoning of the statement in Chandrakīrti's *Supplement to (Nāgārjuna's) "Treatise on the Middle"*:[a]

> This non-produced permanent [self imputed by false systems] is not perceived
> By those spending many eons as animals,
> Yet consciousnesses apprehending "I" are seen to operate in them.[b]

[a] VI.125abc; P5262, vol. 98, 104.1.8; Toh. 3861, *dbu ma*, vol. *'a*, 210a.7; La Vallée Poussin, *Madhyamakāvatāra*, 243.9-243.11; La Vallée Poussin, "*Introduction au traité du milieu*," *Muséon* 12 (1911): 290.

[b] With additions from Tsong-kha-pa's *Illumination of the Thought* (P6143, vol. 154, 84.2.5) in brackets, the full stanza reads:

[it can be understood that] what binds sentient beings in cyclic existence is innate ignorance, and
- because artificial ignorance occurs only in proponents of tenets, it is not feasibly the root of cyclic existence.

Gaining discerning ascertainment about this is crucial. If you do not understand this, you will not know, when delineating [emptiness] through the view, to hold as chief the ascertainment that objects as apprehended by innate ignorance are non-existent and that the objects of artificial apprehensions are refuted as a branch of this [process].[a] If the two selves are negated within neglecting to refute the mode of apprehension by innate ignorance, you will ascertain merely a selflessness that negates imputations only by proponents of tenets mentioned above. Consequently, even during meditation you will have to meditate only on such, since delineation by way of the view is for the sake of meditation.

Therefore, even if [the emptiness of such an artificially apprehended self] were made manifest through meditating on it and even if familiarization with it were brought to completion, it would be subsumed within being only that. And, it would be very absurd to assert

---

> Those who have fallen down senseless into [lives as] animals for many eons also do not perceive this unborn permanent [self]. Having seen that the apprehension of (an inherently existent) "I" operates even in them, [what intelligent being would hold that such an unborn permanent self is the base of the innate apprehension of an (inherently existent) "I"?] Hence, there is no self other than the aggregates.

See also Hopkins, *Maps of the Profound,* 648, 877.

[a] Jam-yang-shay-pa responds to Tak-tsang Shay-rap-rin-chen's criticism of Tsong-kha-pa for this apparent claim that reasoning refuting artificial misapprehensions does not refute the innate. In reply, Jam-yang-shay-pa first explains that Tsong-kha-pa should be understood as saying:

> Although one refuted objects imputed by systems of tenets **that do not involve the mode of apprehension by innate [misapprehensions],** this would not damage innate [misapprehensions] and although one refuted objects imputed **merely and only** by systems of tenets, this would not harm innate [misapprehensions].

Jam-yang-shay-pa's cogent point is that Tsong-kha-pa's meaning is that refuting that the "I," for instance, does not depend on causes and does not change is not itself a refutation of the innate misapprehension of the inherent existence of the "I," because the apprehension that the "I" is independent and immutable does not constitute the innate apprehension that the "I" inherently exists, that is to say, exists in its own right. Rather, refuting such can be a branch of refuting the innate apprehension of inherent existence when it is understood that if things did inherently exist, they could not depend on causes and could not change. See Hopkins, *Maps of the Profound,* 647.

that through seeing the non-existence of the two selves merely as imputed by such artificial apprehensions, the innate afflictive emotions are overcome. Chandrakīrti's *Supplement to (Nāgārjuna's) "Treatise on the Middle"* says:[a]

> [You propound] that when the selflessness [of persons] is realized
> One abandons [only] the permanent self, [but] it is not asserted
> As the base of the [innate] apprehension of "I." Hence, it is amazing to propound
> That through knowing the non-existence of [just a permanent] self the [innate] view of self is eradicated![b]

and Chandrakīrti's commentary also says:[c]

> In order to clarify by way of an example the senselessness [of saying that the innate apprehension of self is abandoned through merely refuting a permanent self, the *Supplement*] says:
>
> > That while seeing a snake living in a hole in a wall of your house,
> > Your fears can be removed and the fright of a snake abandoned
> > By [another's saying, "Do not be afraid of that snake.] There is no elephant here,"
> > Is, alas, laughable to others!

Although he says this about the selflessness of persons, it is the same also with respect to the selflessness of phenomena. [The stanza] could be put together this way:

> [You propound] that when the selflessness [of phenomena] is realized
> One abandons [that is, refutes only] the artificial self [of phenomena, but] it is not asserted

---

[a] Stanza VI.140; Toh. 3861, *dbu ma*, vol. *'a*, 211a.3-211a.4; La Vallée Poussin, *Madhyamakāvatāra*, 264.2-264.5; La Vallée Poussin, "*Introduction au traité du milieu*," *Muséon* 12 (1911): 309. Brackets are from *Four Interwoven Annotations*, vol. 2, 392.4. Cited in *Great Treatise*, vol. 3, 197.

[b] See also Hopkins, *Maps of the Profound*, 646-647, 650, 728-730.

[c] Stanza VI.141 and its introduction; Toh. 3862, *dbu ma*, vol. *'a*, 301b.5-301b.6; La Vallée Poussin, *Madhyamakāvatāra*, 264.9-264.14; La Vallée Poussin, "*Introduction au traité du milieu*," *Muséon* 12 (1911): 309. The stanza is also found at Toh. 3861, *dbu ma*, vol. *'a*, 211a.4-211a.5. Brackets are from *Four Interwoven Annotations*, vol. 2, 392.6. Cited in *Great Treatise*, vol. 3, 197.

As the base of [innate] ignorance. Hence it is amazing to propound
That through knowing the non-existence of [an artificial] self [of phenomena, innate] ignorance is eradicated!

Objection: Nāgārjuna's *Precious Garland* explains that the apprehension of a self of phenomena—the apprehension of the aggregates as truly existent—is the root of cyclic existence:[a]

As long as the aggregates are apprehended [as inherently established],
So long thereby does the apprehension of "I" [as inherently established] exist.
Further, when the apprehension of "I" exists,
There is action, and from it there also is birth.

However, Chandrakīrti's *Supplement to (Nāgārjuna's) "Treatise on the Middle"* explains that the view of the transitory is the root of cyclic existence:[b]

Seeing [through investigating] with their minds that all afflictive emotions [such as desire and so forth] and defects [such as birth, aging, sickness, death, and so on]
Arise from the view of the transitory collection [apprehending "I" and "mine" as inherently established]...

These two explanations are contradictory because it is not feasible to have two discordant roots of cyclic existence.

Answer: There is no fallacy:

- because although this Middle Way Consequentialist system differentiates the two apprehensions of self by way of object of observation, the two do not have different aspects in their mode of apprehension, since they both have the aspect of apprehending [their object] to be established by way of its own character, and

[a] Stanza 35; Hopkins, *Nāgārjuna's Precious Garland,* 98 and corresponding Tibetan text in Part 3. Sanskrit in Hahn, *Ratnāvalī,* 14: *skandhagrāho yāvad asti tāvad evāham ity api / ahaṃkāre sati punaḥ karma janma tataḥ punaḥ //.* Brackets are from *Four Interwoven Annotations,* vol. 2, 189.2. Cited in *Great Treatise,* vol. 3, 122, 208, and 209; Napper, *Dependent-Arising and Emptiness,* 172 and 298-299.

[b] Stanza VI.120ab; Toh. 3861, *dbu ma,* vol. *'a,* 210a.4; La Vallée Poussin, *Madhyamakāvatāra,* 233.16-233.17; La Vallée Poussin, "*Introduction au traité du milieu,*" *Muséon* 12 (1911): 282. Brackets are from *Four Interwoven Annotations,* vol. 2, 180.6; Napper, *Dependent-Arising and Emptiness,* 169 and 290. Cited in *Great Treatise,* vol. 3, 120. For the entire stanza, see 54.

- because [a contradiction of two roots of cyclic existence] is taken to be positing two [consciousnesses] that have **discordant** modes of apprehension in their operation on an object as roots of cyclic existence.

Therefore:

- when it is taught that the apprehension of a self of phenomena is the cause of the view of the transitory, it is being shown that the two inner divisions of ignorance are cause and effect [the apprehension of the inherent existence of phenomena causing the apprehension of inherent existence of the person], and
- when it is taught that both of those are the root of the afflictive emotions, it is being shown that they are the root of all other afflictive emotions whose modes of apprehension are discordant with them.

And since this fact is so for both of them, there is no contradiction, just as there is no contradiction in both former and later [moments] of a similar type of ignorance being the root of cyclic existence.

The honorable Chandrakīrti does not clearly and specifically describe the view of the transitory as ignorance, but:

- he says—without differentiating persons and phenomena—that the apprehension of things in general as truly existent is afflictive ignorance
- also he asserts that an apprehension of a self of persons is an apprehension of persons as established by way of their own character
- also he frequently describes the innate view of the transitory as the root of cyclic existence
- also if he did assert [the view of the transitory] as something other than the ignorance that is the apprehension of true existence, there would be the contradiction of positing two roots of cyclic existence having discordant modes of apprehension.

Therefore, both [apprehensions of the true existence of persons and apprehensions of the true existence of phenomena] should be taken to be ignorance.

All other afflictive emotions—innate and artificial—operate within apprehending **individual features** of just that object on which the innate ignorance described above has superimposed [a sense of inherent existence]. Therefore, it is said that just as the other four sense powers—eyes and so forth—abide in dependence on the body sense power and are not located in a place under their own power other than [where the body sense power is], so even all other afflictive emotions operate in dependence on innate ignorance, due to which bewilderment is chief. [Āryadeva's *Four Hundred* (see also *Illumination,* 212 and 246)] says:[z] [a]

> Just as the body sense power [pervades] the body,
> Bewilderment abides in all [afflictive emotions as their basis].

Chandrakīrti's *Commentary on (Āryadeva's) "Four Hundred"* on this (see also *Illumination,* 246) says:[b]

> Also, desire and so forth engage in superimposing features, such as beauty and ugliness, on just [the appearance of] an inherent nature of things imputed by bewilderment. Hence, they operate non-separately from bewilderment and also depend on bewilderment, because bewilderment is just chief.

Therefore, when bewilderment holds objects to be established by way of their own character:

- If the apprehended object is agreeable to your mind, desire is generated observing it.
- If it seems to be disagreeable to your mind, anger is generated with respect to it.
- If the object does not seem to be either agreeable or disagreeable to your mind but abides as an ordinary thing in the middle, even though the other two are not generated observing it, a continuation of the same type of bewilderment is.

Nāgārjuna's *Sixty Stanzas of Reasoning* says:[c]

> Why would the great poisonous afflictive emotions not arise
> In those whose minds have a basis [that is, an inherently existent object]?
> Even when [the object] is ordinary, [their minds]
> Are grasped by the snake of the afflictive emotions.

Chandrakīrti's commentary (see also *Illumination,* 248) explains it as was just described prior [to the quote].

That the view of the transitory is produced from a consciousness apprehending the aggregates as truly existent appears to be the

[a] The entire stanza as well as the next stanza were cited earlier (45).

[b] Toh. 3865, *dbu ma,* vol. *ya,* 112b.7-113a.2. Brackets are from *Four Interwoven Annotations,* vol. 2, 359.5. Cited in *Great Treatise,* vol. 3, 183.

[c] Stanza 52; Toh. 3825, *dbu ma,* vol. *tsa,* 22a.7; Lindtner, *Master of Wisdom,* 88.

thought also of Nāgārjuna's *Precious Garland* (above, 49). How the remaining afflictive emotions are produced should be known through inferring it from the explanation at the point of beings of medium capacity.[a] This should also be known in accordance with the statement in Dharmakīrti's *Commentary on (Dignāga's) "Compilation of Prime Cognition"*:[b]

> In one who sees self
> There is always adherence to "I."
> Through that adherence there is attachment to pleasure.
> Through attachment faults are obscured
> And advantages seen, whereby there is strong attachment.
> The "mine" are taken up as means of achieving [pleasure].
> Hence, as long as there is attraction to self,
> So long does one revolve in cyclic existence.

Although the system of this [passage] differs from the mode of positing two apprehensions of self [in the Consequence School] as explained above, the stages of how afflictive emotions are produced [according to the Consequence School] can be understood in dependence on it.

Moreover, initially when the "I" that is the object of observation of the thought "I" is apprehended to exist by way of its own character, desire with respect to the self is generated. That generates attachment to the self's pleasure. Also, since the self's pleasure is not independent but depends on the "mine," there is attachment to the "mine." Obscuring the disadvantages of the "mine," this attachment brings about perception of the "mine" as advantageous. Then, the "mine" are taken up as means of achieving the self's pleasure. With afflictive emotions produced in this way, actions are undertaken. Through actions, in turn, the connection is made to [a new] cyclic existence. Nāgārjuna's *Seventy Stanzas on Emptiness* says:[c]

---

[a] This was explained earlier in the *Medium-Length Exposition of the Stages of the Path* prior to the section on special insight; for the same exposition see Tsong-kha-pa, *Great Treatise*, vol. 1, 297-313; see below, 243ff.

[b] *tshad ma rnam 'grel gyi tshig le'ur byas pa, pramāṇavarttikakārikā*, stanza II.217cd-II.219ab; Toh. 4210, *tshad ma*, vol. *ce*, 115b.7-116a.1; Yūsho Miyasaka, "*Pramāṇavarttika-kārikā:* Sanskrit and Tibetan," *Indo Koten Kenkyu (Acta Indologica)* 2 (1971-72): 32-33:
yaḥ paśyaty ātmānaṃ tatrāham iti śāśvataḥ snehaḥ // snehāt sukheṣu tṛṣyati tṛṣṇā doṣāṃ sthirī kurute / guṇadarśī paritṛṣyan mameti tat sādhanāny upādatte // tenātmābhiniveśo yāvat tāvat sa saṃsāre /.

[c] Stanza 37; Toh. 3827, *dbu ma*, vol. *tsa*, 25b.4-25b.5; Lindtner, *Master of Wisdom*, 106; Komito, *Seventy Stanzas*, 149-150. Chandrakīrti's commentary (P5268, vol. 99, 35.4.5-35.5.5; Toh. 3867, *dbu ma*, vol. *ya*, 317a.4-317b.3) is:

> [Contaminated] karmas are caused by afflictive emotions.
> Having a nature of afflictive emotions and karmas,
> The body is caused by [contaminated] karmas.
> Even all three are empty of inherent existence.

You should train in the stages of how beings revolve in cyclic existence in this way, until ascertainment is gained.

Showing that one wishing to abandon the apprehension of self should seek the view of selflessness

This has two parts: the reason why, if you wish to abandon ignorance, you should seek the view realizing selflessness and how to generate the view realizing selflessness.

Reason why, if you wish to abandon ignorance, you should seek the view realizing selflessness

A state of extinguishment in which the two apprehensions of self—the ignorance explained above—have been abandoned should certainly be wanted and appears indeed to be wanted. Nevertheless, despite its being wanted, there are those who do not strive at understanding how the apprehension of self comes to be the root of cyclic existence or, although they see a portion of that, do not strive for the sake of generating the pure view of selflessness in their continuum upon having refuted well—with reasoning and scriptures of definitive meaning—the object apprehended by the apprehension of self. They have very dull faculties, for although they have forsaken the life of the path progressing to liberation and omniscience, they are not concerned about it.

Therefore, the glorious Dharmakīrti's *Commentary on (Dignāga's)*

---

de la ma rig pa'i rkyen gyis 'du byed do zhes bya bas las ni nyon mongs pa'i rgyu mtshan can te nyon mongs pa 'di'i rgyur byas pas/ nyon mongs las bdag las ni 'du byed rnams te/ las dang nyon mongs pa las gang zhig rnam par shes pa la sogs pa'i bdag nyid pas/ rnam par shes pa la sogs pa de rnams 'du byed kyi las dang nyon mongs pa'i bdag nyid de /ma rig pa dang 'du byed kyis bskyed pa'i phyir/ de rnams kyang 'dir 'du byed yongs su rdzogs pa'i skye mched drug gi gnas skabs kyi lus thob pa'i rgyu mtshan du 'gyur ro zhes bya ste/ tha dad pa'i lus 'dzin pa'o// lus de yang 'du byed bzhin du las dang nyon mongs pa'i rgyu can kho na'o zhes byas nas/ gcig gis kyang nye bar mtshon nas las kyi rgyu mtshan can gyi lus zhes bya'o// de las kyang de dag gi las dang de'i 'bras bu lus po ste/ gsum po rnams kyang rten cing 'brel par 'byung ba nyid la/ des na dri za'i grong khyer la sogs pa bzhin du 'di dag gsum yang ngo bo nyid kyis stong pa'o//

"Compilation of Prime Cognition" says:[a]

Without rejecting [through reasoning] the [conceived] object [of the apprehension of self]
This [apprehension of self] cannot be abandoned [by meditating on the self as having defects and so forth].
The abandonment of desire, hatred, and so on
Which are [generated due to being] related with [perceived] advantages [of happiness] and disadvantages [of unhappiness]
Is through not seeing those [advantages and disadvantages] in objects [in accordance with how they are apprehended by desire, hatred, and so forth, that is to say, through properly seeing that those do not exist],
Not through external ways [as when removing a thorn that has pierced the body].

When an external object of abandonment such as a thorn that has pierced oneself is removed, it can be removed from the root with a needle, for instance, without depending on [a process of] rejecting [that is, realizing the non-existence of] the object as it is apprehended. However, when an internal mental object of abandonment is abandoned, it is not done this way. Rather, it must be abandoned through seeing the non-existence of the object as it is apprehended by, for instance, the apprehension of self.

The glorious Chandrakīrti also says that when one sees that all afflictive emotions (desire and so forth) and all defects (birth, death, and so forth) arise from the apprehension of self, a wish to cease and abandon it arises, whereupon a yogi refutes with reasoning the self of persons, the object superimposed by the apprehension of self. His *Supplement to (Nāgārjuna's) "Treatise on the Middle"* clearly says (see also *Illumination*, 212):[b]

Seeing [through investigating] with their minds that all

[a] Stanza II.222-II.223ab; Toh. 4210, *tshad ma*, vol. *ce*, 116a.3; Miyasaka, "*Pramāṇavarttika*," 32-33: *adūṣite 'sya viṣaye na śakyaṃ tasya varjanaṃ / prahāṇir icchādveṣāder guṇadoṣānubandhinaḥ // tayor adṛṣṭir viṣaye na tu bāhyeṣu yaḥ kramaḥ /*. Brackets are from *Four Interwoven Annotations*, vol. 2, 756.1. Cited in *Great Treatise*, vol. 3, 335; Napper, *Dependent-Arising and Emptiness*, 169 and 290.

[b] VI.120; Toh. 3861, *dbu ma*, vol. *'a*, 210a.4; La Vallée Poussin, *Madhyamakāvatāra*, 233.16-233.19; La Vallée Poussin, "*Introduction au traité du milieu*," *Muséon* 12 (1911): 282. Brackets are from *Four Interwoven Annotations*, vol. 2, 180.6 and 755.6. Cited in *Great Treatise*, vol. 3, 120; Napper, *Dependent-Arising and Emptiness*, 169 and 290. The last two lines are cited in *Great Treatise*, vol. 3, 335.

afflictive emotions [such as desire and so forth] and defects
[such as birth, aging, sickness, death, and so on]
Arise from the view of the transitory collection [apprehending
"I" and "mine" as inherently established]
And having realized that the self [or "I"] is the object [of mistake] of this [ignorance],
Yogis [seeking release] refute self [that is to say, inherent establishment, with reasoning].[a]

This must be done by a meditator on suchness; hence, he says "yogis."

This procedure is the excellent thought also of the protector Nāgārjuna because:

- his *Sixty Stanzas of Reasoning* indicates that the apprehension of true existence—called the assertion of inherent existence,[b] which is the cause of all afflicted views and all other afflictive emotions—is abandoned through realizing the suchness of things, the absence of inherently existent production, by means of the reason of dependent-arising:[c]

  That [apprehension of true existence] is the cause of all [bad] views.
  Without it afflictive emotions are not produced.

  Therefore, when that is thoroughly known,
  [Bad] views and afflictive emotions are thoroughly purified.

  Through what is that known?
  The seeing of dependent-arising.
  The supreme knower of suchness said
  That what is dependently produced is not [inherently] produced.

- and the perception that inherent existence does not exist does not occur without rejecting the object of the apprehension of things as inherently established.

[a] "Self" in the third line is taken to be the nominally existent "I" that is mistaken to be inherently established; "self" in the fourth line is taken to be the object of negation itself, inherent establishment.

[b] *dngos por khas len.*

[c] Stanzas 47-48; Toh. 3825, *dbu ma*, vol. *tsa*, 22a.4-5; Lindtner, *Master of Wisdom*, 88, 175: *sa hetuḥ sarvadṛṣṭīnāṃ kleśotpattir na taṃ vinā / tasmāt tasmin parijñāte dṛṣṭikleśaparikṣayaḥ // parijñā tasya keneti pratītyotpādadarśanāt / pratītya jātaṃ cājātam āha tattvavidāṃ varaḥ //*. The last two lines are cited in *Great Treatise*, vol. 3, 187.

A statement by Āryadeva that accords with this was quoted earlier (see also *Insight*, 45). Also, his *Four Hundred* says that through seeing the nonexistence of the self [that is, the inherent existence] of the object of observation apprehended by the apprehension of self, the root of cyclic existence, ignorance, is cut (see also *Illumination*, 211):[a]

> When selflessness, [the absence of inherent establishment,] is seen in objects,
> [The ignorance that is] the seed of cyclic existence is ended.

Moreover, the venerable Shāntideva says [in his *Compendium of Instructions*]:[b]

> The emptiness of the person is thus thoroughly established. Therefore, by cutting their root all afflictive emotions do not arise in any way. It is as the *Sūtra on the Secrecies of the Ones-Gone-Thus*[c] says:
>
>> Shāntamati, it is like this: For example, when the roots of a tree are cut, all the branches, leaves, and twigs dry. Shāntamati, similarly, when the view of the transitory collection is pacified, all afflictive emotions and secondary afflictive emotions are pacified.

He is saying that through having cultivated realization of the person as empty of inherent existence, the view of the transitory is overcome and that when it is overcome, all other afflictive emotions are overcome. Furthermore, without rejecting the object of the apprehension of a self of persons, a realization of selflessness cannot occur. Therefore, [this procedure is also the thought of Shāntideva].

The passage from sūtra indicates that the view of the transitory is the root of all other afflictive emotions. If it were something other than

---

[a] XIV.25cd; Toh. 3846, *dbu ma*, vol. *tsha*, 16a.5; Lang, *Āryadeva's Catuḥśataka*, 134; Sonam Rinchen and Ruth Sonam, *Yogic Deeds of Bodhisattvas*, 275. Brackets are from *Four Interwoven Annotations*, vol. 2, 755.2. Cited in *Great Treatise*, vol. 3, 335.

[b] *bslab pa kun las btus pa, śikṣāsamuccaya;* Toh. 3940, *dbu ma*, vol. *khi*, 133a.7-133b.2; Sanskrit edited by Cecil Bendall, *Çikshāsamuccaya: A Compendium of Buddhistic Teaching*, Bibliotheca Buddhica 1 (Osnabrück, Germany: Biblio Verlag, 1970), 242: *evaṃ hi pudgalaśūnyatā siddhā bhavati / tataśca chinnamūlatvāt kleśā na samudācaranti // yathoktam āryatathāgataguhyasūtre / tadyathāpi nāma śāntamate vṛkṣasya mūlachinnasya sarvaśākhāpattapalāśāḥ śuṣyanti / evam eva śāntamate satkāyadṛṣṭyupaśamāt sarvakleśā upaśāmyantīti //*. English translation in Cecil Bendall and W.H.D. Rouse, *Śikshā-samuccaya: A Compendium of Buddhist Doctrine* (Delhi: Motilal Banarsidass, 1971), 224.

[c] *de bzhin gshegs pa'i gsang ba bsam gyis mi khyab pa bstan pa'i mdo, tathāgatācintyaguhyanirdeśasūtra*, Toh. 47, vol. *ka* (*dkon brtsegs*).

ignorance, there would be two discordant roots of cyclic existence; therefore, it should be taken as ignorance.

In brief, when the many supreme scholars who commented on the meaning of the scriptures on the profound [emptiness] delineated the meaning of suchness, they analyzed by way of scripture and reasoning. They did this from having perceived that selflessness and emptiness cannot be realized without seeing that the self as apprehended by erroneous apprehension does not exist and without seeing the emptiness of that self. It is important to gain ascertainment with respect to this.

For if you do not meditate on the meaning of the negation of the erroneous object that is the root of being bound in cyclic existence, even though you meditate on the meaning of something else that you consider to be profound, it will not harm the apprehension of self at all:

- because unless the mind becomes absorbed in the suchness of selflessness and emptiness, an overcoming of the apprehension of self cannot occur, and
- because without rejecting the object of the apprehension of self, although you perform the mere withdrawal of the mind that moves over there to its object, this cannot be posited as being absorbed in selflessness.

The reason for this is that there are three modes of the mind's operating on an object—(1) apprehending the object of observation to truly exist, (2) apprehending it to not truly exist, and (3) apprehending it without qualifying it with either of those. Hence, just as although one is not apprehending [an object] as not truly existent, one is not necessarily apprehending it as truly existent, so, although one is not involved in the two selves, it is not necessary that one is involved in the two selflessnesses. For there are limitless minds abiding in the third category.

Furthermore, because the two apprehensions of self operate mainly within observing effective things, persons and phenomena, you need to delineate that just those bases—with respect to which the error is made—do not exist in the way that they are apprehended. Otherwise, it is like searching for a robber on the plain after the robber has gone to the woods. Since error is removed by meditating on the meaning that has been delineated in this way, such an emptiness is the supreme meaning of suchness, but delineation of the meaning of suchness as something else forsaking this is reduced to being only imputed by one's own wish. Consequently, keep [in mind] that such is a deviation from the meaning of the scriptures.

Therefore, ignorance apprehending the proliferations of persons, such as man and woman, and of phenomena, such as form and feeling, to be truly existent is overcome by finding the view realizing emptiness—selflessness—and cultivating it in meditation. When that ignorance is overcome, you overcome the conceptuality that is the improper mental application superimposing signs of beauty, ugliness, and so forth upon having observed the objects of the apprehension of true existence. When that is overcome, the other afflictive emotions—desire and so forth—which have the view of the transitory as their root are overcome. When they are overcome, actions motivated by them are overcome. When they are overcome, powerless birth in cyclic existence impelled by actions is overcome, whereby liberation is attained. Thinking about this, you should generate firm ascertainment and then unerringly seek the view of suchness. Nāgārjuna's *Treatise on the Middle* says:[a]

> By extinguishing actions and afflictive emotions [which are the causes producing cyclic existence], there is liberation.
> Actions and afflictive emotions [arise] from conceptualizations [that is, improper mental application superimposing beauty and so forth on objects].
> They arise from proliferations [apprehending true establishment in objects].
> Proliferations cease by [proper knowledge of the mode of] the emptiness [of inherent existence].

You need to value realizing the meaning of suchness upon having understood the stages of how you enter into and disengage from cyclic existence in this way. It will not come through vague involvement in which the points are not differentiated well.

[a] XVIII.5; Toh. 3824, *dbu ma*, vol. *tsa*, 11a.1; de Jong, *Mūlamadhyamakakārikāḥ*, 24: *karmakleśakṣayān mokṣaḥ karmakleśā vikalpataḥ / te prapañcāt prapañcas tu śūnyatāyāṃ nirudhyate //*. Brackets are from *Four Interwoven Annotations*, vol. 2, 715.2. Cited in *Great Treatise*, vol. 3, 321.

3. Order of Realization

How to generate the view realizing selflessness

This section has three parts: the stages generating the two views of selflessness, actual generation of the two views in stages, and presentation of obscurational truths and ultimate truths.

Stages generating the two views of selflessness

With respect to the stages generating the two apprehensions of self, the apprehension of a self of phenomena generates the apprehension of a self of persons, but when entering into the suchness of selflessness, you should first generate the view of the selflessness of persons and then generate the view realizing the selflessness of phenomena. Moreover, this is as Nāgārjuna's *Precious Garland* says (see also *Illumination,* 203):[a]

> A being is not earth, not water,
> Not fire, not wind, not space,
> Not consciousness, and not all of them.
> What person is there other than these?
>
> Just as because of being [only imputed in dependence upon] an aggregation of the six constituents,
> A person is not [established as his/her own] reality,[b]
> So because of being [imputed in dependence upon] an aggregation
> Each of the constituents also is not [established as its own] reality.

He speaks of the absence of inherent existence first of persons and then of the constituents, earth and so forth, which are the bases of imputation of a person. Also, Chandrakīrti's *Clear Words* and Buddhapālita's *Commentary on (Nāgārjuna's) "Treatise on the Middle"*[c] explain that when

[a] Stanzas 80-81; Hopkins, *Nāgārjuna's Precious Garland,* 104-105 and corresponding Tibetan text in Part 3. The Sanskrit is not extant.

[b] For the present Dalai Lama's personal reflections on these lines, see *How to Practice: The Way to a Meaningful Life,* ed. and trans. by Jeffrey Hopkins (New York: Pocket Books, 2002), 166-167, and *How to See Yourself As You Really Are,* 123-124.

[c] *dbu ma rtsa ba'i 'grel pa buddha pā li ta, Buddhapālitamūlamadhyamakavṛtti;* Toh. 3842, *dbu ma,* vol. *tsa;* Tibetan text edited by Max Walleser, *dBu ma rca ba'i 'grel pa Buddha pā li ta (Buddhapālita-Mūlamadhyamakavṛtti) Chapters i-xii.* Bibliotheca Buddhica 16 (St. Petersburg, 1913-14).

entering into suchness, one initially enters by way of the selflessness of persons, and Shāntideva also says the same.

The reason why it must be done this way is that although there is no difference in subtlety with regard to the selflessness to be ascertained in terms of the persons or phenomena that are its substrata, selflessness is easier to ascertain in terms of a person due to essentials of the substratum,[a] whereas it is more difficult to ascertain in terms of [other] phenomena. This is like the fact that, for example, since it is more difficult to ascertain the selflessness of phenomena in terms of an eye, ear, and so forth and easier to ascertain it in terms of a reflection and so forth, the latter are posited as examples for delineating selflessness in terms of the former.[b]

In consideration of this fact, the *King of Meditative Stabilization Sūtra* also says (see also *Insight,* 87; *Illumination,* 204):[c]

> Just as you know [how to generate] discrimination [taking to
> mind the delineation of the mode of subsistence] of a self,
> Apply this mentally to all [phenomena].
> [The reason for this is that] all phenomena are [established as

[a] In his 1972 lectures, the Dalai Lama suggested that a reason for this is that the person is already considered by the other Buddhist systems to be imputedly existent.

[b] In his 1972 lectures, the Dalai Lama noted that Tsong-kha-pa's presentation here differs slightly from that in his *Great Exposition of the Stages of the Path,* where he uses as an example the coarse falsity of a reflection of a face being empty of establishment as a face, which, of course, is realized by ordinary beings who have not realized emptiness. That is used as an example, or analog, of a reflection of a face being empty of inherent existence. However, here the emptiness of inherent existence of a reflection is used as a similar example in the process of realizing the emptiness of inherent existence of phenomena such as an eye, an ear, and so forth. The difference between the two is explained as being for different trainees; the description in the *Great Exposition of the Stages of the Path* is for those whose continuums have not matured, whereas the description in the *Medium-Length Exposition of the Stages of the Path* is for those whose continuums have matured. The Dalai Lama reported that according to Jam-yang-shay-pa it could be that first one contemplates coarse falsity and then as one's understanding becomes more profound, one realizes subtle selflessness with respect to a reflection of a face, whereupon this is used as an example for realizing the subtle selflessness of other phenomena.

[c] *ting nge 'dzin rgyal po'i mdo, samādhirājasūtra,* XII.7; Toh. 127, *mdo sde,* vol. *da,* 44a.2-44a.3; cited in *Prasannapadā,* in commentary to stanza IV.9; Toh. 3860, *dbu ma,* vol. *'a,* 43b.1-43b.2; La Vallée Poussin, *Mūlamadhyamakakārikās (Mādhyamikasūtras) de Nāgārjuna avec la Prasannapadā Commentaire de Candrakīrti* (Osnabrück, Germany: Biblio Verlag, 1970), 128.11-128.13: *yathā jñāta tayā 'tmasaṃjña tathaiva sarvatra peṣitā buddhiḥ / sarve ca tatsvabhāvā dharma viśuddhā gagaṇakalpāḥ // ekena sarvaṃ jñānāti sarvam ekena paśyati /.* Brackets are from *Four Interwoven Annotations,* vol. 2, 686.6. Cited in *Great Treatise,* vol. 3, 311.

having the nature of the mode of emptiness of inherent existence of the self,
Naturally] pure [by way of an elimination of inherent establishment], like space [which is a mere elimination of obstructive contact.
Hence] even through [knowing with reasoning the mode of emptiness of inherent existence of] one [phenomenon the mode of emptiness of inherent existence of] all [phenomena] is known.
Even through [meditatively directly seeing the emptiness of inherent existence of] one [phenomenon the emptinesses of inherent existence of] all [phenomena] are [directly] seen.

It says that:

> When you know well the mode of subsistence of "I" with respect to which the discrimination of self, thinking "I," operates, all phenomena (internal such as eye, ear, and so forth) and external (such as a pot and so forth) are to be understood in the same way upon applying that reasoning to them.[a] Thereby, through knowing and seeing the natural mode of one phenomenon, the nature of all other phenomena also can be known and seen.

[a] For more on this topic, see 77-78.

4. Selflessness of Persons

Actual generation of the two views in stages

This section has two parts: delineating the selflessness of persons and delineating the selflessness of phenomena.

Delineating the selflessness of persons

This section has two parts: identifying persons and delineating them as not inherently existent.

Identifying persons

"Persons" are the persons of the six types—gods, demi-gods, humans, animals, hungry ghosts, and hell-beings—as well as persons who are common beings and Superiors, and so forth. Moreover, they are accumulators of wholesome and unwholesome actions, experiencers of the fruits of those actions, revolvers in cyclic existence, cultivators of paths for the sake of liberation, attainers of liberation, and so forth.

A [Hearer][b] sūtra cited in Chandrakīrti's *Commentary on the "Supplement to (Nāgārjuna's) 'Treatise on the Middle'"* and so forth[c] says:[d]

> [This mind apprehending and viewing an inherently established] self is a devilish mind.
> [Thenceforth] you are under the influence of [devils by way of] viewing [and adhering to an inherently established self].

---

[a] Ge-luk-pa scholars often say that if an object were imputed **to** its basis of designation, it would be its basis of designation; rather, it is imputed **in dependence upon** its basis of designation. Indeed, this is how the sūtra cited below puts it.

[b] *Four Interwoven Annotations*, vol. 2, 594.6.

[c] The *Four Interwoven Annotations* (vol. 2, 594.6) says that Bhāvaviveka cites the same passage.

[d] Commenting on VI.135ab; Toh. 3862, *dbu ma*, vol. *'a*, 299b.6-299b.7; La Vallée Poussin, *Madhyamakāvatāra*, 257.19-258.6; La Vallée Poussin, "*Introduction au traité du milieu*," *Muséon* 12 (1911): 303. Brackets are from *Four Interwoven Annotations*, vol. 2, 594.6. Cited in *Great Treatise*, vol. 3, 278. Khangkar and Yorihito (192 n. 100) call attention to Saṃyuttanikāya I. Sagātha-vagga, V. Bhikkunī-saṃyutta, 10, p. 135:

> *kinnu satto ti paccesi// māra ḍittigataṃ nu te// //*
> *suddhasaṅkhāropuñjo yaṃ// nayiddha sattūpalabhati// //*
> *yathā hi aṅgasambhārā// noti saddo ratho iti// //*
> *evaṃ khandhesu santesu// hoti satto ti sammuti// //*

These compositional[a] aggregates are empty [of inherent existence.
Even if a self is apprehended in dependence upon the five aggregates, the mere collection of these aggregates is not a self or sentient being, and] here [among the aggregates individually separated out] there is no sentient being [or self].

Just as a chariot is spoken of
In dependence upon a collection of parts [such as wheels, axles, and so forth],
So conventionally a sentient being
[Is spoken of] in dependence upon the aggregates.

The first stanza indicates the selflessness of persons—that ultimately persons do not exist. The first line says that the apprehension of a self of persons is a devilish mind. The second, that one who conceives such is under the influence of a bad view. The third and fourth, that the aggregates are empty of a self of persons.

The second stanza indicates that persons exist in conventional terms. The first two lines give an example; the last two connect it to the meaning, indicating that persons are only imputed in dependence on the aggregates.

This sūtra speaks of the collection of the aggregates as the basis of imputation of a person. A basis of imputation is not feasible to be the object imputed, and the collection of the aggregates must be taken as both a collection at one time and a collection over former and later [moments]; therefore, it is not feasible to posit the continuum of the collection of the aggregates as a person. When the collection is posited as the basis of imputation, the possessors of the collection [that is, the parts] are also posited as the bases of imputation, and therefore both of those [that is, the collection and its parts] are not fit to be a person. Chandrakīrti's *Supplement to (Nāgārjuna's) "Treatise on the Middle"* says:[b]

Sūtra says it is in dependence on the aggregates.
Therefore the mere composite of the aggregates is not the self.[c]

---

[a] *'du byed, saṃskāra.* The *Four Interwoven Annotations* (vol. 2, 595.2) explains that the aggregates are called "compositional" because through the force of coming together they produce various manifestations of effects (*tshogs pa'i dbang gis 'bras bu'i rnam 'gyur sna tshogs sgrub*).

[b] VI.135cd; Toh. 3861, *dbu ma,* vol. *'a,* 210b.7; La Vallée Poussin, *Madhyamakāvatāra,* 258.8-258.9; La Vallée Poussin, "*Introduction au traité du milieu,*" *Muséon* 12 (1911): 303.

[c] As Jam-yang-shay-pa (Hopkins, *Meditation on Emptiness,* 694-695 and 897-903) shows, in his *Blaze of Reasoning* (P5256, vol. 96, 36.4.5) Bhāvaviveka explains that the collection

and:[a]

> *Objection:* The Teacher asserts the aggregates as the self
> Because he said, "The aggregates are the self."
> *Answer:* That refutes a self other than the aggregates,
> For other sūtras say that form is not the self, and so forth.

Therefore, even the statement [in sūtra],[b] "Any devotee or Brahmin who views a self is viewing only these five aggregates," refutes through the term "only" that a self that is a different entity from the aggregates exists as the object of observation of an innate apprehension of an [inherently existent] "I." Having refuted such, it also does not indicate that the aggregates are the object of observation of a consciousness apprehending [an inherently existent] "I." If it did, it would contradict the refutation in other sūtras that the five aggregates are the self. For if—from between the object of observation and the subjective aspect of a consciousness apprehending [an inherently existent] "I"—[the aggregates] were the object of observation, they would have to be posited as the self. Hence, the meaning of the statement in sūtra [above] about

of the body and the senses is a basis of the designation "self" and thus is the self. For when another school tries to prove that the mental consciousness is the self, Bhāvaviveka responds that they are proving what is already established for him:

> This is a proof of what is already established [for me] since we also actually impute the term "self" to [the mental] consciousness conventionally. Because [the mental] consciousness takes rebirth, it is called the self.

In his *Great Exposition of Tenets*, Jam-yang-shay-pa says that this statement indicates that for Bhāvaviveka the collection is the basis of designation and thus is the phenomenon imputed. In his *Great Exposition of the Middle* (475b.1-475b.3) he takes it slightly differently, saying that in this passage Bhāvaviveka posits consciousness as the self **that continuously takes rebirth** and indicates (1) that the mere collection of the body and senses is the self and (2) that the five aggregates—the body and so forth—are the basis of designation of that self, just as, for example, (1) the mere collection of the parts of a chariot is the chariot and (2) its parts are the basis of designation.

Jam-yang-shay-pa points out that Bhāvaviveka (P5256, vol. 96, 36.4.6) cites this very sūtra passage as support for his position:

> It is said [in sūtra], "Just as one thinks 'chariot,' for example, with respect to a collection of parts, so in dependence on the aggregates 'sentient being' is imputed conventionally."

[a] Stanza VI.132; P5262, vol. 98, 104.2.6; Toh. 3861, *dbu ma*, vol. *'a*, 210b.5; La Vallée Poussin, *Madhyamakāvatāra*, 254.18-255.2; La Vallée Poussin, "*Introduction au traité du milieu*," *Muséon* 12 (1911): 301.

[b] This passage is quoted in Chandrakīrti's *Commentary on the "Supplement,"* P5263, vol. 98, 142.4.8, commenting on VI.126cd and also in Tsong-kha-pa's *Illumination*, P6143, vol. 154, 84.3.7; La Vallée Poussin, *Madhyamakāvatāra*, 244.16-244.18; La Vallée Poussin, "*Introduction au traité du milieu*," *Muséon* 12 (1911): 291.

viewing the aggregates must be explained as referring to observing the self that is imputed to[a] the aggregates.

Consequently, you should differentiate between references to the "mere "I"," called self, which exists in conventional terms and the inherently existent person, called self, which does not exist even in conventional terms. You should not say that this system asserts that a self [that is, inherent existence] of persons exists in conventional terms [even though self, meaning person, exists in conventional terms].

Such an identification of persons is a distinguishing feature of this unsurpassed system. Ascertaining this well is a good technique for realizing the uncommon selflessness of persons.

Delineating persons as not inherently existent

This has three parts: delineating "I" as not inherently existent, delineating "mine" as not inherently existent, and showing how, in dependence on this, persons appear as like illusions.

Delineating "I" as not inherently existent

Concerning this, the first of the four essentials is to identify the mode of apprehending a self of persons through analyzing your own continuum.[c] It was explained earlier.[d]

The second essential is the decision that if a person is inherently established, it must be established as either one entity with or a

[a] As here, Tsong-kha-pa himself does not always say "imputed in dependence upon"; however, this is taken to be the meaning of "imputed to."

[b] The outline (416.3) mistakenly reads "four."

[c] About Tsong-kha-pa's presentation of the four essentials here in the *Medium-Length Exposition of the Stages of the Path,* which is also called the *Small Exposition of the Stages of the Path,* Jang-kya's *Presentations of Tenets* says:

> The lack of being one or many is applied to both selflessnesses. The extensive teaching of the reasoning that is the lack of being one or many by way of an analysis of four essentials set forth in Tsong-kha-pa's *Small Exposition of the Stages of the Path* is based on the eighteenth chapter of Nāgārjuna's *Treatise on the Middle.* It is said that this chapter teaches the meanings of all the other twenty-six chapters of Nāgārjuna's *Treatise on the Middle,* arranged in stages of practice; hence, [Tsong-kha-pa's teaching of the four essentials] in this way is very important.

See Jeffrey Hopkins, *Emptiness Yoga* (Ithaca, N.Y.: Snow Lion Publications, 1987), 382. In his *Great Exposition of the Stages of the Path* Tsong-kha-pa uses the sevenfold reasoning elaborated by Chandrakīrti; see Hopkins, *Meditation on Emptiness,* 175-196 and 677-697, and *Emptiness Yoga,* 209-281 and 391-408.

[d] See 38ff.

different entity from the aggregates and that there is no mode of establishment other than those two. It is established through experience that when "pot and pillar," for instance, are positively set off as plural,[a] it is eliminated that they are single.[b] And when "pot," for instance, is positively set off as single, it is eliminated that it is plural. Hence, there is no third category that is neither one nor many;[c] thereby, it is determined that something that is not one entity or different entities does not occur.

The third essential is to see the damage to [the position that] a person and the aggregates are one inherently established entity. The fourth essential is to see well the damage [to the position that] those two are inherently different. When in that way the four essentials are complete, then the pure view realizing the suchness that is the selflessness of a person is generated.

Concerning that, if the two—the self and the aggregates—are one inherently established entity, from among three fallacies the first damage to this position is that the assertion of a self [or person] would be senseless. If the sameness of entity of those two were inherently established, then they would become an utterly indivisible one. This is because if a sameness of entity were ultimately established, then to whatever awareness those two appeared, they would necessarily not appear to be different. The reason for this is that although among falsities—conventionalities—it is not contradictory for the mode of appearance and mode of being to be in disagreement, such is necessarily contradictory in what is truly established because the mode of being of what truly exists must appear just as it is to any mind to which it appears.

The assertion of an inherently established self is for the sake of establishing an assumer and discarder of the aggregates; however, if it is one with the aggregates, those are not feasible. About that, Nāgārjuna's *Treatise on the Middle* says:[d]

> When [you say that] there is no [inherently existent] self [who
> is the appropriator of the mental and physical aggregates]
> Separate from the appropriated [aggregates],

---

[a] *zla bcas* literally means having an equivalent, having a mate, and thus not being alone.

[b] *zla med* literally means not having an equivalent, not having a mate, and thus being alone, matchless.

[c] Or, neither singular nor plural; neither one nor different.

[d] XXVII.5; Toh. 3824, *dbu ma*, vol. *tsa*, 18a.1; de Jong, *Mūlamadhyamakakārikāḥ*, 41: *upādānavinirmukto nāsty ātmeti kṛte sati / syād upādānam evātmā nāsti cātmeti vaḥ punaḥ //* Brackets are from *Four Interwoven Annotations*, vol. 2, 628.6. Cited in *Great Treatise*, vol. 3, 290.

Then if [you claim that] just the appropriated [aggregates] are the [inherently existent] self [who is the appropriator,
This is not reasonable because] there is no [meaning to the assertion in] your [system that] the self [inherently exists because the self is reduced to being only a synonym of the aggregates].[a]

The second [damage to the position that the self and the aggregates are one inherently established entity] is that the selves would be manifold. If the self is one with the aggregates, then just as one person has many aggregates, so even one person would have many selves. [Or] just as there is no more than one self, so the aggregates would be one. Those are the fallacies. Chandrakīrti's *Supplement to (Nāgārjuna's) "Treatise on the Middle"* says:[b]

If the aggregates were [inherently] the self, then
Since those [aggregates] are many, the selves also would be [as] many [as the number of the aggregates].

The third [damage to the position that the self and the aggregates are one inherently established entity] is that the self would have production and disintegration. Nāgārjuna's *Treatise on the Middle* says:[c]

If the aggregates were [inherently one with] the self,
Then [just as the aggregates are produced and disintegrate momentarily, the inherently established self also] would have

---

[a] Without the brackets, the stanza reads:

When the self does not exist
Separate from the appropriated,
Then if just the appropriated is the self,
Your self does not exist.

[b] VI.127ab; Toh. 3861, *dbu ma*, vol. *'a*, 210b.1-210b.2; La Vallée Poussin, *Madhyamakāvatāra*, 245.15-245.16; La Vallée Poussin, "*Introduction au traité du milieu*," *Muséon* 12 (1911): 292. Brackets are from *Four Interwoven Annotations*, vol. 2, 629.4. Cited in *Great Treatise*, vol. 3, 290.

[c] Stanza XVIII.1ab; Toh. 3824, *dbu ma*, vol. *tsa*, 10b.6; de Jong, *Mūlamadhyamakakārikāḥ*, 24: *ātmā skandhā yadi bhaved udayavyayabhāg bhavet /*. Brackets are from *Four Interwoven Annotations*, vol. 2, 629.6. Cited in *Great Treatise*, vol. 3, 291. In the eighteenth chapter of the *Treatise*, Analysis of the Self and Phenomena, Nāgārjuna presents the reasoning refuting the inherent existence of persons in abbreviated form, treating just two positions: a person is shown to be inherently neither the same as nor inherently different from the aggregates. In the twenty-second chapter, Analysis of the One-Gone-Thus, a five-cornered reasoning is presented; Chandrakīrti, in turn, expands this to a seven-cornered reasoning. See Hopkins, *Meditation on Emptiness*, 178-193, and *Emptiness Yoga*, 209-281.

production and disintegration [moment by moment].

Just as the aggregates are produced and disintegrate, the self also would be produced and disintegrate because those two are one.[a]

Objection: It is accepted that the self, or person, is produced and disintegrates each moment.

Answer: There is no fault in merely asserting such in conventional terms, but the opponent asserts that persons are established by way of their own character and consequently has to assert that persons are produced and disintegrate by way of their own nature. That has three fallacies, as set out in Chandrakīrti's *Commentary on the "Supplement to (Nāgārjuna's) 'Treatise on the Middle.'"* With respect to the first fallacy, his *Supplement to (Nāgārjuna's) "Treatise on the Middle"* says:[b]

> Those that are separate by way of their own character
> Are not feasible to be included in one continuum.

Hence, it is not feasible for former and later individuals that are established by way of their own nature to have the relationship of the later depending on the former. For, since the former and later would be established as able to set themselves up under their own power, reliance on others would not be suitable. When in that way a sameness of continuum is not feasible, memory of a former life as in "At such-and-such a time in that life I became such-and-such," is not possible. It is like the fact that when Devadatta remembers a [former] life, he does not think, "I became Yajñadatta," who [is his contemporary and] has a separate continuum.

In our own system, although there is [conventionally existent] disintegration in each moment, it is not contradictory for former and later to be one continuum. Due to this, memory of lives is feasible.

Those who do not understand the meaning of the above think that because in the sets of discourses[c] Buddha frequently says, "In the past I became such-and-such [a person]," the two persons—the one after enlightenment and the one at an earlier time—are one. Furthermore, [they think that] it would not be suitable for them to be one if they were compounded phenomena, since they would disintegrate moment by moment, and therefore they say that both are permanent. In this

---

[a] This point is now explained at length.

[b] Stanza VI.61cd; Toh. 3861, *dbu ma*, vol. *'a*, 207a.4; La Vallée Poussin, *Madhyamakāvatāra*, 154.9-154.10; La Vallée Poussin, "*Introduction au traité du milieu*," *Muséon* 11 (1910): 340. In *Four Interwoven Annotations*, vol. 2, 638.5. Cited in *Great Treatise*, vol. 3, 294.

[c] *mdo sde, sūtrānta.*

way the first of the four bad views based on past factors[a] is generated in them. To prevent falling to such [a view], when Buddha remembered a life, he spoke of remembering in general, saying "I" without qualifying it with a specific place, time, or nature.[b] You need to understand well this feature of his mode of remembering [former lives].

The second fallacy [of an inherently produced and disintegrating person] is that actions done would be wasted. The two—the agent of the action and the experiencer of the effect—could not be included within the single substratum of the "mere "I" ."

The [third] fallacy is that one would meet with [the effects of] actions not done [by oneself]. This is the greatly absurd consequence that even all the effects of actions accumulated by another [person] of a different continuum would have to be experienced by [the person of] this continuum.

These two fallacies are incurred by way of the essential—as in the above explanation of Chandrakīrti's *Supplement to (Nāgārjuna's) "Treatise on the Middle"*—that if a person is established inherently, former and later moments are not suitable to be the same continuum. Nāgārjuna's *Treatise on the Middle* also says:[c]

> If the god [of an earlier birth] and the human [of a later birth]
> were others [established by way of their own entities,
> Those two] would not be feasible [to be a single] continuum.

Question: What fallacy is there if the self and the aggregates are asserted to be inherently established as different?

Answer: There is the fallacy described in Nāgārjuna's *Treatise on the Middle:*[d]

---

[a] *sngon gyi mtha' la rten pa'i lta ba.* The four views based on past factors are:

1. The self and the world are permanent.
2. The self and the world are impermanent.
3. The self and the world are both permanent and impermanent.
4. The self and the world are neither permanent nor impermanent.

These are the first four of fourteen views to which Buddha did not respond because the listeners would not comprehend the answers; for discussion see Hopkins, *Maps of the Profound,* 184-187.

[b] He did not say, "When I, the Buddha of this city, in this century, and with this nature, used to be so-and-so..." Rather, he used the general "I," thereby indicating that a mere-I travels from lifetime to lifetime.

[c] Stanza XXVII.16cd; Toh. 3824, *dbu ma,* vol. *tsa,* 18a.6-18a.7; de Jong, *Mūlamadhyamakakārikāḥ,* 42: *devād anyo manuṣyaś cet saṃtatir nopapadyate //.* Brackets are from *Four Interwoven Annotations,* vol. 2, 638.6. Cited in *Great Treatise,* vol. 3, 294.

[d] Stanza XVIII.1cd; Toh. 3824, *dbu ma,* vol. *tsa,* 10b.6; de Jong, *Mūlamadhyamakakārikāḥ,* 24: *skandhebhyo 'nyo yadi bhaved bhaved askandhalakṣaṇaḥ //.* Brackets are from *Four*

> If [the self] is [established as inherently] other than the aggregates,
> [The self] would not have the characteristics of the aggregates [namely, production, abiding, and disintegration].

Concerning that, if the self were inherently different from the aggregates, it would not possess the characteristics that characterize the aggregates as compounded phenomena—production, abiding, and disintegration. For example, because a horse is established as factually other than an ox, it does not have the characteristics of an ox.

If you think, "That indeed is so *but*" [that is, if you are not entirely convinced], then [this so-called self] is not feasible as the object of observation that is the basis of designating the convention "self" by innate apprehension because it is uncompounded, like a sky-flower or like nirvāṇa.

Moreover, if [the self] exists as inherently different from the characteristics of the aggregates—such as being suitable as form,[a] and so forth—it must be observed that way, just as, for example, form and mind are apprehended as different. Further, since there is no such apprehension, the self does not exist as factually other [than the aggregates]. Nāgārjuna's *Treatise on the Middle* says:[b]

Interwoven Annotations, vol. 2, 643.6. Cited in *Great Treatise,* vol. 3, 296.

[a] *gzugs su rung ba, rūpaṇa;* this is the definition, or defining characteristic, of form. "That which is suitable as form" appears to be almost a non-definition since it repeats the very term being defined, form; however, the definition may derive from the notion that reasoning meets back to common experience in that with form we are at a level of common experience with little else to come up with as a definition other than saying that it is what we point to when we identify form.

The definition *rūpaṇa* is rendered by de Jong in *Cinq chapitres de la Prasannapadā,* 4, as "le pouvoir d'être brisé," "capable of being broken." Ajitamitra explains the term this way in his commentary on Nāgārjuna's *Precious Garland* (P5659, vol. 129, notation lost). Therefore, it might be that the translators into Tibetan were aware of both meanings and chose "suitability as form" here.

In oral commentary, Lati Rinbochay explained that "capable of being broken" is not appropriate as a definition of form at least in those schools that assert partless particles as these cannot be broken down either physically or mentally. Perhaps this is the reason why the translation as "that which is suitable as form," meaning whatever one points to when asked what form is, was preferred. Still, the late Geshe Gedün Lodrö opined that partless particles could not be further reduced without disappearing, and thus indicated that they could be broken; therefore, if we take their physical disappearance as their susceptibility to being broken, this reading of *rūpaṇa* as "that which is susceptible to being broken" would be an appropriate definition of form.

[b] Stanza XXVII.7; Toh. 3824, *dbu ma,* vol. *tsa,* 18a.2; de Jong, *Mūlamadhyamakakārikāḥ,* 41: *anyaḥ punar upādānād ātmā naivopapadyate / gṛhyeta hy anupādāno yady anyo na ca gṛhyate //.* Brackets are from *Four Interwoven Annotations,* vol. 2, 645.5. Cited in *Great Treatise,* vol.

It is just not feasible that the self
Be another [entity] from the appropriated [aggregates].
If it were [feasible for the self to be] another [entity from them], it would be reasonable [for the self] to be apprehendable [by the mind]
Without the appropriated [aggregates], whereas it is not apprehended [that way].

and Chandrakīrti's *Supplement to (Nāgārjuna's) "Treatise on the Middle"* says:[a]

Hence there is no self [as] another [factuality] than the aggregates
Because [an innate mind] apprehending [the self as another factuality] aside from the aggregates is not established.

You should train until gaining firm ascertainment, seeing by way of such reasonings the damage to [the position that] the self exists as a different entity from the aggregates. For if you do not induce pure ascertainment regarding the damage to these two positions of sameness and difference, although you might decide that persons do not inherently exist, it would be just a thesis, and hence the pure view would not be found.

Delineating "mine" as not inherently existent

When whether the self has or does not have inherent establishment is sought in this way through reasoning, inherent existence is negated with respect to the self because the self is not found to be either one or many. At that time inherently established "mine" will not be found by the reasoning analyzing suchness, just as, for example, when the child of a barren woman is not observed, the "mine" of the child of a barren woman—eyes and so forth—are not observed. Nāgārjuna's *Treatise on the Middle* says:[b]

If the self does not [inherently] exist,
How could the "mine" [inherently] exist?

3, 296.

[a] VI.124ab; Toh. 3861, *dbu ma*, vol. *'a*, 210a.6-210a.7; La Vallée Poussin, *Madhyamakāvatāra*, 242.1 and 242.6; La Vallée Poussin, "*Introduction au traité du milieu*," *Muséon* 12 (1911): 289. Brackets are from *Four Interwoven Annotations*, vol. 2, 645.6. Cited in *Great Treatise*, vol. 3, 296.

[b] XVIII.2ab; Toh. 3824, *dbu ma*, vol. *tsa*, 10b.6; de Jong, *Mūlamadhyamakakārikāḥ*, 24: *ātmany asati cātmīyaṃ kuta eva bhaviṣyati /*. Brackets are from *Four Interwoven Annotations*, vol. 2, 681.6. Cited in *Great Treatise*, vol. 3, 121 and 307.

and Chandrakīrti's *Supplement to (Nāgārjuna's) "Treatise on the Middle"* also says(see also *Insight,* 165):[a]

> Because [of being like the fact that, for example] an object [such as a pot] of a non-existent agent [such as a potter] does not exist,
> Without [an inherently established] self [inherently established] "mine" does not exist.
> Therefore through the view of "I" and "mine" as empty [of inherent existence]
> A yogi [viewing such] will be released [from cyclic existence upon having abandoned all afflictive emotions conceptualizing inherent establishment].

Through those reasonings settling that the "I" of an apprehending consciousness thinking "I," or self or person, in your own continuum is not established by way of its own nature, you should also realize the entire meaning of the suchness of the selflessness of persons, in which all persons ranging from hell-beings through Buddhas are not inherently established as the same entity with or different entities from the contaminated and uncontaminated aggregates that are [their] bases of imputation. And through this you should understand the fact that all their "mine" is also established as without inherent existence.

[a] VI.165; Toh. 3861, *dbu ma,* vol. *'a,* 212a.7; La Vallée Poussin, *Madhyamakāvatāra,* 287.16-287.19; La Vallée Poussin, "*Introduction au traité du milieu,*" *Muséon* 12 (1911): 328. Brackets are from *Four Interwoven Annotations,* vol. 2, 681.6. Cited in *Great Treatise,* vol. 3, 307-308, and last two lines vol. 3, 193.

5. Illusory-Like Appearance

How, in dependence on delineating "I" and "mine" as not inherently existent, persons appear as like illusions

This section has two parts: indicating the meaning of setting forth illusory-like appearance and the method in dependence on which illusory-like appearance occurs.

Indicating the meaning of setting forth illusory-like appearance

This section has two parts: the unerring mode of illusory-like appearance and the fallacious mode of illusory-like appearance.

Unerring mode of illusory-like appearance

The *King of Meditative Stabilizations Sūtra* says:[a]

> Like a mirage, a city of Scent-Eaters,
> A magician's illusions, and dreams,
> Meditation on signs is empty of inherent existence.
> Know all phenomena to be like that.

and the *Mother of the Conquerors* [that is, *Perfection of Wisdom Sūtra*] says that all phenomena from forms through exalted-knowledge-of-all-

[a] Stanza IX.11; Toh. 127, *mdo sde*, vol. *da*, 26a.6; Sanskrit and Tibetan texts and English translation in Cristoph Cüppers, *The IXth Chapter of the Samādhirājasūtra: A Text-critical Contribution to the Study of Mahāyāna Sūtras*, Alt- und Neu-Indische Studien 41 (Stuttgart: Franz Steiner Verlag, 1990), 27: *yathaiva gandharvapuraṃ marīcikā yathaiva māyā supinaṃ yathaiva / svabhāvaśūnyā tu nimittabhāvanā tathopamāṃ jānatha sarvadharmān //*. The Tibetan is on p. 28, and an English translation on pp. 93-94. Cited in *Great Treatise*, vol. 3, 306. The *Four Interwoven Annotations* (vol. 2, 674.5) explains this stanza in detail:

> With respect to how all phenomena are signless, the *King of Meditative Stabilizations Sūtra* gives examples. Just as there is no water in a mirage but it appears to be water and just as a city of Scent-Eaters [that is, a phantom city] does not exist as the actuality of a city and so forth but appears to be a city and so forth and just as a magician's emanations do not exist as horses, elephants, and so forth but appear to be horses, elephants, and so forth and just as in a dream there are no men, women, and so forth but there appear to be (that is to say, just as mirages and so forth appear to be water and so on but are empty of water and so on), so forms and so forth, which are like signs of capacity to appear and manifest, are meditated on—that is to say, adhered to by way of taking them to mind—as manifestly evident (*mngon rtags*), are empty of inherent existence, and adherers to them are also empty of inherent existence. Know that this mode of emptiness is to be applied to all phenomena.

aspects[a] are like a magician's illusions and dreams.

There are two meanings of such teachings of being like an illusion. In the description of, for instance, an ultimate truth as being like an illusion, it is taken [as meaning] that although [an ultimate truth, that is, an emptiness,] is established as merely existent, truth [that is, its true existence] is negated.[b] [The second] is an illusory-like appearance in which [an object] appears while being empty [of inherent existence]. Between these two, here [being like an illusion refers to] the latter.

Concerning this, two [factors]—appearance of something and emptiness of existing the way it appears—are needed. Moreover, if [objects seem] to be utterly non-existent even as mere appearances, like the horn of a rabbit or the child of a barren woman, and do not dawn as appearing yet empty of existing the way they appear, the meaning of illusory-like appearance has not dawned to the mind.

Therefore, the way to know other phenomena as like the example of an illusion is as follows. For example, the illusions emanated [or conjured] by a magician are from the start empty of being horses and elephants, but appearances as horses and elephants undeniably dawn; and likewise you should know that phenomena, persons and so forth, also are from the start empty of inherent existence—that is, of being established by way of their own nature right with the object—but it is undeniable that they appear as if established that way.

Thus, appearances as a god, human, and so forth are posited as persons, and the objects that are appearances as forms, sounds, and so forth are posited as phenomena. Therefore, although persons and phenomena do not have even a mere particle of an inherent nature,[c] that is to say, establishment by way of their own character, even all the dependently arisen actions, agents, and objects[d]—accumulator of actions[e] and so forth, act of viewing, object of hearing, and so forth—are feasible. Because all actions, agents, and objects are feasible, this is not an annihilatory emptiness. Also, because phenomena, which from the primordial start have been empty in this way, are just being known as empty, this is also not a mentally fabricated emptiness. Furthermore, since **all** objects of knowledge are asserted this way, it is not a partial emptiness. Consequently, meditation on it even serves as the antidote

[a] *rnam mkhyen / rnam pa thams cad mkhyen pa, sarvākārajñāna.*

[b] Just as an illusory horse exists but is not established as a horse, so an ultimate truth exists but is not inherently established.

[c] *rang bzhin, svabhāva.*

[d] *bya byed;* short for *bya byed las gsum.*

[e] *las, karma.*

to all the exaggerated adherences of the apprehension of true existence.

It is not that the meaning of the profound [emptiness] is not suitable to be the object of any awareness. Through delineating it by means of the correct view and through meditating on the meaning of the reality [that has been delineated], it can be taken as an object [of the mind]. Therefore, it is also not a vacuousness that cannot be practiced during the time of the path and about which there is nothing to be known and nothing to be realized.

Objection: If this ascertainment that reflections and so forth are empty of what they appear to be is a realization of their absence of inherent existence, then the direct perceptions of common beings would realize the absence of inherent existence [since they know, for instance, that that reflection of a face is empty of being an actual face], and due to that, they would be Superiors.[a] If the ascertainment that reflections and so forth are empty of what they appear to be is not a realization of their absence of inherent existence, how could these be suitable as examples of the absence of inherent existence?

Answer: Concerning this, Āryadeva's *Four Hundred* says:[b]

> Whoever is a viewer[c] of one thing [as without inherent existence]
> Is described as a viewer of all [as without inherent existence.
> The reason for this is] that that which is the emptiness [of inherent existence] of one [thing]
> Is the emptiness [of inherent existence] of all [things].

He explains that a viewer, or realizer, of the emptiness of one thing also can realize the emptiness of other things. However, the realization that a reflection of a face is empty of a face does not do any damage to the object of a [consciousness] apprehending true existence, that is to say, which apprehends a reflection to be established by way of its own nature. Furthermore, without rejecting the object of that apprehension, the emptiness of inherent establishment of the reflection is not realized. Hence, that awareness [realizing that a reflection of a face is empty of a face] does not realize the suchness of the reflection. Due to this, though one realizes magical illusions to be empty of beings horses

[a] Superiors (*'phags pa, āryan*) are those who have realized emptiness directly.

[b] VIII.16; Toh. 3846, *dbu ma*, vol. *tsha*, 9b.6; Lang, *Āryadeva's Catuḥśataka*, 82: *bhāvasyaikasya yo draṣṭā draṣṭā sarvasya sa smṛtaḥ / ekasya śūnyatā yaiva saiva sarvasya śūnyatā //.* See Sonam Rinchen and Ruth Sonam, *Yogic Deeds of Bodhisattvas*, 194. Brackets are from *Four Interwoven Annotations*, vol. 2, 670.6. Cited in *Great Treatise*, vol. 3, 304-305.

[c] *lta po, draṣṭā.*

and elephants and realizes dream appearances and so forth to be empty of what they appear to be, one has not found the Middle Way view realizing [objects] to be like illusions and dreams.

Nonetheless, these are used as examples due to the fact that realization that these do not inherently exist is easier than realization that other phenomena such as forms, sounds, and so forth do not inherently exist. If an object is truly established, it is not suitable for it to appear to a mind in any way other than just what its mode of subsistence is; therefore, that these [reflections and magical illusions] are empty of an inherent nature in the sense of being established by way of their own nature is proven through showing the contradiction in those two [that is, being truly established and appearing to be something they are not].

Initially, one is caused to enter into realizing that these examples, which are renowned as false in the world, are without inherent existence, whereupon one must generate realization that other phenomena not renowned as false in the world are without inherent existence. Since these must have a temporal order, it is not [Āryadeva's] thought [in the passage cited just above] that when the emptiness of one phenomenon is realized, the emptinesses of all other phenomena are **explicitly** realized. Rather, his meaning is that when [after realizing the emptiness of one phenomenon] one's awareness is directed toward whether another phenomenon truly exists or not, it is able realize [its emptiness through the functioning of the former reasoning].

Thus, the two:

- within knowing a dream to be a dream, to realize that appearances as men, women, and so forth [in the dream] are empty of being men, women, and so forth, and
- to view in dreams all phenomena as like dreams as described in Maitreya's *Ornament for Clear Realization,*[a] "Viewing all phenomena even in dreams as like dreams, and so forth,"

do not have the same import [since the latter involves realization of their emptiness, whereas the former does not]. Similarly:

- to realize that appearances as pots, woolen cloth, and so forth in the visions of one who has cultivated meditative stabilization are empty of being what they appear to be, and

[a] *mngon par rtogs pa'i rgyan, abhisamayālaṃkāra,* stanza V.1ab; Toh. 3786, *sher phyin,* vol. *ka,* 9a.7; Sanskrit and Tibetan in E. Obermiller, *Abhisamayālaṅkāra-Prajñāpāramitā-Upadeśa-Śāstra* (Osnabrück, Germany: Biblio Verlag, 1970), 27 and 48: *svapnāntare 'pi svapnābhasarvadharmekṣaṇādikam /.* English translation in Edward Conze, *Abhisamayālaṅkāra* (Rome: Istituto Italiano per il Medio ed Estremo Oriente, 1954), 77.

- to realize them to be like magical illusions and dreams that are not inherently established

also do not have the same import. Therefore, you should investigate well the uncommon mode of illusory-like appearance in the prescriptions in definitive scriptures and treatises to realize [phenomena] as like illusions and dreams.

This being the case, no matter whether

(1) a mirror-image is apprehended to be a face, and so forth, by an infant not versed in language,
(2) magical appearances are apprehended to be horses, elephants, and so forth by a member of the audience unfamiliar with magic,
(3) dream appearances of mountains, houses, and so forth are apprehended as real by one who does not recognize dreams as such,

or whether those appearances are known as untrue by

(1) mature persons trained in language,
(2) magicians,
(3) those who know dreams as dreams,

they are all similar; neither set has found the view of suchness.

Fallacious mode of illusory-like appearance

When the measure of the object of negation explained above is not grasped well and an object is analyzed with reasoning, breaking it down:

- Initially the thought arises, "This object does not exist."
- Then, seeing the same also with respect to the analyzer, there is even no ascertainer of non-existence.
- Thereby it comes that there is nothing to ascertain as, "It is this, not that."

The dawning, thereupon, of shimmering ephemeral appearances[a] arises in dependence on not differentiating **inherent** existence from **mere**

[a] *snang ba ban bun*. In his 1972 lectures, the Dalai Lama described these appearances as like insubstantial drawings. In his *Instructions on the Profound View of the Middle Way: Clearing Away All Extremes* (*zab mo dbu ma'i lta khrid mthar 'dzin kun sel*), 555.5, Mön-lam-pel-lek-pay-lo-drö (*smon lam dpal legs pa'i blo gros*) says that experiences subsequent to meditation in which appearances are shimmering and ephemeral, lack any hardness and obstructiveness, or are unidentifiable as this or that are good meditative experiences (*nyams bzang po*) but are not what it means for phenomena to dawn as like illusions.

existence and the absence of **inherent** existence from non-existence. Hence, such an emptiness is an emptiness destroying dependent-arising. Therefore, even the dawning of shimmering ephemeral appearances, induced by realizing those, is not at all the meaning of being like an illusion.

Therefore, it is not difficult, when analyzing with reasoning to think, "Persons and so forth do not in the least have an objective mode of abiding[a] which is their being established by way of their own nature," and in dependence on this, for these appearances to shine forth ephemerally.[b] Such happens to all who are interested in Middle Way tenets and have heard a few scattered doctrines teaching the mode of the absence of inherent existence. However, the difficult point is that you must, from the depths, be able to induce ascertainment with respect to the negation, without residue, of an inherent nature—establishment by way of [the object's] own nature—and be able to posit those very persons and so forth, lacking inherent existence, as the accumulators of actions, experiencers of effects, and so forth. A composite of these two hardly occurs; hence, the Middle Way view is very difficult to find.

Therefore, it is said that because production and so forth, when analyzed with the reasoning analyzing suchness, are not found, inherently existent production and so forth are refuted, but all whatsoever production, cessation, and so forth are not refuted, and if they were refuted, there would be the fallacy that [everything] would be like the horns of a rabbit or the child of a barren woman, empty of all performance of function, and all dependently arisen agents, actions, and objects would not be feasible within the mere illusory-like appearance that is left over. In commentary on the statement in Āryadeva's *Four Hundred:*[c]

> If that were the case [that phenomena become utterly nonexistent due to not being found by reasoning analyzing suchness],
> Cyclic existence would not be like an illusion.

Chandrakīrti says:[d]

---

[a] *yul steng nas sdod tshul.*

[b] *ban bun du 'char ba.*

[c] XV.10cd; Toh. 3846, *dbu ma*, vol. *tsha*, 16b.3-16b.4; Lang, *Āryadeva's Catuḥśataka*, 138; Sonam Rinchen and Ruth Sonam, *Yogic Deeds of Bodhisattvas*, 281. Brackets are from *Four Interwoven Annotations*, vol. 2, 659.2. Cited in *Great Treatise*, vol. 3, 301.

[d] In his *Commentary on (Āryadeva's) "Four Hundred Stanzas on the Yogic Deeds of Bodhisattvas,"* Toh. 3865, *dbu ma*, vol. *ya*, 225a.1-225a.3. Brackets are from *Four Interwoven Annotations*, vol. 2, 659.3 and 289.1. Cited in *Great Treatise*, vol. 3, 301, and all but the first sen-

> When dependent-arisings are seen as they are, they become like a magician's illusory creations, not like the child of a barren woman. If [you proponents of inherent existence] assert that [merely not being found] by this [reasoned] analysis [of suchness] indicates the non-production of compounded phenomena by way of refuting production in all respects, then those [compounded phenomena] would not be like a magician's illusions [such as horses and elephants which appear to be horses and elephants but do not exist as such] but would be comprehended by way of [examples] such as the [utterly non-existent] child of a barren woman, [the horns of a donkey,] and so forth. Due to fearing the consequence that dependent-arisings would not exist, [we] do not make comparison with those, but use magical illusions and so forth, which do not contradict this [dependent-arising].

and says [in the same commentary]:[a]

> Therefore, when thoroughly analyzed in this way, an inherent existence of things is non-established, whereby just an illusory-like [appearance] remains left over with respect to the individual things [that are analyzed].

Hence, apprehending dependent-arisings, which are illusory-like appearances, to be merely existent is not a faulty apprehension of illusion. However, if illusory-like appearances are apprehended to be established by way of their own nature or to be true, it is faulty.

The *King of Meditative Stabilizations Sūtra* also says:[b]

> Transmigrators in cyclic existence are like dreams; [just as in a dream a person appears to be born and to die but there is no birth and death,
> So] here [in this world of cyclic existence although there appear to be inherently existent birth and death,] no one is [inherently] born and no one [inherently] dies.
> [Since] a sentient being [who is a basis for accumulating the

tence, vol. 3, 159.

[a] Toh. 3865, *dbu ma,* vol. *ya,* 229a.4-229a.5. Brackets are from *Four Interwoven Annotations,* vol. 2, 660.4. Cited in *Great Treatise,* vol. 3, 302.

[b] Cited in Chandrakīrti's *Clear Words,* in commentary to stanza IX.12; Toh. 3860, *dbu ma,* vol. *'a,* 68a.5-68a.6; Louis de La Vallée Poussin, *Mūlamadhyamakakārikās (Mādhyamikasūtras) de Nāgārjuna avec la Prasannapadā Commentaire de Candrakīrti* (Osnabrück, Germany: Biblio Verlag, 1970), 200.7-200.16. Brackets are from *Four Interwoven Annotations,* vol. 2, 665.1. Cited in *Great Treatise,* vol. 3, 303.

karma that is the cause of a birth], a human [which is a type of transmigration taken through the force of karma], and even life [that causes the human life-support to abide do not inherently exist, they] are not found [when properly investigated].
These phenomena are like bubbles [appearing adventitiously and disintegrating even due to tiny conditions], banana[a] trees [without an essence when separated out and investigated],
Magician's illusions [appearing variously but empty of the nature of those appearances], lightning in the sky [appearing and disintegrating moment by moment,
Reflections of] the moon in water [though not shifting from one spot to another but appearing to do so], and mirages [appearing to be inherently established objects of use but not established from their side as objects of use in accordance with their appearance.
Just as the moon indeed does not shift from the sky and enter into the water but a reflection like the moon appears in water,] so although when a human dies in this world
[That very human him/herself] does not [in the least] transmigrate and go to another world [that is a place of rebirth],
The actions done [by that human] are never wasted,
Ripening as effects [projected by] white [virtues] and black [nonvirtues] in the cyclic existence [of six transmigrations].

When sought with reasoning analyzing suchness, persons—who are born and transmigrate—and so forth, able to withstand analysis, are not found, not even a particle. Nevertheless, phenomena give rise to white and black effects within being illusory-like. You need to form understanding of such statements.

Moreover, instead of sustaining in meditative equipoise a setting within the view penetrating the mode of being, [some] gain a stability of mere one-pointedness in which the mind does not conceive anything, and when they rise from it, through its power appearances of mountains and so forth—rather than appearing as they did before, as hard and obstructive—appear insubstantially, like rainbows or light smoke, but even this is not the illusory-like appearance mentioned in scripture. This is because those are appearances as empty of gross

[a] *chu shing;* plantain or banana.

obstructiveness and those appearances of objects are not dawning as empty of inherent establishment, and because the non-existence of obstructive hardness is not at all fit to be the meaning of the emptiness that is the absence of inherent existence. Otherwise, there would be the fallacies that:

- when rainbows and so forth are taken as substrata, it would not be possible to generate a consciousness apprehending true existence [with respect to them], and
- when obstructive objects are taken as substrata, it would not be possible to generate a consciousness realizing the absence of true existence.[a]

Method in dependence on which illusory-like appearance occurs

Question: What has to be done for the meaning of illusion to dawn unerringly?

Answer: For example, in dependence on the eye consciousness seeing illusory horses and elephants [conjured by a magician] and the mental consciousness ascertaining the non-existence of those horses and elephants in accordance with how they appear, one generates ascertainment that the appearance of horses and elephants is an illusory, or false, appearance. Similarly, in dependence on the two—undeniable appearance of persons and so forth to a conventional consciousness and ascertainment of them by a rational consciousness[b] as empty of an inherent nature, that is, establishment by way of their own nature—one generates ascertainment of persons as illusory, or false, appearances. Due to this fact:

- when in meditative equipoise one has become successful at meditating on space-like emptiness, [realizing that] the target aimed at by the apprehension of signs [that is, inherent existence,] does not

[a] Gedün Lodrö (*Calm Abiding and Special Insight,* trans. and ed. by Jeffrey Hopkins [Ithaca, N.Y.: Snow Lion Publications, 1998], 119) indicates that nevertheless there is a relationship between the two types of realizations:

> *Question:* Tsong-kha-pa's *Great Exposition of the Stages of the Path* says that it is a mistake to consider impedance to be the object of negation of emptiness. How can this be?
>
> *Answer:* Impedance, or obstructiveness, is coarser than inherent existence, which is the subtle meaning of the object of negation. It is inherent existence, not impedance, that is being refuted. However, if the person does not first understand an absence of impedance, it is doubtful that she or he could understand the absence of inherent existence.

[b] *rigs shes.*

exist, not even a particle,
- then upon rising from [this meditative realization], when one views the dawning of objects, an illusory-like emptiness dawns subsequent to meditative equipoise.

In that way, through analyzing phenomena frequently with the reasoning analyzing whether they are established by way of their own nature or not, strong ascertainment with respect to the absence of inherent existence is generated, and when, after that, one views the dawning of appearances, they dawn as like illusions. There is no separate way of delineating illusory-like emptiness.

Consequently, even when engaging in the class of behavioral practices, such as prostration, circumambulation, and so forth, you should do them within being affected by the force of analytical ascertainment as [explained] above and thereby train in illusory-like appearance. They should be done within this. Through having become proficient in this, even by merely becoming mindful of the view those will dawn as like illusions.

To describe how to seek that ascertainment in a way easy to understand:

- As explained earlier, cause the generality of the object of negation by reasoning to appear well, and contemplating well inherent existence as it is superimposed by the ignorance in your own continuum, identify it.
- Then, with particular emphasis contemplate the fact that if such inherent establishment exists, it does not pass beyond oneness and difference, and with particular emphasis contemplate the mode of the presence of damage to assertions [of the self and aggregates] as either one or different, inducing ascertainment seeing the damage.
- Finally, make firm the ascertainment thinking, "A person does not in the least have inherent establishment."

Frequently train this way in the factor of emptiness. Then:

- Let the undeniable appearances of the conventions of persons dawn as objects of your awareness.
- Take to mind the dependently arisen factors of positing persons as the accumulators of actions and the experiencers of effects.
- Gain ascertainment with respect to how dependent-arisings are feasible within the absence of inherent existence.

When those two [dependent-arising and the absence of inherent existence] seem to be contradictory, within taking as examples [mirror] images and so forth, contemplate how they are non-contradictory as follows:

> The image of a face is an aggregate in one common locus[a] of (1) undeniably being produced in dependence on a face and a mirror even though it is empty of the eyes, ears, and so forth it appears to have and (2) disintegrating when either of those two conditions [face or mirror] is absent. Similarly, even though a person does not have inherent establishment—not even a particle—it is not contradictory for the person to be the accumulator of actions, the experiencer of effects, and to be born in dependence on former contaminated actions, afflictive emotions, and so forth.

Contemplating this, you should train [in the non-contradiction of appearance and emptiness]. Such should be understood in all similar situations.

[a] That is, in one object.

6. Selflessness of Phenomena

Delineating the selflessness of phenomena

The bases of imputation as a person—the five aggregates,[a] six constituents (earth and so forth),[b] six sense spheres (eye and so forth),[c] and so forth are phenomena. Their emptiness of an inherent nature—establishment by way of their own nature—is the selflessness of those phenomena. The delineation of that selflessness has two parts: refutation through moving over the reasoning explained earlier and refutation through another reasoning not explained earlier.

Refutation through moving over the reasoning explained earlier

There are two types within the phenomena of the aggregates, constituents, and sense spheres, [these being the physical and the non-physical. Their inherent existence] is to be refuted, as before, through:

- analyzing with respect to the physical whether the parts—their directional parts such as the eastern part, and so forth—and the whole are established as inherently one or different
- analyzing with respect to consciousnesses whether the parts—their own temporal parts such as earlier and later—and the whole are established as inherently one or different.

This is the meaning of the sūtra quoted earlier (see also *Insight,* 60; *Illumination,* 204):

> Just as you know [how to generate] discrimination [taking to
> mind the delineation of the mode of subsistence] of a self,
> Apply this mentally to all [phenomena].

Refutation through another reasoning not explained earlier

This section has two parts: showing the reasoning of dependent-arising and establishing uncompounded phenomena also as not truly existent through the reasoning of dependent-arising and the former reasoning.

---

[a] That is, forms, feelings, discriminations, compositional factors, and consciousnesses.

[b] That is, earth, water, fire, wind, space, and consciousness.

[c] That is, eye, ear, nose, tongue, body, and mental sense powers.

Showing the reasoning of dependent-arising

With regard to the reasoning of dependent-arising,[a] the *Questions of Sāgaramati Sūtra* clearly describes a refutation of inherent establishment by the sign of dependent-arising:[b]

> Those which arise dependently
> Do not exist by way of [their own] nature.

Also, the *Questions of Anavatapta King of Nāgas Sūtra* clearly says:[c]

---

[a] For Jam-yang-shay-pa's lengthy discussion of the formation of the term *pratītyasamutpāda,* see Hopkins, *Meditation on Emptiness,* 662-668. From that discussion and the source materials cited, it is clear that Tibetan and Indian translators of Sanskrit into Tibetan adopted a code for handling the three-part discussion of the formation of *pratītyasamutpāda:*

> *prati* = *rten cing*
> *i* or *itya* = *'brel bar*
> *samutpāda* = *'byung ba*

Their overriding concern was with having a three-part translation equivalent that makes sense in Tibetan when the parts are put together. As a result, the individual equivalents often make no sense when associated with the various explanations of the formation of the term by Indian scholars.

Some Tibetan scholars mistakenly claim that *rten cing* and *'brel bar* have different meanings; however, since Chandrakīrti says that *prati* (*rten cing*), which itself means *prāpti* (*phrad pa*), modifies the meaning of *itya* (*'brel ba*) into meaning *prāpti* (*phrad pa*), the two words come to have just one meaning, and thus the two were separated out in Tibetan merely in order to convey the discussion of the meaning of the individual parts. (An alternative to the three-part code would have been to transliterate the individual parts into Tibetan script rather than attempt to translate each part, but this avenue was not chosen.)

In Chandrakīrti's explanation, *pratītya* has just one meaning: a continuative meaning "having depended." In Tibetan this is *rten nas* as in the commonly used *rten nas 'byung ba* or *rten* in *rten 'byung.* Strictly speaking, therefore, in the Consequence School *rten nas 'byung ba* or *rten 'byung* is the most appropriate general term, with *rten cing 'brel bar 'byung ba* suitable only as a code equivalent for the three-part discussion. *rten 'brel* is a common usage that is neither. The point is that all three—*rten nas 'byung ba, rten 'byung,* and *rten cing 'brel bar 'byung ba*—have the same meaning, dependent-arising.

[b] *blo gros rgya mtshos zhus pa'i mdo, sāgaramatiparipṛcchāsūtra;* Toh. 152, *mdo sde,* vol. *pha,* 48a.4.

[c] *klu'i rgyal po ma dros pas zhus pa'i mdo, anavataptanāgarājaparipṛcchāsūtra;* Toh. 156, *mdo sde,* vol. *pha,* , 224a.1; cited in *Prasannapadā,* in commentary on stanza XIII.2; Toh. 3860, *dbu ma,* vol. *'a,* 81b.3-81b.4; La Vallée Poussin, *Mūlamadhyamakakārikās (Mādhyamikasūtras) de Nāgārjuna avec la Prasannapadā,* 239.10-239.13; J.W. de Jong, "Text-critical Notes on the Prasannapadā," *Indo-Iranian Journal* 20, nos. 1/2 (1978): 55: *yaḥ pratyayair jāyati sa hy ajāto na tasya utpādu svabhāvato sti / yaḥ pratyayādhīnu sa śūnyu ukto yaḥ śūnyatāṃ jānāti sā prasamanta iti //.* Brackets are from *Four Interwoven Annotations,* vol. 2, 368.2. Cited in *Great Treatise,* vol. 3, 188.

Those which are produced from [causes and] conditions are not produced;
They have no inherent nature of production.
[Therefore] those which rely on [causes and] conditions are said [by the Conqueror] to be empty.
[A person] who knows the emptiness [of inherent existence] is conscientious [overcoming the unpeacefulness of the afflictive emotions].

This occurs with great frequency in the precious scriptures.

Concerning this, the meaning of "not produced" mentioned in the first line is explained by "no inherently existent production" in the second line. Thereby, a qualification of the object of negation ["inherently existent"] is affixed to the refutation of production. Also, Chandrakīrti's *Clear Words*[a] cites the *Descent into Laṅkā Sūtra,*[b] "Thinking of no **inherently existent** production I said, 'All phenomena are not produced.'" From the qualm that his statements of no production without a qualification affixed might be held [as indicating that] all production whatsoever does not exist, the Teacher [Buddha] himself identifies the thought of the sūtras, explaining that it means the absence of **inherently existent** production.

Then, the third line says that depending[c] and relying on conditions is the meaning of being empty of inherent establishment. Thereby, it indicates that being empty of inherent establishment is the meaning of dependent-arising, and not an emptiness of the capacity to perform a function, which is a negative of mere production. Also, Nāgārjuna's *Fundamental Treatise on the Middle, Called "Wisdom"* says that by reason of being dependent-arisings [phenomena] are quiescent of, or empty of, inherent existence:[d]

That which arises dependent [upon causes and conditions]

[a] In commentary on stanza XXIV.18; Toh. 3860, *dbu ma,* vol. *'a,* 167b.1; La Vallée Poussin, *Mūlamadhyamakakārikās avec la Prasannapadā,* 504.5-504.6: *svabhāvānutpattiṃ saṃdhāya mahāmate sarvadharmāḥ śūnyā iti mayā deśitā iti /.*

[b] *lang kar gshegs pa'i mdo, laṅkāvatārasūtra;* Toh. 107, *mdo sde,* vol. *ca;* Sanskrit text edited by Bunyiu Nanjio, Bibl. Otaniensis, vol. 1 (Kyoto: Otani University Press, 1923), 76.3: *anutpattiṃ saṃdhāya mahāmate niḥsvabhāvāḥ sarvasvabhāvāḥ.* Compare with the citation in *Prasannapadā* given in the previous note. *Four Interwoven Annotations,* vol. 2, 369.2. Cited in *Great Treatise,* vol. 3, 188.

[c] *rag las.*

[d] VII.16ab; Toh. 3824, *dbu ma,* vol. *tsa,* 5a.5; de Jong, *Mūlamadhyamakakārikāḥ,* 9: *pratītya yad yad bhavati tat tac chāntaṃ svabhāvataḥ /.* Brackets are from *Four Interwoven Annotations,* vol. 2, 702.5. Cited in *Great Treatise,* vol. 3, 316.

Is [empty and] quiescent by [its own] nature.

Consequently, you should know that this statement also clears away any and all propositions that are emanations of darkness such as that the Middle Way system must propound that by reason of dependent production there is no production, and so forth.

Such reasoning of dependent-arising is greatly praised; the *Questions of Anavatapta King of Nāgas Sūtra* says:[a]

Realizing the [meaning of] dependently arisen phenomena,
The wise do not at all rely on extreme views.

Chandrakīrti's *Supplement to (Nāgārjuna's) "Treatise on the Middle"* sets forth the meaning of this statement that through realizing dependent-arising as it actually is, one does not rely on views holding to extremes:[b]

Since things arise dependent [upon causes and conditions],
They cannot sustain these conceptions [of being produced from self, other, and so forth].
Therefore this reasoning of dependent-arising
Cuts through all the webs[c] of bad views.

This is an unsurpassed feature of the great beings, the father Nāgārjuna and his spiritual sons. Therefore, from among the reasonings, I will describe here the reasoning of dependent-arising.

Here, the principal places of possible error that serve as obstacles to the pure view are two. One is the view of permanence, or superimposition, which has the target of apprehensions by a consciousness apprehending true establishment, this being to apprehend phenomena as truly established. The second is the view of annihilation, or deprecation, in which the measure of the object of negation has not been delimited and one has gone too far, whereby it is impossible to induce ascertainment in one's own system with respect to the dependent-

[a] Toh. 156, *mdo sde*, vol. *pha*. Khangkar and Yorihito (202 note 179) give the Sanskrit from Chandrakīrti's *Clear Words* XXIV. Brackets are from *Four Interwoven Annotations*, vol. 2, 712.6. Cited in *Great Treatise*, vol. 3, 186 and 320.

[b] VI.115; Toh. 3861, *dbu ma*, vol. *'a*, 209b.7-210a.1; La Vallée Poussin, *Madhyamakāvatāra*, 228.1-228.4; La Vallée Poussin, "*Introduction au traité du milieu*," *Muséon* 12 (1911): 278. Brackets are from *Four Interwoven Annotations*, vol. 2, 702.5. Cited in *Great Treatise*, vol. 3, 316.

[c] *dra ba*. In Dharmakīrti's *Commentary on (Dignāga's) "Compilation of Prime Cognition"* one meaning of *dra ba* is "web" or "net." The other is a grass that prevents the growing of other things, just as bad views prevent the (growth of) good views. Notice that Chandrakīrti speaks of cutting through the nets of **bad** views (*lta ngan*), not of all views in general.

arising of cause and effect, without any way of identifying, "It is this, not that."

Those two are abandoned without residue when inherent establishment is refuted based on a reason in which ascertainment has been induced with respect to the arising of such-and-such an effect from such-and-such causes and conditions. For through ascertaining the reason, the view of annihilation is eradicated, and through ascertaining the meaning of the thesis, the view of permanence is eradicated.

Therefore, external things such as sprouts and internal things such as compositional activity[a] arise in dependence, respectively, on seeds and so forth, and on ignorance[b] and so forth. This being so, that those [sprouts, compositional activity, and so forth] are established by way of their own character is not feasible because whatever is established by way of its own nature must be inherently established—that is, be able to set itself up under its own power—due to which it is contradictory for it to rely on causes and conditions. Āryadeva's *Four Hundred* says:[c]

> Those which have a dependent arising
> Are not under their own power.
> All these are not under their own power;
> Therefore, they do not have self [that is to say, establishment
> by way of their own nature].

Through this you should understand that persons, pots, and so forth also are without inherent establishment because of being imputed in dependence on their own collection [of parts]. Those are two presentations of the reasoning of dependent-arising.[d]

What is dependently produced or dependently imputed does not exist as an inherently existent one with that upon which it depends; [for] if it did, all agents and objects[e] would be one. Those two also do not exist as inherently existent others because if they did, a

[a] The second of the twelve links of dependent-arising.

[b] The first of the twelve links of dependent-arising.

[c] XIV.23; P5246, vol. 95, 139.2.7; Toh. 3846, *dbu ma*, vol. *tsha*, 16a.4; Lang, *Āryadeva's Catuḥśataka*, 134; see Sonam Rinchen and Ruth Sonam, *Yogic Deeds of Bodhisattvas*, 274. Brackets from Chandrakīrti's commentary, P5266, vol. 98, 270.3.6, and *Four Interwoven Annotations*, vol. 2, 704.6. Cited in *Great Treatise*, vol. 3, 317.

[d] The two are (1) arising in dependence upon causes and conditions and (2) being imputed in dependence on their own collection of parts.

[e] Jam-yang-shay-pa's *Great Exposition of Tenets* (Hopkins, *Maps of the Profound*, 832, and *Meditation on Emptiness*, 642) says, "It [absurdly] follows that the agents and the objects of cause and effect [that is, producer and produced] would be one because something would produce itself."

relationship [between them] could be refuted, whereby reliance on those [causes or a basis of imputation] would be contradictory.

Moreover, Nāgārjuna's *Fundamental Treatise on the Middle, Called "Wisdom"* says:[a]

> That which arises dependently
> Respectively is not one [with that on which it depends]
> And is also not [inherently] other than that.
> Hence, it is not annihilated and not permanent.

and Nāgārjuna's *Praise of the Supramundane* says:[b]

> Logicians [ranging from Outsider Non-Buddhists to our own Buddhists who propound inherent existence] assert that suffering
> Is created by itself [or by what is its own entity as the Sāṃkhyas assert], created by [what is inherently] other [as most of our own and others' sects who propound that things are inherently established assert],
> Created by both [self and other], or causelessly [as the Nihilists assert].
> You said it is dependently arisen.
>
> That which arises dependently
> You asserted as empty.
> That things do not exist under their own power
> Is the roar of the lion, you unequalled.

He says that apprehensions of oneness, difference, the extremes of permanence and annihilation, as well as the four extreme types of production are refuted by the reasoning of dependent-arising.

Inducing ascertainment in that way about the emptiness of all the targets aimed at by the apprehension of signs [that is, inherent existence], one does not forsake ascertainment of the relationship of actions and their effects, whereby one relies on discarding [non-virtues] and assuming [virtues]. This is greatly praised; Nāgārjuna's *Essay on the*

---

[a] XVIII.10; Toh. 3824, *dbu ma*, vol. *tsa*, 11a.4; de Jong, *Mūlamadhyamakakārikāḥ*, 24-25: *pratītya yad yad bhavati na hi tāvat tad eva tat / na cānyad api tat tasmānnocchinnaṃ nāpi śāśvatam //.*

[b] *'jig rten las 'das par bstod pa, lokātītastava*, stanzas 21-22; Toh. 1120, *bstod tshogs*, vol. *ka;* Sanskrit and Tibetan texts edited by Lindtner, *Master of Wisdom*, 8 and 161: *svayaṃkṛtaṃ parakṛtaṃ dvābhyāṃ kṛtam ahetukam / tārkikair iṣyate duḥkhaṃ tvayā tūktaṃ pratītyajam // yaḥ pratītyasamutpādaḥ śūnyatā saiva te matā / bhāvaḥ svatantro nāstīti siṃhanādas tavātulaḥ//.* Brackets are from *Four Interwoven Annotations*, vol. 2, 218.5. Cited in *Great Treatise*, vol. 3, 133; Napper, *Dependent-Arising and Emptiness*, 187 and 336-337.

Mind of Enlightenment says:[a]

> Reliance on actions and their fruits
> Within knowing this emptiness of phenomena
> Is more wonderful than even the wonderful,
> More fantastic than even the fantastic.

In order for such to happen, it is necessary to differentiate between:

- inherent existence and mere existence
- absence of existence by way of its [the object's] own character and non-existence.

It is as Chandrakīrti's *Commentary on the "Supplement to (Nāgārjuna's) 'Treatise on the Middle'"* says:[b]

> While knowing even the presentation of causes and effects, which are reflections without inherent existence, what wise person would—through observing that forms, feelings, and so forth, which do not abide separately from causes and effects, are merely existent—ascertain them as having inherent existence? Therefore, although observed to exist, they have no inherently existent production.

When those are not differentiated, you do not pass beyond the two extremes of superimposition and deprecation since then once a thing exists, it exists by way of its own nature, and once something does not exist by way of its own nature, it is totally non-existent. Chandrakīrti's *Commentary on (Āryadeva's) "Four Hundred"* says:[c]

> According to the proponents of [inherently existent] things, as long as a thing's existence occurs, [its establishment by way of] its own entity also exists, and when devoid of [establishment by way of] their own entity, things do not exist in all ways, like the horns of a donkey. Thereby, since they do not pass beyond propounding the two [extremes of permanence and annihilation], it is difficult to fit together all their assertions.

---

[a] *byang chub sems kyi 'grel pa, bodhicittavivaraṇa,* stanza 82; P2665, vol. 61, 46b.6; Toh. 1800/1801, *rgyud 'grel,* vol. *ngi;* Tibetan text edited by Lindtner, *Master of Wisdom,* 62.

[b] Commenting on VI.38ab; Toh. 3862, *dbu ma,* vol. 70, 259b.3-259b.4; La Vallée Poussin, *Madhyamakāvatāra,* 123.18-124.3; La Vallée Poussin, "*Introduction au traité du milieu,*" *Muséon* 11 (1910): 316.

[c] Toh. 3865, *dbu ma,* vol. *ya,* 175b.2-175b.3; for the Sanskrit see Khangkar and Yorihito, 205 note 195. Brackets are from *Four Interwoven Annotations,* vol. 2, 243.6. Cited in *Great Treatise,* vol. 3, 142; Napper, *Dependent-Arising and Emptiness,* 199 and 364-365.

Therefore, you are released from all extremes of existence through the absence of inherent existence, and you are released from all extremes of non-existence through being able to posit, with respect to that, causes and effects that do not inherently exist.

Concerning *anta*[a] [that is, "end," "extreme," "limit," "pole," and the like] Vasubandhu's *Principles of Explanation* says:[b]

> *Anta* is used for finish, end,
> Proximity, direction, and lowliness.

The *anta*s mentioned this way [in Vasubandhu's text] are also indeed accepted in our own system, but with respect to the *anta* (extreme) that is a place of going wrong with respect to the view, as in "devoid of the extremes," Kamalashīla's *Illumination of the Middle* says:[c]

> If in the middle there were any ultimate nature of inherent existence of the mind,[d] then since it had that, how could even manifest adherences to "permanence" and "impermanence" with regard to it be extremes (*anta*)? It is not reasonable to say that proper mental application in accordance with the suchness of things is a situation of falling [to an extreme (*anta*)].

As he says, mental application in accordance with how an object actually is, is not a situation of falling [to an extreme]. Hence, just as in the world an abyss is called an extreme and falling into it is called "falling into an extreme," the apprehension of phenomena as truly existent and the apprehension that nothing at all is established and nothing exists are [cases of] falling to extremes of permanence and annihilation—the opposite of the correct fact. However, apprehensions that phenomena do not ultimately exist and that actions and their effects, and so on, in conventional terms exist and so forth are not apprehensions of extremes because the objects abide in the way that they are apprehended. For, Nāgārjuna's *Refutation of Objections* says that if [something] is not ultimately non-existent, then it ultimately exists:[e]

---

[a] *mtha'.*

[b] *rnam par bshad pa'i rigs pa, vyākhyāyukti;* Toh. 4061, *sems tsam,* vol. *shi,* 34b.5.

[c] *dbu ma snang ba, madhyamakāloka;* Toh. 3887, *dbu ma,* vol. *sa,* 158a.4.

[d] *dbu ma la sems kyi rang gi ngo bo'i bdag nyid kyi dngos po don dam pa ba.*

[e] *rtsod pa bzlog pa'i tshig le'ur byas pa, vigrahavyāvartanīkārikā,* stanza 26cd; Toh. 3828, *dbu ma,* vol. *tsa,* 27b.6-27b.7; Sanskrit in Lindtner, *Master of Wisdom,* 210: *naiḥsvābhāvyanivṛttau svābhāvyaṃ hi prasiddhaṃ syāt //;* Tibetan on p. 222. Brackets are from *Four Interwoven Annotations,* vol. 2, 258.2 and 377.5. Cited in *Great Treatise,* vol. 3, 146-147 and 191; Napper, *Dependent-Arising and Emptiness,* 206 and 380.

> If the absence of inherent existence were disposed of [with respect to any phenomenon],
> Then [that phenomenon] would be established as inherently existent.

and:[a]

> We [Proponents of the Middle] do not make explanations
> Without asserting the conventions [of the world].

and his *Seventy Stanzas on Emptiness* says:[b]

> This worldly mode of "Depending on that,
> This arises" is not refuted.

Therefore, distinctions:[c]

- between the two—that something is not existent (*yod pa min pa*) and that something does not exist (*med pa*) [whereas these actually have the same meaning], and
- between the two—that something is not non-existent (*med pa min pa*) and that something exists (*yod pa*) [whereas these actually have the same meaning]

are reduced to merely being differences in mode of expression. No matter how much one analyzes how the meanings of both of those appear to the mind, there is no difference at all; hence, to propound that one falls or does not fall to extremes through those modes [of expression] is exhausted as fixation on mere words.

Establishing uncompounded phenomena also as not truly existent through the reasoning of dependent-arising and the former reasoning

Thinking that when in this way compounded things—persons and other phenomena—have been established as not truly existent by way of the reasonings described earlier, it can be established with little difficulty that uncompounded phenomena such as space, analytical cessations, non-analytical cessations, thusness, and so forth are not truly existent, Nāgārjuna says in the *Fundamental Treatise on the Middle Called*

---

[a] Stanza 28cd; Toh. 3828, *dbu ma*, vol. *tsa*, 27b.7-28a.1; Lindtner, *Master of Wisdom*, 211: *saṃvyavahāraṃ ca vayaṃ nānabhyupagamya kathayāmaḥ //;* Tibetan on p. 222. Brackets are from *Four Interwoven Annotations*, vol. 2, 520.1. Cited in *Great Treatise*, vol. 3, 247.

[b] Stanza 71ab; Toh. 3827, *dbu ma*, vol. *tsa*, 26b.6; Lindtner, *Master of Wisdom*, 116; Komito, *Seventy Stanzas*, 179-180.

[c] These distinctions are made in a futile attempt to propound that an object is not existent, is not non-existent, is not both, and is not either.

"Wisdom":[a]

> Since compounded phenomena are thoroughly not established,
> How could the uncompounded be established?

With regard to how it is easy to establish [uncompounded phenomena as not truly existent], when the inherent establishment of compounded phenomena is refuted as before, it is established that even though [phenomena] do not inherently exist, it is permissible to posit agents, activities, and objects—bondage and liberation, cause and effect, object comprehended and comprehender, and so forth—with respect to them. When that is established, even though uncompounded phenomena such as the noumenon and analytical cessations also do not truly exist, it is permissible to posit well the presentations of them as the objects of attainment and objects of comprehension of the path, as well as the doctrine jewel that is a source of refuge for trainees, and so forth. Hence, when those are not asserted to truly exist, there is no way to say that these presentations of the necessity for positing them as those are not feasible. Consequently, there is no point in asserting them to truly exist.

Even those who assert that [the noumenon, cessations, and so forth] truly exist must indeed assert and do indeed assert—with respect to those—presentations of definiendum and definition, separative cause[b] and separative effect,[c] comprehension by such-and-such valid cognition, and so forth. Then, if [it is claimed that the noumenon, cessations, and so forth] are not related with one's object of attainment, definition, means of comprehension, and so forth, it could not be refuted that all unrelated [phenomena] would be [in the relationship of] definition and definiendum, and so forth. If a relation is asserted, then since dependence on another is not suitable in what truly exists, that is to say, is inherently established, a relationship cannot be posited [since it is being claimed that the noumenon, cessations, and so forth truly exist].[d]

---

[a] VII.33cd; Toh. 3824, *dbu ma*, vol. *tsa*, 5b.6-5b.7; de Jong, *Mūlamadhyamakakārikāḥ*, 11: *saṃskṛtasyāprasiddhau ca kathaṃ setsyaty asaṃskṛtam //.*

[b] *bral rgyu.*

[c] *bral 'bras.*

[d] Lo-sang-dor-jay's *Decisive Analysis of (Tsong-kha-pa's) "Stages of the Path to Enlightenment": Ship for Entering into the Ocean of Textual Systems* rephrases these points (adapted from Elizabeth Napper's unpublished translation, 91-92):

> When the inherent establishment of compounded phenomena is refuted as [explained] previously, then even though they are not established inherently, all activities such as bondage and liberation with respect to these [com-

Similarly, [the inherent existence of an uncompounded phenomenon] should also be refuted through analyzing whether [it and its basis of imputation] are one or different. If the assertion of these as truly existent could not be refuted by this reasoned analysis, then since it would also be the same in all respects with regard to compounded phenomena, true existence could not even in the least be refuted.

Objection: The meaning of the statement that compounded phenomena are empty of their own inherently existent entity is that those phenomena do not have their own entities, whereby this is an annihilatory emptiness. However, since thusness has its own entity, it truly exists.

Answer: [The first part of that assertion] is the final place of going wrong with respect to delineating compounded phenomena as empty of inherent establishment, a view deprecating the dependent-arising of compounded phenomena. The latter [part of that assertion] is an awful view of permanence superimposing true existence on whatever has its own entity. Therefore, [the proponents of this] are wrongly perspected with respect to the correct meaning of emptiness.

If [an object's] emptiness of its own inherently established entity [meant that] it did not exist within itself, then since not existing within itself [means] that existence would not occur anywhere, holders of the thesis that some phenomena truly exist as well as the scriptures and reasonings proving this, and so forth, would not be established bases [that is, would not exist] due to being empty of their own inherently established entity. Therefore, the positing of a tenet that some

---

pounded phenomena] are established as positable. And, if these are established, then also with respect to uncompounded phenomena, such as suchness and analytical cessations, even though they are not truly established, the presentations of positing these as objects of attainment of the path, as objects of ascertainment [of the path], and as the doctrine jewel that is a source of refuge can be well posited.

Therefore, the subjects, uncompounded phenomena, are not inherently established because of being related with their objects of attainment, their definitions, their positers, and so forth. There is entailment [that if something is related with its objects of attainment, its definition, its positers, and so forth, it is necessarily not inherently established] because since reliance on something else is unsuitable in that which is truly established—that is, inherently established—relationship cannot be posited [with respect to it].

The above reason [—that it is established that uncompounded phenomena are related with objects of attainment, definitions, positers, and so forth—] is confirmed because if these were unrelated with those, one could not avoid [the problem] that all unrelated things would be definition and definiendum.

phenomena truly exist[a] is an unexamined propounding of whatever appears to mind.

Seeing well the implications of the reasoning of this situation, all our own [Buddhist] sects in the country of Superiors [India] who propound that phenomena truly exist are called proponents of [truly existent] things[b] since they definitely propound that things truly exist. Once things are propounded as not truly existent, not to assert any phenomenon [as truly existent] appears to be a sign of greatly surpassing those who propound foolishness in this area.

Also, with respect to those here [in Tibet] who propound two discordant [positions] regarding suchness,[c] you should, through the above explanation, understand well the status of their modes of debate—as to whether the ultimate is ultimately established or not—in the context of their affinity for the former mode of conventionalities being empty of their own inherently established entity [mistaking this to mean that phenomena are empty of themselves and wanting to avoid holding that the ultimate is empty of itself and hence non-existent, which would be a view of deprecatory nihilism]. For the two—(1) [correctly] not asserting true existence with respect to all things and all phenomena, having refuted with reasoning true existence in phenomena, and (2) [incorrectly] propounding that all things and all phenomena do not truly exist based on an annihilatory emptiness in which the way of understanding emptiness is faulty—are dissimilar in all respects.

Objection: If the meaning of the statement [in Nāgārjuna's *Treatise on the Middle*]:

> Since compounded phenomena are thoroughly not established,
> How could the uncompounded be established?

is as you have explained above (96), does it not contradict (1) the statement in his *Sixty Stanzas of Reasoning* that only nirvāṇa is true and that the others are not:[d]

> When the Conqueror said

[a] Dol-po-pa Shay-rap-gyel-tsen holds that suchness, the matrix-of-One-Gone-Thus, and all ultimate Buddha attributes of body, speech, and mind ultimately, or truly, exist, whereas all conventional phenomena are empty of themselves.

[b] *dngos por smra ba.* For extended discussion of this term, see Napper, *Dependent-Arising and Emptiness,* 50-51 and 666-667 n.73.

[c] In his 1972 lectures, the Dalai Lama speculated that the two might be those who wrongly hold that the ultimate is not an object of knowledge and those who wrongly hold that emptiness truly exists, or, alternatively, those who hold the combined position that conventionalities are self-empty and the ultimate is other-empty.

[d] Stanza 35; Toh. 3825, *dbu ma,* vol. 68, 21b.5; Lindtner, *Master of Wisdom,* 84.

That only nirvāṇa is a truth,
What wise person would think,
"The rest are not unreal"?

and (2) the statement also in his *Praise of the Element of Attributes* that the sūtras teaching emptiness—the absence of inherent existence—are for the sake of abandoning the afflictive emotions and do not teach the non-existence of the naturally pure basic constituent:[a]

All the sūtras teaching emptiness
Set forth by the Conqueror
Overcome the afflictive emotions.
[These sūtras] do not diminish this basic constituent.

Answer: Those [who say such] are wrongly perspected with respect to the meaning of the scriptures as follows. The meaning of the former scripture is expressed [in sūtra]:[b]

The Supramundane Victor said "Monastics, this ultimate truth is one—non-deceptive nirvāṇa. All compositional things[c] have the attribute of falsity, deceptiveness."

This sūtra passage also says that nirvāṇa is a truth and all compositional things are false. The early part of the passage very clearly explains that truth means non-deceptive, and the latter part very clearly explains that falsity means deceptive. Furthermore, nirvāṇa [here refers] to ultimate truth,[d] as is explained in Chandrakīrti's *Commentary on (Nāgārjuna's) "Sixty Stanzas of Reasoning."* Hence, an ultimate truth is

[a] *chos kyi dbyings su bstod pa, dharmadhātustotra;* Toh. 1118, *bstod tshogs,* vol. *ka,* 64b.2-64b.3.

[b] This passage is cited in Chandrakīrti's *Clear Words (dbu ma tshig gsal, prasannapadā)* commenting on stanza I.1; Toh. 3860, *dbu ma,* vol. *'a,* 13a.4-13a.5, which reads: *dge slong dag 'di ni bden pa dam pa ste 'di lta ste slu ba med pa'i chos can mya ngan las 'das pa'o,* as does Dol-po-pa's citation (Gangtok edition, 318.3); Tsong-kha-pa's citation differs in minor ways: *dge slong dag bden pa dam pa 'di ni gcig ste/ 'di lta ste mi slu ba'i chos can mya ngan las 'das pa'o.* Tsong-kha-pa also cites this passage in his *Explanation of (Nāgārjuna's) "Treatise on the Middle": Ocean of Reasoning* (P6153, vol. 156, 64.2.3). The Sanskrit is in La Vallée Poussin, *Mūlamadhyamakakārikās (Mādhyamikasūtras) de Nāgārjuna avec la Prasannapadā Commentaire de Candrakīrti* (Osnabrück: Biblio Verlag, 1970), 41: *tattvadarśanāpekṣayā tūktaṃ bhagavatā / etaddhi bhikṣavaḥ paramaṃ satyaṃ yaduta amoṣadharma nirvāṇaṃ / sarvasaṃskārāś ca mṛṣā moṣadharmāṇaḥ /.*

[c] *'du byed, saṃskāra;* this term is often used as an equivalent for compounded things (*'dus byas, saṃskṛta*).

[d] The ultimate truth is called the "natural nirvāṇa," which is the emptiness of inherent existence, and not the nirvāṇa that is the cessation of obstructions attained through practice of the path.

without the deception of appearing—in the perspective of an awareness directly perceiving it—as if being established inherently whereas it is not. The remaining [phenomena], compositional things, have the deceptiveness of appearing—in the perspective of an awareness directly perceiving them—to be established inherently whereas they are not. Therefore, when [an ultimate truth] is analyzed with the reasoning investigating whether it is truly established or not, it is not truly established in the sense of being able to withstand analysis. Hence, what point is there in not thinking about the meaning in detail and being attached to mere words!

Moreover, Nāgārjuna's *Sixty Stanzas of Reasoning* says:[a]

> These two, cyclic existence and nirvāṇa,
> Do not [inherently] exist.
> The thorough knowledge itself of cyclic existence
> Is called "nirvāṇa."

He explains that **both** cyclic existence and nirvāṇa are not inherently existent and that [the emptiness which is] just the object of the knowledge that cyclic existence is not inherently established is posited as nirvāṇa. Therefore, how could this be a position asserting that the emptiness that is the absence of true existence of cyclic existence is an annihilatory emptiness!

Moreover, the passage from Nāgārjuna's *Praise of the Element of Attributes* (see also *Insight*, 99) means:

> For the sake of overcoming the apprehension of things as truly existent—the root of all other afflictive emotions—the sūtras teaching emptiness, the absence of inherent establishment, teach that the conceived object of the apprehension of true existence does not exist. They do not teach that emptiness—the naturally pure basic constituent, the negative of the two selves that are the objects of the apprehension of true existence—does not exist.

Since although this emptiness exists, it is not truly established, that passage serves as a source refuting the proposition that the emptiness that is a negative of true existence—its object of negation—does not exist. It also refutes the proposition that it is not necessary to realize emptiness, the ultimate suchness, in order to exhaustively abandon the

[a] Stanza 6; Toh. 3825, *dbu ma*, vol. *tsa*, 20a.4-20a.5; Lindtner, *Master of Wisdom*, 74, 174: *nirvāṇaṃ ca bhavaś caiva dvayam etan na vidyate / parijñānaṃ bhavasyaiva nirvāṇam iti kathyate //*.

afflictive emotions. Hence, Nāgārjuna's *Praise of the Element of Attributes* itself says:[a]

> Through the three called impermanence, [coarse] emptiness,
> And suffering, the mind is purified.
> The doctrine supremely purifying the mind
> Is naturelessness [that is, the absence of inherent existence].

and:

> The naturelessness of phenomena
> Should be meditated upon as the element of attributes.

He says that the absence of an inherently established nature in these phenomena is the element of attributes that is the object of meditation, and he says that just meditation on it is the supreme purifier of the mind. Therefore, how could it be suitable to cite this [*Praise of the Element of Attributes*] for the position that the emptiness that is the absence of the inherent establishment of phenomena appearing in this way[b] is an annihilatory emptiness and that, therefore, a truly existent emptiness separate from it is to be posited as the emptiness that is the object of meditation!

This is like propounding that in order to remove the suffering of fright upon apprehending a snake in the east despite there being no snake there, the demonstration that there is no snake in the east will not serve as an antidote to it, but rather one should indicate, "There is a tree in the west." For, one is propounding that in order to remove the suffering upon adhering to the true existence of what appears in this way to sentient beings, realization that those bases [that is, objects]—which are apprehended to truly exist—do not truly exist will not serve as an antidote, but that rather one must indicate that some other senseless base truly exists.

[a] Toh. 1118, *bstod tshogs*, vol. *ka*, 64b.5 and 65a.6-65a.7.

[b] That is to say, appearing to be inherently established.

7. Basis of Division of the Two Truths

Presentation of obscurational truths and ultimate truths

This section has four parts: the basis of division of the two truths, number of divisions, meaning of dividing them that way, and meaning of the individual divisions.

Basis of division of the two truths

With respect to the basis of division of the two truths there are many modes of assertion among earlier [scholars];[a] however, here objects of

---

[a] Jam-yang-shay-pa's *Great Exposition of Tenets* (Hopkins, *Maps of the Profound,* 894-895) gives a clear presentation of these:

> There are many systems of assertion with regard to the basis of division of the two truths—that is, what is divided into the two truths. These incorrect systems hold that:
>
> 1. Mere appearances are the basis of division of the two truths because ultimate truths are not objects of knowledge.
> 2. The entities of form through to omniscience are the basis of division because Chandrakīrti explains that phenomena have two entities.
> 3. Non-superimpositional objects are the basis of division.
> 4. Non-investigated and non-analyzed objects of knowledge are the basis of division.
> 5. Truths are the basis of division, and when truths are divided, there are two, obscurational truths and ultimate truths.
> 6. There is no necessity for a basis of division, but there is much to be said about the two truths that are the divisions.
>
> Those are not correct because:
>
> 1. If [according to you] ultimate truths do not exist [because they are not objects of knowledge, and hence not existents]:
>   - It [absurdly] follows that the final mode of subsistence of forms and so forth does not exist.
>   - It [absurdly] follows that because what is seen now is the final mode of subsistence, all sentient beings are already liberated.
>
>   and so forth.
> 2. Just as the two truths are not among the entities of a form, so it is [for all phenomena] through to omniscience. [If the two truths were both included within, for instance, form, then the ultimate truth of a form, which is its emptiness, would be a form, due to which emptiness absurdly would not be an uncompounded phenomenon which it actually is.]
> 3. Existing superimpositional systems [such as the Sāṃkhya system] are obscurational truths. [Even though the superimpositions of the Sāṃkhya

knowledge are the basis of division, since Shāntideva's *Compendium of Instructions*[a] says (see also *Illumination*, 220):

Furthermore, objects of knowledge[b] are exhausted as these

---

system, like the principal, do not exist even as obscurational truths, the system itself exists and is not an emptiness, whereby it is an obscurational truth].

4. The two truths have much to be analyzed, and, therefore, the fourth is bad talk and the worst mistake.
5. Obscurational truths, falsities, and so forth are synonymous. [If the basis of division of the two truths is truth, then everything divided from it is a truth in which case obscurational truths would be truths. Then how could they be falsities?]
6. If the base of division and the mode of division are not known, then [the two truths] become attributes without a substratum...

Therefore, that objects of knowledge are the basis of division [of the two truths] is proved by:

- scripture: The *Meeting of the Father and Son Sūtra* which says, "Furthermore, objects of knowledge [that is, objects to be known] are exhausted as these two truths, obscurational and ultimate." [See the following note.]
- and reasoning: [The two truths] are objects of two types of awareness—that is, objects to be known and objects of analysis by those two types of awareness.

[a] *bslab pa kun las btus pa, śikṣāsamuccaya;* Toh. 3940, vol. *khi*, 142b.2; Sanskrit in Bendall, *Çikshāsamuccaya*, 256: *etāvaccaitat jñeyam / yaduta saṃvṛtiḥ paramārthaśca /*. English translation in Cecil Bendall and W.H.D. Rouse, *Śikṣā Samuccaya* (Delhi: Motilal Banarsidass, 1971), 236. Shāntideva is citing the *Meeting of Father and Son Sūtra* (*yab dang sras mjal ba'i mdo, pitāputrasamāgamasūtra;* P760.16, vol. 23; Toh. 60, vol. *nga* (*dkon brtsegs*), which Tsong-kha-pa cites in his *Illumination of the Thought* (220):

It is thus: Ones-Gone-Thus thoroughly understand the two, fraudulences and ultimates. Furthermore, objects of knowledge are exhausted as these obscurational truths and ultimate truths. Moreover, it is because Ones-Gone-Thus have thoroughly perceived, known, and actualized well [those which have the aspect of]* emptiness that they are called "omniscient."

*The bracketed addition is taken from Tsong-kha-pa's commentary later in the *Illumination* (97.5). Without the addition, the passage seems to say that a Buddha is called omniscient only because of having thoroughly realized emptiness; by taking the word emptiness as a *bahuvṛhi* compound meaning "those which have emptiness" or "those which have the aspect of emptiness," the term comes to refer to all those that are empty and thus all fraudulent truths and ultimate truths. The addition does indeed seem strained, but the sūtra itself, just above, has spoken about both truths.

[b] Or, "those that are to be known," that is to say, what is to be known by those seeking liberation and omniscience. As Lo-sang-dor-jay's *Decisive Analysis* says (adapted from Elizabeth Napper's unpublished translation, 94):

A basis of division into the two truths exists because objects of knowledge are that [basis of division], since what are to be known by hearing, thinking, and obscurational[a] truths and ultimate truths."

Number of divisions

Nāgārjuna's *Treatise on the Middle* says:[b]

> Worldly obscurational truths [which are posited in the perspective of conventional consciousnesses of the world and are true in the perspective of consciousnesses apprehending true existence]
> And ultimate truths [which are objects of ultimate pristine wisdom and are true, non-deceptive].

Accordingly, [objects of knowledge] are divided into the two truths—obscurational truths and ultimate truths.[c]

Meaning of dividing them that way

Question: Since the two of the division into two must be different, what kind of difference is this?

Answer: With respect to this, many earlier [scholars] propounded:[d]

> meditating for the sake of attaining release are exhausted as those two [truths].

[a] As Tsong-kha-pa says below (109), "Chandrakīrti's *Clear Words* describes three [meanings] for *saṃvṛti*—(1) obstructing suchness, (2) mutually dependent objects, and (3) worldly conventions."

Thus, *saṃvṛtisatya* (*kun rdzob bden pa*) could be translated as "obscurational truth," "relative truth," or "conventional truth." Because the first is the predominant usage, I only occasionally use "conventional truth" depending on the import of the passage.

[b] XXIV.8cd; Toh. 3824, *dbu ma*, vol. *tsa*, 15a.1; de Jong, *Mūlamadhyamakakārikāḥ*, 34: *loka-saṃvṛtisatyaṃ ca satyaṃ ca paramārthataḥ //*. Brackets are from *Four Interwoven Annotations*, vol. 2, 452.3. Cited in *Great Treatise*, vol. 3, 218.

[c] There is no other category, and nothing is both; Lo-sang-dor-jay's *Decisive Analysis* says (adapted from Elizabeth Napper's unpublished translation, 94):

> Further, this definite enumeration is one eliminating any possible third category because there does not exist a third category of objects of knowledge that is not either of the two truths. That the reason is so follows because the two, truth and falsity, are explicitly contradictory in the sense of mutual exclusion. That this is so follows because the two, deceptive and non-deceptive, are such. That this is so follows because when a particular basis is positively included as being non-deceptive, it is eliminated that that basis is deceptive, and when it is eliminated that a particular basis is non-deceptive, it is positively included that it is deceptive. The reason for this is that the meaning of true and false on this occasion refers to deceptiveness and non-deceptiveness.

[d] For Jam-yang-shay-pa's exposition of four positions on this topic, see Hopkins, *Maps*

> Pot and woolen cloth, for instance, are different entities.[a] Product and impermanent thing, for instance, are one entity and different isolates.[b] In these two cases, the two that are different are both effective things; however, in cases of difference when either is a non-effective thing [that is, a permanent phenomenon] they have a difference that [merely] negates sameness.[c] Among these three [modes of] difference, the two truths are different in the sense of negating sameness.

However, some [correctly] asserted that the two truths are one entity and different isolates.

It is good to take this in accordance with the statement in Kamalashīla's *Illumination of the Middle* that the relationship of one essence[d] is not contradictory even among non-effective things [that is, permanent phenomena].[e] Therefore, a oneness of entity and difference of isolates is not contradictory even in both cases—when both of the different phenomena are non-effective things or when one is. This is:

- because Chandrakīrti's *Commentary on the "Supplement to (Nāgārjuna's) 'Treatise on the Middle'"* says,[f] "Two types of natures of all these things are taught, obscurational and ultimate," and hence with regard to the natures of each substratum there are two, obscurational and ultimate, and
- because if the two truths were not one entity, then since it would also be very unreasonable for them to be different entities,[g] the two truths would have to be entityless, whereby they would not exist, for whatever exists necessarily exists as one entity or many entities.

Moreover, Nāgārjuna's *Essay on the Mind of Enlightenment* says (see also

of the Profound, 896-902.

[a] *ngo bo tha dad.*

[b] *ngo bo gcig la ldog pa tha dad.*

[c] *gcig pa dkag pa'i tha dad.*

[d] *bdag gcig pa'i 'brel pa.*

[e] *dbu ma snang ba, madhyamakāloka;* Toh. 3887, *dbu ma*, vol. *sa*, 221a.1-221a.2.

[f] Commenting on VI.23; Toh. 3862, *dbu ma*, vol. *'a*, 253a.6; La Vallée Poussin, *Madhyamakāvatāra*, 102.14-102.15; La Vallée Poussin, "*Introduction au traité du milieu*," *Muséon* 11 (1910): 300.

[g] Tsong-kha-pa spells out this point in his *Illumination of (Chandrakīrti's) Thought:*

> ...if phenomena were different entities from [their respective] emptinesses of true existence, they would be truly established.

Tsong-kha-pa makes this very point after the citation from Nāgārjuna's *Essay on the Mind of Enlightenment.*

Illumination, 221):[a]

> Conventionalities[b] are described as emptiness [that is, as empty of inherent existence]
> And just emptiness is [posited in relation to] the conventional,
> Because of the definiteness that [the one] would not occur without [the other],
> Like product and impermanent thing.

If a sprout, for instance, were a different entity from its own ultimate, then since it would be a different entity also from its own emptiness of true existence, it would be truly established. Therefore, since it is not a different entity [from its own emptiness of true existence], it is the same entity. A sprout is empty of its own true existence but is not its own ultimate truth.[c]

Some texts say that the two truths are neither one nor different.[d] Among these, some are in consideration [that the two truths lack] inherently established oneness and difference; others are in consideration [that the two truths are] not either different entities or one isolate.[e]

---

[a] Stanza 68; Lindtner, *Master of Wisdom*, 54.

[b] Or, obscurationals.

[c] *myu gu ni rang gi bden stong yin yang rang gi don dam bden pa ni min no.*

[d] Such a passage is the first of two concluding stanzas to chapter three, The Questions of Suvishuddhamati, in the *Sūtra Unraveling the Thought:*

> The character of the compounded realm and of the ultimate
> Is a character devoid of sameness and difference.
> Those who consider that they are the same or different
> Are improperly oriented.

[e] About the relationship of the two truths Jam-yang-shay-pa's *Great Exposition of Tenets* (Hopkins, *Maps of the Profound*, 901-902) says:

> Therefore, the two truths are one entity and different isolates, like product and impermanent phenomenon. If the two truths are different without even a sameness of entity there are four fallacies:
>
> - It [absurdly] follows that the absence of true existence of form must not be the final mode of subsistence of form.
> - It [absurdly] follows that realization of the absence of true existence of form must not suppress with its power the apprehension of [truly existent] signs of form.
> - It [absurdly] follows that yogis' meditation of high paths is senseless.
> - It [absurdly] follows that even a Buddha has not abandoned all the bonds of apprehending [truly existent] signs and defilements of assumption of bad states.
>
> and so forth...If the two truths are one such that not even their isolates are individually differentiable:

- It [absurdly] follows that just as mistaken obscurational truths, [polluted] actions, and afflictive emotions are abandoned, so even the ultimate, the noumenon of those phenomena, is abandoned.
- It [absurdly] follows that like obscurational truths, the ultimate has dissimilar, different aspects.
- It [absurdly] follows that just as obscurational truths are defiled, so even the ultimate would be suitable to be tainted with defilements.
- It [absurdly] follows that even common beings are able to apprehend ultimates manifestly.

and so forth...Therefore, although the two truths are undifferentiable in entity as empty of true existence, they are established as different from the viewpoints of their respective isolates that are their bases of dependence.

8. Obscurational Truths

Meaning of the individual divisions

This section has three parts: obscurational truths, ultimate truths, and indicating the definiteness of the number of the truths as two.

Obscurational truths

This section has three parts: the meanings of the terms *saṃvṛti* (*kun rdzob*) and *satya* (*bden pa*), definition of an obscurational truth, and divisions of conventionalities.

Meanings of the terms saṃvṛti (kun rdzob) and satya (bden pa)

Chandrakīrti's *Clear Words*[a] describes three [meanings] for *saṃvṛti*—(1) obstructing suchness,[b] (2) mutually dependent objects,[c] and (3) worldly conventions.[d] Since he explains the last as having the character of object of expression and means of expression, knower and object of knowledge, and so forth, it is not just subjective conventions—consciousnesses and expressions—[but also objects known and objects expressed]. Nevertheless, [this is just an etymology and not a definition since] not all whatsoever objects of knowledge and objects of expression should be held to be obscurational truths [because an emptiness is an object of knowledge and object of expression but is an ultimate truth].[e]

[a] La Vallée Poussin, *Mūlamadhyamakakārikās (Mādhyamikasūtras) de Nāgārjuna avec la Prasannapadā*, 492.11-492.12.

[b] *de kho na nyid la sgrib pa, tattvāvacchādana.*

[c] *phan tshun brten pa, parasparasaṃbhavana.*

[d] *'jig rten gyi tha snyad, lokavyavahāra.*

[e] Jam-yang-shay-pa's *Great Exposition of Tenets* (Hopkins, *Maps of the Profound*, 904-905) says:

> In the Sanskrit original of *'jig rten kun rdzob bden pa* (worldly obscurational truth) *lokasaṃvṛtisatya:*
>
> - *Loka* (*'jig rten;* world) on this occasion is taken to be persons and also dualistic awarenesses...A person imputed in dependence on the aggregates is called "world"...but it is not suitable to take all occurrences of "world" as referring to common beings—it refers to both common beings and Superiors [depending on context]...Still, "world" on this occasion is not just persons because there are many instances of its referring to dualistic consciousness...acting in both erroneous and non-erroneous ways with regard to conventionalities...

The *saṃvṛti* that is the obscuring consciousness with respect to which forms and so forth are posited as truths [in the sense that ignorance takes them to exist the way they appear to be inherently existent] is the first among the three [meanings]. It is the ignorance superimposing on phenomena the existence of their own inherently established entity, whereas they do not have such.[a] This is because:

- true establishment does not occur in objects, and therefore the positing of [objects that appear to be truly existent] as truths is in the perspective of an awareness, and
- there is no positing [of objects that appear to be truly existent] as truths in the perspective of a mind that is not an apprehender of true existence.

In that way moreover, Chandrakīrti's *Supplement to (Nāgārjuna's)*

- In general, *saṃvṛti* is used in many ways, but on this occasion *saṃvṛti* is obscurational (*kun rdzob*), or *samantavṛti* [meaning] concealing all (*kun sgrib*), or concealing reality (*yang dag sgrib*), that is to say, ignorance; "obscurational truths" (*kun rdzob bden pa*) are so called since they are true in the perspective of ignorance...Hence, *saṃvṛti* is used for "concealing reality" (*yang dag sgrib*), "concealing all" (*kun sgrib*), and "concealing the nature" (*rang bzhin sgrib*)...

  Saṃvṛti also means mutual dependence—falsity...[Because they are mutually dependent, that they have a self-instituting nature is untrue.] Hence, the world's mutual dependence is called *saṃvṛti*, and "relative truths" (*kun rdzob bden pa, saṃvṛtisatya*) are so called since they exist just in mutual dependence.

  In addition, *saṃvṛti* means terminology (*brda*), or conventions (*tha snyad*), which include both objects expressed and means of expression, objects known and consciousnesses, and so forth...Because the world's objects expressed and means of expression and the world's objects known and consciousnesses are the world's terminology, or conventions, they are called "conventional" (*saṃvṛti*); "conventional truths" (*kun rdzob bden pa, saṃvṛtisatya*) are so called since their mode of appearance and mode of abiding accord with the world's terminology, or conventions.

[a] Nga-wang-pel-den (Hopkins, *Maps of the Profound*, 904) describes how conventionalities are falsities:

> Ultimate truths necessarily are established in accordance with how they appear to the awarenesses to which they clearly appear. Thus, obscurational truths are necessarily falsities. The meaning of falsity is "deceptive," and the meaning of deceptive is "discordance between the mode of appearance and the mode of abiding." [This conflict] is taken to be that although they appear—to the awarenesses to which they clearly appear—to be truly established, they are without true establishment.

"Treatise on the Middle" (see also *Illumination,* 235) says:[a]

> The Subduer said that because bewilderment [that is, the apprehension of inherent existence] obscures [direct perception of] the nature [of the mode of subsistence of phenomena],
> [This ignorance] is all-obscuring (*kun rdzob*)[b] and he said that those fabrications appearing
> To be true due to this [ignorance] are obscurational truths (*kun rdzob bden*) [because of being true in the perspective of the obscurational apprehension of inherent existence].
> Things that are fabrications [exist] conventionally (*kun rdzob tu*).

Concerning this, Chandrakīrti's *Commentary on the "Supplement to (Nāgārjuna's) 'Treatise on the Middle'"* says (see also *Illumination,* 240):[c]

> In that way, respectively, obscurational truths are posited through the force of the afflictive ignorance that is included within the [twelve] links [of the dependent-arising] of cyclic existence. Moreover, for Hearer [Foe Destroyers], Solitary Realizer [Foe Destroyers], and [eighth ground] Bodhisattvas, who have [entirely] abandoned afflictive ignorance and who see that [although] compositional phenomena [are empty of being established by way of their own character but appear to be established by way of their own character] like the existence of reflections and so forth, these have [only] a fabricated [false] nature and are not truths, because they do not exaggerate [forms

[a] VI.28; Toh. 3861, *dbu ma,* vol. *'a,* 205b.2-205b.3; La Vallée Poussin, *Madhyamakāvatāra,* 107.1-107.4; La Vallée Poussin, "*Introduction au traité du milieu,*" *Muséon* 11 (1910): 303. For Tsong-kha-pa's detailed commentary, see below, 235ff. The Sanskrit, as cited from Prajñākaramati's *Commentary on the Difficult Points of (Shāntideva's) "Engaging in the Bodhisattva Deeds"* in Khangkar and Yorihito, 211 note 245, reads: *mohaḥ svabhāvāvataṇād dhi saṃvṛtiḥ satyaṃ tayā khyāti yad eva kṛtrimam/ jagād tat saṃvṛtisatyam ity asau muniḥ padārthaṃ kṛtakaṃ ca saṃvṛtim//.* Brackets are from *Four Interwoven Annotations,* vol. 2, 356.5. The first three lines cited in *Great Treatise,* vol. 3, 182.

[b] The *Four Interwoven Annotations* (357.1) gives an etymology of *kun rdzob:*

> *Kun* means "*all* of the nature of the mode of subsistence of phenomena" (*chos kyi gnas lugs kyi rang bzhin kun*), and *rdzob* means "obstructing" (*sgrib pa*) and "covering/veiling" (*'gebs pa*).

[c] Commenting on VI.28; Toh. 3862, *dbu ma,* vol. *'a,* 255a.1-255a.3; La Vallée Poussin, *Madhyamakāvatāra,* 107.17-108.6; La Vallée Poussin, "*Introduction au traité du milieu,*" *Muséon* 11 (1910): 304. Brackets are from *Four Interwoven Annotations,* vol. 2, 722.2. Cited in *Great Treatise,* vol. 3, 323, except for the first sentence.

> and so forth] into being truly [established]. To childish [common beings] these are deceptive, but to the others [that is, to the Hearers, Solitary Realizers, and Bodhisattvas described above] they are mere conventionalities[a] due to being dependent-arisings, like a magician's illusions and so forth [appearing to truly exist while not truly existing the way they appear].

This passage does not indicate (1) that the positing of obscurational truths as existent is a positing of their **existence** by ignorance or (2) that obscurational truths are not posited in the perspective of Hearers, Solitary Realizers, and Bodhisattvas who have abandoned afflictive ignorance. The reasons for the first point are:

> because, as explained before, afflictive ignorance is a consciousness apprehending true existence, due to which the object apprehended by it does not exist even in conventional terms, and because whatever is an obscurational truth necessarily exists in conventional terms.

Therefore, whatever is the conventionality (*kun rdzob, saṃvṛti*) that is the ground from which phenomena are posited as existing conventionally[b] (*kun rdzob tu yod pa, saṃvṛtisat*) must be something that is not the afflictive ignorance that is taken as the obscurer (*kun rdzob, saṃvṛti*) [in "obscurational truth" (*kun rdzob bden pa, saṃvṛtisatya*)].

The reason for the second point is:

> Chandrakīrti is establishing that those who have abandoned the obscurer, afflictive ignorance, do not have the obscurer—a consciousness adhering to true existence—in the perspective of which [objects appearing to exist inherently] are posited as truths, and, therefore, compositional phenomena are not truths for them. He is not establishing that compositional phenomena are not obscurational truths.[c]

Consequently, Chandrakīrti's statement that compositional phenomena are mere conventionalities for them means that, between conventionality and truth, those are not positable as truths for them, and therefore the term "mere" [in "mere conventionalities"] eliminates truth,

[a] Or, "mere fraudulences" (*kun rdzob tsam, saṃvṛtimātra*).

[b] *kun rdzob tu yod par 'jog sa'i kun rdzob.*

[c] Even for Hearers, Solitary Realizers, and Bodhisattvas who have abandoned afflictive ignorance and who see compositional phenomena as like the existence of reflections and so forth, compositional phenomena are obscurational truths, since they know that others take them to be truths and since these exist but are not ultimate truths.

not obscurational truth. Hence, Chandrakīrti's thought in speaking of the two—mere conventionality and obscurational truth—should be understood in that way.

Chandrakīrti's *Clear Words* says,[a] "Truths for a worldly obscurer are worldly obscurational truths."[b] With respect to this, Chandrakīrti's *Commentary on the "Supplement to (Nāgārjuna's) 'Treatise on the Middle'"* says:[c]

> Those which are perceived as true by the obscurer and are individually perceived as having inherent existence, whereas they do not, are truths for a worldly **erroneous** obscurer; hence, they are worldly obscurational truths.

Therefore, the statement in Chandrakīrti's *Clear Words* should be taken in accordance with this clear description of truths in the perspective of that obscurer which is the ignorance described earlier, and it should not be taken as true establishment in conventional terms:

- because otherwise it would contradict the system of the non-occurrence of establishment by way of [the object's] own character even in conventional terms,[d] and
- because the refutation of true establishment and the proof of the absence of true existence are done in conventional terms.

Through this way, you should also understand the master Jñānagarbha's explanation of abiding as obscurational truths [not mistaking it for "abiding as truths conventionally"].

Objection: Then, since the noumenon [which actually is the ultimate

---

[a] Commenting on XXIV.8; Toh. 3860, *dbu ma*, vol. *'a*, 163b.2; La Vallée Poussin, *Mūlamadhyamakakārikās (Mādhyamikasūtras) de Nāgārjuna avec la Prasannapadā*, 493.5: *lokasaṃvṛtyā satyaṃ lokasaṃvṛtisatyaṃ /.*

[b] *'jig rten gyi kun rdzob tu bden pa ni/ kun rdzob bden pa ste.* Tsong-kha-pa's concern is that Chandrakīrti's statement might be mistaken to mean that whatever ignorance takes to be truly established is an obscurational truth or that obscurational truths are truly established conventionally. He addresses these mistakes in what follows.

[c] Commenting on VI.28; Toh. 3862, *dbu ma*, vol. *'a*, 254b.5-254b.6; La Vallée Poussin, *Madhyamakāvatāra*, 107.8-107.10; La Vallée Poussin, "*Introduction au traité du milieu*," *Muséon* 11 (1910): 304. In La Vallée Poussin's edition, the final clause, which reads in the sDe dge *'jig rten gyi kun rdzob kyi bden pa ste*, is omitted.

[d] As Chandrakīrti's *Supplement to (Nāgārjuna's) "Treatise on the Middle"* (VI.36) says:

> By that reasoning through which [it is seen] on the occasion of analyzing suchness
> That production from self and other are not reasonable,
> [It is seen] that [production] is not reasonable even in conventional terms.
> If so, by what [reasoning] would your production be [established]?

truth] and the two selves [which do not exist at all] are truths in the perspective of an obscuring consciousness apprehending true existence, they would be obscurational truths.

Answer: If that which is merely true in the perspective of the obscurer—a consciousness apprehending true existence—were posited as an obscurational truth, such would indeed be so, but that is not propounded. This is merely an explanation of the obscurer with respect to which the truths of "obscurational truths" are truths, and the mode of truth in its perspective.[a]

Definition of obscurational truth

Each of these external and internal things has two natures, ultimate and conventional. If this is illustrated with, for instance, a sprout, there is the nature of a sprout found by a rational consciousness perceiving the meaning of suchness, a real object of knowledge, and there is the nature of a sprout found by a conventional consciousness comprehending a deceptive object, a false object of knowledge. The former of those is the nature of the sprout's ultimate truth; the latter is the nature of the sprout's obscurational truth. In that way also Chandrakīrti's *Supplement to (Nāgārjuna's) "Treatise on the Middle"* (see also *Illumination,* 217 and 219) says:[b]

> [Buddha] said that all things have two natures,
> Those found by perceptions of the real and of the false—
> Objects of perceptions of reality are suchnesses,
> [And] objects of perceptions of the false are obscurational truths.

This indicates that with regard to the natures of a sprout there are two—the natures of the two truths—and that the ultimate is found by the former consciousness, whereas the conventional is found by the latter consciousness. It does not indicate that one nature of a sprout itself is the two truths in relation to the former and latter consciousnesses.[c] Chandrakīrti's *Commentary on the "Supplement to (Nāgārjuna's)*

[a] It is not a complete definition of obscurational truth, for which see the next section.

[b] VI.23; Toh. 3861, *dbu ma,* vol. *'a,* 205a.5-205a.6; La Vallée Poussin, *Madhyamakāvatāra,* 102.8-102.11; La Vallée Poussin, "*Introduction au traité du milieu,*" *Muséon* 11 (1910): 299. The Sanskrit, as cited from Prajñākaramati's *Commentary on the Difficult Points of (Shāntideva's) "Engaging in the Bodhisattva Deeds"* in Khangkar and Yorihito, 212 note 251, reads: *samyagmṛṣādarśaṇalabdhabhāvaṃ rūpadvayam bibhrati sarvabhāvāḥ / samyagdṛśāṃ yo viṣayaḥ sa tattvaṃ mṛṣādṛśāṃ saṃvṛtisatyam uktam //.*

[c] This clears away the notion that the two truths are one object viewed two different ways.

'Treatise on the Middle,'" differentiating two natures for each thing, says that the ultimate is found by a consciousness perceiving the meaning of reality and the conventional is found by a consciousness perceiving falsities,[a] "Two types of natures of all things are taught, conventional and ultimate."

Since an obscurational truth is not a truth in fact but is a truth only in the perspective of a consciousness apprehending true existence, it is necessary to ascertain it as a falsity in order to ascertain the very meaning[b] of obscurational truth. In order to ascertain an illustration [of an obscurational truth], such as a pot, as a false object of knowledge, a deceptive object, it is necessary to gain the view that—with respect to that substratum—causes disbelief[c] in the conceived object of the apprehension of true existence through a rational consciousness. For without having refuted trueness through reasoning, falsity cannot be established by valid cognition.

Although pots, woolen cloth, and so forth are obscurational truths, it is not necessary—when they are established by an awareness [as existing]—that the meaning of obscurational truth be established by the awareness.[d] It is like the fact that although pots, woolen cloth, and so forth are illusory-like appearances seeming to be inherently existent whereas they are not, an awareness that establishes them [as existing] does not have to establish the meaning of being illusory-like.

Therefore, it is not feasible to propound that in this system pots, woolen cloth, and so forth are posited as obscurational truths in relation to the perspective of a consciousness of a common being who does not have the Middle Way view and that the same are posited as ultimate truths in relation to a Superior. For that would be propounded opposite to what Chandrakīrti says in his *Commentary on the "Supplement to (Nāgārjuna's) 'Treatise on the Middle'"* (see also *Illumination,* 253):[e]

> Regarding this, those which are ultimates for common beings are mere conventionalities for Superiors acting on objects

[a] Commenting on VI.23; Toh. 3862, *dbu ma,* vol. *'a,* 253a.6; La Vallée Poussin, *Madhyamakāvatāra,* 102.14-102.15; La Vallée Poussin, "*Introduction au traité du milieu,*" *Muséon* 11 (1910): 300. Cited above, 106.

[b] *don ldog;* literally, "meaning-isolate," that is to say, the meaning itself and not its instances and so forth.

[c] *sun phyung ba.*

[d] Tsong-kha-pa's point is that one can know a pot without knowing *with valid cognition* that it is an obscurational truth.

[e] Commenting on VI.28; Toh. 3862, *dbu ma,* vol. *'a,* 255a.5; La Vallée Poussin, *Madhyamakāvatāra,* 108.13-108.16; La Vallée Poussin, "*Introduction au traité du milieu,*" *Muséon* 11 (1910): 305.

> involving appearance [outside of meditative equipoise directly realizing emptiness]. That which is the nature of those [objects]—emptiness—is the ultimate for them.

Common beings apprehend pots and so forth to be true, and just that is also an apprehension [of pots and so forth] as existing ultimately. Hence, in relation to the perspective of these consciousnesses of those [common beings], pots and so forth are ultimately established and are not conventional objects. Pots and so forth—the bases that for them are ultimately established—are conventionalities in relation to the perception by the pristine wisdom in the continuum of a Superior comprehending illusory-like appearance. In relation to this consciousness, these cannot be posited as true, whereby they are mere conventionalities. This is what Chandrakīrti is saying.

Nevertheless, since he says that their nature is the ultimate truth, a differentiation should be made, saying, "Pots and so forth are conventionalities, and their nature is the ultimate of Superiors." However, it should not be propounded that pots and so forth are ultimates for Superiors:

- because their rational consciousnesses seeing the meaning of reality do not find pots and so forth, and
- because that which is found by a rational consciousness seeing the meaning of reality is said to be the meaning of an ultimate truth.

Divisions of conventionalities

The Middle Way Autonomists assert that since a consciousness appearing to be established by way of its own character is ascertained to exist the way it appears, a differentiation of real and unreal is not made with respect to subjects [that is, consciousnesses]. Rather, appearances of objects are differentiated by whether they exist or not by way of their own character in accordance with how they appear. It is as Jñānagarbha's *Differentiation of the Two Truths* says:[a]

> Though similar in appearing, there are those
> Able and not able to perform functions as they appear,
> Whereby a division of real and unreal
> Conventionalities is made.

[a] *bden pa gnyis rnam par 'byed, satyadvayavibhaṅga,* stanza 12; Toh. 3881, *dbu ma,* vol. *sa,* 2a.4-2a.5; Tibetan text edited by Malcolm David Eckel, *Jñānagarbha's Commentary on the Distinction between the Two Truths: An Eighth Century Handbook of Madhyamaka Philosophy* (Albany, NY: State University of New York Press, 1987), 163; Eckel's translation is on p. 54.

[However] this [Consequentialist] system asserts that all appearances as being established by way of their own character to those who possess ignorance are appearances belonging to a consciousness polluted by ignorance. Therefore, they do not divide conventional objects into the two—real and unreal.

With respect to this, Chandrakīrti's *Commentary on the "Supplement to (Nāgārjuna's) 'Treatise on the Middle'"* says,[a] "That which is false even conventionally is not an obscurational truth." [This means that] since an image of a face, for instance, is not true as a face for a worldly conventional [consciousness] of one versed in language, it is not an obscurational truth in relation to it. Nonetheless, because it is an object found by a [consciousness] perceiving a false object of knowledge—a deceptive object—it is an obscurational truth. Just as a consciousness to which a reflection appears is mistaken with respect to its appearing object [in that the reflection appears to be a face], so among those who possess ignorance [their consciousnesses to which] blue and so forth appear as established by way of their own character also are similarly mistaken with respect to their appearing object.

When a true object of comprehension is posited, it would be contradictory for [a consciousness] mistaken in that way to posit it; however, this itself acts as an aid in positing a false object of comprehension. Otherwise, whatever in conventional terms is not truly established could not be posited as an obscurational truth, and therefore when falsities such as illusory-like [appearances] are posited in conventional terms, they could not be posited as obscurational truths.[b]

The Consequentialist system:

- posits the six consciousnesses[c] not affected by superficial causes of mistake and the six objects[d] apprehended by those consciousnesses as real conventionalities, and
- posits the six consciousnesses affected by superficial causes of mistake[e] and the six objects apprehended by those consciousnesses as

[a] Commenting on VI.28; Toh. 3862, *dbu ma*, vol. *'a*, 254b.7-255a.1; La Vallée Poussin, *Madhyamakāvatāra*, 107.16-107.17; La Vallée Poussin, "*Introduction au traité du milieu,*" *Muséon* 11 (1910): 304.

[b] That is, whatever is not truly established for a conventional valid cognition could not be posited as an obscurational truth, and therefore when falsities such as illusory-like appearances are posited in the perspective of conventional valid cognition, they could not be posited as obscurational truths and hence would not exist, since they are not ultimate truths either and objects of knowledge are exhausted as the two truths.

[c] Eye, ear, nose, tongue, body, and mental consciousnesses.

[d] Visible forms, sounds, odors, tastes, tangible objects, and phenomena.

[e] Lo-sang-dor-jay's *Decisive Analysis* describes these superficial causes of mistake

unreal conventionalities, but

- posits real and unreal conventionalities in relation to **just** worldly or conventional valid cognitions, not in relation to a rational consciousness following a Superior's perception.[a]

Therefore, since in the Middle Way's own system[b] the two

(adapted from Elizabeth Napper's unpublished translation, 96-97):

> Superficial causes of mistake are twofold: those harming the physical sense powers and those harming the mental sense power. Those harming the physical sense powers are two types: those in which the cause of error is internal and those in which it is external. The first are, for example, opthomalia, jaundice, and eating *dadhura* [a poison]. External causes of mistake are mirrors; a sound in an empty cave; in the summer the contact of sunlight with pale yellow sand; medicines and spells used by a magician; and so forth.
>
> The way these generate mistaken consciousnesses is as follows. Opthomalia acts as the cause of a mistaken sense consciousness seeing falling hairs; jaundice acts as the cause of a mistaken sense consciousness seeing a white conch shell as yellow; eating *dadhura* acts as the cause of a mistaken sense consciousness to which the ground appears gold; the coming together of a mirror and a face acts as the cause of a mistaken sense consciousness to which the reflection of a face within the mirror appears to be a face; a sound in an empty cave acts as the cause of a mistaken sense consciousness to which an echo appears to be an expressive sound; the contact of summer sunlight and the pale yellow sand acts as the cause of a mistaken sense consciousness to which a mirage appears to be water; and the medicines and mantras used by a magician act as causes of a mistaken sense consciousness to which pebbles and twigs appear to be horses and elephants.
>
> The second, causes of mistake harming the mental sense power, are wrong tenets, counterfeit reasons, sleep, and so forth. As to how they generate error, wrong tenets and counterfeit reasons act as the cause of mistaken mental consciousnesses apprehending the general principal (*spyi'i gtso bo, sāmānya-pradhāna*) [of the Sāṃkhya system] and so forth to be existent; sleep acts as the cause of a mistaken mental consciousness apprehending the appearance of an elephant in a dream as an elephant.

[a] *'phags pa'i gzigs pa'i rjes su 'brang ba'i rigs shes.* For expansion on this, see the objection and answer in *Illumination,* 229.

[b] Jam-yang-shay-pa's *Great Exposition of Tenets* (Hopkins, *Maps of the Profound,* 908-909) says:

> [The phrase] "In the Middle Way's own system" is to be taken as "in the perspective of the Middle Way rational consciousness of the unique Middle Way system." In its perspective it is not suitable to make a division of obscurational truths into the real whose mode of appearance and mode of subsistence agree and the unreal whose mode of appearance and mode of subsistence do not agree because not only Superiors' meditative equipoise but also their pristine wisdom subsequent to meditative equipoise perceive forms and so forth as like illusions and do not perceive their mode of appearance and mode of subsistence as in agreement...Therefore, obscurational truths are

appearances—of (1) reflections, and so forth, and (2) blue, and so forth—to those who possess ignorance do not differ with respect to whether [consciousnesses of them] are mistaken or not in relation to their appearing object, they do not make a division into the two—real and unreal conventionalities. Chandrakīrti's *Supplement to (Nāgārjuna's) "Treatise on the Middle"* says (see also *Illumination*, 227):[a]

> Objects realized by the world that are apprehended
> By [the consciousnesses of] the six sense powers unimpaired [by superficial causes of mistake]
> Are true [or real] just [relative] to the world [because of being phenomena that prior to realizing emptiness cannot be realized to be a combination of appearing to be inherently existent but being empty of such].
> The rest [that is, those apprehended by sense consciousnesses

---

divided into the two—real and unreal—relative to the perspective of coarse, innate, worldly consciousnesses because:

- the six senses free from superficial damage and the six objects apprehended by them are posited as real in the perspective of innate coarse consciousnesses and
- the six senses having superficial damage and the six objects apprehended by them are posited as unreal in the perspective of worldly consciousnesses...

Proponents of the Middle themselves also assert such real and unreal [conventionalities relative to worldly valid cognition], but they conventionally do not assert the former type of real [conventionalities relative to a rational consciousness] in their own system...Therefore:

- The worldly perspective in "existing conventionally," the worldly perspective in "existing in the world's conventions," the convention in "conventional truth," and the noble [or superior] in "noble truth" are conventional valid cognitions.
- The worldly perspective in [Chandrakīrti's statement about real conventionalities] "They are true in just the world," is an innate ordinary [consciousness].
- The obscurational [consciousness] (*kun rdzob, saṃvṛti*) in the perspective of which forms and so forth are posited as true must be ignorance.

For a thorough discussion of this topic see Guy Newland, *The Two Truths* (Ithaca, N.Y.: Snow Lion Publications, 1992), 136-157. For Nga-wang-pel-den's refinements of these points (*Annotations, dbu, ka,* 190.8ff) see Hopkins, *Maps of the Profound*, 909-911.

[a] Stanza VI.25; Toh. 3861, *dbu ma*, vol. *'a*, 205a.7; La Vallée Poussin, *Madhyamakāvatāra*, 104.4-104.7; La Vallée Poussin, "*Introduction au traité du milieu*," *Muséon* 11 (1910): 301. The Sanskrit, as cited from Prajñākaramati's *Commentary on the Difficult Points of (Shāntideva's) "Engaging in the Bodhisattva Deeds"* in Khangkar and Yorihito, 211 note 245, reads: *vinopaghātena yad indriyāṇāṃ saṇṇām api grāhyam avaiti lokaḥ/ satyaṃ hi tal loyata evaṃ śeṣaṃ vikalpitaṃ lokata eva mithyā//*. Brackets are from *Four Interwoven Annotations*, vol. 2, 314.5. Cited in *Great Treatise*, vol. 3, 167.

impaired by superficial causes of mistake such as reflections, echoes and so forth] are posited as unreal just [relative] to the world.

With respect to the apprehension of persons and phenomena as being established by way of their own character, there are two types [innate and artificial]. The opposite of an [artificial] mode of apprehension arising, for instance, from the mind's being superficially affected by one's own bad system of tenets is not established by a conventional valid cognition.[a] Hence, it is an exception.[b]

Furthermore, although a pristine wisdom knowing the diversity, which has separated from all causes of pollution due to the predispositions of ignorance, has dualistic appearance, it is not mistaken with respect to its appearing objects. I have explained the reasons elsewhere.

[a] The emptiness that is the opposite of the mode of apprehension that objects are established by way of their own character—whether the apprehension is innate or artificial—cannot be established by conventional valid cognition; it must be established by ultimate valid cognition.

[b] Lo-sang-dor-jay's *Decisive Analysis* offers definitions in terms of subjects—that is, consciousnesses—and objects (adapted from Elizabeth Napper's unpublished translation, 97):

> The definition of something's being a conventionality that is a real (or correct) subject in relation to a worldly consciousness is:
>
> > (1) It is a consciousness, and (2) a conventional valid cognition in the continuum of a person who has not experienced realization of emptiness cannot realize it as a mistaken consciousness.
>
> The definition of a something's being a conventionality that is an unreal (or wrong) subject in relation to a worldly consciousness is:
>
> > (1) It is a consciousness, and (2) [a conventional valid cognition in the continuum of a person who has not experienced realization of emptiness] can realize that it is a wrong consciousness.
>
> The definition of something's being a conventionality that is a real object in relation to a worldly consciousness is:
>
> > (1) It is a conventionality that is an object, and (2) a conventional valid cognition in the continuum of a person who has not experienced realization of emptiness cannot realize that it is not established as it appears.
>
> The definition of something's being a conventionality that is an unreal object in relation to a worldly consciousness is:
>
> > (1) It is a conventionality that is an object, and (2) a conventional valid cognition in the continuum of a person who has not experienced realization of emptiness can realize that it is not established as it appears.
>
> Conventional truths are not divided into the two, real conventionalities and unreal conventionalities, because real conventionalities do not exist.

9. Ultimate Truths

Ultimate truths

This section has three parts: explaining the meaning of *paramārtha* and *satya*, explaining the definition of ultimate truth, and explaining the divisions of ultimate truths.

Explaining the meaning of paramārtha (don dam) and satya (bden pa)

Chandrakīrti's *Clear Words* says:[a]

> Because it both is an object[b] and also is ultimate,[c] it is the ultimate object.[d] Because just it is a truth,[e] it is the ultimate-object truth.[f]

Hence, he asserts both object and ultimate as [applying to emptiness,] the ultimate-object truth [that is, truth which is the ultimate object].[g]

The mode of truth of an ultimate truth is non-deceptiveness. Moreover, it does not deceive the world through its mode of subsistence abiding one way and its appearing another way.[h] Hence, Chandrakīrti's

---

[a] Commenting on stanza XXIV.8; Toh. 3860, *dbu ma*, vol. *'a*, 163b.5-163b.6; La Vallée Poussin, *Mūlamadhyamakakārikās (Mādhyamikasūtras) de Nāgārjuna avec la Prasannapadā*, 494.1: *paramaścāsāvarthaśceti paramārthaḥ / tadeva satyaṃ paramārthasatyaṃ /.*

[b] *don, artha.*

[c] *dam pa, parama.*

[d] *don dam pa, paramārtha.*

[e] *bden pa, satya.*

[f] *don dam bden pa, paramārthasatya.*

[g] Jam-yang-shay-pa's *Great Exposition of Tenets* (Hopkins, *Maps of the Profound*, 903-904) says:

> In the Sanskrit original of *don dam bden pa* (ultimate truth), *paramārthasatya:*
> - *parama* is used for ultimate, supreme, and so forth
> - *artha* is used for object
> - *satya* is used for truth, permanence, and so forth.
>
> On this occasion:
> 1. "object" (*don, artha*) does not mean purpose but means the object known, analyzed, and found by pristine wisdom.
> 2. Because of being both such an object and the supreme, or ultimate, of objects, it is ultimate.
> 3. It is called "truth" since it does not deceive trainees [by] not abiding the way it appears or since the mode of appearance and the mode of abiding are concordant—not being discordant like false conventionalities.

[h] Nga-wang-pel-den's *Annotations for (Jam-yang-shay-pa's) "Great Exposition of Tenets"*

Commentary on (Nāgārjuna's) "Sixty Stanzas of Reasoning" says that an ultimate truth is merely posited as existing through the force of worldly conventions.[a] Therefore, the meanings of the term "truth" differ in the two:

- in "obscurational truth," "truth" [means] "truth for a consciousness apprehending true existence," and
- in "ultimate truth," ["truth" means non-deceptive].

Explaining the definition of ultimate truth

This section has two parts: actual definition of ultimate truth and dispelling objections.

Actual definition of ultimate truth

The definition of ultimate truth is that given in Chandrakīrti's *Supplement*[b] (see also *Illumination,* 217 and 219) as explained earlier (114)[c]—that which is found by a perception of a real object of knowledge. Chandrakīrti's commentary on that says:[d]

> Concerning that, with respect to the ultimate its own entity[e] is found through being the object of the specific pristine wisdom

(Hopkins, *Maps of the Profound,* 904) expands on Tsong-kha-pa's meaning:

> Ultimate truths necessarily are established in accordance with how they appear to the awarenesses to which they clearly appear. Thus, obscurational truths are necessarily falsities. The meaning of falsity is "deceptive," and the meaning of deceptive is "discordance between the mode of appearance and the mode of abiding." [This conflict] is taken to be that although they appear—to the awarenesses to which they clearly appear—to be truly established, they are without true establishment.

[a] In his *Commentary on (Nāgārjuna's) "Sixty Stanzas of Reasoning,"* commenting on stanza 5cd; Toh. 3864, *dbu ma,* vol. *ya,* 7b.6; Scherrer-Schaub, *Yuktiṣaṣṭikāvṛtti,* 36.

[b] VI.23.

[c] The complete stanza is:

> [Buddha] said that all things have two natures,
> Those found by perceptions of the real and of the false—
> That objects of perceptions of reality are suchnesses,
> [And] that objects of perceptions of the false are obscurational truths.

VI.23; Toh. 3861, *dbu ma,* vol. *'a,* 205a.5-205a.6; La Vallée Poussin, *Madhyamakāvatāra,* 102.8-102.11; La Vallée Poussin, "*Introduction au traité du milieu,*" *Muséon* 11 (1910): 299.

[d] Commenting on VI.23; Toh. 3862, *dbu ma,* vol. *'a,* 253a.6-253a.7; La Vallée Poussin, *Madhyamakāvatāra,* 102.16-102.18; La Vallée Poussin, "*Introduction au traité du milieu,*" *Muséon* 11 (1910): 300.

[e] *rang gi ngo bo.*

> of those perceiving the real. It is not established by way of its own selfhood. This is one nature [of an object, the other being its conventional nature].

His saying that it is found by the uncontaminated pristine wisdom comprehending suchness and that it is not established by way of its own nature refutes the proposition that if there is anything found by uncontaminated meditative equipoise, it is truly established. His speaking of a "**specific** pristine wisdom" indicates that what is found by any pristine wisdom of Superiors is not sufficient, but rather what is found by a specific pristine wisdom—the pristine wisdom knowing the mode [of being]—is an ultimate truth. "Found" means "established thus by that consciousness"; it is the same also for conventionalities.[a]

Furthermore, with respect to its way of finding:

- When the eyes of one with cataracts[b] see falling hairs—the

---

[a] About the definition of ultimate truth, Jam-yang-shay-pa's *Great Exposition of Tenets* (Hopkins, *Maps of the Profound,* 902-903) says:

> An object explicitly found by an awareness, that is, a rational consciousness distinguishing the ultimate—[called] a rational consciousness since it is a logical consciousness—is feasible as [the definition of] an ultimate truth...This is a general [definition]; it covers all those for whom meditative equipoise and the state subsequent to meditative equipoise have not become one, that is, those at the end of the continuum [of being a sentient being with obstructions yet to overcome] and below.
>
> The convention of "finding" does not apply in cases when the aspect of an object does not appear to that awareness; hence, that which is implicitly realized is not suitable to be an object found...Since it is explained that the qualities of a Buddha's exalted body, speech, and mind are inconceivable, the idea that whatever is an object found by an omniscient consciousness distinguishing a conventionality necessarily is an object found by a rational consciousness distinguishing a conventionality is a fool's over-extension [of the above, limited definition to include the mode of perception of a Buddha]...
>
> Hence, if you wish to include even the separate positing of the two truths by one pristine wisdom [of a Buddha] in which meditative equipoise and the state subsequent to meditative equipoise have become one, then [the definitions] should be put together this way:
>
> - ultimate truth: object found with respect to which [an awareness] comes to be a rational consciousness distinguishing the ultimate
> - obscurational truth: object found with respect to which [an awareness] comes to be a rational consciousness distinguishing a conventionality.

[b] *rab rib, timira;* the term means "dimness" and thus "dim sightedness," the technical name in English perhaps being "amblyopia." Since Tsong-kha-pa uses the example of floating hairs, the Tibetan and Sanskrit general terms include a disease resulting in the perception of floaters as if they are external to the eye. It seems also to include glaucoma, as in Dol-po-pa's citation of the *Great Drum Sūtra* where it speaks of "eyes dark-

appearance of intermediate space serving as the base—the eyes of one without cataracts do not see even an appearance of falling hairs with respect to that base.

- In the same way, those damaged by the cataracts of ignorance apprehend the own-entities[a] of the aggregates and so forth; [however,] in terms of the mode of perception of suchness by [Buddhas], who have removed all predispositions of ignorance, and by a Learner Superior's pristine wisdom of uncontaminated meditative equipoise, not even subtle dualistic appearance is perceived, like the eyes of one without cataracts.
- The nature perceived in this manner is the ultimate truth.

Chandrakīrti's *Supplement to (Nāgārjuna's) "Treatise on the Middle"* (see also *Illumination,* 256) says:[b]

> Where just those wrong entities such as falling hairs and so forth
> Are imputed through the force of cataracts,
> What is seen by one with clear eyes is the suchness [of those falling hairs].
> Understand it similarly here.

Also, Chandrakīrti's commentary on that says:[c]

> The nature of the aggregates and so forth perceived by the Supramundane Buddhas, separated from the predispositions of ignorance, in the manner of those without cataracts seeing falling hairs,[d] is the ultimate truth of those [Buddhas].[e]

The ultimate perceived in that way is the ultimate nature from among the two natures of each phenomenon. Furthermore, it is the two—the

ened by yellow and blue eye film" (Hopkins, *Mountain Doctrine,* 150).

[a] *rang gi ngo bo.*

[b] VI.29; Toh. 3861, *dbu ma,* vol. *'a,* 205b.3; La Vallée Poussin, *Madhyamakāvatāra,* 109.6-109.9; La Vallée Poussin, "*Introduction au traité du milieu,*" *Muséon* 11 (1910): 305. The Sanskrit, as cited from Prajñākaramati's *Commentary on the Difficult Points of (Shāntideva's) "Engaging in the Bodhisattva Deeds"* in Khangkar and Yorihito, 215 note 272, reads: *vikalpitaṃ yat timiraprabhāvāt keśādirūpaṃ vitathaṃ tad eva / yenātmanā paśyati śuddhadṛṣṭis tattvam itya evam ihāpy avehi //.*

[c] Commenting on VI.29; Toh. 3862, *dbu ma,* vol. *'a,* 255b.5-255b.6; La Vallée Poussin, *Madhyamakāvatāra,* 110.8-110.11; La Vallée Poussin, "*Introduction au traité du milieu,*" *Muséon* 11 (1910): 306.

[d] Those without cataracts see falling hairs in the manner of not seeing falling hairs.

[e] Tsong-kha-pa's *Illumination of the Thought* identifies "of those" as "of those Buddhas"; see 257.

naturally pure nirvāṇa, which is the emptiness of inherent existence of substrata, and the nirvāṇa that is a true cessation, this being just that [natural emptiness of the mind] separated from any of the seeds of the defilements.

Hence, the meaning of Chandrakīrti's *Commentary on (Nāgārjuna's) "Sixty Stanzas of Reasoning"* where it says,[a] "Is a nirvāṇa also an obscurational truth? It is so," and, "Therefore, a nirvāṇa is only imputed as an obscurational truth," is that with regard to positing a nirvāṇa, an ultimate truth, as **existing**, it is posited as merely existent in the perspective of a conventional consciousness, an obscurational truth. This system does not assert that a nirvāṇa is an obscurational truth:

- because even that very commentary explains that the three truths [true sufferings, sources, and paths] are obscurational truths and a nirvāṇa is an ultimate truth and Chandrakīrti's *Commentary on the "Supplement to (Nāgārjuna's) 'Treatise on the Middle'"* also speaks of the other three truths as obscurational truths and true cessations as ultimate truths,[b] and
- because in answer to the objection that if a nirvāṇa is posited as existing conventionally, this would contradict the statement that it is an ultimate truth, he says,[c] "It is said to be an ultimate truth just by way of worldly conventions."

Therefore, all that are posited as existing are posited through the force of worldly conventions. The *One Hundred Thousand Stanza Perfection of Wisdom Sūtra* says,[d] "All these phenomena are imputed in dependence on worldly conventions, not ultimately." Also, Nāgārjuna's *Seventy Stanzas on Emptiness* says:[e]

> Through the force of worldly expressions
> Buddha spoke of abiding, production, or disintegration,

[a] Commenting on stanza 5cd; Toh. 3864, *dbu ma,* vol. *ya,* 7b.3, 7b.5; Scherrer-Schaub, *Yuktiṣaṣṭikāvṛtti,* 35 and 36.

[b] In his commentary on stanza V.1cd; Toh. 3862, *dbu ma,* vol. *'a,* 243b.1; La Vallée Poussin, *Madhyamakāvatāra,* 71.3-71.5: *de la sdug bsngal dang kun 'byung dang lam gyi bden pa ni kun rdzob kyi bden pa'i khongs su gtogs so/ /'gog pa'i bden pa ni don dam pa'i bden pa'i rang gi ngo bo'o/;* La Vallée Poussin, "*Introduction au traité du milieu,*" *Muséon* 8 (1907): 313.

[c] In his *Commentary on (Nāgārjuna's) "Sixty Stanzas of Reasoning,"* commenting on stanza 5cd; Toh. 3864, *dbu ma,* vol. *ya,* 7b.6; Scherrer-Schaub, *Yuktiṣaṣṭikāvṛtti,* 36.

[d] *shes rab kyi pha rol tu phyin pa stong phrag brgya pa'i mdo, śatasahāsrikāprajñāpāramitā,* Toh. 8, vols. *ka-'a (sher phyin).*

[e] Stanza 1; Toh. 3827, *dbu ma,* vol. *tsa,* 24a.6-24a.7; Lindtner, *Master of Wisdom,* 94; Komito, *Seventy Stanzas,* 97. Brackets are from *Four Interwoven Annotations,* vol. 2, 451.3. Cited in *Great Treatise,* vol. 3, 217.

Existence or non-existence, low, equal, or special—
Not through the force of [those being] real [that is, truly established].

He says that:

- all the various presentations of the three (production, disintegration, and abiding) and of the three (low, medium, and supreme) as well as, "This exists, that does not exist" are only posited by the Conqueror through the force of worldly conventions
- they are not posited through the force of a real status that is not just posited through the force of conventions.

Moreover, with respect to the master Jñānagarbha's statement [in his *Commentary on the "Differentiation of the Two Truths"*],[a] "Because of being a truth ultimately, it is an ultimate truth," since he also describes a rational consciousness as the ultimate, he is saying that what is non-deceptive in its perspective is a truth.[b] His thought is not that [an ultimate truth] is **truly established** in the sense of being able to withstand analysis because in his text the true establishment of all phenomena is refuted. Therefore:

- we accept the proposition that "If an ultimate is not true ultimately [that is, in the perspective of a rational consciousness called the ultimate], then a conventionality is not a truth conventionally [that is, in the perspective of a conventional valid cognition],"[c]
- but to propound [as Dol-po-pa does] that "If the ultimate is not ultimately established, then a conventionality is not conventionally established," is to [absurdly] say that if the negation of truth [that is, the absence of true establishment] is not truly established, then [the conventionalities that are] the substrata of the negation [would not be conventionally established and thus] would be truly

---

[a] See Jñānagarbha's *Commentary on the "Differentiation of the Two Truths"* (*bden pa gnyis rnam par 'byed pa'i 'grel pa, satyadvayavibhaṅgavṛtti*); Toh. 3882, *dbu ma*, vol. *sa*, 4a.4; Eckel, *Jñānagarbha's Commentary*, 156 (Tibetan) and 71 (English).

[b] Nga-wang-pel-den's *Explanation of the Obscurational and the Ultimate in the Four Systems* (173.1) reframes this (he refers to the *Medium-Length Exposition* as the "*Small Exposition*," as it is often called):

> Tsong-kha-pa's *Small Exposition of the Stages of the Path* says that the explanation in Jñānagarbha's *Autocommentary on the "Two Truths"* that "Because of being true ultimately, it is an ultimate truth," refers to being undeceiving in the perspective of the ultimate in the context of the description of a rational consciousness as the ultimate.

[c] *don dam don dam du mi bden na kun rdzob kun rdzob tu mi bden no:* 468.6.

established.

This is because an ultimate truth is posited as just the negation of truth [that is, the absence of true establishment] in the substratum of negation and because the implication of substrata not being conventionally established is that they are not falsely established [and hence are truly established].[a] Thus, [to propound such] would be even extremely senseless because the bases of negation [of true establishment] must be established as false due to the very fact that the substrata—appearances—do not exist as truly established, that is to say, are not truly established.[b]

Therefore, although to posit something as existing in conventional terms it is not necessary that it be established by a rational consciousness of suchness, it is necessary that there be no damage by any valid cognition, conventional or rational. Chandrakīrti's *Commentary on (Nāgārjuna's) "Sixty Stanzas of Reasoning"*[c] explains that since the appropriated aggregates conventionally abide as the four—impermanent and so forth[d]—the apprehension of those four is non-erroneous in relation to that [conventional consciousness], and since the aggregates do not abide even conventionally as the four—permanent and so forth[e]—the apprehension of those four is erroneous in relation to that [conventional consciousness]. Also, Chandrakīrti's *Supplement to (Nāgārjuna's) "Treatise on the Middle"* (see also *Illumination*, 230) says:[f]

Entities [such as a permanent self, principal, and so forth] as

---

[a] *chos can rnams kun rdzob tu ma grub par 'phen pa ni rdzun par ma grub par 'phen pa:* 469.2

[b] *chos can snang ba rnams bden grub tu med pa bden par ma grub pa nyid kyis dgag gzhi rnams brdzun par 'grub dgos pa'i phyir ro.* I take *bden par ma grub pa* as glossing and emphasizing *bden grub tu med pa.* Otherwise, the clause would mean "because the bases of negation must be established as false due to the very fact that the absence of true existence of the substrata—appearances—is not truly established"; in that case the point would be that only by the fact that ultimate truths are not truly existent—that is, falsely established—can it be said that all bases of negation are falsely established.

[c] Commenting on stanza 5cd; Toh. 3864, *dbu ma,* vol. *ya,* 7b.1; Scherrer-Schaub, *Yuktiṣaṣṭikāvṛtti,* 35.

[d] The aggregates are impermanent, miserable, unclean, and non-self. For Chandrakīrti's lengthy exposition of these four and their opposite misconceptions in his *Commentary on (Āryadeva's) "Four Hundred,"* see Karen Lang, *Four Illusions: Candrakīrti's Advice to Travelers on the Bodhisattva Path* (New York: Oxford University Press, 2003).

[e] The aggregates are misconceived to be permanent, pleasurable, clean, and self.

[f] Stanza VI.26; Toh. 3861, *dbu ma,* vol. *'a,* 205b.1; La Vallée Poussin, *Madhyamakāvatāra,* 105.9-105.12; La Vallée Poussin, "*Introduction au traité du milieu,*" *Muséon* 11 (1910): 302. Brackets are from *Four Interwoven Annotations,* vol. 2, 343.1. Cited in *Great Treatise,* vol. 3, 178.

they are imputed by [the assertions of] Forders [driven by bad tenets and quasi-reasons],
Strongly affected by the sleep of ignorance,
And [those horses and elephants, water, and so forth] imputed to magical illusions, mirages, and so forth
Are just non-existent even in [the conventions of] the world.

Since he says that the self, principal,[a] and so forth imputed by [non-Buddhist] Forders as well as the objects apprehended as the horses, elephants, and so forth in magical illusions do not exist even in conventional terms, the proposition that it is the Consequentialist system that what merely exist for a mistaken mind are posited as existing conventionally is pithless talk. Not even any other great Proponent of the Middle Way[b] asserts such.

In Chandrakīrti's *Supplement to (Nāgārjuna's) "Treatise on the Middle"* object and subject are taken to be similarly existent or non-existent; this is done in reference not to mere existence or non-existence in general but to object and subject that are not inherently existent and are inherently existent.[c]

Therefore, although what are posited as existent in conventional terms are posited as existing through the force of nominal conventions, all that are posited through the force of nominal conventions are not asserted as existing in conventional terms.[d] [Phenomena] are asserted as only posited through the force of conventions, but the term "only" eliminates anything that is not a subjective convention; it does not at

---

[a] *gtso bo, pradhāna.* This is the three qualities (*yon tan gsum, triguṇa*) in equilibrium as asserted in the Sāṃkhya system, also called the nature (*rang bzhin, prakṛti*); it is the source of all material manifestations.

[b] *dbu ma pa chen po.*

[c] Nāgārjuna's *Essay on the Mind of Enlightenment* says:

> A consciousness realizes an object of knowledge.
> Without an object of knowledge consciousness does not exist.

Chandrakīrti's *Clear Words* (La Vallée Poussin, *Madhyamakāvatāra,* 75.10; Napper, *Dependent-Arising and Emptiness,* 109) says:

> Those are established through mutual dependence. When valid cognitions exist, then there are objects that are objects of comprehension; when objects that are objects of comprehension exist, then there are valid cognitions. However, the two, valid cognitions and objects of comprehension, are not established by way of [their own] entities.

I have not located where such a statement is made in Chandrakīrti's *Supplement to (Nāgārjuna's) "Treatise on the Middle."*

[d] In his 1972 lectures, the Dalai Lama commented, "Otherwise, the horns of a rabbit would exist."

all eliminate that the object posited is established by valid cognition. It is as follows. This system does not act in accordance with [those systems that]:

- posit something as existing if, not satisfied with positing it through the force of the imputation of conventions, it is found upon investigating how the object imputed—which is not just posited through the force of imputation—exists in factuality
- but posit something as not existing if not found.

Rather:

- This system asserts that if something were found upon searching by way of this mode of searching, it would be truly established.
- Therefore, it does not accept even in conventional terms that anything is found as existing upon such analysis.
- It puts right there the boundary of analyzing and not analyzing with respect to suchness.
- Hence, it sees that if establishment by way of its own character existed, objects that are not just posited by the force of subjective conventions would have to exist by way of their own nature.
- Thereupon, even in conventional terms it does not assert inherent existence, existence by way of its [the object's] own character, or existence by way of its own nature.

I have explained this at length elsewhere.[a]

Dispelling objections

Objection: If the ultimate truth is found by a Buddha's pristine wisdom knowing the mode [of being of phenomena], then how does this not contradict:

1. Chandrakīrti's description of not seeing anything as seeing suchness in his *Commentary on the "Supplement to (Nāgārjuna's) 'Treatise on the Middle'"* which (see also *Illumination,* 259) says:[b]

> *Question:* Is such a nature not unseen? Therefore, how could they see it?
> *Answer:* That indeed is true, but it is expressed that they

[a] See his *Great Treatise* (vol. 3, 139ff., 169ff., 177ff., and so forth) and *The Essence of Eloquence* at the beginning of the section on the Consequence School.

[b] Commenting on VI.29; Toh. 3862, *dbu ma,* vol. *'a,* 255b.6-255b.7; La Vallée Poussin, *Madhyamakāvatāra,* 110.12-110.14; La Vallée Poussin, "*Introduction au traité du milieu,*" *Muséon* 11 (1910): 306.

see it in the manner of non-seeing.

and his quoting as a source an explanation [in the *Introduction to the Two Truths Sūtra*][a] (see also *Illumination*, 262) that the ultimate truth is beyond even the objects of omniscient wisdom;

2. his explanation[b] (below, 134) that on the Buddha ground the movement of mind and mental factors has utterly stopped;
3. and his explanation at the point of discussing the ten powers[c] that when Buddhas do not see the aggregates and so forth, they know all phenomena?

Answer: "They see it in the manner of non-seeing" does not refer to not seeing any and all objects but indicates that if these that are observed through the power of the cataracts of ignorance existed as [their own] suchness, they would have to be observed by the pristine wisdom of uncontaminated meditative equipoise of Superiors, whereas they are not, and thus their seeing suchness is by way of not seeing any of those. For due to not observing the object of negation—despite the fact that if it did exist, it would be suitable to be observed—it is posited that the negative of the object of negation is realized [and hence emptiness is seen and it is not that nothing at all is seen]. The meaning of "Non-seeing is the excellent seeing" (see also *Illumination*, 259) is to be understood similarly.

Moreover, in that way the *Verse Summary of the Perfection of Wisdom* (see also *Illumination*, 260) says:[d]

[a] *bden pa gnyis la 'jug pa / bden pa po'i le'u, satyakaparivarta;* P813, vol. 32.

[b] *Commentary on the "Supplement to (Nāgārjuna's) 'Treatise on the Middle,'"* commenting on stanza XII.5; Toh. 3862, *dbu ma*, vol. *'a*, 331a.6-331a.7; La Vallée Poussin, *Madhyamakāvatāra*, 359.20-360.4: *sprul pa dag las 'byung ba 'ba' zhig tu ma zad kyi gzhan yang de'i mthus* ***sems dang sems las byung ba 'jug pa med du zin kyang*** */ nam mkha' dang gzhan rtsa dang shing dang rtsig pa dang brag la sogs pa las de'i mthus sgra gang zhig byung ba las kyang 'jig rten gyi de nyid rig pa yin no/.*

[c] *Commentary on the "Supplement to (Nāgārjuna's) 'Treatise on the Middle,'"* following stanza XII.22; Toh. 3862, *dbu ma*, vol. *'a*, 334a.6ff; La Vallée Poussin, *Madhyamakāvatāra*, 369.17.

[d] *sañcayagāthāprajñāpāramitā, shes rab kyi pha rol tu phyin pa sdud pa,* stanzas XII.9-10; Toh. 13, vol. *ka* (*shes rab sna tshogs*); Sanskrit and Tibetan texts edited by Akira Yuyama, *Prajñā-pāramitā-ratna-guṇa-saṃcaya-gāthā (Sanskrit Recension A): Edited with an Introduction, Bibliographical Notes and a Tibetan Version from Tunhuang* (London: Cambridge University Press, 1976), 52 and 171: *rūpasy' adarśanu adarśanu vedanāye saṃjñāy' adarśanu adarśanu cetanāye / vijñāna-citta-manu-darśanu yatra nāsti ayu dharma-darśanu nidiṣṭu tathāgatena // ākāśa-dṛṣṭu iti sattva pravyāharanti kha-nidarśanaṃ kutu vimṛṣyata etam arthaṃ / tatha dharma-darśanu nidiṣṭu tathāgatena na hi darśanaṃ bhaṇitu śakya nidarśanena //.* English translation in Edward Conze, *The Perfection of Wisdom in Eight Thousand Lines and its Verse Summary* (Bolinas, Calif.: Four Seasons Foundation, 1973), 32.

> The One-Gone-Thus teaches that one who does not see forms,
> Does not see feelings, does not see discriminations,
> Does not see intentions, does not see
> Consciousness, mind, or sentience sees the *dharma*.[a]
>
> Analyze how space is seen as in the expression
> By sentient beings in words, "Space is seen."
> The One-Gone-Thus teaches that seeing the *dharma* is also like that.
> The seeing cannot be expressed by another example.

This says that the unseen is the aggregates, and the seen is the *dharma*,[b] which means suchness,[c] as in the statement, "Whoever sees dependent-arising sees the *dharma*."

Furthermore, it is like, for example, the fact that space is a mere elimination of obstructive tangible objects, and that seeing—or realizing—it is taken as not seeing the preventive obstruction that is the object of negation and is suitable to be observed if it were present. In that [example], the seen is space, and the unseen is preventive obstruction. The last two lines refute that suchness is seen while seeing blue [for instance], which would be not to see in accordance with the example [of seeing space]. The statement that the five aggregates are not seen indicates that the substrata[d] [that is, these phenomena,] are not seen in the perspective of perception of suchness by uncontaminated meditative equipoise.

The *Introduction to the Two Truths Sūtra* (see also *Illumination*, 262) says:[e]

> Devaputras, the ultimate truth is passed beyond [the objects of all consciousnesses] ranging right through the objects of omniscient pristine wisdoms endowed with the supreme of all aspects; it is not as expressed in the phrase "ultimate truth."

---

[a] *chos*, which here means *chos nyid* (*dharmatā*), the noumenon, as Tsong-kha-pa says just below when he equates it with suchness.

[b] *chos*, *dharma*.

[c] *de kho na nyid*, *tathatā*.

[d] *chos can;* the substrata that possess the attribute of emptiness.

[e] *bden pa gnyis la 'jug pa / bden pa po'i le'u*, *satyakaparivarta;* P813, vol. 32. This passage is cited by Chandrakīrti in his *Commentary on the "Supplement to (Nāgārjuna's) 'Treatise on the Middle,'"* commenting on VI.29; Toh. 3862, *dbu ma*, vol. *'a*, 256a.2; La Vallée Poussin, *Madhyamakāvatāra*, 111.1-111.4; La Vallée Poussin, "*Introduction au traité du milieu*," *Muséon* 11 (1910): 306-307. For the Sanskrit as cited in Prajñākaramati's *Commentary on the Difficult Points of (Shāntideva's) "Engaging in the Bodhisattva Deeds,"* see Khangkar and Yorihito, 219 note 296.

It explains that [the ultimate truth] is not seen in accordance with the individual appearance, to an awareness, of the two—subject and object—when one says "ultimate truth." Therefore, it is a source for the disappearance of dualistic appearance, not a source for a Buddha's not realizing the ultimate.

Moreover, Chandrakīrti's *Commentary on the "Supplement to (Nāgārjuna's) 'Treatise on the Middle'"* (see also *Illumination*, 259) says:[a]

> Without contacting produced things, it actualizes solely the nature,[b] whereby suchness is understood; therefore, [a being who possesses such knowledge] is called "Buddha."

Chandrakīrti says that in terms of the perception of suchness by a Buddha's pristine wisdom knowing the mode [of being of phenomena], only the noumenon is realized, without contacting other-powered phenomena.

The disappearance of the movement of minds and mental factors means that when suchness is actualized, the movement of conceptuality stops; it does not indicate that there are no minds and mental factors [at that time]. Chandrakīrti's *Clear Words* explains that the statement that there is no movement of the mind refers to the absence of the movement of conceptuality (see also *Illumination*, 252):[c]

> If conceptuality is the movement of the mind, due to being devoid of it suchness is non-conceptual. Sūtra says, "What is ultimate truth? If it is without even the movement of the mind, what need is there to mention letters?"

Furthermore, Chandrakīrti's *Commentary on the "Supplement to (Nāgārjuna's) 'Treatise on the Middle'"* says that during a Learner Superior's meditative equipoise [the movement of conceptuality] does not stop forever but at Buddhahood stops forever.

Moreover, Chandrakīrti's *Commentary on the "Supplement to (Nāgārjuna's) 'Treatise on the Middle'"* proves, together with a source, that if the

---

[a] Commenting on VI.97; Toh. 3862, *dbu ma*, vol. *'a*, 283a.2; La Vallée Poussin, *Madhyamakāvatāra*, 201.17-201.19; La Vallée Poussin, "*Introduction au traité du milieu*," *Muséon* 12 (1911): 255.

[b] *rang bzhin, svabhāva.* This is not the object of negation in emptiness, but the final nature of phenomena.

[c] Commenting on XVIII.9; Toh. 3860, *dbu ma*, vol. *'a*, 120a.3-120a.4; La Vallée Poussin, *Mūlamadhyamakakārikās avec la Prasannapadā*, 374.1-374.2: *vikalpaścittapracāraḥ / tadrahitatvāt tat tattvaṃ nirvikalpaṃ // yathoktaṃ sūtre / paramārthasatyaṃ katamat / yatra jñānasyāpyapracāraḥ kaḥ punar vādo 'kṣarāṇāmiti /*. Tibetan in de Jong, *Cinq chapitres de la Prasannapadā*, 104-105; his French translation is on p. 30.

nature was not existent, Bodhisattvas' hard work in order to realize it would be senseless:[a]

> *Question:* Moreover, what is their nature [that is, what is the nature realized by Bodhisattvas]?
>
> *Answer:* It is that which is unfabricated and has no reliance on another, the nature realized by a consciousness free from the cataracts of ignorance.
>
> *Question:* Does it exist?
>
> *Answer:* Who would propound that it does not exist? If it did not exist, for what purpose would Bodhisattvas cultivate the paths of the perfections? For in order to realize that noumenon Bodhisattvas undergo hundreds of hardships.

As a source he cites the [*Cloud of Jewels*] *Sūtra:*[b]

> Child of good lineage, if the ultimate did not exist, behavior for purity would be senseless, and the arising of Ones-Gone-Thus would be senseless. Because the ultimate exists, Bodhisattvas are said to be skilled with respect to the ultimate.

He quotes this sūtra proving that the ultimate truth exists due to the fact that if the ultimate truth did not exist:

1. performing practice for the sake of the purity of the final nirvāṇa would be senseless;
2. Buddha's coming to the world in order that trainees might realize the ultimate would be senseless, since realization of the ultimate by trainees would not occur;
3. the great Conqueror Children would not be skilled in the ultimate truth.

Therefore, that the system of this great master propounds that the ultimate truth is not an object of knowledge[c] and that there is no pristine wisdom realizing suchness in a Superior's meditative equipoise are only wrong propositions.

---

[a] Commenting on VI.182; Toh. 3862, *dbu ma,* vol. *'a,* 314a.7-314b.1; La Vallée Poussin, *Madhyamakāvatāra,* 306.5-306.12; sūtra quote at vol. *'a,* 314b.4-314b.5, La Vallée Poussin, *Madhyamakāvatāra,* 307.4-307.7.

[b] *dkon mchog sprin gyi mdo, ratnameghasūtra;* P897, vol. 35, 214.3.6-214.3.7.

[c] Jam-yang-shay-pa describes the Autonomist Ngok Lo-den-shay-rap (*rngog blo ldan shes rab,* 1059-1109) as holding that the ultimate is not an object of knowledge; see Hopkins, *Maps of the Profound,* 562 and 745. Dol-po-pa (*Mountain Doctrine,* 33-35) holds that the ultimate is an object of knowledge but not either an effective thing or a non-effective thing.

Furthermore, Chandrakīrti's *Commentary on the "Supplement to (Nāgārjuna's) 'Treatise on the Middle'"* says:[a]

> Therefore, that "suchness is realized" is posited from imputation; actually something is not known by something because even both knower and object known are just non-produced.

The meaning of the first part is that the positing of a realization of suchness with the two—the pristine wisdom and suchness—being taken as separate subject and object is a positing in the perspective only of a conventional consciousness, not in the perspective of that pristine wisdom. That the knower is non-produced means that it has become like water put in water with respect to the meaning of the absence of inherently existent production.[b]

About the statement [in Chandrakīrti's *Commentary on the "Supplement to (Nāgārjuna's) 'Treatise on the Middle'"*]:[c]

> Because minds and mental factors do not operate with respect to suchness—the object of pristine wisdom—it is actualized only by the body.[d]

---

[a] Commenting on XII.4; Toh. 3862, *dbu ma,* vol. *'a,* 330b.6-330b.7; La Vallée Poussin, *Madhyamakāvatāra,* 358.15-358.17.

[b] The object is the absence of inherently existent production, and the subject is pristine wisdom; in direct realization these are indivisibly fused, like water poured into water.

[c] Commenting on XII.8; Toh. 3862, *dbu ma,* vol. *'a,* 332a.1-332a.2; La Vallée Poussin, *Madhyamakāvatāra,* 362.6-362.8.

[d] In La Vallée Poussin's edition (*Madhyamakāvatāra,* 362.6-362.9; also, Toh. 3862, vol. *'a,* 332a.1-332a.2), the passage reads in full (Tsong-kha-pa's omissions in bold):

> ***de ltar na*** *ye shes kyi yul de kho na nyid la* ***rnam pa thams cad du de'i yul na*** *sems* ***dang*** *sems* ***las*** *byung* ***ba rnams*** *mi 'jug pas sku kho nas mngon sum du mdzad* ***par kun rdzob tu rnam par bzhag go/***
>
> **In that case,** because minds and mental factors**, which have it as their object,** do not operate **in any way** with respect to suchness—the object of pristine wisdom—**it is conventionally posited that** it is actualized only by the body.

Since Tsong-kha-pa's point is that minds and mental factors do indeed operate with respect to suchness, the dropping of "in any way" (*rnam pa thams cad du*) seems to skew the topic in his favor, allowing him to immediately qualify the stoppage as being of conceptual minds and mental factors. However, Tsong-kha-pa indicated that he is sensitive to this charge when he showed earlier (132) that Chandrakīrti himself limits the scope of reference to conceptual minds and mental factors. Also, Tsong-kha-pa's own commentary on this line in his *Illumination of the Thought* says:

> On the Buddha ground, conceptual minds and mental factors that have suchness as their object have in all respects stopped and do not operate with regard to the meaning of suchness as the object of exalted wisdom. Hence, the

the object to be actualized is suchness; the subject, pristine wisdom, is the means of actualization, and the Complete Enjoyment Body is the agent of actualization, the knower. Its mode of actualizing suchness is in the manner of the stoppage of conceptual minds and mental factors as explained earlier (132); this is known from the explanation in Chandrakīrti's *Commentary on the "Supplement to (Nāgārjuna's) 'Treatise on the Middle'"* that the exalted body through which suchness is actualized has a nature of quiescence due to being free from minds and mental factors.[a]

If a Buddha did not perceive the aggregates and so forth, it would deprecate the exalted knowledge of the diversity and all the diverse objects because the existent and what is not known by a Buddha are mutually exclusive. Consequently, the diverse objects must appear to an exalted knower of the diversity [of phenomena]. Since exalted knowledge without the aspect [of the object appearing] is not this [Consequentialist] system, [objects are known by an omniscient consciousness] upon the appearance of their aspect. Also, the diversity that are the appearing objects are twofold—(1) the marks and beauties and so forth of a Buddha, which are not polluted by the latencies of ignorance, and (2) impure environments and inhabitants, and so forth, which are polluted by the latencies of ignorance. There is no sense of the vanishing of the first of those on the Buddha ground, whereas the second have vanished due to the reversal of their causes on that ground.

With respect to the mode of appearance, when the marks and beauties of a Buddha appear to persons who have not abandoned ignorance, their appearance as established by way of their own character—despite not being so established—is not by reason of those objects' having arisen through the force of the latencies of ignorance but is an appearance due to the [perceiving] subject's being polluted by the latencies of

---

> two—non-conceptual exalted wisdom and suchness—are undifferentiably merged like water poured into water. Consequently, that state is conventionally presented as initially actualized, that is, gained, by the Complete Enjoyment Body.

See Hopkins, *Maps of the Profound*, 990.

[a] Commenting on XII.9; Toh. 3862, *dbu ma*, vol. *'a*, 332a.3; La Vallée Poussin, *Madhyamakāvatāra*, 362.14-362.16. In the *sde dge* edition (Toh. 3862, vol. *'a*, 332a.3) and in La Vallée Poussin, *Madhyamakāvatāra* (362.14-362.16), the passage reads in full (Tsong-kha-pa's omissions from his paraphrase in bold):

> *sku gang gis de* ***kho na*** *nyid* ***'di*** *mngon* ***sum*** *du mdzad par* ***bshad pa*** *de* ***ni*** *zhi ba'i rang bzhin can du* ***'dod de*** */ sems dang sems las byung ba dang bral ba'****i phyir*** *ro*

> **That** Body through which suchness is **described as** actualized is **asserted** as having a nature of peace due to being devoid of minds and mental factors.

ignorance. For those [marks and beauties of a Buddha] do not appear to that subject [that is, a Buddha's consciousness] from the viewpoint of merely appearing thus[a] to other persons but appear thus from [a Buddha's] own viewpoint.[b]

The appearance of objects such as forms and sounds[c]—which appear in the perspective of those who have not abandoned ignorance as established by way of their own character whereas they are not so established—to a Buddha's pristine wisdom knowing the diversity is an appearance to a Buddha **only** from the viewpoint of [these phenomena] appearing to persons who have the pollutions of ignorance. Without depending on their appearing thus to others, they do not appear from a Buddha's own viewpoint. Therefore, a Buddha's knowing forms and so forth—which appear to be inherently established whereas they are not so established—is also from the viewpoint of their appearing thus to those who possess ignorance. Without depending on the appearance of them to those persons, Buddhas from their own viewpoint do not know them in the manner of their appearing this way; hence, there is no sense in which [a Buddha's consciousness] could become mistaken through their appearing. This is because, although they do not appear within the context of the pristine wisdom's having pollution, they appear by way of the essential point that the pristine wisdom must know all objects of knowledge.

From the viewpoint of an exalted knower of the diversity itself, all things appear in the perspective[d] of selflessness and the absence of inherent existence, whereby they appear as falsities, like illusions; they do not appear as truths. When [phenomena] appear to that pristine wisdom from the factor of[e] appearing to those who have ignorance, this is a mere becoming visible[f] of the appearance [of those] as true to

[a] That is, as the marks and beauties of a Buddha.

[b] *rang ngos nas.* This could also be correctly translated as "from [a Buddha's] own side," which would highlight the similarity with the phrase *rang ngos nas grub pa* (established from its own side), the object of negation in the doctrine of emptiness, and thus perhaps illuminate a little the meaning of the latter. However, it is awkward to use that translation in place of the word "viewpoint" in the earlier part of the sentence.

[c] The false appearance of objects such as forms and sounds as if they inherently exist is itself something that exists, and thus it must be known by an omniscient consciousness and hence must appear to a Buddha. However, this appearance occurs to a Buddha not because of a fault in that Buddha, but only because it occurs this way for beings who have the pollutions of ignorance. From a Buddha's own viewpoint, only endless purity is perceived.

[d] *ngor;* 479.4.

[e] *cha nas;* 479.5.

[f] *shar ba;* 479.5.

other persons.

Furthermore, Nāgārjuna's *Sixty Stanzas of Reasoning* says:[a]

> Those skilled with respect to things
> See things as impermanent, deceptive phenomena,
> Conglomerate,[b] empty,
> Selfless, and void.

Also, Chandrakīrti's commentary on this[c] says that one who has completed the deeds [of practice, that is to say, a Buddha,] perceives in that way.

In that way Jñānagarbha's *Differentiation of the Two Truths* explains that [this pristine wisdom] vividly perceives directly all the diversity:[d]

> An omniscient knower directly perceives
> All the dependently produced
> Just as they appear
> Devoid of the superimposed entity.

and he explains that [Buddhas] never rise from the meditative stabilization in which dualistic appearance has been pacified:

> Because that which does not see knowers,
> Objects known, and selfhood has a stable abiding
> Due to the non-arising of signs,
> [Buddhas] do not rise [from meditative stabilization].

Although to those who do not properly understand these two descriptions it seems to be contradictory to assert both—rather than just one of the two—there is no contradiction. This is because although the two pristine wisdoms perceiving suchness and perceiving the diversity are one entity, there is not the slightest contradiction that in relation to individual objects [that is, the ultimate and the conventional] there come to be two—a rational consciousness and a conventional consciousness.

Moreover, this depends on knowing well that there is not the slightest contradiction in there being two different modes of finding [objects] by the two valid cognitions—rational and conventional—in terms of one substratum [that is, one object] at the time of the view of

---

[a] Stanza 25; Toh. 3825, *dbu ma*, vol. *tsa*, 21a.7; Lindtner, *Master of Wisdom*, 80.

[b] *gsog*, a collection, and thus essenceless, hollow, false.

[c] Toh. 3864, *dbu ma*, vol. *ya*, 18a.7; Scherrer-Schaub, *Yuktiṣaṣṭikāvṛtti*, 64.

[d] Stanzas 37 and 39; Toh. 3881, *dbu ma*, vol. *sa*, 3a.4-3a.5 and 3a.5-3a.6; Eckel, *Jñānagarbha's Commentary*, 186 and 187; Eckel's English translation is found on pp.100-101.

the basal state. If, concerning the time of the fruit when the two pristine wisdoms comprehend objects, you know well not only that point but also which of the two valid cognitions[—ultimate or conventional—a pristine wisdom] becomes with regard to an object, you also can know that the two subjects [that is, the exalted knower of the mode and the exalted knower of the diversity] do not become a common locus [that is, one consciousness that is both an exalted knower of the mode and an exalted knower of the diversity][a] even though the objects [of those two] are not limited separately. Through this you will also understand the fine points of the definitions of the two truths.

Explaining the divisions of ultimate truths

When ultimate truths are divided, it is as Chandrakīrti's *Commentary on the "Supplement to (Nāgārjuna's) 'Treatise on the Middle'"* says—an extensive division into the sixteen emptinesses,[b] a middling division into the four emptinesses of things, non-things, self-entity, and other-entity, and a brief division into the two, selflessness of persons and selflessness of phenomena.

Other texts speak of two—actual ultimates and concordant

[a] Both an exalted knower of the mode and an exalted knower of the diversity are omniscient consciousnesses and thus realize both the ultimate and the conventional; however, they are individually specified from the viewpoint of the objects, which are, respectively, the ultimate and the conventional.

[b] The sixteen emptinesses are:

1. emptiness of the internal
2. emptiness of the external
3. emptiness of the internal and external
4. emptiness of emptiness
5. emptiness of the great
6. emptiness of the ultimate
7. emptiness of the compounded
8. emptiness of the uncompounded
9. emptiness of what has passed beyond extremes
10. emptiness of what is beginningless and endless
11. emptiness of the indestructible
12. emptiness of nature
13. emptiness of all phenomena
14. emptiness of definitions
15. emptiness of the unapprehendable
16. emptiness of the inherent existence of non-things.

For identifications of these, see the list of eighteen emptinesses in Hopkins, *Meditation on Emptiness*, 204-205.

ultimates:[a]

- Kamalashīla's *Illumination of the Middle* says:[b]

  > Because this absence of production moreover accords with the ultimate, it is called an "ultimate," but it is not actually so because actually the ultimate is beyond all proliferations.[c]

- Shāntarakṣhita's *Ornament for the Middle* also says:[d]

  > Because of according with the ultimate,
  > This is called an "ultimate."
  > In reality [the ultimate] is free from all
  > The collections of proliferations.

- The same is also said in Jñānagarbha's *Differentiation of the Two Truths.*[e]

---

[a] *don dam pa dngos dang mthun pa'i don dam;* 481.5. The issue that Tsong-kha-pa is dealing with in the rest of this section is that in his system the absence of inherently existent production is an actual ultimate truth, and thus he must explain away several statements indicating that it is only a concordant ultimate; he does this through contextualizing those statements.

[b] Toh. 3887, *dbu ma,* vol. *sa,* 149a.5.

[c] Nga-wang-pel-den's *Annotations for (Jam-yang-shay-pa's) "Great Exposition of Tenets"* (*dbu,* 189.4) explains this quote first in terms of subjects—that is to say, consciousnesses—refuting truly existent production and so forth:

> Because this ultimate [conceptual rational consciousness] in "absence of ultimate production" accords with an actual ultimate subject [that is, consciousness] in its elimination of the proliferations of the apprehension of true existence, it is called an "ultimate subject," but it is not an actual ultimate subject because an actual ultimate subject must be a [non-conceptual] awareness beyond all proliferations of dualistic appearance.
>
> The meaning of this passage from Shāntarakṣhita's *Ornament for the Middle* is also similar.

For Nga-wang-pel-den's explanation of these quotes in terms of the object, emptiness, see the end of the next footnote.

[d] *dbu ma rgyan, madhyamakālaṃkāra,* stanza 70; Toh. 3884, *dbu ma,* vol. *sa,* 55b.2; Tibetan text edited by Masamichi Ichigō, "Śāntarakṣita's Madhyamakālaṃkāra," in *Studies in the Literature of the Great Vehicle,* Michigan Studies in Buddhist Literature No. 1, eds. Luis O. Gómez and Jonathan A. Silk (Ann Arbor: Collegiate Institute for the Study of Buddhist Literature and Center for South and Southeast Asian Studies, University of Michigan, 1989), 214; Ichigō's English translation is found on p. 215.

[e] Jñānagarbha's *Differentiation of the Two Truths* (9ab) says:

> We assert that a negation of production and so forth also
> Is [an ultimate] due to being concordant with the real.
> (*skye la sogs pa bkag pa yang / yang dag pa dang mthun phyir 'dod*)

His autocommentary says:

- Jñānagarbha's own commentary on that text as well as Maitreya's *Ornament* speak of the negative of ultimately [existent] production and so forth as conventional.[a]

With respect to the meaning of those, many earlier [Tibetans]—in their treatment of the two, enumerative and non-enumerative ultimate truths[b]—asserted that:

- the emptinesses that are negatives of the ultimate[ly existent] production and so forth of forms and so on are enumerative ultimates, which are imputed ultimate truths[c] and fully qualified obscurational truths,[d] and

---

> We assert that by reason of negating conceptualization of really [existent] production and so forth it is an ultimate due to being concordant with the real.

Nga-wang-pel-den's *Annotations for (Jam-yang-shay-pa's) "Great Exposition of Tenets"* (*dbu*, 189.2) explains this quote first in terms of subjects—that is to say, consciousnesses—refuting truly existent production and so forth:

> We assert moreover that a conceptual rational consciousness that, upon having analyzed through reasoning, has refuted ultimate production, cessation, and so forth is concordant with a non-conceptual pristine wisdom—a real subject [that is, a correct consciousness]—and hence is an ultimate subject. Its concordance is that by reason of negating conceptualization of really [existent] production and so forth—that is, the proliferations of the apprehension of true existence—it accords with non-conceptual pristine wisdom.

He also explains this and the previous two quotes in terms of the object, emptiness:

> With respect to how to explain the meaning of these passages within applying them to the object, emptiness: this absence of truly established production moreover is called an ultimate concordant with the ultimate due to being free from only a portion of proliferations in the perspective of a conceptual rational consciousness, because freedom from the proliferations of the apprehension of true existence in its perspective accords only partially with freedom from the proliferations of dualistic appearance in the perspective of an uncontaminated consciousness. It is not an actual ultimate free from both proliferations in the perspective of a non-conceptual rational consciousness because whatever is an *actual* ultimate—a rational consciousness—in the perspective of which an ultimate truth is free from both proliferations must be a rational consciousness in the perspective of which [an ultimate truth] is beyond both proliferations.

[a] Below (146), Tsong-kha-pa explains that this statement is misread as meaning that a negative of ultimately existent production is a conventionality, whereas he holds that it is an ultimate truth; Tsong-kha-pa asserts that the meaning of this quote is that a negative of ultimately existent production **exists** conventionally.

[b] *rnam grangs pa yin min gyi don dam bden pa;* 482.2.

[c] *don dam bden pa btags pa ba;* 482.3.

[d] *kun rdzob bden pa mtshan nyid pa;* 482.3.

- the non-enumerative ultimate truth cannot be taken as an object of any awareness and therefore is not an object of knowledge.[a]

Since that is not the meaning of those [passages], they are to be explained as follows. Though indeed the object, the noumenon, is to be taken as the ultimate, there are also many descriptions of the subject—the rational consciousness—as an ultimate, as is set forth in:

- Jñānagarbha's *Differentiation of the Two Truths:*[b]

---

[a] This is not aimed at Dol-po-pa Shay-rap-gyel-tsen, since he (below, 298) asserts that the ultimate is an object of knowledge.

Jam-yang-shay-pa's *Great Exposition of Tenets* (Hopkins, *Maps of the Profound*, 908) says:

> Many earlier Tibetans asserted that:
>
> - The emptiness that is a negative of forms' ultimately existent production and so forth is an enumerative ultimate, an imputed ultimate truth (*don dam bden pa btags pa ba*), and a fully qualified obscurational truth (*kun rdzob bden pa mtshan nyid pa*).
> - The non-enumerative ultimate truth cannot be taken as an object of any awareness and therefore is not an object of knowledge.
>
> Those are very incorrect because not only does each ultimate—enumerative and non-enumerative—have, [when taken] as object [from between object and subject], the absence of true existence [which is an ultimate truth and hence not an obscurational truth], but also the enumerative ultimate has, [when taken] as subject [from between object and subject], awarenesses of hearing and thinking, and the non-enumerative ultimate has, as subject, pristine wisdoms of meditative equipoise [which take the absence of true existence as their object, and, therefore, even the non-enumerative ultimate, as object, is an object of knowledge, and thus it is wrong to hold that the non-enumerative ultimate truth cannot be taken as an object of any mind]...
>
> Although the absence of ultimately existent production, which is the mode of subsistence, does not have proliferations from its own side, an inference of determinative realization [of the absence of ultimately existent production] comprehends [the absence of ultimately existent production] together with proliferations of dualistic appearance in the perspective of its appearance factor despite the fact that proliferations have disappeared in the perspective of its ascertainment factor. Hence, since it accords with the ultimate that is the object of a Superior's meditative equipoise, it is called a "concordant ultimate." Since the absence of ultimately existent production is without all of the collections of proliferations both in the perspective of the ascertainment factor of meditative equipoise and even in the perspective of its appearance factor, it is called an "actual ultimate" or "non-enumerative ultimate." Therefore, how could even the object found by inference—the absence of truly existent production—be a conventionality!

[b] Stanza 4ab; Toh. 3881, *dbu ma*, vol. *sa*, 1a.4; Tibetan in Eckel, *Jñānagarbha's Commentary*, 156; his English translation is on p. 71. For the Sanskrit see Khangkar and Yorihito, 222 note 319.

> Because of being undeceiving, a rational [consciousness] is an ultimate.

- and moreover in Kamalashīla's *Illumination of the Middle:*[a]

> The statements also that production and so forth do not **ultimately** exist are asserted to mean the following: All consciousnesses arisen from correct hearing, thinking, and meditating are non-erroneous subjects; hence, they are called "ultimates" because of being the ultimate among these [consciousnesses. Production and so forth do not exist for such consciousnesses and in this sense do not exist ultimately.]

There are two types of rational consciousnesses:

1. non-conceptual: a Superior's non-conceptual pristine wisdom of meditative equipoise
2. conceptual: a rational consciousness comprehending suchness in dependence on a reason, and so forth.[b]

The thought of Bhāvaviveka's *Blaze of Reasoning*[c] in describing the ultimate as twofold—a non-conceptual pristine wisdom and a wisdom concordant with that—and the thought of Kamalashīla's *Illumination of the Middle* in describing two ultimates are the same. Therefore, it is not the meaning of those texts that the explanation of two ultimates should be taken as ultimates only in terms of objects and not in terms of subjects.

Concerning this, when the first [that is, a Superior's non-conceptual pristine wisdom of meditative equipoise] understands suchness, it is able to simultaneously eliminate with respect to its object the proliferations of [the apprehension of] true [existence] and the proliferations of dualistic appearance; hence, [a Superior's non-conceptual pristine wisdom of meditative equipoise] is an actual ultimate; also, that is the meaning of being "beyond all proliferations" (see the quote on 139). Although the second [that is, a conceptual rational consciousness comprehending suchness in dependence on a sign, and so forth] is able to cease the proliferations [of the apprehension] of true [existence] with respect to its own object [that is, emptiness], it cannot eliminate the proliferations of dualistic appearance; hence, it is an ultimate that accords in aspect with the supramundane ultimate.

It is necessary to set forth two modes also with respect to the

[a] Toh. 3887, *dbu ma*, vol. *sa*, 229b.1-229b.2.

[b] In his 1972 lectures, the Dalai Lama speculated that "and so forth" might include consequences.

[c] *rtog ge 'bar ba, tarkajvālā;* Toh. 3856, *dbu ma*, vol. *dza*, 60b.4-60b.5.

object-ultimate[a] that is the negative of ultimately [existent] production—and so forth—of forms and so on. Concerning this:

- In the perspective of a non-conceptual rational consciousness, the object-emptiness is the actual ultimate free from both proliferations.
- In the perspective of a conceptual rational consciousness, the object-emptiness is not the actual ultimate free from both proliferations, since it is free from only one class of proliferations. However, this is not to say that **in general** it is not an actual ultimate truth.

Therefore, except for the case of being free from all proliferations of dualistic appearance **in the perspective of certain awarenesses**, an emptiness of true existence free from all proliferations of appearance does not occur, and hence the meaning of those texts is not that whatever is an ultimate truth is necessarily free from all proliferations of dualistic appearance.[b]

[The proponents of] establishment of illusion by a rational [consciousness[c] wrongly] assert that a composite of the two, the appearance of a base, such as an aggregate, and of its emptiness of true existence—[this composite according to them] being the mere meaning established by an inferential rational consciousness[d]—is an ultimate truth. [However] it is a concordant ultimate, not an ultimate truth.

Moreover, with respect [to their misguided attempt] to prove the

[a] *yul gyi don dam;* 483.6. This is the ultimate that is the object of the wisdom consciousness, not the wisdom consciousness that is called an ultimate.

[b] For Nga-wang-pel-den's explication of the meaning of this and the previous paragraph see 347.

[c] Tsong-kha-pa mentioned this position earlier (29). For an exhaustive discussion of the usage of the term "Thoroughly Non-Abiding Proponents of the Middle" for Consequentialists and "Reason-Established Illusionists" for Autonomists, see Appendix One in Napper, *Dependent-Arising and Emptiness,* 403-440.

[d] *rigs shes rjes dpag gis grub pa'i don tsam;* in his *Great Exposition of the Stages of the Path* Tsong-kha-pa uses the phrase "the mere meaning **comprehended** by an inferential rational consciousness" (*rigs shes rjes dpag gis* ***gzhal ba'i*** *don tsam*). In his 1972 lectures, the Dalai Lama explained that once an inferential rational consciousness has realized the absence of inherent existence, then through the force of that realization a combination of appearance and emptiness is established. Thus, an inferential rational consciousness itself realizes only the absence of inherent existence, not a combination of appearance and emptiness; later, through its force phenomena dawn as like illusions. It seems to me that it is perhaps in this sense that a combination of appearance and emptiness is **established** through the force of an inferential rational consciousness even though it is not **comprehended** by an inferential rational consciousness, and therefore Tsong-kha-pa switched from his earlier usage of "comprehended" in the *Great Exposition of the Stages of the Path* to "established" here in the *Medium-Length Exposition*.

appearance of the absence of the true existence of sprouts and so forth through the appearance of the lack of being a true one or many:

- There is no point in proving such [a combination of an object and the appearance of its emptiness] to an intelligent person[a] who has not eliminated doubt with respect to whether or not those bases [that is, sprouts and so forth] truly exist [in that it will not help in realizing the absence of inherent existence, which has to be done first]. Also, for one who has eliminated such doubt, the sign [that is to say, reason] is not a correct sign [since that person would have no need to realize "appearance of the absence of true existence of sprouts and so forth" in dependence upon this or any other reasoning, because the person has already realized the absence of true existence].
- Furthermore, Kamalashīla's *Illumination of the Middle* says that both the sign—lacking being one or many—and the predicate [that is, the absence of true existence] are mere eliminations and that whatever is taken as the sign—"is not one or many" or "does not exist as one or many"—it is the same. That he is not referring to affirming negatives is known from the examples given there. Hence, it is not at all the assertion of the masters—the father Shāntarakṣhita, his spiritual son [Kamalashīla], and the master Haribhadra—[that the **appearance** of the absence of true existence of sprouts and so forth is proven through the **appearance** of the lack of being a true one or many, since such a proof would make the reason and the predicate of the thesis affirming negatives. Therefore, those who claim that these masters are proponents of establishment of illusion by a rational consciousness are mistaken.]

Also, there is no great Proponent of the Middle Way who asserts that the mere object comprehended by an inferential consciousness[b]—the

[a] *rtogs ldan.*

[b] *rjes dpag gi gzhal ba'i don tsam;* 485.3. This seems contrary to Tsong-kha-pa's own position that inference realizes the actual ultimate; however, it may be possible to take his usage of this term to be referring to the **appearing object** (*snang yul*) of a conceptual consciousness—a meaning-generality (*don spyi, arthasāmānya*) or sound-generality (*sgra spyi, śabdasāmānya*), that is, a conceptual image through the route of which a conceptual consciousness understands its object. My identification is based on Tsong-kha-pa's usage of the term "objects of comprehension of an inferential valid cognition" (*rjes dpag tshad ma'i gzhal bya*) in his *The Essence of Eloquence,* which Gung-ru Chö-jung (*Garland of White Lotuses,* 19b.3) cogently identifies as the appearing objects of inferential cognition, these being sound-generalities and meaning-generalities; see Hopkins, *Emptiness in the Mind-Only School of Buddhism,* 198 and the accompanying notes, as well as Jeffrey Hopkins, *Absorption in No External World: 170 Issues in Mind-Only Buddhism* (Ithaca, N.Y.: Snow

latter from between the two, an exclusionary elimination[a] and an inclusionary elimination[b] with regard to the elimination of the proliferations that are the object of negation with respect to appearances—is an ultimate truth.[c] Through these ways[d] you should also understand in more refinement [my] explanation of the presentation of these in the extensive *Stages of the Path.*[e]

In connection with the explanation of the negative of production and so forth as a concordant ultimate,[f] Jñānagarbha's *Autocommentary on the "Differentiation of the Two Truths"* says:[g]

> Others [that is, Proponents of Mind-Only] hold [that emptiness is] only real; therefore, "also" [in the root text][h] has the meaning of a conjunction. [However,] when analyzed with reasoning, it is only conventional. Why?

Lion Publications, 2005), issue #125. A meaning-generality, rather than being a mere elimination of the object of negation, is an affirming negative and thus an inclusionary elimination.

[a] *rnam bcad.* This is a non-affirming negative.

[b] *yongs gcod.* This is an affirming negative.

[c] The position of those propounding thorough non-abiding was briefly mentioned earlier (30).

[d] *tshul 'dis.*

[e] The explanations here and earlier in this text (30) of the problems in the position of the proponents of establishment of illusion by a rational consciousness and in the position of the proponents of the thoroughly non-abiding middle should be used to understand Tsong-kha-pa's briefer explanations in his *Great Exposition of the Stages of the Path.*

[f] This point is in response to an objector's position given earlier (140):

> Jñānagarbha's own commentary on that text as well as Maitreya's *Ornament* speak of the negative of ultimately [existent] production and so forth as conventional.

The misguided claim is that for Jñānagarbha and Maitreya the emptiness of ultimately existent production is a conventional truth, not an ultimate truth; Tsong-kha-pa's opinion is that for these scholars it is an ultimate truth that, like everything else, **exists** conventionally.

[g] Commentary on stanza 9b, followed by the half-stanza 9cd; Toh. 3882, *dbu ma,* vol. *sa,* 6a.2-6a.3; Eckel, *Jñānagarbha's Commentary,* 161; Eckel's English commentary is found on p. 76. For the Sanskrit see Khangkar and Yorihito, 223 note 325.

[h] Jñānagarbha's *Differentiation of the Two Truths* (9ab) says:

> We assert that a negation of production and so forth also
> Is [an ultimate] due to being concordant with the real.
> (*skye la sogs pa bkag pa* ***yang*** */ yang dag pa dang mthun phyir 'dod*)

Jñānagarbha is contrasting his assertion with the assertion by the Proponents of Mind-Only that emptiness ultimately exists.

> Since the object of negation [that is, a self of phenomena,] does not exist,
> It is clear that the negative does not exist in reality.[a]

He says that:

- others—Proponents of Mind-Only—assert that an emptiness, which is a negative of a self of phenomena in a base of negation, is established in reality,
- but his own system asserts that since the self of phenomena, which is the object of negation, does not exist, the negation that is the negative of this is not established in reality.[b]

Therefore, [Jñānagarbha's] explanation that a negative of ultimately existent production and so forth is conventional means that it **exists** conventionally; it does not indicate that such is a conventionality.

Also, Jñānagarbha's *Autocommentary on the "Differentiation of the Two Truths"* says:[c]

> [*Objection:*] Because when a thing appears, its really existent production and so forth do not appear, such [really existent production and so forth] are unreal conventionalities. Similarly, a negative of really existent production and so forth also would be an unreal conventionality, for when the thing that is the basis of negation appears, it does not appear.
>
> *Answer:* It is not that [a negative of really existent production and so forth] does not appear because it is not different from the entity of a thing.

With respect to his explanation that when blue, for instance, appears, its emptiness of true existence appears, it is not that the mere elimination that is a negative of true existence appears to an eye consciousness and so forth; rather, [he says this] in consideration of an affirming negative.[d] Therefore, even though such is a fully qualified

---

[a] *yang dag tu na;* 485.5. Ge-luk-pa scholars often explain this phrase as meaning "existing as its own reality," that is to say, ultimately. By demonstrating that the negative of the object of negation—emptiness—does not exist ultimately, Jñānagarbha indicates that since emptiness exists, it must exist conventionally.

[b] In Jñānagarbha's system, "the self of phenomena" is ultimate existence, or establishment in reality; since ultimate existence is negated, the emptiness of ultimate existence also cannot ultimately exist; it must exist conventionally.

[c] Commentary on stanza 8d; Toh. 3882, *dbu ma,* vol. *sa,* 5b.7; Eckel, *Jñānagarbha's Commentary,* 160; Eckel's English is on p. 76.

[d] In his 1972 lectures, the Dalai Lama indicated that this is the combination of appearance of the object and appearance of emptiness that occurs for someone who sees

conventionality, it is not contradictory that an emptiness that is a mere elimination of truth is an ultimate truth.

Shāntarakṣhita's *Ornament for the Middle*[a] explains that although a negative of ultimately existent production and so forth is included among real conventionalities, it is a concordant ultimate, since it accords with the ultimate. The nets of proliferations—in his statement that the ultimate has abandoned all the nets of proliferations such as existent thing, non-existent thing, and so forth—are in accordance with the description in Jñānagarbha's *Autocommentary on the "Differentiation of the Two Truths"* of the nets of conceptuality as the nets of proliferations:[b]

> Therefore, the Supramundane Victor said
> It is not empty, not non-empty,
> Not existent and non-existent,
> Not non-produced and not produced, and so on.

and:

> Why? It is without proliferations; suchness is free from all nets of conceptuality.

Furthermore, because those have vanished in the perspective of direct realization of suchness, [a negative of ultimately existent production in its perspective] is an actual ultimate, and a rational consciousness as well as its object, which are not like that, are concordant with the former, and so forth, as explained earlier.

Also, with respect to the negation of really existent production and so forth, there are two—the rational consciousness by which it is negated and its object of comprehension. Therefore, the mode of inclusion as a real conventionality also should be known in terms of those.[c] This way of explaining freedom from the nets of all whatsoever proliferations with respect to the two truths is important on many occasions.

---

phenomena as like illusions.

[a] See above, 139.

[b] Commentary on stanza 11ab, including stanza 11b; Toh. 3882, *dbu ma,* vol. *sa,* 6a.6; Eckel, *Jñānagarbha's Commentary,* 162; Eckel's English is on p. 77.

[c] The point is that although the object of comprehension of a conceptual rational consciousness is an actual ultimate, from the viewpoint of how it is realized by such a consciousness, it is called a concordant ultimate.

Indicating the definiteness of the number of the truths as two

If a base [that is, any phenomenon] is positively set off[a] as a false deceptive object, its being a non-deceptive object is necessarily eliminated.[b] Therefore, deceptive and non-deceptive are mutually exclusive contradictories. Because they apply to all objects of knowledge in the manner of mutual abandonment, a third category is also excluded.[c] Therefore, you should know that with respect to objects of knowledge the enumeration is definite as the two truths.

Moreover, the *Meeting of Father and Son Sūtra* says that all objects of knowledge are exhausted in the two truths (see also *Illumination*, 220):[d]

> It is thus: Ones-Gone-Thus thoroughly understand the two, fraudulences and ultimates. Furthermore, objects of knowledge are exhausted as these obscurational truths and ultimate truths.

Furthermore, the *Superior Sūtra of the Meditative Stabilization Definitely Revealing Suchness* clearly says that the enumeration is definite as the two truths (see also *Illumination*, 224):[e]

> The obscurational and likewise the ultimate—
> There is not at all a third truth.[f]

---

[a] *yongs su bcad.*

[b] *rnam par bcad.*

[c] Dol-po-pa Shay-rap-gyel-tsen asserts that the ultimate is a third category beyond effective thing and non-effective thing, but he asserts that there are only two truths; therefore, this passage is not aimed at refuting him.

[d] *yab sras mjal ba, pitāputrasamāgama;* Toh. 60, vol. *nga* (*dkon brtsegs*), 60b.4; cited in Shāntideva's *bslab pa kun las btus pa, śikṣāsamuccaya;* Toh. 3940, vol. *khi*, 142b.2; Sanskrit, which is missing the first sentence, in Bendall, *Çikshāsamuccaya*, 256.4: *etāvaccaitat jñeyam / yaduta saṃvṛti: paramārthaśca /*. English translation in Bendall and Rouse, *Śikṣā Samuccaya*, 236.

[e] *de kho na nyid nges par bstan pa'i ting nge 'dzin, tattvanirdeśasamādhi.* Cited in Chandrakīrti's *Commentary on the "Supplement to (Nāgārjuna's) 'Treatise on the Middle,'"* commenting on stanza VI.80; Toh. 3682, *dbu ma*, vol. *'a*, 243a.4; La Vallée Poussin, *Madhyamakāvatāra*, 175.11-175.12; La Vallée Poussin, "*Introduction au traité du milieu,*" *Muséon* 11 (1910): 356. For the Sanskrit see Khangkar and Yorihito, 224 note 332.

[f] Concerning the limitation to two truths, Jam-yang-shay-pa's *Great Exposition of Tenets* (Hopkins, *Maps of the Profound*, 896-897) says:

> The divisions [of the two truths] are two, obscurational truths—objects of operation of a worldly person who has dualistic appearance and objects of operation of worldly awareness that has dualistic appearance—and ultimate truths. Further, objects of knowledge have those two categories, and this is a definite number eliminating a third category that is not either of those two:
>
> - because, within the context of objects of knowledge, if something is

It is said that if the division of the two truths is known, one is not obscured with regard to the Subduer's word, and if the division of the two truths is not known, one will not know the suchness of the teaching. Furthermore, it must be known in accordance with how the protector Nāgārjuna delineated it. Chandrakīrti's *Supplement to (Nāgārjuna's) "Treatise on the Middle"* says:[a]

> There is no method of pacification for those outside
> The path of the honorable master Nāgārjuna.
> They fall from the truths of the obscurational and of suchness.
> Due to falling from those, liberation is not achieved.
>
> One who does not know the division of the two—
> Conventional truths[b] as the method
> And ultimate truths as arisen from the method—
> Has entered on a bad path through wrong conceptions.

Hence, it is very important for those wishing liberation to become skilled in the two truths.

---

established as any one of the two truths—for instance, an ultimate truth—then it is perforce blocked in an exclusionary way from being the other one, that is, an obscurational truth, and if something is established as an obscurational truth, it is perforce blocked in an exclusionary way from being the other one, that is, an ultimate truth, and hence the two truths are explicit contradictories by way of mutual exclusion, and

- because if any one of the two truths were not existent, then all objects of knowledge would not be included in the truths, and it is established by both scripture and reasoning that a third and so forth truth that is not any of those two does not exist.

The determination of the count is not like mere inclusion into a count, as is the case with the Four [Buddha] Bodies, but is a definite count eliminating a third category...Hence, saying that Proponents of the Middle and Consequentialists have no explicit contradictories has been refuted earlier.

[a] Stanzas VI.79-80; Toh. 3861, *dbu ma*, vol. *'a*, 208a.1-208a.3; La Vallée Poussin, *Madhyamakāvatāra*, 174.15-174.19 and 175.3-175.6; La Vallée Poussin, "*Introduction au traité du milieu*," *Muséon* 11 (1910): 355-356. For the Sanskrit see Khangkar and Yorihito, 224 note 334.

[b] *tha snyad bden pa.*

10. Procedures of Special Insight

Divisions of special insight

When, from observing the prerequisites for special insight as explained above (27ff.), you have found the view realizing the two selflessnesses, you should cultivate special insight.

Question: How many [types of] special insight are there?

Answer: Here I will not mainly indicate the special insights of those on high grounds but will predominantly indicate those to be cultivated while a common being. All inclusively, the divisions of the special insights to be cultivated while a common being are those of the four natures, the three approaches, and the six examinations.

The four natures[a] are those described in the *Sūtra Unraveling the Thought,*[b] differentiation[c] and so forth. About them:

- differentiation observes the diversity [of phenomena]
- intense differentiation[d] observes the mode [of being of phenomena, emptiness].

Differentiation has two types, thorough investigation[e] and thorough analysis;[f] intense differentiation also has two types, [thorough] investigation and [thorough] analysis, which are analyses of coarse and subtle objects [respectively]. Identifications of those four are given in Asaṅga's *Grounds of Hearers,*[g] Ratnākarashānti's *Quintessential Instructions on the Perfection of Wisdom,*[h] and so forth.

---

[a] The four are coarse and subtle differentiation and coarse and subtle intense differentiation.

[b] *dgongs pa nges par 'grel pa'i mdo, saṃdhinirmocana;* Toh. 106, *mdo sde,* vol. *ca;* Tibetan and English in John Powers, *Wisdom of Buddha* (Berkeley, Calif.: Dharma Publishing, 1995), 150-151; Tibetan and French in Étienne Lamotte, *Saṃdhinirmocana Sūtra. L'Explication des mystères* (Louvain and Paris: Université de Louvain and Adrien Maisonneuve, 1935), 89 and 210.

[c] *rnam par 'byed pa, vicaya.*

[d] *rab tu rnam par 'byed pa, pravicaya.*

[e] *yongs su rtog pa, paritarka.*

[f] *yongs su dpyod pa, paricāra.*

[g] *nyan sa, śrāvakabhūmi;* P5537 101.1.6-101.1.7; for the passage see Tsong-kha-pa, *Great Treatise,* vol. 3, 328.

[h] *she rab kyi pha rol tu phyin pa'i man ngag, prajñāpāramitopadeśa;* Toh. 4079, *sems tsam,* vol. *hi.*

The three approaches are those described in the *Sūtra Unraveling the Thought:*[a]

1. arisen from a sign[b] [that is to say, an imagistic recollection of experience gained earlier]
2. arisen from thorough examination[c]
3. arisen from individual investigation.[d]

To illustrate identifications of these with respect to, for instance, the meaning of selflessness:

1. The special insight arisen from a sign is a case of observing the selflessness already ascertained and taking to mind its sign [that is, a conceptual image of it]; one does not perform much [additional] delineation [of the meaning].
2. The special insight arisen from thorough examination is a delineation for the sake of ascertaining what was not ascertained earlier.
3. The special insight arisen from individual investigation is a performing of analysis on a meaning already ascertained in the way it was done earlier.

The six examinations are thorough examinations concerning meanings, things, characteristics, classes, times, and reasonings, as well as individual investigation after examination. Concerning those:

1. Examination concerning the meaning is to examine, "The meaning of this word is such-and-such."
2. Examination of things is to examine, "This is an internal thing; that is an external thing."
3. Examination concerning characteristics is twofold—to examine, "This is a specific characteristic; that is a general characteristic," or shared and unshared.[e]
4. Examination concerning classes is to examine the unwholesome class from the viewpoint of faults and disadvantages and the wholesome class from the viewpoint of good qualities and advantages.
5. Examination concerning times is to examine, "Such-and-such

[a] P744, 14.2.3-14.2.5; for the passage see Tsong-kha-pa, *Great Treatise,* vol. 3, 328; Tibetan and English in Powers, *Wisdom of Buddha,* 156-159; Tibetan and French in Lamotte, *Saṃdhinirmocana Sūtra,* 92 and 213.

[b] *mtshan ma las byung ba, nimitta-mayī.*

[c] *yongs su tshol ba las byung ba, paryeṣaṇā-mayī.*

[d] *so sor rtog pa las byung ba, pratyavekṣaṇā-mayī.*

[e] "Unshared" means unique.

occurred in the past; such-and-such will occur in the future; and such-and-such exists in the present."

6. Examination concerning reasonings[a] is of four types.
    - The reasoning of dependence[b] is [from the viewpoint] that the arising of effects depends on causes and conditions. It is also an examination of the conventional, the ultimate, and their bases [that is, instances,] individually.
    - The reasoning of performance of function[c] is [from the viewpoint] that phenomena perform their respective functions, such as fire performing the function of burning. Moreover, one examines, "This is the phenomenon; this is the functioning; this phenomenon performs this function."
    - The reasoning of tenable proof[d] is to prove a meaning without contradicting valid cognition. It is an examination within considering whether or not [the meaning] has valid cognition—direct, inferential, or believable scripture.
    - The reasoning of nature[e] is to examine [from the viewpoint] of (1) natures renowned in the world, such as heat being the nature of fire and moisture being the nature of water, (2) inconceivable natures [such as a Buddha's placing a world-system in a single hair-pore],[f] and (3) the subsisting nature [such as phenomena's emptiness of inherent existence]. It is done by way of believing in them and not contemplating other reasons for their being[g] like that.

Through positing six types in that way, the objects to be known by a yogi are limited to three—the meanings of utterances, the diverse objects of knowledge, and the mode [that is to say, *how* things are]. The first examination [examination concerning the meaning] is posited in terms of the first [the meanings of utterances]. The examination of things and examination of specific characteristics are posited in terms of the second [the diverse objects of knowledge]. The remaining three

[a] These are four analytical procedures.

[b] *ltos pa'i rigs pa, apekṣā-yukti.*

[c] *bya ba byed pa'i rigs pa, kārya-kāraṇa-yukti.*

[d] *'thad pas sgrub pa'i rigs pa, upapatti-sādhana-yukti.*

[e] *chos nyid kyi rigs pa, dharmatā-yukti.*

[f] This and the next bracketed additions are drawn from the *Four Interwoven Annotations,* vol.2, 738.6.

[g] In the dga' ldan shar rtse edition (491.6) read ***yin*** *pa'i rgyu mtshan* for ***min*** *pa'i rgyu mtshan* in accordance with the Sera Je Library edition (363.19) and the *Four Interwoven Annotations,* (vol. 2, 739.1).

[examination concerning classes, times, and reasonings] as well as examination of general characteristics are posited in terms of the third [the mode].

The approaches of the four special insights, which were described initially [namely, the four natures—differentiation observing the diversity that is thorough investigation, differentiation observing the diversity that is thorough analysis, intense differentiation observing the mode that is thorough investigation, and intense differentiation observing the mode that is thorough analysis], are said to be threefold [arisen from a sign, from thorough examination, and from individual investigation], and their modes of examination are said to be sixfold [examination concerning meaning, things, characteristics, classes, times, and reasonings]. Therefore, the three approaches and the six examinations are included in the former four [natures].

Asaṅga's *Grounds of Hearers* says that the four mental engagements[a] explained earlier [on the occasion of cultivating calm abiding], forcible engagement[b] and so forth [namely, interrupted engagement,[c] uninterrupted engagement,[d] and spontaneous engagement[e]], are common to both calm abiding and special insight. Therefore, special insight also involves the four mental engagements.[f]

How to cultivate special insight

This section has three parts: (1) showing the meaning of statements that special insight is cultivated in dependence on calm abiding, (2) from the viewpoint of which paths of which vehicle—great or small—this is the system, and (3) actual way to cultivating special insight in dependence on calm abiding.

---

[a] *yid la byed pa, manaskāra.* For discussion of these on the occasion of cultivating calm abiding, see Tsong-kha-pa, *Great Treatise,* vol. 3, 27-90, and Gedün Lodrö, *Calm Abiding and Special Insight,* 90-91.

[b] *sgrim ste 'jug pa, balavāhana.*

[c] *bar du chad cing 'jug pa, sacchidravāhana.*

[d] *chad pa med par 'jug pa, niśchidravāhana.*

[e] *lhun grub tu 'jug pa, anābhogavāhana.*

[f] In his 1972 lectures, the Dalai Lama explained that since one is now engaging in analytical meditation, problems and modes of procedure arise similar to those encountered during cultivation of calm abiding but in lesser form, such as not wanting to analyze and thus requiring forcible engagement, for instance.

Showing the meaning of statements that special insight is cultivated in dependence on calm abiding

The *Sūtra Unraveling the Thought*[a] says that having first achieved calm abiding, one should afterward cultivate special insight, and similarly many texts—such as those by the holy Maitreya, Asaṅga's *Grounds of Bodhisattvas,*[b] his *Grounds of Hearers,* Bhāvaviveka, Shāntideva, Kamalashīla's three works on the *Stages of Meditation,* Ratnākarashānti's *Quintessential Instructions on the Perfection of Wisdom,* and so forth—also say this.

The thought of these texts is not that first one generates calm abiding observing any object of observation but not the meaning of selflessness, and then the later sustaining [of calm abiding] within observing selflessness is special insight:

- because the two—calm abiding and special insight—are not differentiated by way of object of observation, and
- because Ratnākarashānti's *Quintessential Instructions on the Perfection of Wisdom* also explains that first one generates calm abiding within observing suchness—the emptiness of duality of apprehended object and apprehending subject—and later generates special insight through analytical meditation within observing that same object of observation, and
- because the Superior Asaṅga also describes a special insight observing the diversity and says that after having first generated calm abiding, in dependence on it [mundane] special insight is cultivated having the aspect of [viewing the lower level as] gross and [the upper level as] peaceful, and
- because Asaṅga moreover speaks of this [mundane special insight] as a path common to both non-Buddhists and Buddhists, as well as both common beings and Superiors.

Therefore, when one who has not earlier achieved calm abiding is newly achieving it, it is to be achieved within setting [the mind] one-pointedly on whatever the object of observation is. Except for this, [calm abiding] is not achievable within analyzing the object of observation in many ways. For if you do it the former way [within setting the mind one-pointedly on any object of observation], you will achieve calm abiding, whereas if you do it the latter way [within analyzing the

[a] Tibetan and English in Powers, *Wisdom of Buddha,* 150-153; Tibetan and French in Lamotte, *Saṃdhinirmocana Sūtra,* 89-90 and 210.

[b] *byang chub sems dpa'i sa, bodhisattvabhūmi;* Toh. 4037, *sems tsam,* vol. *dzi.*

object of observation in many ways], achievement is impossible.

When one who has first achieved calm abiding does not just extend the conditioning to mere stabilizing meditation as before but performs analytical meditation in which the object appropriate to the occasion—the mode or the diversity—is individually analyzed with wisdom, finally a special one-pointed meditative stabilization can be induced. Therefore, since the former [mode of mere stabilization] cannot induce a very powerful one-pointed meditative stabilization as achieved through analytical meditation, analytical meditation is praised.

Just that mode of achievement is how, in dependence on first having sought calm abiding, to cultivate special insight afterwards. Hence, it is the general reason for there being two different modes of procedure in calm abiding and special insight, even though the object of observation—selflessness, for instance—might be the same.

In particular, cultivation of special insight having the aspect of grossness/peacefulness—individually analyzing the faults of a lower realm and advantages of an upper realm[a]—and the cultivation of special insight having the aspect of selflessness, in which the meaning of selflessness is sustained within analysis through the wisdom of individual investigation, necessarily involve generation of strong and steady ascertainment. Consequently, they have great power with respect to abandoning their individual objects of abandonment.

Not only is there cultivation of special insight observing the diversity that has the aspect of grossness/peacefulness for the sake of abandoning the manifest afflictive emotions, but also, as is explained in Ratnākarashānti's *Quintessential Instructions on the Perfection of Wisdom,* there is analytical meditation thoroughly differentiating the character of the eighteen constituents.[b] Therefore, using this as an illustration you should understand that there are other special insights that involve meditation differentiating the objects comprising the diversity.

Ratnākarashānti's *Quintessential Instructions on the Perfection of Wisdom* explains that prior to generating calm abiding and special insight

[a] In brief, about this process, Gedün Lodrö (*Calm Abiding and Special Insight,* 231) says:

> For example, someone who is cultivating an actual absorption of the first concentration views the afflictive emotions pertaining to the Desire Realm as gross relative to the afflictive emotions of the Form Realm. The afflictive emotions of the Form Realm are also viewed as peaceful in comparison to those of the Desire Realm; other qualities of the Form Realm are seen as even more peaceful.

For a detailed and evocative description of the faults of the Desire Realm drawn from Gedün Lodrö's book, see the Appendix (363ff.).

[b] These are the six objects, six senses powers, and six consciousnesses.

observing the mode [emptiness], calm abiding and special insight on the ground [or level] of yoga observing the diversity is to be generated. However, here according to the assertions of Shāntideva, Kamalashīla, and so forth, first any calm abiding is generated and then special insight is generated, and they indicate that this, moreover, is just the special insight observing the mode.[a]

From the viewpoint of which paths of which vehicle, great or small, this is the system

Question: From the viewpoint of which vehicles—Great or Small and Sūtra or Mantra—is this the mode of serially generating calm abiding and special insight?

Answer: It is common to the two vehicles—that of the Hearers and Solitary Realizers and that of the Perfections—and moreover is common to the four schools of tenets,[b] and in my *Great Exposition of Secret Mantra* I have explained that the assertion of the individual tantras and their great commentators is that it is similar also for the three lower tantra sets within the Mantra [Vehicle].[c]

With respect to Highest Yoga [Mantra], Ratnākarashānti's *Quintessential Instructions on the Perfection of Wisdom*[d] explains that the three grounds of yoga—observing mind-only, observing suchness, and without appearance—taught in the *Descent into Laṅkā Sūtra:*[e]

[a] In his 1972 lectures, the Dalai Lama indicated that for those who have attained the stability of calm abiding, except for cultivating special insight observing emptiness, it is not necessary to cultivate special insight observing an upper realm as gross and a lower realm as peaceful. He added that for someone practicing Highest Yoga Tantra, cultivation of mundane special insight would be to stray into a diversionary path in that one would become separated from desire for the attributes of the desire realm, his point being that desire for the attributes of the desire realm is needed for certain levels of the completion stage.

[b] Great Exposition School, Sūtra School, Mind-Only School, and Middle Way School.

[c] For translations of the sections on Action Tantra and Performance Tantra see His Holiness the Dalai Lama, Tsong-kha-pa, and Jeffrey Hopkins, *Deity Yoga* (Ithaca, N.Y.: Snow Lion Publications, 1987); for Yoga Tantra see His Holiness the Dalai Lama, Tsong-kha-pa, and Jeffrey Hopkins, *Yoga Tantra: Paths to Magical Feats* (Ithaca, N.Y.: Snow Lion Publications, 2005).

[d] Toh. 4079, *sems tsam,* vol. *hi,* 161a.5-161b.1.

[e] Tsong-kha-pa quotes only the first two lines and indicates the rest by "and so forth." The Sanskrit, in Nanjio's *Laṅkāvatāra Sūtra,* 298-299, reads: *cittamātraṃ samāruhya bāhyamarthaṃ na kalpayet / tathatālambane sthitvā cittamātramatikramet // cittamātramatikramya nirābhāsamatikramet / nirābhāsasthito yogī mahāyānaṃ na paśyate //.* Toh. 107, *mdo sde,* vol. *ca,* 270a.1-270a.2.

Dol-po-pa Shay-rap-gyel-tsen (Hopkins, *Mountain Doctrine,* 236-237) cites this passage

> Relying on mind-only,
> One does not imagine external objects.
> Relying on non-appearance,
> One passes beyond mind-only.
>
> Relying on observing reality,
> One passes beyond non-appearance.
> If yogis dwell in non-appearance,
> They do not perceive the Great Vehicle.

are indicated even by the statement in the *Guhyasamāja Tantra:*[a]

> When one's own mind is analyzed,
> All phenomena dwell in one's own mind.
> These phenomena dwell as vajras of space.
> Phenomena and noumenon do not exist.

and it appears that he explains how to achieve calm abiding and special insight through stabilizing and analytical meditation on the first two grounds [of yoga] in the manner explained above. Therefore, he asserts that the way special insight observing the mode [that is, emptiness] is generated in the mental continuum is similar [in Highest Yoga Mantra and in the Perfection Vehicle].

Our own system is as follows: Even in the context of Highest Yoga [Mantra] the system of generating understanding of the view must be done in accordance with what occurs in the Middle Way texts. With respect to how it is sustained, on some occasions during states subsequent to meditative equipoise on the stages of generation and completion, one takes suchness to mind within analyzing it, but when those on the stage of completion who have attained the capacity to put penetrative focus on essential points in the body sustain suchness in meditative equipoise, although they definitely must meditate within setting [the mind] in the context of the view, they do not perform the analytical meditation of special insight as it occurs in other texts. Therefore, with respect to that occasion, do not posit analytical meditation as

---

to show that *Descent into Laṅkā Sūtra* teaches the Great Middle Way, which is beyond consciousness, as the finality of a three-staged teaching:

> Similarly, the *Descent into Laṅkā Sūtra* also says that, for the time being, one is taught mind-only, but finally having thoroughly passed beyond that, one is taught the middle without appearance, and that, having also passed beyond this, one is taught the middle with appearance, and it says that if one does not arrive at that, one has not seen the profound meaning of the Great Vehicle.

[a] XV.135; *gsang ba 'dus pa, guhyasamāja;* Toh. 442, *rgyud,* vol. *ca.* For the Sanskrit see Khangkar and Yorihito, 228 note 359.

one-pointed meditation on suchness from within the context of the view ancillary to[a] stabilizing [meditation].[b] Since it is not appropriate here to show clearly the reasons why doing such [stabilizing meditation that is one-pointed meditation on suchness performed within the context of the view in certain Highest Yoga Mantra practices] is sufficient, I will explain here the reasons for what is to be done on the other paths.

Actual way to cultivate special insight in dependence on calm abiding

If the view of selflessness is not found, no matter what system of meditation you perform, that meditation will not dwell in the meaning of suchness. Therefore, it is necessary to find the view.

If although you have understanding of the view, during meditation on suchness you do not meditate within being set in its context—not becoming mindful of it—such will not serve as meditation on suchness. Therefore, even to set [the mind] without contemplating anything at the end of first doing a little analysis of the view is not a sustaining of suchness. Even to become accustomed to a mere placement within the view upon becoming mindful of it is reduced to being just the way to sustain calm abiding explained earlier.[c] Therefore, such is not the meaning of texts describing the way to sustain special insight, which is distinct from that.

For this reason, within individually analyzing the meaning of selflessness by means of wisdom as explained before [when presenting the reasonings establishing selflessness], you should sustain [the view]. Moreover, if analytical meditation is solely done, the calm abiding generated earlier will degenerate. Therefore, having mounted the horse of calm abiding, you should sustain [the view] within analysis and then periodically alternate it with stabilizing meditation.

Furthermore, if due to too much analytical meditation stability lessens, you should perform more stabilizing meditation and reinstate the factor of stability. If due to too much stabilizing meditation you do not want to analyze or, despite analyzing, it is unworkable and the mind entirely goes into the factor of stability, you should perform more

---

[a] *zhar la.*

[b] One-pointed meditation on suchness from within the context of the view is stabilizing meditation, not analytical meditation. For discussion of Highest Yoga Mantra practices related with these topics, see Gedün Lodrö, *Calm Abiding and Special Insight*, 162-165.

[c] It is just stabilizing meditation as explained in the section on calm abiding.

analytical meditation. It is very powerful when [in this way] the two—calm abiding and special insight—are cultivated within continuously making them equal; therefore, you should do it this way. The last of Kamalashīla's [three works on the] *Stages of Meditation* says:[a]

> Moreover, when due to having cultivated special insight [too much], the wisdom [of individual analysis] becomes excessive, [the stability of] calm abiding diminishes. Due to this, like a butter-lamp set in a breeze, the mind fluctuates [and becomes unstable], whereby suchness is not seen very clearly. Therefore [in order to achieve stability seeing suchness clearly], at that time you should cultivate [just] the calm abiding [of non-analytical fixation]. Also, when [the stability of] calm abiding is excessive, you will, like a person asleep, not see suchness very clearly [due to the diminishment of individual analysis]. Therefore, at that time also you should cultivate the wisdom [of individual analysis].

With respect to sustaining [meditation] within analysis in this way, it is not correct to stop analytical meditation upon holding that all conceptuality whatsoever is apprehension of signs—that is, apprehension of true existence. For earlier[b] [I] have proven in many ways that conceptuality apprehending true existence is just one class of conceptuality. It is established that to regard that whatever conceptuality apprehends incurs the damage of reasoning is a deprecation in which the object of reasoned negation is excessive[c] and also is not the meaning of the scriptures. If with regard to other subjects you do not assert that whatever conceptuality apprehends incurs the damage of reasoning, but you think that whatever the mind apprehends with respect to the noumenon is a consciousness apprehending signs that is an adherence to true existence, this also is a fallacy in which the mode of estimation is faulty. All whatsoever apprehensions [about the noumenon] are not [apprehensions of true existence] because it is said that one of limited perspective[d] who is seeking release must inquire into suchness through

---

[a] Toh. 3917, *dbu ma*, vol. *ki*, 59b.2-59b.4; Giuseppe Tucci, *Minor Buddhist Texts, III*, Serie Orientale Roma 43 (Rome: Istituto Italiano per il Medio ed Estremo Oriente, 1971), 9. Brackets are from *Four Interwoven Annotations*, vol. 2, 801.1. Cited in *Great Treatise*, vol. 3, 352.

[b] See 57. Tsong-kha-pa is likely also referring to other texts where he has made this point; see 319ff.

[c] For thoroughgoing discussion of an overly broad object of negation, see Napper, *Dependent-Arising and Emptiness.*

[d] *tshur mthong;* 500.3. That is, someone who has not yet realized emptiness.

multiple approaches of scripture and reasoning.

Objection: Concerning this, if meditation on suchness is for the sake of generating the non-conceptual, it will not be generated from individual analysis because the two—cause and effect—must accord.

Answer: About this, the Supramundane Victor himself gave a clear answer; the *Kāshyapa Chapter* says:[a]

> Kāshyapa, it is thus: For example, from the rubbing together of two branches by the wind fire arises, and once arisen, the two branches are burned up. Similarly, Kāshyapa, if one has correct individual analysis [of things, through its force] a Superior's faculty of wisdom is generated. Through its generation correct individual analysis itself is consumed.

This says that a Superior's wisdom is generated from individual analysis.

Also, Kamalashīla's middle [of three works on the] *Stages of Meditation* says:[b]

> When analyzing in that way with wisdom, yogis [meditating on emptiness] definitely do not apprehend an inherent nature of anything [being analyzed] as ultimately [existing], they enter into meditative stabilization [of emptiness] not conceptualizing [that objects truly exist]. They also realize the naturelessness of all phenomena. The conceptualization [of true existence]—of those who do not cultivate individual analysis of the nature of things with wisdom but only cultivate just a mere thorough abandonment of mental application—will never be reversed, and they will never realize naturelessness because of not having the illumination of wisdom. It is thus: The Supramundane Victor said [in the *Kāshyapa Chapter*] that when the fire of knowing the real just as it is arises from correct individual analysis itself, the wood of conceptuality is burned, like the fire of sticks rubbed together.

---

[a] *'od srung gi le'u, kāśyapaparivarta;* Toh. 87, *dkon brtsegs,* vol. *cha,* 133a.7-133b.1; Tibetan and Chinese edited by Alexander von Staël-Holstein, *Kāçyapaparivarta: A Mahāyanasūtra of the Ratnakūṭa Class* (Shanghai: Commercial Press, 1926; reprint, Tokyo: Meicho-fukyū-kai, 1977), 102; Sanskrit of this passage not extant. Brackets are from *Four Interwoven Annotations,* vol. 2, 782.1. Cited in *Great Treatise,* vol. 3, 344.

[b] Toh. 3916, *dbu ma,* vol. *ki,* 49b.4-49b.6; see Geshe Lhundup Sopa, Elvin W. Jones, and John Newman, *The Stages of Meditation: Bhāvanākrama II* (Madison, Wisconsin: Deer Park Books, 1998) and Geshe Lobsang Jordhen, Lobsang Choephel Ganchenpa, and Jeremy Russell, *Stages of Meditation* (Ithaca, N.Y.: Snow Lion Publications, 2001). Brackets are from *Four Interwoven Annotations,* vol. 2, 782.4. Cited in *Great Treatise,* vol. 3, 344-345.

If such were not the case, then the arising of the uncontaminated from the contaminated, of the supramundane from the mundane, of a Buddha from a sentient being, or a Superior from a common being, and so forth, would not occur because of the dissimilarity of cause and effect.

Nāgārjuna's statement in the *Essay on the Mind of Enlightenment,*[a]

> How could emptiness be where
> Conceptuality has appeared?
> The Ones-Gone-Thus do not perceive
> Minds having the aspect of object analyzed and analyzer.
> Enlightenment is not present where
> Object of analysis and analyzer exist.

indicates that those who have apprehension of true existence with respect to object analyzed and analyzer have no attainment of enlightenment. For if it refuted the wisdom of individual analysis and refuted mere object analyzed and analyzer, it would contradict delineation of suchness in that text through many approaches of investigation in individual analysis, and if Buddhas did not perceive those two,[b] they would not exist.

Also, the statement in the same text,[c]

> One is not to meditate on the emptiness
> Called "non-production," "emptiness,"
> And "selflessness" that is meditated upon
> As having a low nature.

does not refute meditation observing selflessness—the emptiness that is the non-existence of inherently existent production—but refutes meditation on a low emptiness that has the low nature of being apprehended to truly exist. It is as Nāgārjuna's *Praise of the Supramundane* says:[d]

> When in order to remove all conceptuality
> The ambrosia of emptiness was taught,
> One who adheres to it [as truly existent]
> Is greatly derided by you.

---

[a] Stanzas 44cd-45; Lindtner, *Master of Wisdom,* 46-47, 172 (stanza 45): *na bodhyabodhakākāraṃ cittaṃ dṛṣṭaṃ tathāgataiḥ / yatra boddhā ca bodhyaṃ ca tatra bodhir na vidyate //.*

[b] That is, mere object analyzed and analyzer.

[c] Stanza 49; Lindtner, *Master of Wisdom,* 48.

[d] Stanza 23; Lindtner, *Master of Wisdom,* 8, 161: *sarvasaṃkalpanāśāya śūnyatāmṛtadeśanā / yasya tasyām api grāhas tvayāsāv avasāditaḥ //.*

Similarly, the statement also in Nāgārjuna's *Precious Garland,*[a]

> Thus neither self [inherent existence] nor non-self [absence of inherent existence]
> Are to be apprehended as real [that is, as inherently existent].
> Therefore the Great Subduer rejected
> Views of self and of non-self [as inherently existent].

means that since both self and selflessness are not established as [their own] reality, [Buddha] rejected views that those two really exist, but he did not refute the view of selflessness. For like the passage from Nāgārjuna's *Refutation of Objections* quoted earlier (94), if [phenomena] were not without an inherently established nature, [their] inherent establishment would exist.

The meaning of the statements:

- in the *Verse Summary of the Perfection of Wisdom:*[b]

  > Even if Bodhisattvas conceive, "This aggregate is empty," they are coursing in signs and do not have faith in the abode of [emptiness that is] the absence of [inherently existent] production.

- and in the Great Mothers [that is, Perfection of Wisdom Sūtras][c] that if one considers "Form is empty and selfless," one is coursing in signs and is not coursing in the perfection of wisdom.

is to be taken as holding emptiness and so forth to truly exist.

If that were not the case, it would even not be right for [Buddha to say just above] "they do not have faith in the abode of non-production" because to have faith in [the abode of the absence of production] also would be to course in signs, and it would contradict many statements:

---

[a] Stanza 103; Hopkins, *Nāgārjuna's Precious Garland,* 109 and corresponding Tibetan text in Part 3. Sanskrit in Hahn, *Nāgārjuna's Ratnāvalī,* 40 (stanza II.3): *naivam ātmā na cānātmā yāthābhūtyena labhyate / ātmānātmakṛte dṛṣṭī vavārāsmān mahāmuniḥ //.* Brackets are from *Four Interwoven Annotations,* vol. 2, 381.5. Last two lines cited in *Great Treatise,* vol. 3, 193.

[b] Stanza I.9cd; Toh. 13, vol. *ka* (*she rab sna tshogs*), 2a.6-2b.1; Sanskrit and Tibetan in Yuyama, *Saṃcaya-gāthā,* 10 and 160: *imi skandha śūnya parikalpayi bodhisattvo caratī nimitti anupāda-pade asakto //.* Conze, *Perfection of Wisdom in Eight Thousand Lines,* 10. Brackets are from *Four Interwoven Annotations,* vol. 2, 381.4. Cited in *Great Treatise,* vol. 3, 193.

[c] Khangkar and Yorihito (231 note 376) give the Sanskrit from the *Eight Thousand Stanza Perfection of Wisdom Sūtra. Four Interwoven Annotations,* vol. 2, 785.4. Similar statement in *Great Treatise,* vol. 3, 345.

- the same [*Verse Summary of the Perfection of Wisdom*] says:[a]

  Who thoroughly knows all phenomena as without inherent existence
  This one is coursing in the supreme perfection of wisdom.

- and:[b]

  When wisdom breaks down compounded and uncompounded phenomena [in general]
  As well as wholesome and unwholesome phenomena [in particular] and not even particles are observed.
  In [the conventions of] the world this comes to be counted as the perfection of wisdom.

- and the *King of Meditative Stabilizations Sūtra* also says:[c]

  If [upon having attained calm abiding] phenomena are individually analyzed as selfless
  And what has been analyzed is meditated upon,
  That is the cause of the fruit, attaining nirvāṇa.
  Peace [that is, nirvāṇa] is not [attained] through any other cause.

- and also in the *Heart of the Perfection of Wisdom Sūtra* Shāriputra asks,[d] "How should Bodhisattvas who wish to course in the

---

[a] Stanza I.28cd; Sanskrit and Tibetan in Yuyama, *Saṃcaya-gāthā*, 16 and 162: *prakṛti-asanta parijānayamāna dharmān eṣā sa prajña-vara-pāramitāya caryā //*. English translation in Conze, *Perfection of Wisdom in Eight Thousand Lines*, 12. *Four Interwoven Annotations*, vol. 2, 382.3. Cited in *Great Treatise*, vol. 3, 193.

[b] Stanza VII.3abc; Sanskrit and Tibetan in Yuyama, *Saṃcaya-gāthā*, 35-36 and 167: *yada dharma saṃskṛta-asaṃskṛta-kṛṣṇa-śuklā aṇu-mātru no labhati prajña vibhāvamānaḥ / tada prajña-pāramita gacchati saṃkhya loke*. English translation in Conze, *Perfection of Wisdom in Eight Thousand Lines*, 23. Brackets are from *Four Interwoven Annotations*, vol. 2, 787.2. Cited in *Great Treatise*, vol. 3, 346.

[c] Stanza IX.37; Toh. 127, *mdo sde*, vol. *da*, 27a.7-27b.1; Sanskrit, Tibetan, and English in Cristoph Cüppers, *The IXth Chapter of the Samādhirājasūtra*, Alt- und Neu-Indische Studien, 41 (Stuttgart: Franz Steiner Verlag, 1990), 53: *nairātmya dharmān yadi pratyavekṣate tāṃ pratyavekṣya yadi bhāvayeta / sa hetu nirvāṇaphalasya prāptaye ya anyahetū na sa bhoti śāntaye //*. The Tibetan is on p. 54, and English translation on p. 100. Brackets are from *Four Interwoven Annotations*, vol. 2, 21.5 and 142.1. Cited in *Great Treatise*, vol. 3, 23 and 108.

[d] *shes rab kyi pha rol tu phyin pa snying po, prajñāpāramitāhṛdaya;* Toh. 21, vol. ka (*shes rab sna tshogs*), 145a.4-145a.5. Sanskrit in Edward Conze, *Thirty Years of Buddhist Studies* (Columbia, S.C.: University of South Carolina Press, 1968), 149-150: *atha-āyuṣmāñc chāriputro buddha-anubhāvena ārya-avalokiteśvaraṃ bodhisattvaṃ mahāsattvam etad avocat / yaḥ kaścit kūlaputro vā kuladuhitā vā asyāṃ gambhīrāyāṃ prajñāpāramitāyāṃ caryāṃ cartukāmas tena*

> profound perfection of wisdom train?" And Avalokiteshvara replies, "They should thoroughly and correctly view even these five aggregates as empty of inherent existence."[a]

and so forth.

Therefore, in accordance with the statements in Nāgārjuna's *Praise of the Element of Attributes* (above, 101; see also *Illumination,* 211):[b]

> The doctrine supremely purifying the mind
> Is naturelessness [that is, the absence of inherent existence].

and (see also *Illumination,* 211):

> As long as "self" and "mine" are apprehended,
> So long is there [false] imputation of the external.
> When the two types of selflessness are seen,
> The seed of cyclic existence ceases.

and also the statement in Chandrakīrti's *Supplement to (Nāgārjuna's) "Treatise on the Middle"* (above, 73):[c]

> Therefore through the view of "I" and "mine" as empty [of inherent existence]
> A yogi [viewing such] will be released [from cyclic existence upon having abandoned all afflictive emotions conceptualizing inherent establishment].

you should understand this and should sustain the continuum of ascertainment of selflessness and the absence of inherent existence.

About this, the first of Kamalashīla's [three works on the] *Stages of Meditation* says that even the statements in scriptures to abandon the apprehension of signs through meditatively cultivating the absence of mental application are in consideration of:

---

kathaṃ śikṣitavyam / evam ukta ārya-avalokiteśvaro bodhisattvo mahāsattvo āyuṣmantaṃ śāriputram etad avocat / yaḥ kaścic chāriputra kulaputro vā kuladuhitā vā asyāṃ gambhīrāyāṃ prajñāpāramitāyāṃ caryāṃ cartukāmas tenaivaṃ vyavalokitavyam / pañcaskandhās tāṃś ca svabhāva-śūnyān paśyati sma. Four Interwoven Annotations, vol. 2, 382.1. Cited in *Great Treatise,* vol. 3, 193.

[a] For the context of this citation, see His Holiness the Dalai Lama, *How To Practice: The Way to a Meaningful Life,* 159-165; and Donald S. Lopez Jr., *The Heart Sūtra Explained* (Albany, N.Y.: State University of New York Press, 1988), 49-56.

[b] Toh. 1118, *bstod tshogs,* vol. *ka,* 64b.5 and 66a.3-66a.4.

[c] Stanza VI.165cd; Toh. 3861, *dbu ma,* vol. *'a,* 212a.7; La Vallée Poussin, *Madhyamakāvatāra,* 287.18-287.19; La Vallée Poussin, "*Introduction au traité du milieu,*" *Muséon* 12 (1911): 328. Brackets are from *Four Interwoven Annotations,* vol. 2, 681.6. Cited in *Great Treatise,* vol. 3, 193 and 307-308.

- realizing—through analysis by way of the proper analytical wisdom—the non-apprehension of even a particle of the target of the apprehension of true existence and
- setting in meditative equipoise on the meaning realized.

He says:[a]

> Also, the statement in the *Non-Conceptual Retention Sūtra,*[b] "Through not performing mental application, the signs of forms and so forth [these being adherences to phenomena as truly existent] are abandoned" is in consideration that when you analyze with wisdom, you should not take to mind that which is unobservable [and non-established in the perspective of that analysis] in that manner [as truly existent]. It does not [at all] mean that [you remain in] a mere absence of mental application [in general]. This is not an abandonment through merely having forsaken mental application [by stopping taking to mind] the adherence to forms and so forth [as truly existent that has operated] since beginningless time, like that of one in the meditative absorption of non-discrimination [who cannot at all abandon adherence to forms and so forth as truly existent although being without mental application].

Moreover, the middle [of Kamalashīla's three works on the] *Stages of Meditation* says:[c]

> [The *Cloud of Jewels Sūtra* says,[d]] "When they examine the mind [that scatters to objects], they realize it as [only] empty [of inherent existence]. When they also examine the nature of the mind that realizes [that the places to which the mind scatters and the scattering mind are empty of inherent existence], they

---

[a] Toh. 3915, *dbu ma,* vol. *ki,* 34a.2-34a.4; Tucci, *Minor Buddhist Texts I,* 212 and 261: *yat punar uktam avikalpapraveśadhāraṇyāṃ amanasikārato rūpādinimittaṃ varjayatīti / tatrāpi prajñayā nirūpayato yo 'nupalambhaḥ sa tatrāmanasikāro 'bhipreto na manasikārābhāvamātram / na hy asaṃjñisamāpattyādir iva anādikāliko rūpādyabhiniveśo manasikāraparivarjanamātrāt prahīyate /.* Brackets are from *Four Interwoven Annotations,* vol. 2, 795.5. Cited in *Great Treatise,* vol. 3, 348-349.

[b] *rnam par mi rtog par 'jug pa'i gzungs, avikalpapraveśanāmadhāraṇī;* Toh. 142, *mdo sde,* vol. *pa.*

[c] Toh. 3916, *dbu ma,* vol. *ki,* 49b.7-50a.2. Brackets are from *Four Interwoven Annotations,* vol. 2, 776.6. Cited in *Great Treatise,* vol. 3, 342-343.

[d] *dkon mchog sprin gyi mdo, ratnameghasūtra;* Toh. 231, *mdo sde,* vol. *wa,* 92a.5. Just prior to this quote, the sūtra says, "When they examine the nature of the abodes [or objects] to which the mind scatters and takes delight, they realize that [those objects] are [only] empty [of inherent existence]."

> realize it [also] as empty [of inherent existence]. Through realizing in that way [that those are empty of inherent existence], they enter the yoga of [emptiness that is] without [the proliferations of] the signs [of the apprehension of inherent existence and so forth]." This indicates that just those who [meditate by way of] previously analyzing [phenomena with reasoning] enter into signlessness. It most clearly indicates that through [meditation] merely abandoning mental application and without analyzing the nature of things with wisdom, entry into non-conceptuality does not [at all] occur.

[Kamalashīla] says that the statement thus in the *Cloud of Jewels Sūtra* explains that if one does not find the view of suchness through prior analysis in the proper way, non-conceptual entry into the meaning of suchness does not occur.

Also, it is very important to understand through the explanations in the last [of Kamalashīla's three works on the] *Stages of Meditation* how to refute the Chinese master who propounded that suchness can be realized through setting in meditative equipoise without taking anything at all to mind but the view ascertaining suchness cannot be gained in dependence upon scripture and reasoning. With regard to the [sūtra] statements [that the ultimate] is inconceivable, beyond the mind, and so forth, [Kamalashīla] explains that:[a]

1. In order to refute claims that the profound meaning [of emptiness] can be realized merely through hearing and thinking, it is taught that because those are objects known by a Superior's own individual [meditative equipoise], they are inconceivable **by others** [namely, hearing and thinking], and so forth.
2. These were spoken for the sake of refuting improper contemplation

[a] This is a paraphrase of Toh. 3917, *dbu ma*, vol. *ki*, 63b.7-64a.4; Tucci, *Minor Buddhist Texts, III*, 18-19. The full quote is:

> *de ltar gang dang gang du bsam gyis mi khyab pa la sogs pa'i tshig thos na de dang der thos pa dang bsam pa tsam kho nas de kho na rtogs par gang dag sems pa de dag gi mngon pa'i nga rgyal dgag pa'i phyir chos rnams so so rang gis rig par bya ba nyid du bstan par byed do/ /tshul bzhin ma yin pa'i sems pa yang dgag par byed par khong du chud par bya'i/ yang dag par so sor rtog pa de dgag par ni ma yin no/ /de lta ma yin na rigs pa dang lung shin tu mang po dang 'gal bar 'gyur ro zhes sngar bshad pa bzhin no/ /yang thos pa dang bsam pa las byung ba'i shes rab kyis rtogs pa gang yin pa de nyid bsgom pa las byung ba'i shes rab kyi bsgom par bya'i/ gzhan du ni ma yin te/ rta dkyus kyi sa bstan nas rgyug pa bzhin no/ /de lta bas na yang dag par so sor brtag par bya'o/ /de rnam par rtog pa'i ngo bo nyid yin du zin kyang tshul bzhin du yid la byed pa'i ngo bo nyid yin pa'i phyir de las rnam par mi rtog pa'i ye shes 'byung bar 'gyur pas na ye shes de 'dod pas de la brten par bya'o/*

upon apprehending the meaning of the profound [emptiness] to truly exist, but they do not refute proper mental application by means of the wisdom of individual analysis.

3. If such [proper mental application by means of the wisdom of individual analysis] were refuted, it would contradict a great many reasonings and scriptures.
4. [Individual analysis] is an entity of conceptuality, but because it is an entity of proper mental application, non-conceptual pristine wisdom arises [from it], and consequently since one wants that pristine wisdom, one should rely on it.

These ways of meditation occur in earlier guiding-advice on the stages of the path, such as Po-to-wa's[a] *Small Vessel:*[b]

Some say during hearing and thinking
To delineate the absence of inherent existence through reasoning
And when meditating to cultivate only the non-conceptual.
In that case, because an unrelated emptiness
Is meditated separately, it will not serve as an antidote.
Therefore, even during meditation
Analyze individually with whatever you are familiar—
The lack of being one or many, dependent-arising, and so forth—
And stay a little also [on the meaning investigated] within non-conceptuality [without analyzing].
If you meditate in this way,
It is the antidote to the afflictive emotions.
The system of meditatively cultivating wisdom
By those wishing to follow the Sole Deity [Atisha] and by those
Wishing to course in the system of the perfections is this.
Moreover, one who has [initially] familiarized with the selflessness of persons
Should then enter [into the selflessness of phenomena] in such [a way].

[a] *po to ba rin chen gsal* (1027/31-1105), a student of Atisha's chief disciple Drom-tön-pa (*'brom ston pa*).

[b] *be'u bum*. See dge bshes po to ba sogs, *gangs can rig brgya'i sgo 'byed lde mig (deb bcu drug pa)—bka gdams be'u bum sngon po'i rtsa 'grel* (mi rigs dpe skrun khang, 1991), 28, this being the sayings of *dge bshes po to ba,* which likely was arranged by *dol po shes rab rgya mtsho* (1059-1131) with a commentary by *lha 'bri sgang pa.* Thanks to Dr. Amy Sims Miller for the above. Brackets are from *Four Interwoven Annotations,* vol. 2, 804.1. Cited in *Great Treatise,* vol. 3, 353.

About this moreover, the Elder [Atisha] says [in his *Introduction to the Two Truths*]:[a]

> Who realized emptiness?
> Nāgārjuna, who was prophesied by the One-Gone-Thus
> And saw the noumenal truth;
> The student [of Nāgārjuna who realized his thought exactly as it is] is Chandrakīrti.
> Through quintessential instructions transmitted
> From him the noumenal truth will be realized.

Also, with regard to the mode of instruction [I] have expanded on what appear to be similar in the two, [Atisha's] statements in the manner of Middle Way guiding-advice and the thought of the master Kamalashīla.

For sustaining special insight you should know how to observe the six preparatory practices,[b] how to sustain the actual session and its conclusion, how to act between sessions, and especially how to sustain the session free from laxity and excitement as explained before.[c]

Measure of having established special insight through meditative cultivation

When you have meditated in that way analyzing by way of the wisdom of individual analysis, up to the point prior to generating the pliancies described earlier[d] it is a similitude of special insight. Then the pliancies

---

[a] *bden gnyis la 'jug pa, satyadvayāvatāra,* stanza 14; P5380, 7b.2-7b.3; Toh. 3902, *dbu ma,* vol. *a,* 72b.4-72b.5; Tibetan and English in Richard Sherburne, *The Complete Works of Atīśa* (New Delhi: Aditya Prakashan, 2000), 354-355. Brackets are from *Four Interwoven Annotations,* vol. 2, 805.5. Cited in *Great Treatise,* vol. 3, 353.

[b] See Geshe Lhundup Sopa and Jeffrey Hopkins, *Cutting through Appearances: The Practice and Theory of Tibetan Buddhism* (Ithaca, N.Y.: Snow Lion Publications, 1989), 19-23, 46-64.

[c] These were explained in the section on calm abiding prior to the discussion of special insight, and thus are not translated here. For teachings by His Holiness the Dalai Lama based on that exposition, see *How to See Yourself As You Really Are,* Part Three, 85-120.

[d] The mental and physical pliancies are described in the section on calm abiding earlier in the *Medium-Length Exposition of the Stages of the Path to Enlightenment;* for his even more extensive treatment of the pliancies, see Tsong-kha-pa, *Great Treatise,* vol. 3, 80-86. For a thoroughgoing discussion of the pliancies see Gedün Lodrö, *Calm Abiding and Special Insight,* 96ff. In brief, as His Holiness the Dalai Lama says in *How to See Yourself As You Really Are* (pp.116-117) about mental and physical pliancy, or flexibility:

> First, your brain feels heavy, though not in an unpleasant way. Also, a tingly sensation is felt at the top of the head, like the feeling of a warm hand put on top of the head after it has been shaved. This is a sign that the *mental flexibility* that removes mental dysfunctions preventing completely easy meditative fo-

having been generated, it is fully qualified special insight. The entities and modes of generating the pliancies are as explained earlier. Moreover, because one even has the pliancy induced by calm abiding that has already been achieved and has not deteriorated, [the achievement of special insight] is not the mere presence of pliancy.

Question: Then, what is it?

Answer: When the power of having performed analytical meditation itself is able to induce pliancy, it then becomes special insight. This is the same for both special insight observing the diversity and special insight observing the mode [of being of phenomena]. Furthermore, in that way the *Sūtra Unraveling the Thought* says:[a]

> "Supramundane Victor, until a Bodhisattva has attained physical and mental pliancy [induced through the power of analysis], what is the mental contemplation—that is an internal taking to mind of an image, an object of meditative stabilization, of those

cus is about to be generated. It is a mental lightness generated only from meditation when the mind happily stays on its object.

This mental flexibility causes a favorable energy to circulate throughout the body, thereby producing *physical flexibility* removing all physical awkwardness and dysfunction producing fatigue that leads to a lack of enthusiasm for meditation. Your body feels light like cotton. This physical flexibility immediately engenders a *bliss of physical flexibility*, a feeling of comfort pervading the body. Now you can use your body in virtuous activities in accordance with your wish.

This physical pleasure leads to mental pleasure, called "bliss of mental flexibility," making the mind full of joy that initially is a little too buoyant, but then gradually becomes more steady. At this juncture you attain an *unfluctuating flexibility*. This marks the attainment of true calm abiding. Prior to this, you just have a similitude of calm abiding.

With fully qualified calm abiding, your mind is powerfully concentrated enough to purify destructive emotions when it is joined with insight. When you enter into meditative equipoise, mental and physical flexibility are quickly generated, and it is as if your mind is mixed with space itself. Leaving meditation, your body is like new to you, and aspects of mental and physical flexibility remain. Outside of meditation your mind is firm like a mountain and so clear that it seems you could count the particles in a wall, and you have fewer counter-productive emotions, being mostly free from desire for pleasant sights, sounds, odors, tastes, and touches, as well as free from harmful intent, lethargy, sleepiness, excitement, contrition, and doubt. Also, sleep easily turns into meditation, in which you have many wonderful experiences.

[a] Toh. 106, *mdo sde,* vol. *ca,* 26b.7-27a.1; Tibetan and English in Powers, *Wisdom of Buddha,* 152 and 153; Tibetan and French in Lamotte, *Saṃdhinirmocana Sūtra,* 90 and 211. Brackets are from *Four Interwoven Annotations,* vol. 2, 808.1. Cited in *Great Treatise,* vol. 3, 354.

> phenomena that have been contemplated [and analyzed] well—called?"
>
> "Maitreya, it is not special insight; it should be said that it is [a mental contemplation that] is associated with determined attention[a] that is a similitude of special insight."

and Ratnākarashānti's *Quintessential Instructions on the Perfection of Wisdom* also says:[b]

> Abiding in just that attainment of physical and mental pliancy [induced by calm abiding], they individually analyze the meaning of just what was contemplated through determined attention to the object, which is an internal image of meditative stabilization. As long as physical and mental pliancy [induced through the power of analysis] are not generated, [this analytical meditation] is a mental contemplation that is a similitude of special insight. When those [pliancies] are generated, it is special insight.

When the power of [analysis] itself is able to induce pliancy, it is also able to induce one-pointedness of mind. Therefore, this inducing of calm abiding through analytical meditation of individual analysis by its own power is a quality of previously having achieved calm abiding.

Since in that way calm abiding becomes far more developed through analytical meditation performed by one who has already achieved calm abiding well, you should not hold onto thinking that if analytical meditation of individual analysis is performed, the factor of stability will diminish.

How calm abiding and special insight are unified[c]

If calm abiding and special insight are not attained as they were described above at the point of [discussing] the measure of their establishment, there will be nothing to be unified. Therefore, those two must definitely be attained in order for them to be unified.

Concerning this, from the start of attaining special insight a union [of calm abiding and special insight] is attained. Hence, with regard to

---

[a] *mos pa;* 510.1.

[b] Toh. 4079, *sems tsam,* vol. *hi,* 154b.6-154b.7. Brackets are from *Four Interwoven Annotations,* vol. 2, 809.5. Cited in *Great Treatise,* vol. 3, 354.

[c] This is the third of three topics: how to train in calm abiding, how to train in special insight, and how calm abiding and special insight are unified.

how this is done: When, through the force of having performed analytical meditation in dependence on calm abiding [gained] earlier, one attains the mental activity of natural engagement[a] without the activity [of applying antidotes to laxity and excitement] as was explained earlier in the section on calm abiding, it becomes a union. As [indicated in the following two citations, the attainment of a union of calm abiding and special insight] is from the point of attaining fully qualified special insight:

- Asaṅga's *Grounds of Hearers* says:[b]

> *Question:* Concerning this, at what point are calm abiding and special insight mixed and equalized, and why is it called a "path of unification" [of those two]?
> *Answer:* It is by way of the nine mental abidings. It is thus: In dependence upon having thoroughly established the meditative stabilization [of calm abiding induced by] having attained the ninth [mental abiding called] "equipoise," one [repeatedly performs analytical meditation by way of making] intense effort at higher wisdom differentiating phenomena. At that time the path of the differentiation of phenomena comes to [continuously] operate naturally and without exertion, and similar to [when] the path of calm abiding [was attained] there is no activity [of exertion[c]]. Due to this, special insight is conjoined with thorough purity [from laxity and excitement], thorough refinement [without any discomfort or unserviceability], subsequence to calm abiding [that is to say, one-pointed stability like calm abiding], and blissful experience [due to having generated pliancy induced by the power of analysis]. Thereby, the two, calm abiding and special insight, become mixed and operate equally, and this is called the path of unification of calm abiding and special insight.

- and the last of Kamalashīla's [three works on the] *Stages of Meditation* also says:[d]

> You should know that when [your mind] is set in equipoise

[a] *rang gis ngang gis 'jug pa;* 511.3.

[b] Toh. 4036, *sems tsam,* vol. *dzi,* 148b.4-148b.7. Brackets are from *Four Interwoven Annotations,* vol. 2, 819.5. Cited in *Great Treatise,* vol. 3, 358.

[c] This is the exertion of applying the antidotes to laxity and excitement.

[d] Toh. 3917, *dbu ma,* vol. *ki,* 59b.1-59b.2; Tucci, *Minor Buddhist Texts, III,* 9. Brackets are from *Four Interwoven Annotations,* vol. 2, 821.3. Cited in *Great Treatise,* vol. 3, 358.

> due to being devoid of laxity and excitement [through having analytically meditated well with wisdom] and is naturally operating whereby a very clear [and unfluctuating] mind arises with respect to suchness and you abide in equanimity through loosening exertion,[a] the path of a union of calm abiding and special insight has at that time been [attained and] established.

Also, Ratnākarashānti's *Quintessential Instructions on the Perfection of Wisdom* says:[b]

> After [accustoming to individual analysis within calm abiding], when—observing just the image that is being analyzed—[calm abiding is induced] through the continuum of mental engagement of unsevered continuous [attention to the object of observation] and uninterrupted [force of analytical meditation, and] both [calm abiding and special insight] are experienced [in equal strength] in that very mind, this is called a "path of a union[c] of calm abiding and special insight." Concerning that, calm abiding and special insight are the pair; joining means possession, that is, operating within mutual bonding [that is to say, depending on and influenced by each other such that calm abiding operates like special insight and special insight operates like calm abiding].

In that, "uninterrupted" means that [the power of] analytical meditation itself [at the point of attaining special insight] induces the non-conceptuality [of calm abiding], without needing to set aside the run of that analytical meditation itself and to stabilize in non-conceptuality.

"Both are experienced" means that both calm abiding observing the unanalyzed image and special insight observing the image along with analysis are experienced. "Through the continuum" is in reference to the fact that analytical special insight and the calm abiding that is a stabilizing **at the end** of analysis do not arise simultaneously, but at the time of the calm abiding that is the actual one induced through the power of analysis, special insight—intense differentiation of phenomena observing the mode [of being of phenomena]—and calm abiding, which is the meditative stabilization of one-pointed steady abiding on

[a] That is to say, you cease the exertion involved in applying the antidotes to laxity and excitement.

[b] Toh. 4079, *sems tsam*, vol. *hi*, 154b.7-155a.2. Brackets are from *Four Interwoven Annotations*, vol. 2, 822.4. Cited in *Great Treatise*, vol. 3, 358.

[c] *zung du 'brel*, literally, "joining as a pair."

the mode, operate in mutual association. At such a time, calm abiding and special insight are mixed; they operate equally.

For this, realization that is a state arisen from meditation must be attained. Therefore, a composite of the two—the suitability of (1) individually analyzing the meaning of selflessness within the non-destruction of the influence of (2) non-conceptuality that is the steady factor of abiding, these being like the small fish [of analysis] moving about while staying in the unmoving water [of mental stability]—is posited as a **similitude** of calm abiding and special insight. Except for [being a similitude], such a composite does not have the meaning of a union of actual calm abiding and special insight.

You should understand how calm abiding and special insight are unified in that way according to what appears in reliable texts and not put confidence in explanations that make superimpositions in other ways. Reasoned final decisions, scriptural sources, and modes of cultivation concerning the stages of the path to enlightenment should be known in extensive form from my *Great Exposition of the Stages of the Path.*

11. The Way

Now [I] will set forth a brief summation of the general path.[a] Initially, the root of the path derives from reliance on a spiritual guide; hence, it should be carefully taken to heart. Then, [a purpose of relying on a spiritual guide is] to generate a non-artificial wish to extract the essence with respect to the leisure [already gained in this human lifetime], and when this is generated, it will urge you to continual practice from within. Hence, in order to generate it you should meditate on the topics concerning leisure and fortune.[b]

Then, [a purpose of being urged on to continual practice from within is] to reverse the attitude of seeking the purposes of this lifetime and to seek the purposes of future lives. Hence] if you do not reverse the attitude of seeking the purposes of this lifetime, a strong seeking of the purposes of future lives will not arise, and therefore you should strive at meditating on impermanence—the fact that the gained [human] body will not last long [and how the time of death is indefinite and how when dying nothing helps except religious practice]—and at meditating on how you will [have to] wander in bad transmigrations upon dying [making this inference from your karmic predispositions over beginningless lives and from your actions in this lifetime]. Since at that time a genuine attitude mindful of the frights [of bad transmigrations] will be generated [through the power of meditatively cultivating that attitude], you should from the depths of the heart generate ascertainment with respect to the qualities of the three refuges [that are capable of protecting you from those frights—that is, the qualities of exalted body, speech, and mind and, in particular, knowledge, sympathy, and power—] and should dwell in the vow of common refuge and train in its precepts.

Then [like the fact that one must ingest medicine as an antidote to a disease, it is necessary to perform the practices that are the antidotes to those frights—these being to abandon nonvirtues in order to prevent bad transmigrations and to achieve virtues in order to attain happy transmigrations. Thus] from many approaches you should generate the faith of conviction in actions and their effects—this being the basis for all wholesome practices. Having made that faith firm, you should do whatever you can to strive at engaging in [the ten] virtues and

[a] This summation is in *Great Treatise*, vol. 3, 361-363, with slight variations. Brackets are from *Four Interwoven Annotations*, vol. 2, 827.4-836.1.

[b] See *Great Treatise*, vol. 1, 117ff.

disengaging from [the ten] non-virtues and enact continual engagement in the path of the four powers [in order to purify previously committed nonvirtues].[a]

When in that way the topics of practice by a being of small capacity have been internalized firmly, you should frequently contemplate the faults of cyclic existence in general and in particular [concerning the entire range from the peak of cyclic existence to the most torturous hell by way of reflecting on such topics as how there is no happiness even in high states within cyclic existence, thereby generating discouragement with it], and [strive at] turning your mind away from cyclic existence in its entirety as much as possible. Then [since if you to not want cyclic existence, you need to abandon its causes, you should investigate] the causes from which cyclic existence arises, identifying karma and afflictive emotions [as those causes], and thereupon generate a non-artificial wish to abandon them. [Induced by such an attitude] strive at the three trainings[b] in general—the paths of release from cyclic existence—and in particular at the (vow of) individual liberation that you have taken [since it is the foundation of all trainings].

When in that way the topics of practice by a being of medium capacity have been internalized firmly, you also should take to mind [transmigrating beings—your kind] mothers who have fallen into the ocean of cyclic existence [undergoing limitless suffering] just as you have and are undergoing such [a state]. Doing this, train in the altruistic intention to become enlightened [having the aspect of wishing to attain perfect enlightenment for the sake of others' welfare], which has as its roots the love [of cherishing them induced by recognizing them as your mothers, becoming mindful of their kindness, and developing an intention to reciprocate their kindness] and the compassion [that is a bearing the burden of others' welfare yourself, induced by the power of that love]. You must strive to generate [the altruistic intention to become enlightened] as much as you can, for without it the six perfections, the two stages [of generation and completion in Mantra], and so forth are like trying to [erect many] stories [of a building] lacking a foundation. When a little experience is generated with respect to it, assume it through the rite [of the aspirational mind of enlightenment], striving at its training-precepts [that are for not losing it and increasing it], making the aspirational attitude as [developed and] steady as

[a] See ibid., 209ff. and 247ff.; and Jeffrey Hopkins, *Cultivating Compassion* (New York: Broadway Books, 2001), 53-59.

[b] See His Holiness the Dalai Lama, *How to Practice: The Way to a Meaningful Life,* 21ff., and Tsong-kha-pa, *Great Treatise,* vol. 1, 341ff.

you can.

Then, listen [to sūtras, commentaries, quintessential instructions, and so forth teaching] about the great waves of [Bodhisattva] deeds and generate [unconfused, proper] understanding of the boundaries of what to disengage from and what to engage in [with respect to the Bodhisattva deeds], engendering a wish to train in them. When that is generated, through the rite take the vow to practice [the Bodhisattva deeds]. Train in [all the points of training of the Bodhisattva deeds,] the six perfections,[a] which ripen your own continuum, and in the four means of gathering [students][b] and so forth, which ripen others' continuums. In particular risk even your life [to avoid] the root infractions [of the Bodhisattva vows]. Strive at not being polluted by the lesser and medium contaminations and [other] faults; even if [powerlessly] polluted by such [because of too many afflictive emotions and so on, do not disregard it but] work at restoration.

Then, since you must train in particular in the latter two perfections [of concentration and of wisdom, or calm abiding and special insight]:

- become skilled in how to sustain concentration and achieve the meditative stabilization [of calm abiding], and
- understand (1) how to gain the view [of the middle] upon generating in your continuum—as much as you can—the pure view of the two selflessnesses [of persons and of other phenomena] and (2) how to sustain it within setting [the mind] in the context of the view. Thereupon, sustain [the continuum of the view].

Such concentration and wisdom are designated with the names of calm abiding and special insight, which, since they are not separate from those two, fall within the precepts of training of the Bodhisattva vow once it has been taken.

---

[a] Giving, ethics, patience, effort, concentration, and wisdom.

[b] As Nāgārjuna says in the *Precious Garland of Advice* (stanza 133), the four modes of gathering students are by way of giving gifts, giving doctrine, teaching others to fulfill their aims, and oneself acting according to that teaching:

> You should cause the assembling
> Of the religious and the worldly
> Through giving, speaking pleasantly,
> Purposeful behavior, and concordant behavior.

"Giving" means to give material things; "speaking pleasantly" is to converse on the topics of high status and definite goodness; "purposeful behavior" is to cause others to practice what is beneficial; "concordant behavior" is for one to practice what one teaches others. See Hopkins, *Nāgārjuna's Precious Garland*, 113.

About these [modes of practice ranging from relying on a spiritual guide to calm abiding and special insight] moreover, it should be such that when meditatively cultivating the lower paths, the wish to attain the higher paths increases, and when hearing [from others] about the higher [paths such as the functions and so forth of special insight], the wish to achieve the lower increases. Also, when those are cultivated in meditation, you need [to achieve all the lower, intermediate, and higher] attitudes in a balanced way, having become skilled[a] in examining [what is needed for any specific path. With regard to how to achieve them in a balanced way:]

- If it appears that you are less intent [on the ways to rely] on the spiritual guide leading you on the path [than you are on other practices], then since the root of the collections [for achieving] good [fruits in this and future lives] is severed, you should strive at [the topics concerning] how to rely [on a spiritual guide].
- Similarly, if you have little force of enthusiasm for achievement in practice, mainly work at meditating on the topics of leisure and fortune.
- If you come to have great attachment to this life, mainly work at meditating on impermanence and the faults of bad transmigrations.
- If it appears that you are neglecting the ethical formulations that you have accepted, mainly work at meditating on actions and their effects.
- If you have little discouragement about cyclic existence, then since your seeking liberation has come to be merely verbal, contemplate the faults of cyclic existence [from all points of view].
- If it appears that you do not have a strong force of mind making everything you do be for the sake of sentient beings, then since the root of the Great Vehicle has been severed, train in the aspirational mind of enlightenment together with its causes.
- If even when, upon taking the Bodhisattva vows, you train in the [Bodhisattva] deeds, it appears that you have the fetters of apprehensions of signs [that is, apprehensions of inherent existence which are contrary to special insight] in strong force, with a rational consciousness break down the target of the apprehension of signs and train in [the two emptinesses,] the emptiness that is like space [in that it is a vacuity that is a mere negative of the object of negation] and [in states subsequent to meditative equipoise the

[a] This edition (516.6) reads *spyang* as does the *Four Interwoven Annotations,* vol. 2, 833.6.

emptiness that is] like a magician's illusions [in that it is a composite of appearance and emptiness].

- If it appears that your mind is not staying on its object of observation and has become a servant of distraction, mainly train in the factor of one-pointed stability [generating mindfulness and introspection and exertion].

This is what the earlier [lamas of these stages of the path] said.

Using those as illustrations you should also understand with regard to those that have not been mentioned [how to make equal whatever have become weaker]. In brief, without allowing [factors of the path] to become partial, your [mental] continuum should be serviceable in all virtuous directions.

THE OBJECT OF NEGATION

From Tsong-kha-pa Lo-sang-drak-pa's
Extensive Explanation of (Chandrakīrti's) "Supplement to (Nāgārjuna's) 'Treatise on the Middle'": Illumination of the Thought

Commentary near the beginning of chapter six

1. Importance of Identifying What Is Negated in Emptiness

How the meaning of reality is explained through scripture

This section has two parts: stating how reality is set out in scripture and identifying what is discordant with knowing suchness.

Stating how reality is set out in scripture

The *Sūtra on the Ten Grounds* says:[a]

> When fifth grounders enter the sixth ground, they do so by way of the ten samenesses of phenomena. What are the ten? (1) All phenomena are the same in being signless; (2) all phenomena are the same in being characterless, likewise in (3) being productionless, (4) non-produced, (5) void, (6) pure from the very beginning, (7) without proliferations, and (8) non-adopted and non-discarded; and (9) all phenomena are the same in being like a magician's illusions, dreams, optical illusions, echoes, moons in water, reflections, and emanations; and (10) all phenomena are the same in being without the duality of effective things and non-effective things. When in that way they thoroughly realize the nature of all phenomena, through sharp and concordant forbearance they attain the sixth Bodhisattva ground, the Manifest.[b]

The word "likewise" [means that] "all phenomena" is to be applied up to [the eighth which is the sameness in being] non-adopted and non-discarded. [With regard to how the list is taken as ten samenesses] those two samenesses [of being non-adopted and non-discarded] are taken as one, and the seven samenesses of being like an illusion, and so

---

[a] *mdo sde sa bcu pa, daśabhūmikasūtra,* chapter VI; P761.31, vol. 25; cited in Chandrakīrti's *Commentary on the "Supplement to (Nāgārjuna's) 'Treatise on the Middle,'"* commenting on stanza VI.7; Toh. 3862, *dbu ma,* vol. *'a;* La Vallée Poussin, *Madhyamakāvatāra,* 80.10-81.3; La Vallée Poussin, "*Introduction au traité du milieu,*" *Muséon* 11 (1910): 278.

[b] None of the material after this quote up to the two truths section is found in Chandrakīrti's text. Chandrakīrti directly proceeds to the refutation of inherently existent production, whereas Tsong-kha-pa has a long excursus on the object negated in the view of selflessness in the Middle Way Schools.

forth, are taken as one sameness, and the last two [the sameness of being without the duality of things and non-things] are taken as one.

With respect to the identification of the ten samenesses, even [Vasubandhu's] *Commentary on the "Sūtra on the Ten Grounds"*[a] and Asaṅga's *Bodhisattva Grounds*[b] do not appear to agree. Because these two [texts] do not accord with the mode of commenting on emptiness in this [Middle Way Consequence] system, [the ten samenesses] are to be explained differently here.

Concerning this, the first sameness is that all phenomena are similar in that appearances of [their] dissimilar characteristics [such as white, red, and so forth][c] do not exist in the perspective of a Superior's meditative equipoise [on thusness]. The second is that all phenomena are the same in being without establishment by way of their own character. These two are the general teaching; the other eight are taught in the context of making distinctions within the meaning of the general teaching itself.[d]

"Productionless"[e] refers to future [production in that all phenomena are the same in not being produced by way of their own character in the future], and "non-produced"[f] refers to the other times [past and present in that all past and present phenomena are the same in not being produced and not ceasing by way of their own character]. That these are the same, or similar, *with respect to all phenomena* also should be understood about the other [samenesses]. Voidness is an emptiness of the produced and the to-be-produced, that is, void of being taken to be qualified by being established by way of their character as on the occasion of the second sameness. That such is not created adventitiously by scripture or reasoning but [phenomena] abide in such purity primordially is the sixth [sameness].

The seventh [sameness, that all phenomena are the same in] lacking the proliferations of dualistic appearance, applies to the first

[a] *sa bcu'i rnam par bshad pa, daśabhūmi-vyākhyāna;* P5494, vol. 104. Jam-yang-shay-pa's *Great Exposition of the Middle* (199.2) cites the passage in Vasubandhu's commentary.

[b] *byang chub sems dpa'i sa, bodhisattvabhūmi;* Toh. 4037, *sems tsam,* vol. *dzi.* Jam-yang-shay-pa's *Great Exposition of the Middle* (199.2) cites the passage in Asaṅga's *Grounds of Bodhisattvas.*

[c] The bracketed additions are drawn from Jam-yang-shay-pa's *Great Exposition of the Middle,* 197b.3ff.

[d] Jam-yang-shay-pa's *Great Exposition of the Middle* (198.2) explains, "The seventh sameness is a distinction (*khyad par*) of the first; the third, fourth, and fifth are distinctions of the second sameness; and the rest are distinctions of the second."

[e] *skye ba med pa.*

[f] *ma skyes pa.*

[sameness in the sense of being that way in the perspective of meditative equipoise on suchness], whereas [that all phenomena are] the same in not being proliferated by terms and thoughts should be affixed with the qualification of the second [sameness, in the sense that all phenomena are the same in that their being proliferated by terms and thoughts is not established by way of its own character]. Such [latter] qualification should also be applied to the eighth sameness [that all phenomena are the same in not involving adopting and discarding that exist by way of their own character]. The ninth [sameness, that all phenomena are the same in being empty of establishment by way of their own character in accordance with seven examples of illusion,] is many forms of examples for ascertaining the meanings explained earlier. The tenth [sameness] is the similarity of all phenomena in not being inherently existent as effective things or non-effective things [that is, compounded phenomena and uncompounded phenomena are the same in being without inherent existence as effective things and non-effective things respectively].

"Sharp" means quickness of wisdom. "Concordant" means concordant with an eighth grounder's forbearance with respect to the doctrine of non-production. There appear to be many different [explanations] of "concordant forbearance" due to [different] contexts.[a]

Although there are many scriptures that teach the suchness of phenomena, [the explanation] here is in the context of describing how suchness is realized by a sixth grounder's wisdom; hence [Chandrakīrti] cites a scripture that describes entry into the sixth ground by way of the ten samenesses.

[a] Jam-yang-shay-pa's *Great Exposition of the Middle* (198a.5) explains:

> There are three levels of forbearance that are non-fright with respect to emptiness—the forbearance [attained at the third rung of] the path of preparation, the forbearance [attained at] the path of seeing, and the forbearance [attained at] the eighth ground.

Identifying what is discordant with knowing suchness

With regard to delineating the absence of true existence in phenomena, if you do not understand well just what true establishment is, as well as how [phenomena] are apprehended as truly existent, the view of suchness will definitely go astray. Shāntideva's *Engaging in the Bodhisattva Deeds* says that if the thing imputed, the generality [or image] of the object of negation, does not appear well to your awareness, it is impossible to apprehend well the non-existence of the object of negation:[a]

> Without making contact with the thing imputed,
> The non-existence of that thing is not apprehended.

Therefore, unless true establishment (which is what does not exist) and the aspect of the object of negation (which is that of which [phenomena] are empty) do not appear—just as they are—as objects of [your] awareness, good ascertainment of the lack of true establishment and of the entity of emptiness cannot occur.

Furthermore, mere identification of (1) a true establishment that is superficially imputed by proponents of tenets and (2) [the consciousness] apprehending such true establishment is not sufficient. Because of this, it is most essential to identify well the innate apprehension of true establishment that has operated beginninglessly and exists both in those whose awarenesses have been affected through [study of] tenets and in those whose awarenesses have not been affected in this way, and to identify the true establishment apprehended by this [mind]. For if you have not identified these, even if you refute an object of negation through reasoning, the adherence to true establishment that has operated beginninglessly is not harmed at all, due to which the meaning at this point would be lost.[b]

---

[a] *byang chub sems dpa'i spyod pa la 'jug pa, bodhi[sattva]caryāvatāra,* stanza IX.140; Toh. 3871, *dbu ma,* vol. *la,* 36a.6. The Sanskrit is:

> *kalpitaḥ bhāvamaspṛṣṭvā tadabhāvo na gṛhyate//*

See Vidhushekara Bhattacharya, ed., *Bodhicaryāvatāra,* Bibliotheca Indica vol. 280 (Calcutta: The Asiatic Society, 1960), 221.

[b] Jam-yang-shay-pa (Hopkins, *Maps of the Profound,* 737) summarizes this:

> Identification of the object of negation is extremely important because unless the generality of the object of negation—true establishment—and the way it is conceived by a consciousness conceiving true establishment appear well [to your mind], you might utter many term-generalities such as, "True establishment does not occur, and establishment in the manner of the conceived object of a consciousness conceiving true establishment does not occur," and "If [phenomena] were established that way, there is such-and-such damage,

Furthermore, having initially identified the apprehension of true establishment in your own [mental] continuum, you ought to know[a] how the reasonings serve to disprove the object of that [apprehension] directly and indirectly. For, refutation and proof only directed outside are of very little benefit.

If you know well the identification of this [apprehension of true establishment and true establishment itself] by both the Middle Way Autonomy and Middle Way Consequence systems, you will discriminate them well. Hence, the explanation of these is in two parts: identification of the apprehension of true establishment in the Middle Way Autonomy School and identification of the apprehension of true establishment in the Middle Way Consequence School.

and the proofs of non-establishment are such-and-such," but you would not have understood the meaning well.

[a] Read *shes* ***dgos*** *kyi* for *shes kyi* in accordance with P6143, vol. 154, 30.5.7.

2. Autonomy School on True Existence

Identification of the apprehension of true establishment in the Middle Way Autonomy School

This section has three parts: identifying true establishment and the apprehension of true establishment, indicating truth and falsity relative to worldly persons through the example of a magician's illusion, and explanation within applying the example to the meaning.

Identifying true establishment and the apprehension of true establishment

A clear identification of the object of negation does not emerge in other reliable sourcebooks of the Autonomy School, but the existence that is the opposite of the mode of conventional existence described in Kamalashīla's *Illumination of the Middle* is to be known as ultimate or true existence, and, therefore, let us explain it that way. This text says:[a]

> A mistaken awareness that superimposes—on things that in reality [or ultimately] are natureless—an aspect opposite to that [naturelessness] is called an "obscurer" (*kun rdzob, saṃvṛti*) because it obstructs [itself] from [perception of] suchness or because it veils [other awarenesses] from perception of suchness. [The *Descent into Laṅkā*] *Sūtra* (see also *Illumination*, 236) also says:[b]
>
> > The production of things [exists] conventionally (*kun rdzob tu, saṃvṛtyā*);
> > Ultimately it lacks inherent existence.
> > That [consciousness] mistaken with regard to the lack of inherent existence
> > Is asserted as the obscurer of reality (*yang dag kun rdzob, satyaṃ saṃvṛti*).[c]

[a] *dbu ma snang ba, madhyamakāloka;* Toh. 3887, *dbu ma,* vol. *sa,* 228a.7-228b.3.

[b] *lang kar gshegs pa'i mdo, laṅkāvatārasūtra,* stanza X.429; Sanskrit in Bunyiu Nanjio, *Laṅkāvatāra Sūtra,* 319: *bhāvā vidyanti saṃvṛtyā paramārthe na bhāvakāḥ / niḥsvabhāveṣu yā bhrāntistatsatyaṃ saṃvṛtirbhavet //.*

[c] This sūtra passage is also cited below (236) to elucidate Candrakīrti's understanding of obscurational truth.

All false things seen displayed by that [consciousness apprehending them as if they are truly established] due to having arisen from it[a] are called "just obscurational."[b] Moreover, that [apprehension of true existence] arises through the maturation

[a] I take it that what arise from a consciousness conceiving true existence are not the false things themselves but the display, or appearance, of them as truly existent. Nga-wang-pel-den, on the other hand, holds that what arises from a consciousness apprehending true existence is an artificial apprehension of true existence in the continuum of a Proponent of True Existence. In his *Annotations for (Jam-yang-shay-pa's) "Great Exposition of Tenets"* (Hopkins, *Maps of the Profound*, 740-742) he recasts the meaning of this passage as follows:

> The subject, an innate consciousness conceiving true existence, which conceives that phenomena ultimately exist inherently whereas they do not, is called an "obscurer" (*kun rdzob, saṃvṛti*) or obstructor (*sgrib byed*) because a consciousness conceiving true existence, like an eye obstructed by an eye disease, obstructs itself from seeing suchness [or] this consciousness conceiving true existence veils other awarenesses from seeing suchness, like covering something with a cloth. This is because the *Descent into Laṅkā Sūtra* says:
>
> > The production of things [exists] conventionally (*kun rdzob tu, saṃvṛtyā*);
> > Ultimately it lacks inherent existence.
> > That [consciousness] mistaken regarding the lack of inherent existence
> > Is asserted as the obscurer of reality (*yang dag kun rdzob, satyaṃ saṃvṛti*).
>
> ...Since an artificial awareness in the continuum of a Proponent of True Existence arises from that consciousness conceiving true existence, all false things such as forms and so forth—which are the observed objects of such an artificial awareness that sees them displayed by that consciousness conceiving true existence as if they are truly existent—exist only conventionally, not ultimately. Not only does that artificial awareness arise from a consciousness conceiving true existence but also this consciousness conceiving true existence arises through the maturation of beginningless predispositions for mistake. This consciousness conceiving true existence displays truly established phenomena to all living beings as if they exist, whether their awarenesses are affected by systems of tenets or not, and those living beings also perceive them that way.
>
> Therefore, since it would not be suitable to posit phenomena as existing through the force of appearing to a consciousness conceiving true existence, existence that is posited through the force of appearing to a non-defective awareness—its factors of appearance and conception not being affected by the force of a consciousness conceiving true existence—is the meaning of existing conventionally. Hence, the object of negation, true existence, does not appear to sense consciousnesses.

Nga-wang-pel-den's reading strikes me as excessively complicated, but the matter requires more analysis.

[b] *kun rdzob pa kho na.*

of beginningless predispositions for mistake, whereby all living beings see [phenomena] displayed as if they had an inherent nature in reality. Therefore, all entities of false things—[existing] through the power of those [sentient beings' non-defective] thoughts [that is, conceptual and non-conceptual consciousnesses unaffected by superficial causes of mistake[a]]—are said "only to exist conventionally."

[In that quotation:]

The passage "A mistaken awareness that superimposes—on things that in reality [or ultimately] are natureless—an aspect opposite to that [naturelessness]" refers to [a consciousness] mistaking what does not ultimately exist inherently to exist ultimately.

The passage "...is called an 'obscurer' (*kun rdzob, saṃvṛti*) because it obstructs [itself] from [perception of] suchness or because it veils [other awarenesses] from perception of suchness" is the meaning of "the obscurer of reality (*yang dag kun rdzob, satyaṃ saṃvṛti*)" [in the quote from the *Descent into Laṅkā Sūtra*]. *Saṃvṛti* [here] is taken as [meaning] "obstructor" (*sgrib byed*), obstructing reality.

That which sees the display by a consciousness conceiving true existence—due to having arisen from it—as if [objects] are truly established is a conceptual consciousness, not a sense consciousness. For, Jñānagarbha's[b] *Autocommentary on "Differentiation of the Two Truths"*[c] explains that true [existence]—the object of negation—

[a] Four types of consciousnesses affected by superficial causes of mistake are enumerated:

- cause of mistake existing in the object: for instance, a consciousness perceiving a circle of fire due to a firebrand being twirled quickly
- cause of mistake existing in the basis: for instance, an eye consciousness that sees a single moon as double due to a fault in the eye
- cause of mistake existing in the abode: for instance, an eye consciousness that sees trees as moving when a person is riding in a boat (causing stationary objects on the shore to appear to move)
- cause of mistake existing in the immediately preceding condition: for instance, an eye consciousness that sees everything as red when a person is overcome by anger.

See Lati Rinbochay and Elizabeth Napper, *Mind in Tibetan Buddhism* (London: Rider, 1980; Ithaca, N.Y.: Snow Lion Publications, 1980), 51-52.

[b] Jñānagarbha is taken to be a proponent of the Sūtric Middle Way Autonomy School.

[c] *bden pa gnyis rnam par 'byed pa'i 'grel pa, satyadvayavibhaṅgavṛtti;* Toh. 3882, *dbu ma,* vol. *sa,* 5b.3-6a.2; Tibetan and English in Eckel, *Jñānagarbha's Commentary,* 160-161 and 75-76. Jñānagarbha states in his autocommentary to stanza 8abc that "Imputed objects are production [existing] in reality, and so forth" (*brtags pa'i don ni yang dag par skye ba la sogs pa*) and that "Production [existing] in reality, and so forth, do not appear" (*yang dag*

does not appear to sense consciousnesses, and it is the same here [in Kamalashīla's Yogic Middle Way Autonomy School].

The passage "Moreover, that [apprehension of true existence] arises through the maturation of beginningless predispositions for mistake" indicates that this apprehension of true existence is innate. Therefore, [Kamalashīla] speaks of "all living beings."

The "thoughts" of those living beings are not just conceptual consciousnesses but also are to be taken as non-conceptual consciousnesses.

False things—that is to say, that do not exist ultimately but are posited as existing through the force of those two [conceptual and non-conceptual consciousnesses]—exist only conventionally. This is the meaning of the statement in the *[Descent into Laṅkā Sūtra],* "The production of things [exists] conventionally (*kun rdzob tu, saṃvṛtyā*)." Moreover, this does not mean that [such falsities] exist conventionally in the sense of existing for a *saṃvṛti* (*kun rdzob*) that is an apprehender of true existence. [Rather, they exist for a *saṃvṛti* (*kun rdzob*) that is a conventional valid consciousness.]

Since this is the case, [in the Autonomy School] "to exist in the manner of an objective mode of abiding without being posited through appearing to an awareness, or through the force of an awareness"[a] is to truly exist, to ultimately exist, and to exist as [the object's own] reality, and apprehending such is an innate apprehension of true existence.

Objection: Implicit to the statement in Kamalashīla's *Illumination of the Middle:*[b]

> That "ultimately there is no production" is to be explained as that "the production of these is not established by a consciousness of reality."

is an explanation that to be ultimately existent and ultimately produced is to be established—as existent and as produced—by a rational

par skye ba la sogs pa ni mi snang ste). In stanza 9ab, he states that "Since the negation of production, and so forth, is concordant with reality, we assert it" (*skye la sogs pa bkag pa yang / yang dag pa dang mthun phyir 'dod*). His autocommentary explains "production" (*skye*) as "real production" (*yang dag par skye ba*), and that the negation of real production "we assert as the ultimate" (*don dam pa yin par kho bo cag 'dod do*). Putting these assertions together, one can see why Tsong-kha-pa states that Jñānagarbha's object of negation—the negation of which is the ultimate—does not appear to sense consciousnesses.

[a] *blo la snang ba'am blo'i dbang gis bzhag pa min par don gyi sdod lugs su yod pa.*

[b] Toh. 3887, *dbu ma,* vol. *sa,* 229b.3.

consciousness[a] understanding suchness. [Since, just above, you have explained that the meaning of being ultimately existent is to exist in the manner of an objective mode of abiding without being posited through appearing to an awareness or through the force of an awareness,] how [do you take Kamalashīla's explanation]?

Answer: That is true. You need to understand that the qualification "ultimately" is affixed in two ways to the object of negation:

1. Rational consciousnesses of hearing, thinking, and meditating are taken as the ultimate [consciousness], and what is not established by them [is not ultimately established, that is to say, not established for an ultimate consciousness], as described [by Kamalashīla just] above.
2. Existing in an objective mode of abiding without being posited through the force of an awareness is posited as [the meaning of] ultimately existing [and not existing this way is posited as the meaning of not being ultimately established].

The first of these two ultimates [that is, a rational consciousness of hearing, thinking, or meditating], as well as something that is established in its perspective [namely, emptiness], exists. However, both the latter ultimate [that is, existence in an objective mode of abiding without being posited through the force of an awareness] and something that exists that way do not occur.[b]

Therefore, although whatever exists ultimately in the latter sense

[a] *rigs shes.*

[b] Nga-wang-pel-den (Hopkins, *Maps of the Profound,* 743-744) rephrases this:

The "ultimate" in "not existing ultimately" has two types:

1. A conceptual rational consciousness of hearing, thinking, or meditating that analyzes suchness is taken as the ultimate, and not existing as able to bear analysis by that conceptual rational consciousness is posited as "not existing ultimately."
2. Existing in an objective mode of subsistence without being merely posited through the force of appearing to a non-defective awareness is posited as "existing ultimately," and not existing in that way is posited as "not existing ultimately."

Concerning these:

1. Both the ultimate in the first mode of positing [that is, a conceptual rational consciousness analyzing suchness] and something established in its perspective [namely, emptiness] exist.
2. Both the ultimate of the second mode of positing [that is, existing in an objective mode of subsistence without being merely posited through the force of appearing to a non-defective awareness] and something established as it do not exist.

would exist ultimately in the former sense,[a] the apprehension of the former type of existence [that is, the apprehension that an object is established for a rational consciousness] is not an innate apprehension of true existence.[b] To have such an [innate] apprehension of true existence, one must apprehend the latter type of existence [that is, one must apprehend that an object has an objective mode of abiding not posited through the force of an awareness].

Not differentiating these [two meanings of "ultimate"], many have held that the measure of the object of negation is "that which is able to bear reasoned analysis"[c] or "a thing able to bear analysis."[d] In dependence upon this, it appears that many mistakes asserting that ultimate truths are not established bases [that is, do not exist] or that ultimate truths are truly established have arisen. If these [facts] are understood well, you will understand the essential points that the statements that "[the noumenon] does not exist as [its own] basic disposition" and that "[the noumenon] does not exist ultimately"[e] do not contradict the assertion that the noumenon[f] exists and the proposition that it is the basic disposition [of phenomena] and is the ultimate.[g]

[a] Nga-wang-pel-den (Hopkins, *Maps of the Profound,* 744-745) expands on this:

> Whatever is established as the ultimate of the second mode of positing [that is, as existing in an objective mode of subsistence without being posited through the force of an awareness] would [hypothetically] be established for the ultimate of the former mode of positing [that is, would be established in the perspective of a conceptual rational consciousness of hearing, thinking, or meditating that analyzes suchness] because whatever truly exists must be established as the final mode of subsistence, and whatever is established as the final mode of subsistence must be found by a rational consciousness examining the final mode of being.
>
> Whatever is established in the perspective of the former ultimate [that is, in the perspective of a conceptual rational consciousness] is not necessarily established as the latter ultimate [as existing in an objective mode of subsistence without being posited through the force of an awareness] because having analyzed whether or not something truly exists, a rational consciousness finds non-establishment of true existence, and it does not find true existence.

[b] Emptiness is established for a rational consciousness but is not truly established, and the apprehension that any other phenomenon is established for such a rational consciousness is artificial and not innate.

[c] *rigs pas dpyad bzod.*

[d] *dpyad bzod pa'i dngos po.*

[e] *gshis lugs la dang don dam du med.*

[f] *chos nyid, dharmatā.*

[g] Nga-wang-pel-den (Hopkins, *Maps of the Profound,* 745) gives more detail:

> If these are understood well, you will know that it is not contradictory:
>
> - to say that something is not established as [its own] mode of disposition

Indicating truth and falsity relative to worldly persons through the example of a magician's illusion

Since for understanding the styles of existence posited and not posited through the force of an awareness, making these known in terms of the example of a [magician's] illusion is praised, let us explain it. When a magician causes a pebble, twig, or the like to appear as a horse or elephant, there are three [types of persons present]:

1. the magician
2. the audience whose eyes have been affected [by the mantra the magician has cast]
3. [a person who comes later and thus] whose eyes have not been affected [by the mantra].

For the first [that is, the magician] there is the mere appearance as a horse or elephant, but he/she does not adhere to such [as being true]. The second [the audience whose eyes have been affected] have both the appearance [as horse or elephant] and adherence to that appearance. The third [a person whose eyes have not been affected] has neither the appearance as a horse or elephant nor adherence to it.

When, for example, a rope is mistaken for a snake, it is said that the rope is a snake in the perspective of that consciousness but in general is not a snake. However, it is not suitable to say that similarly, when a basis of conjuring appears as a horse or elephant, the appearance as a horse or elephant is only in the perspective of a mistaken consciousness but in general the basis of conjuring **does not appear** as a horse or elephant [because it does]. Even though that qualification [that is, "in general"] is not affixed, it must be asserted that the basis of conjuring

---

(*gshis lugs su ma grub pa*) and is not ultimately established

- and to assert that ultimate truths exist and to propound that ultimate truths are the mode of subsistence and are ultimates.

Due to not distinguishing these, there arose explanations such as:

- The great translator Ngok [Lo-den-shay-rap (*blo ldan shes rab, rngog lo chen po*, 1059-1109)], sole eye of the snowy land, said that ultimate truths are not objects of knowledge.
- The lord of reasoning Cha-pa Chö-kyi-seng-ge (*cha pa* or *phywa pa chos kyi seng ge*, 1109-1169) asserted that ultimate truths are truly established in the sense of being able to bear analysis by reasoning.
- Dro-lung-pa's (*gro lung pa blo gros 'byung gnas*, eleventh century) *Stages of the Teaching* and so forth explain that through dividing one awareness by way of conceptually isolatable factors [it can be said that] there is no object of a rational consciousness, but there is an object of an inferential consciousness.

does appear as a horse or elephant [even though it only appears so for a mistaken consciousness] because if this were not the case, mistakes regarding appearances would not occur.

Therefore, that the basis of conjuring can be posited as appearing as a horse or elephant is, according to the magician, through the force of appearing that way to a mistaken awareness; it is not posited otherwise through the force of the mode of abiding of the basis of conjuring itself. As for the audience, the appearance as a horse or elephant does not seem to be posited through the force of an internal awareness; rather, they conceive that there is a fully qualified horse or elephant dwelling on that place where the appearance is, covering that spot.

In terms of the example, those are how something is apprehended to be posited through the force of an awareness and is apprehended not to be posited through the force of an awareness. When a basis [that is, an object] appears in a certain way, there are two [types]—those that do and do not correspond with the mode of subsistence as it appears.

When you understand well this [presentation of how phenomena are posited through the force of the mind according to the Autonomy School], you will come to differentiate the two positions [of the Autonomy School and the Proponents of True Existence which some] confuse. They think:

> Objects of comprehension [that is, all objects] are posited through the force of valid cognitions, and since valid cognitions are awarenesses, the positing of objects of comprehension through them is a case of positing [objects] through the force of an awareness. Hence, even the systems of the Proponents of True Existence refute true establishment.

[However,] that objects of comprehension are posited [that is, certified] through the force of valid cognitions means that valid cognitions realize the mode of abiding of the two [types of] objects of comprehension.[a] Therefore, the two—this [meaning of positing or certifying objects of comprehension] and the former [meaning of positing objects through the force of an awareness according to the Autonomy School] are utterly dissimilar.

According to the Yogic Middle Way Autonomists [who do not assert external objects], the appearance of such an illusion is established [or certified] by a self-knowing direct perception, and according to [the Sūtra Middle Way Autonomists] who assert external objects, the

[a] The two types of objects of comprehension are specifically and generally characterized objects, or impermanent and permanent objects, or manifest and hidden objects.

appearance of such an illusion is established [or certified] by a sense direct perception apprehending the basis—for instance, the area [on which the illusion appears] or intermediate space [in which it appears].

With respect to its not existing in accordance with how it appears, [that the illusory horse or elephant exists as it appears] is refuted with signs [that is, reasons] such as, "If it did exist that way, it would be seen by those whose eyes are not affected [by the mantra], but they do not see it," and so forth. At this time, a combination of the two—appearing that way and an emptiness of that—is established, at which point [the illusion] is established as a falsity relative to an ordinary conventional awareness not involved in [philosophical] tenets. Hence, an awareness that establishes [or certifies] this [composite of appearance and emptiness] and a reflection's emptiness of what it appears to be is not asserted to be either a coarse or a subtle rational consciousness.[a]

Even if something is truly established in terms of a conventional ordinary awareness,[b] if [an object] appears as that, it could not be empty of it, and also if it is empty of that, it could not appear that way. Hence, if a combination of those two [that is, appearing one way and existing another] occurs, it is only a falsity in terms of an ordinary awareness.

Explanation within applying the example to the meaning

When external and internal phenomena appear as truly existent, sentient beings, like the audience of magic whose eyes are affected [by the mantra cast by the magician], apprehend that there is a mode of subsistence of those phenomena not posited through the force of an awareness. This apprehension is the innate apprehension of true existence which has operated beginninglessly.

What the Autonomists posit this way is very coarse relative to the Consequentialists' apprehension of the object of negation; hence, it is not the innate subtle apprehension of true existence [according to the

[a] *rigs shes*. A coarse rational consciousness establishes a coarse selflessness, whereas a subtle rational consciousness establishes a subtle selflessness.

[b] "True establishment *in terms of a conventional ordinary awareness*" does not refer to the object of negation as the term "true establishment" usually does but to something that is true on the conventional level. Even on the conventional level, if something is true, there will be no conflict between how it appears and how it is; it will not appear to be something and yet not be that, and correspondingly if it is empty of something, that is, if it is not something, it will not appear to be that. Therefore, a magician's illusion, since it appears to be a real object and yet is not, cannot be true (or truly established) in a conventional sense of true establishment and thus must be a falsity, appearing one way and existing another.

Consequentialists].

When the true existence apprehended by the apprehension of true existence is refuted through reasoning, one—like the magician—does not apprehend external and internal phenomena as having a mode of abiding that is not posited through the force of an internal awareness; rather, one understands [external and internal phenomena] as mere existents posited through the force of an awareness. Moreover, those posited through the force of an awareness that are not damaged by valid cognition are asserted as existing in conventional terms; however, everything posited through the force of an awareness is not asserted as existing in conventional terms.

Although the production of a sprout from a seed is posited through the force of an awareness, it is not contradictory that the sprout also is produced from the seed from its own side. This is like the fact that there is an appearance as a horse or an elephant even from the side of the basis of conjuring [that is, a pebble or twig]. Through this, all phenomena existing in conventional terms are to be understood.

Even the noumenon is posited as existing through the force of the awareness to which it appears. Hence, it is not an exception to being posited as existing in conventional terms.

Therefore, the significance of applying the example, a magician's illusion, to the meaning—other phenomena—is not at all that just as a magician's illusion appears to be a horse or an elephant but is empty of being such, so all [phenomena] such as pots and so forth appear to be pots and so forth, but are empty of being pots and so forth. For, if that were the case, being that phenomenon [for example, being a pot] would not occur, and the application of the example to the meaning would be that [phenomena] appear to be such-and-such but are not the actual thing.

When non-conceptual pristine wisdom of meditative equipoise is generated, in its perspective all dualistic appearances are quiescent. This is like one whose eyes, not having been affected [by the magician's mantra], have neither the illusory appearance nor adherence to it.

Later [in Chandrakīrti's text] there is no indication of the Autonomists' uncommon modes of refuting [true existence] by reasoning; therefore, let us here express briefly and in a way easy to understand how through this system all phenomena are caused to appear as like a magician's illusions.

Objects of knowledge are inclusively divided into the two: effective things and non-effective things [or impermanent and permanent phenomena]. Let us explain this with respect to effective things first.

Effective things are inclusively divided into the physical and non-physical. Applying the refutation, as explained elsewhere, of physical things that are directionally partless—eastern direction, and so forth—and of consciousnesses that are temporally partless, [the Autonomists] prove that effective things necessarily have parts. Then, if parts and whole were different entities, they would be unrelated; thereby [a difference of entity of parts and whole] is refuted, and [parts and whole] are shown to be one entity.

At that time, no matter how the mind looks into it, it is undeniable that although the mode of being [of parts and whole] is to be one entity, in their mode of appearance [to thought] they appear to be different entities. Thereby, it is delineated that [effective things] are, like a magician's illusions, a combination of the two—appearing one way and being empty of [existing] that way.

Then, although such is not contradictory in the context of the mode of abiding of a falsity posited through the force of appearing to an awareness, if a certain base [that is, a certain phenomenon] had a mode of subsistence not posited through the force of appearing to an awareness, [such a combination of appearance and emptiness] would not at all be reasonable because discordant modes of abiding and of appearance cannot occur in what is truly established, as was explained earlier, because if something is truly established, it must abide in a manner devoid of falsity in all respects and because [since appearance and mode of being would necessarily be concordant,] the awareness to which [parts and whole] appear as different entities would have to be unmistaken, thereby damaging their being one entity.

Once this is established [with respect to effective things], in dependence on that reasoning it can be refuted that non-effective things are truly established. For, even with respect to uncompounded space, it must be asserted that it pervades certain physical objects, and regarding this it must be asserted that it has a part pervading the east and parts pervading the other directions. Likewise, the noumenon [or emptiness] also has many parts pervading [phenomena], as well as many different parts realized by different former and later awarenesses. Also, other uncompounded [phenomena] are similar. Therefore, since the two—the many parts and the whole—are not fit to be different entities, they are one entity. Also, that [same discrepancy between modes of being and of appearance] is suitable in a falsity but not suitable in what is truly established. Hence, [the true establishment of uncompounded phenomena] is refuted as before [with compounded phenomena], whereby all objects of knowledge are established to be without true existence. Since this treatment is the assertion of the father Shāntarakṣhita and his spiritual son [Kamalashīla], reckoning part and whole only for effective things is a flaw of those with small intelligence.

The falsity renowned among those whose awarenesses have not been affected by tenets does not have the same meaning as the falsity asserted by the Middle Way School; therefore, although it is posited by an awareness, [this type of being posited by an awareness] is in accordance with how that is renowned to them. However, in the [Autonomists'] own system merely this is not asserted as [the meaning of being] posited by an awareness.

[Concluding remarks]

In that way, even though there is no mode of subsistence not posited by the force of appearing to an awareness, in this system it is not contradictory for there to be a mode of subsistence that is posited by the force of appearing to an awareness but is not merely nominally imputed,[a] [whereas such is contradictory in the Consequence School]. Hence, the objects of negation in the two Middle Way Schools come to differ greatly with regard to the perspective of the awareness [in the face of which objects are posited].[b]

Having seen that contemporary persons—who have been briefly instructed well in [the Autonomists'] identification of true [existence] and [their estimation of] the apprehension of true existence as well as [their] reasonings refuting those—discern the Consequentialists' view well when, afterwards, that system is taught, [I] have explained these here.

[a] *ming tu btags pa tsam min pa.*

[b] For the Autonomists the awareness is any consciousness, either conceptual or non-conceptual, not affected by superficial causes of mistake, whereas for the Consequentialists it must be only conceptual, as will be described below.

3. Consequence School on True Existence

Identification of the apprehension of true establishment in the Middle Way Consequence School

If you understand how in this system phenomena are assigned as merely posited through the force of conceptuality, you will easily understand the apprehension of true existence that apprehends opposite to this. Hence, this has two parts: indicating how phenomena are posited through the force of conceptuality and the apprehension of true existence that apprehends opposite to this.

Indicating how phenomena are posited through the force of conceptuality

The *Questions of Upāli Sūtra* says that phenomena are posited through the force of conceptuality (see also *Insight*, 39):[a]

> Here the various mind-pleasing blossoming flowers
> And attractive, shining, supreme golden houses
> Have no [inherently existent] maker at all.
> They are posited through the power of conceptuality.
> Through the power of conceptuality the world is imputed.

There are also many other statements that phenomena are merely imputed by conceptuality and are posited through the force of conceptuality.

Furthermore, Nāgārjuna's *Sixty Stanzas of Reasoning* says (see also *Insight*, 39):[b]

> The perfect Buddha stated that the world
> Has the condition of ignorance.
> Therefore, how could it not be feasible
> That this world is [imputed by] conceptuality?

[a] *nye bar 'khor gyis zhus pa, upālipariprcchā*, stanzas 69-70a; Toh. 68, vol. *ca* (*dkon brtsegs*); Python, *Vinaya-Viniścaya-Upāli-Paripṛcchā*, 59-60: *citra manorama sajjita puṣpāḥ svarṇavimāna jalanti manojñāḥ / teṣvapi kāraku nāst'iha kaści te 'pi ca sthāpita kalpavaśena // kalpavaśena vikalpitu lokaḥ.*

[b] *rigs pa drug cu pa, yuktiṣaṣṭikā*, stanza 37; Toh. 3825, *dbu ma*, vol. *tsa*, 21b.6; Tibetan edited by Lindtner, *Master of Wisdom*, 84.

The meaning of this statement is explained in Chandrakīrti's commentary[a] as being that the worlds [that is, beings and environments] are imputed by conceptuality, not established by way of their own nature.

Moreover, Āryadeva's *Four Hundred* says (see also *Insight,* 39):[b]

> Since desire and so forth
> Do not exist without conceptuality,
> Who with intelligence would hold
> That these are real objects and are [also] conceptual?[c]

Also, Chandrakīrti's *Commentary on (Āryadeva's) "Four Hundred"* says (see also *Insight,* 39):[d]

> Those which exist only when the conceptuality [imputing them] exists and do not exist when conceptuality does not are without question definite as not established by way of their own nature, like a snake imputed to a coiled rope.

"Real objects" are those established by way of their own nature. "Conceptual" [means] "produced in dependence upon that [conceptuality]".

The statement in the commentary that *desire and so forth* are [imputed] like the imputation of a snake to a rope is just an illustration; all other phenomena are also described as posited by conceptuality like

---

[a] *rigs pa drug cu pa'i 'grel pa, yuktiṣaṣṭikāvṛtti;* Toh. 3864, *dbu ma,* vol. *ya,* 23a.2-23a.4; Scherrer-Schaub, *Yuktiṣaṣṭikāvṛtti,* 77.

[b] *bstan bcos bzhi brgya pa zhes bya ba'i tshig le'ur byas pa, catuḥśatakaśāstrakārikā,* stanza VIII.3; P5246, vol. 95, 136.2.1; Tibetan text and Sanskrit fragments edited by Lang, *Āryadeva's Catuḥśataka,* 78: *vinā kalpanayāstitvaṃ rāgādīnāṃ na vidyat / bhūtārthaḥ kalpanā ceti ko grahīṣyati buddhimān //.* See Sonam Rinchen and Ruth Sonam, *Yogic Deeds of Bodhisattvas,* 186.

[c] With material added in brackets from Chandrakīrti's commentary (*byang chub sems dpa'i rnal 'byor spyod pa bzhi brgya pa'i rgya cher 'grel pa, bodhisattvayogacaryācatuḥśatakaṭīkā;* P5266, vol. 98, 229.5.3), the passage reads:

> Without [imputation by] thought [like the imputation of a snake to a rope] there is no [finding of] the existence of desire and so forth. If so, who with intelligence would maintain that a real object is [produced dependent on] thought? [For, being imputed by thought and existing as its own reality are contradictory.]

Gyel-tsap (*rgyal tshab dar ma rin chen,* 1364-1432) quotes this passage from Āryadeva and the next citation in his *Illumination of the Essential Meanings of (Nāgārjuna's) "Precious Garland of Madhyamaka"* (*dbu ma rin chen 'phreng ba'i snying po'i don gsal bar byed pa;* edition of 78 folios in library of H.H. Dalai Lama), 20b.6-21a.2. See also Sonam Rinchen and Ruth Sonam, *Yogic Deeds of Bodhisattvas,* 186-187.

[d] *byang chub sems dpa'i rnal 'byor spyod pa bzhi brgya pa'i rgya cher 'grel pa, bodhisattvayogacaryācatuḥśatakaṭīkā,* commenting on stanza VIII.3; P5266, vol. 98, 229.5.3. Cited in *Great Treatise,* vol. 3, 213.

the imputation of a snake to a rope. [The rope's] speckled color and mode of coiling are similar to those of a snake, and when this is perceived in a dim area, the thought arises with respect to the rope, "This is a snake." As for the rope, at that time [when it is imputed to be a snake], the collection and parts of the rope are not even in the slightest way positable as an illustration of a snake [that is, positable as a snake]. Therefore, that snake is merely imputed by conceptuality.

In the same way, when the thought "I" arises in dependence upon the [mental and physical] aggregates, nothing in terms of the aggregates—neither the collection that is the continuum of the earlier and later [moments], nor the collection [of the parts] at one time, nor the parts of those [mental and physical aggregates]—is even in the slightest way positable as an illustration of that "I" [that is, positable as "I"]. This will be explained at length below.

Because of this and because there is not even the slightest something that:

- is an entity different from the parts of the aggregates or the whole, and
- is apprehendable as an illustration[a] of that ["I"]

the "I" is merely posited by conceptuality in dependence upon the aggregates; it is not established by way of its own nature. This is also said in Nāgārjuna's *Precious Garland* (see also *Insight,* 59):[b]

> A being is not earth, not water,
> Not fire, not wind, not space,
> Not consciousness, and not all of them.
> What person is there other than these?

In that, a "being"[c] is a person,[d] sentient being,[e] "I,"[f] and self.[g] "Not earth, not water, not fire, not wind, not space, not consciousness" refutes positing the parts—which are a sentient being's six constituents—as a person, and "not all of them" refutes positing the collection of the constituents as a person. The last line ["What person is there other

[a] *gzhir* here means *mtshan gzhir.*

[b] *rgyal po la gtam bya ba rin po che'i phreng ba, rājaparikathāratnāvalī,* stanza 80; Hopkins, *Nāgārjuna's Precious Garland,* 104 and corresponding Tibetan text in Part 3. The Sanskrit is not extant.

[c] *skyes bu, puruṣa.*

[d] *gang zag, pudgala.*

[e] *sems can, sattva.*

[f] *nga, ahaṃ.*

[g] *bdag, ātman.*

than these?"] refutes positing something that is a different entity from the constituents as a person.

Nevertheless, it is not that persons are not asserted [to exist]. Also, a mind-basis-of-all[a] and so forth are not asserted to be a person. Therefore, in accordance with the commentary by the commentator [Chandrakīrti],[b] Superiors are also asserted.

When the system of positing persons through conceptuality is understood in this way, the system of positing all other phenomena through conceptuality is also similar to that. The *King of Meditative Stabilizations Sūtra* (see also *Insight,* 60 and 87) says:[c]

> Just as you know [how to generate] discrimination [taking to
> mind the delineation of the mode of subsistence] of a self,
> Apply this mentally to all [phenomena].[d]

and the *Verse Summary of the Perfection of Wisdom* also says:[e]

> Understand all sentient beings as like the self,
> Understand all phenomena as like all sentient beings.

and Nāgārjuna's *Precious Garland* (see also *Insight,* 59) clearly says:[f]

> Just as because of being [only imputed in dependence upon] an
> aggregation of the six constituents
> A being is not [established as his/her own] reality,
> So because of being [imputed in dependence upon] an aggregation

[a] *kun gzhi rnam par shes pa, ālayavijñāna.*

[b] *'grel pa mdzad pas bkral pa ltar.* I presume this to refer to Chandrakīrti's *Commentary on (Āryadeva's) "Four Hundred Stanzas on the Yogic Deeds of Bodhisattvas"* and most likely not to Ajitamitra's commentary on Nāgārjuna's *Precious Garland.*

[c] *ting nge 'dzin rgyal po'i mdo, samādhirājasūtra,* XII.7; Toh. 127, *mdo sde,* vol. *da,* 44a.2; cited in *Prasannapadā,* in commentary to stanza IV.9; Toh. 3860, *dbu ma,* vol. *'a,* 43b.1-43b.2; La Vallée Poussin, *Mūlamadhyamakakārikās (Mādhyamikasūtras) de Nāgārjuna avec la Prasannapadā,* 128.11: *yatha jñāta tayā 'tmasaṃjña tathaiva sarvatra peṣitā buddhiḥ /.*

[d] Tsong-kha-pa's two citations of these lines in his Medium-Length Exposition of Special Insight are in terms of extending knowledge of the absence of the inherent existence of persons to other phenomena. Here he cites it in the context of extending understanding of the imputed nature of the person to other phenomena.

[e] Stanza I.26ab; Sanskrit and Tibetan in Yuyama, *Saṃcaya-gāthā,* 15 and 161: *yatha ātmanaṃ tatha prajānati sarva-sattvān yatha sarva-sattva tatha jānati sarva-dharmān /.* English translation in Conze, *Perfection of Wisdom in Eight Thousand Lines,* 12.

[f] Stanza 81; Hopkins, *Nāgārjuna's Precious Garland,* 105, and corresponding Tibetan text in Part 3. The Sanskrit is not extant. The bracketed material is from Nga-wang-pelden's *Annotations for (Jam-yang-shay-pa's) "Great Exposition of Tenets"* (*dbu,* 67b.4-67b.8; Hopkins, *Maps of the Profound,* 888).

Each of the constituents also is not [established as its own] reality.[a]

The meaning of the first line [that is, "because a being is an aggregation of the six constituents"] is "because a being is imputed in dependence upon an aggregation of the six constituents."[b] The meaning of the third and fourth lines is that because there is no occurrence of [a phenomenon] devoid of parts and a whole, each of the constituents is also imputed in dependence upon an aggregation of its own many parts and, therefore, is not established as [its own] reality—that is to say, is not established by way of its own nature.

Furthermore, with regard to whatever is imputed in dependence upon an aggregation of parts, the parts or the whole are not suitable to be posited as an illustration of it [that is, as something that is it], and anything that is a different entity from those two also could not be an illustration of it either.

The mere factor of how a pot and so forth are posited by conceptuality is similar to the imputation of a rope as a snake. However, whether those two—a pot, and so forth, and a rope-snake—exist or do not exist, are able or unable to perform functions, and so forth are not at all similar. This is because they are in all ways not similar in terms of:

- whether or not the designations of those two must be made
- whether or not making those designations is invalidated [by conventional valid cognition]

and so forth.

The feasibility of [an object's] respective functionality within the context of being posited by conceptuality is an uncommon mode of commentary by Buddhapālita, Shāntideva, and this master [Chandrakīrti] from among the commentators on the words and meaning [of the works] of the two—the father, the Superior [Nāgārjuna], and his spiritual son [Āryadeva]. Just this is also the final difficult point in the view of the Middle Way.

This being the case, Nāgārjuna's *Precious Garland* says that even mere nominality does not exist ultimately and that nothing exists except for only being posited in conventional terms through the force of

---

[a] For the present Dalai Lama's personal reflections on these lines, see *How to Practice: The Way to a Meaningful Life*, 166-167.

[b] If the person were the composite or aggregation of the mental and physical aggregates or even if it were designated *to* the composite or aggregation of the mental and physical aggregates, that composite would be the person. Rather, the person is designated *in dependence upon* the mental and physical aggregates.

nominal conventions and, accordingly, [phenomena] abide as mere nominal imputations:[a]

> Because the phenomena of forms are only names,[b]
> [Uncompounded] space too is only a name.
> Without the elements how could forms exist?
> Therefore, even name-only-ness does not [inherently] exist.[c]
>
> Feelings, discriminations, compositional factors,
> And consciousnesses are to be considered
> As like the elements and the self.
> Hence the six constituents[d] are selfless.

and:[e]

> Except for being a convention designated,
> What world exists in fact [that is, ultimately]
> Which would be "is" or "is not"?

If you understand those [points] well, you will understand well:

- that all phenomena must be posited dependently,

---

[a] Stanzas 99-100; Hopkins, *Nāgārjuna's Precious Garland,* 108, and corresponding Tibetan text in Part 3. Sanskrit of stanza 99 in Hahn, *Nāgārjuna's Ratnāvalī,* 38 (the Sanskrit of stanza 100 is not extant): *rūpasyābhāvamātratvād ākāśaṃ nāmamātrakam / bhūtair vinā kuto rūpaṃ nāmamātrakam apy ataḥ //.*

[b] *gzugs kyi dngos po ming tsam phyir.* Chandrakīrti's citation of this in his *Prasannapadā* has a different reading, "because of being just the non-existence of form" (*rūpasyābhāvamātratvād*). This reading is not reflected in any of the Tibetan texts, either of the *Ratnāvalī* or of the *Prasannapadā* (Tibetan Cultural Printing Press, 346.6) or in their commentaries. Though both readings make sense, I am following the Tibetan because it was checked against three Sanskrit editions, reflected also in Gyel-tsap's commentary (25.5).

"Only name" means "merely nominally existent," the word "merely" eliminating that phenomena are established by way of their own character. In Ge-luk-pa scholastic literature it is said that "only name" does not mean "merely sounds" even though names are sounds, since otherwise the only phenomena that would exist would be sounds.

[c] Nga-wang-pel-den (*Annotations, dbu,* 67a.1) recasts this stanza as:

> Because the phenomena of forms [which have the obstructiveness of which space is the absence] are only names, space also is just a name [and does not exist inherently. If someone said that forms exist inherently, then] when the elements do not exist [inherently], how could form exist [inherently]? Therefore, even name-only-ness does not exist [inherently because that which possesses a name does not exist inherently].

[d] The constituents are earth, water, fire, wind, space, and consciousness, which are the basis in dependence upon which a person is imputed.

[e] 114bcd.

- that because they are just dependently imputed and dependently produced, they are not established by way of their own nature and do not have a self-powered entity, not being posited through the force of conventions which are other [than themselves], and
- that no matter what phenomenon is posited as existing, it is posited in the context of not seeking the object imputed.

The apprehension of true existence that apprehends the opposite to this

The apprehension of existence not posited merely through the force of nominal conventions, which was described above, is the innate apprehension of true establishment, ultimate establishment, or establishment as [the object's own] reality as well as the innate apprehension of existing by way of [the object's] own nature, existing by way of [the object's] own character, and existing inherently. The conceived object apprehended by that [consciousness] is the hypothetical measure of true [establishment].

The need to know the two modes of the ultimate in the qualification of the object of negation with [the term] "ultimately" is also the same here [in the Consequence School as in the Autonomy School, explained in the previous chapter, 193ff.]. However, although the Middle Way Autonomists assert that the three (true, ultimate, and real establishment) do not occur in objects of knowledge, they assert that the three (establishment by way of [the object's] own nature, establishment by way of [the object's] own character, and inherent establishment) exist in conventional terms. This is seen to be a very skillful means for leading those who are temporarily unable to easily realize the very subtle suchness toward [realizing] it.

In this way, just that inherent existence[a] that is an entity of phenomena not depending on or not posited through the force of another—a subjective terminological conceptual consciousness[b]—is called the self that is the object of negation. The non-existence of just this with a person as the substratum is said to be a selflessness of persons, and the non-existence of it with a phenomenon such as an eye or ear [as the substratum] is said to be a selflessness of phenomena.

Thereby, it is implicitly understood that the apprehensions of this inherent existence as existing in persons and in phenomena are the apprehensions of the two selves [of persons and of other phenomena].

---

[a] *rang bzhin, svabhāva.*

[b] *yul can tha snyad kyi rtog pa.*

It is as Chandrakīrti's *Commentary on (Āryadeva's) "Four Hundred"* says (see also *Insight*, 41):[a]

> Concerning that, "self" is inherent existence, an entity of things that does not rely on [being posited by] others [that is, conceptuality]. The non-existence of that [inherent existence] is selflessness. Through the division of [its substrata,] phenomena and persons, it is understood as twofold, "selflessness of phenomena and selflessness of persons."

Also, just this [Chandrakīrti's *Supplement to (Nāgārjuna's) "Treatise on the Middle"*] speaks of the two selflessnesses as divided not by way of the object negated but by way of the subjects that are the substrata [of selflessness—persons and other phenomena],[b] "Through a division of persons and [other] phenomena, it is said to be of two aspects."

With respect to the innate view of the transitory collection that is a consciousness apprehending [an inherently existent] self, in the root text [Chandrakīrti's *Supplement to (Nāgārjuna's) "Treatise on the Middle"*][c] it is refuted that the object of observation is the [mental and physical] aggregates, and in the commentary[d] [Chandrakīrti] says that the dependently imputed self is the object of observation.[e] Therefore, the mere "I" or mere person, which is the object of observation generating the mere thought "I," is to be taken as the object of observation.

With respect to the subjective aspect [of a consciousness misapprehending the inherent existence of "I"], Chandrakīrti's *Autocommentary*

[a] P5266, vol. 98, 103.4.4, chapter 12. This is quoted in Tsong-kha-pa's *Ocean of Reasoning, Explanation of (Nāgārjuna's) "Treatise on the Middle,"* P6153, vol. 156, 66.1.4. Brackets are from *Four Interwoven Annotations*, vol. 2, 439.6. Cited in *Great Treatise*, vol. 3, 213. For the Sanskrit see Khangkar and Yorihito, 181 note 39.

[b] Stanza VI.179b; Toh. 3861, *dbu ma*, vol. *'a*, 213a.6; La Vallée Poussin, *Madhyamakāvatāra*, 301.20.

[c] See stanzas VI.124cd-128; Toh. 3861, *dbu ma*, vol. *'a*, 210b.1-210b.3; La Vallée Poussin, *Madhyamakāvatāra*, 242.17ff; La Vallée Poussin, "*Introduction au traité du milieu*," *Muséon* 12 (1911): 289.

[d] P5263, vol. 98, 141.1.2; Toh. 3862, *dbu ma*, vol. *'a*, 292b.3-292b.4; La Vallée Poussin, *Madhyamakāvatāra*, 234.13; La Vallée Poussin, "*Introduction au traité du milieu*," *Muséon* 12 (1911): 283.

[e] Commenting on stanza VI.120, Chandrakīrti says:

> The object of observation of [a consciousness viewing the transitory collection as an inherently existent self] is the [nominally existent] self. For, that which apprehends an [inherently existent] "I" has as its object [an inherently existent] self.

Bracketed material is from Tsong-kha-pa's *Illumination*, P6143, vol. 154, 82.2.8.

on the "Supplement to (Nāgārjuna's) 'Treatise on the Middle'" says:[a]

> Having imputed that a self—which is [actually] non-existent—exists, a [consciousness] apprehending "I" manifestly adheres to just this as true.

Hence, it apprehends the "I" to be truly established. Moreover, Chandrakīrti's *Autocommentary* says:[b]

> With respect to this, the view of the transitory collection is an afflicted intelligence[c] engaged in such thoughts of [inherently existent] "I" and "mine."

Accordingly, the object of observation of an innate view of the transitory collection must naturally generate an awareness thinking "I"; therefore, the innate apprehension of persons—who are of a different continuum [from your own continuum]—as established by way of their own character is an innate apprehension of a self of persons but not an innate view of the transitory collection [as an inherently existent "I"].

[In the citation, just above, from Chandrakīrti] "...engaged in such thoughts of 'I' and 'mine'" does not indicate that mere "I" and mere "mine" are the objects of the subjective aspect of the mode of apprehension.[d] Rather, it indicates that [a view of the transitory collection] has the aspect of apprehending those two to be established by way of their own character.

The object of observation of an innate view of the transitory collection apprehending [inherently existent] "mine" is just the "mine"; it should not be held that one's own eyes, and so forth, are the objects of observation. The subjective aspect is, upon observing that object of observation, to conceive the "mine" to be established by way of its own character.

Objection: In Chandrakīrti's *Autocommentary* on "This is mine,"[e] he

---

[a] Commenting on stanza I.3; Toh. 3862, *dbu ma*, vol. *'a*, 223a.4; La Vallée Poussin, *Madhyamakāvatāra*, 9.12-9.13; La Vallée Poussin, "*Introduction au traité du milieu*," *Muséon* 8 (1907): 258.

[b] Commenting on stanza VI.120; Toh. 3862, *dbu ma*, vol. *'a*, 292a.7-292b.1; La Vallée Poussin, *Madhyamakāvatāra*, 234.1-234.2; La Vallée Poussin, "*Introduction au traité du milieu*," *Muséon* 12 (1911): 282.

[c] *shes rab nyon mongs pa can*, *kliṣṭaprajñā.

[d] *'dzin stangs kyi rnam pa'i yul.*

[e] This is the last line of stanza I.3:

> Homage to that compassion for transmigrating beings
> Powerless like a bucket traveling in a well
> Through initially adhering to a self, "I,"

says, "Thinking, 'This is mine,' one adheres to all aspects of things other than the object of the apprehension of an [inherently existent] 'I.'" [Given your explanation above that the object of observation of a false view of the transitory collection as inherently existent "mine" is not eyes, and so forth, but the "mine" itself,] how do you take [Chandrakīrti's] explanation that upon observing a base such as eyes and so forth, adherence to it thinking, "This is mine," is an apprehension of [inherently existent] "mine"?

Answer: This refers to adherence to the "mine" as truly established **upon perceiving eyes and so forth as "mine"**; it does not indicate that illustrations of "mine"—eyes and so forth—are the objects of observation. For, if that were not the case, the two—the view of the transitory collection and the apprehension of a self of phenomena—would not be mutually exclusive [whereas they are].[a]

The objects of observation of an innate apprehension of a self of phenomena are the form aggregate, and so on, and eyes, ears, and so on, in your own and others' continuums, as well as the environment that is not included in the [personal] continuum. Its subjective aspect is as explained before [to apprehend these to be established by way of their own character].

In this way, the apprehension of the two selves [of persons and other phenomena] is the ignorance binding one in cyclic existence. Nāgārjuna's *Seventy Stanzas on Emptiness* says (see also *Insight,* 44):[b]

> That [consciousness] which apprehends things produced
> From causes and conditions to be real [that is, to be established
> by way of their own entities]
> Was said by the Teacher to be ignorance.
> From it the twelve links arise.

This says that the apprehension that a thing, which is a phenomenon [other than a person], is established as [its own] reality is the ignorance

---

And then generating attachment for things, "This is mine."

See Hopkins, *Compassion in Tibetan Buddhism*, 116. Toh. 3861, *dbu ma,* vol. *'a,* 201b.3-201b.4; La Vallée Poussin, *Madhyamakāvatāra,* 9.7-9.10; La Vallée Poussin, "*Introduction au traité du milieu,*" *Muséon* 8 (1907): 258.

[a] For extended discussion of what "mine" in this context means, see Hopkins, *Maps of the Profound,* 865-875.

[b] *stong pa nyid bdun cu pa'i tshig le'ur byas pa, śunyatāsaptatikārikā,* stanzas 64-65; Toh. 3827, *dbu ma,* vol. *tsa,* 26b.3-26b.4; Tibetan text edited by Lindtner, *Master of Wisdom,* 114; Tibetan text, English translation, and contemporary commentary in Komito, *Seventy Stanzas,* 175-176. Brackets are from *Four Interwoven Annotations,* vol. 2, 426.5. Cited in *Great Treatise,* vol. 3, 209.

that is the root of cyclic existence. Since the ignorance that is the apprehension of a self of persons arises from the apprehension of a self of phenomena, the twelve [links of dependent-arising] are described as arising from it.

In order to overcome this ignorance, you must see that [phenomena] are empty of how they are apprehended by it, and you must see that self [that is, inherent existence] apprehended in this way does not exist. Nāgārjuna's *Seventy Stanzas on Emptiness* says (see also *Insight*, 44):[a]

> If through seeing reality one knows well
> That things are empty [of inherent existence], the ignorance
> [mistaking inherent existence] does not arise.
> That is the cessation of ignorance,
> Whereby the twelve links [of the dependent-arising of cyclic
> existence] cease.

and Nāgārjuna's *Praise of the Element of Attributes* also says (see also *Insight*, 165):[b]

> As long as "self" and "mine" are apprehended,
> So long is there [false] imputation of the external.
> When the two types of selflessness are seen,
> The seed of cyclic existence ceases.

and (see also *Insight*, 165):

> The doctrine supremely purifying the mind
> Is the absence of nature [that is, inherent existence].

and Āryadeva's *Four Hundred* (see also *Insight*, 56) moreover says:[c]

> When selflessness [the absence of inherent establishment] is
> seen in objects,
> [The ignorance that is] the seed of cyclic existence is ended.

and (see also *Insight*, 45):[d]

---

[a] Stanza 65; Toh. 3827, *dbu ma*, vol. *tsa*, 26b.3-26b.4; Lindtner, *Master of Wisdom*, 114; Komito, *Seventy Stanzas*, 176. Brackets are from *Four Interwoven Annotations*, vol. 2, 426.5. Cited in *Great Treatise*, vol. 3, 209.

[b] *chos dbyings bstod pa, dharmadhātustotra;* Toh. 1118, *bstod tshogs*, vol. *ka*, 66a.3-66a.4 and 64b.5.

[c] XIV.25cd; Toh. 3846, *dbu ma*, vol. *tsha*, 16a.5; Lang, *Āryadeva's Catuḥśataka*, 134; Sonam Rinchen and Ruth Sonam, *Yogic Deeds of Bodhisattvas*, 275. The Sanskrit is not extant. Brackets are from *Four Interwoven Annotations*, vol. 2, 755.2. Cited in *Great Treatise*, vol. 3, 335.

[d] Stanzas VI.10c-11; Toh. 3846, *dbu ma*, vol. *tsha*, 7b.2-7b.3; Lang, *Āryadeva's Catuḥśataka*,

Therefore, all afflictive emotions are overcome
Through overcoming bewilderment.

When dependent-arising is seen,
Bewilderment does not arise.
Therefore, with all endeavor here [in this text]
I will set forth just discourse on this.[a]

Since the bewilderment mentioned [in that stanza] is on the occasion of identifying the bewilderment that is one of the three poisons [desire, hatred, and bewilderment], it is **afflictive** ignorance. Also, [Āryadeva] states that in order to overcome this ignorance, one must realize the meaning of profound dependent-arising in which emptiness dawns as the meaning of dependent-arising.

Furthermore, the commentator[b] [Chandrakīrti] says[c] [when commenting on the line in his *Supplement to (Nāgārjuna's) "Treatise on the Middle"* (see also *Insight*, 54)], "Yogis [seeking release] refute self [that is to say, inherent establishment],"[d] that selflessness must be realized in the manner of eradicating the object of the apprehension of self [that is, inherent existence]. Therefore, although you merely withdraw the mind here from going there to its objects without eradicating the object of the apprehension of self, through this it cannot be posited that you are engaged in selflessness. The reason is this:

- When the mind operates on an object, there are three [modes of apprehension]:
  1. apprehending that the object of observation is truly established
  2. apprehending that it is not truly established
  3. apprehending it without qualifying it as either of these two.
- Therefore, although [the object] is not apprehended to be without

66; Sonam Rinchen and Ruth Sonam, *Yogic Deeds of Bodhisattvas*, 156-157. The Sanskrit is not extant.

[a] The translation of the last two lines is confirmed by Chandrakīrti's commentary, Toh. 3865, vol. *ya*, 113b.2; Ren-da-wa Shön-nu-lo-drö's (*red mda' ba gzhon nu blo gros*, 1349-1412) commentary, 172.12-13; and Gyel-tsap Dar-ma-rin-chen's (*rgyal tshab dar ma rin chen*, 1364-1432) commentary, chap. 6, 8.2-8.4.

[b] *'grel pa mdzad pas.*

[c] Commenting on VI.120; Toh. 3862, *dbu ma*, vol. *'a*, 292b.4; La Vallée Poussin, *Madhyamakāvatāra*, 234.14; La Vallée Poussin, "*Introduction au traité du milieu*," *Muséon* 12 (1911): 283.

[d] VI.120d.

true establishment, it is not necessarily apprehended to be truly established.

- Similarly, although [by merely withdrawing the mind] you are not engaged in [apprehending] the two selves, you are not necessarily engaged in the two selflessnesses because there are limitless [ways of] dwelling in a third category of awareness.

Having identified the two apprehensions of self in your own continuum, you need to settle that the bases with respect to which you make the mistake [of apprehending the two selves] do not exist as they are apprehended. Otherwise, refutation and proof that are directed outward are like searching for a robber on the plain after he has gone to the woods and hence are not to the point.

When, in that way, you have identified well the apprehension of true existence, you will understand that there are many apprehensions that are not the two apprehensions of self. Consequently, all wrong ideas of asserting that reasonings analyzing suchness refute all objects apprehended by conceptuality will be overcome.

Although there are many [points] stemming from these [topics] that should be explained, I will not elaborate on them here as some have already been explained at length elsewhere [in my *Great Exposition of the Stages of the Path to Enlightenment, The Essence of Eloquence*, and *Explanation of (Nāgārjuna's) "Treatise on the Middle"*] and some will be discussed below.

THE TWO TRUTHS

From Tsong-kha-pa Lo-sang-drak-pa's
Extensive Explanation of (Chandrakīrti's) "Supplement to (Nāgārjuna's) 'Treatise on the Middle'": Illumination of the Thought

Commenting on chapter six of Chandrakīrti's *Supplement to (Nāgārjuna's) "Treatise on the Middle,"* stanzas 23-29

1. What the World Invalidates

General Presentation of the Two Truths

This section has four parts: (1) stating that because phenomena are divided into two truths, phenomena each have two natures, (2) indicating other presentations of the two truths, (3) explaining the divisions of obscurational truths in relation to the world, and (4) showing that the conceived object, with respect to which [a wrong consciousness] is mistaken, does not exist even in conventional terms.

Stating that because phenomena are divided into two truths, phenomena each have two natures

> Chandrakīrti's *Supplement to (Nāgārjuna's) "Treatise on the Middle"* [a] says (see also *Insight*, 114):[b]
>
> > [Buddha] said that all things have two natures,
> > Those found by perceptions of reality and of falsities—

Concerning this, the Supramundane Victors, who non-erroneously know the natures of the two truths, teach that the entities of all things—internal things such as the compositional factor of intention and external things such as sprouts—are twofold. What are these? An entity that is an obscurational truth and an entity that is an ultimate truth.

This indicates that when the entities of one thing, such as a sprout, are divided, there are two entities, [one] fraudulent and [the other] ultimate, but this does not at all indicate that just the single entity of a sprout is the two truths in relation to common beings and Superiors [respectively].[c] Taken that way, since there is no occurrence of a phenomenon lacking an entity, whatever are established bases [that is, are existents] do not pass beyond being either one entity or different entities, and although entities are asserted to exist, it is not contradictory

[a] Tsong-kha-pa does not cite Chandrakīrti's root text; the stanzas have been added in double indent for the sake of clarity.

[b] VI.23ab; Toh. 3861, vol. 'a, 205a.5-205a.6; La Vallée Poussin, *Madhyamakāvatāra*, 102.8-102.9; La Vallée Poussin, "*Introduction au traité du milieu*," *Muséon* 11 (1910): 299.

[c] That is, this does not at all indicate that just the single entity of a sprout is an obscurational truth in relation to common beings and is an ultimate truth in relation to Superiors.

that an inherently established entity does not exist.

With respect to this, the ultimate entity of things such as sprouts and so forth gains its own entity[a] through being the object itself of a specific pristine wisdom of those who directly see the meaning of reality [that is, emptiness]; it is not established by way of its own selfness.[b] This is one of the two entities being explained.

[An ultimate truth] is not found by just any pristine wisdom of a Superior; rather, [it is found by] a "specific pristine wisdom" which is to be taken as a specific type, or a particular type, of pristine wisdom. It is found, moreover, by a pristine wisdom comprehending the mode [of being of phenomena, emptiness.]

When [Chandrakīrti] indicates that [an ultimate truth] is found, or established, by that pristine wisdom, it might be held that if there is something established by that pristine wisdom, it is truly established. To refute that, he says, "It is not established by way of its own selfness." Hence, those who propound that it is the system of this master that if a pristine wisdom of meditative equipoise comprehended an ultimate truth, [the ultimate] would be truly established and that, therefore, [the ultimate] is not an object of knowledge[c] have not at all realized the meaning of [Chandrakīrti's] explanation that although [ultimate truth] is found by [a consciousness in] meditative equipoise, it is not truly established. Not realizing such, they cause the degeneration of a wise being's system.

The entity of the conventional,[d] which is other than the ultimate, gains the existence of its own entity through the force of perceptions of falsities by common beings whose mental eyes are completely covered over by the darkening cataracts[e] of ignorance. Its own entity does not exist in accordance with how it appears to be established by way of its own character as an object seen by childish beings. This is one of the two entities.

[Chandrakīrti's] statement thus that, as regards the finding of ultimate truths, the finders are Superiors [that is, beings on the path of seeing or above] is made in consideration that the **main** [of those who realize ultimate truths] are Superiors. However, he is not asserting that [ultimate truths] are not found also by common beings who possess the

---

[a] *bdag gi rang gi ngo bo.*

[b] *rang gi bdag nyid kyis ma grub pa.*

[c] The opponent here is not Dol-po-pa, who holds that the ultimate is an object of knowledge and, being the ultimate, must also be ultimately established.

[d] *kun rdzob;* this could also be translated as "the fraudulent."

[e] *rab rib kyi ling tog.*

Middle Way view in their [mental] continuums.[a]

Also, as regards the finding of conventionalities, [Chandrakīrti's] statement that the finders are ordinary[b] common beings is made in consideration that they are the **main** perceivers of external and internal things—illustrations of conventionalities—through being under the other-influence of ignorance. He is not asserting that these things are not found by conventional valid cognitions in the continuums of Superiors.[c]

The finding [that is, realization] of pots and so forth, which are illustrations of obscurational truths, does indeed occur among those who have not found the view of the Middle Way; however, in order to find with valid cognition that something is an obscurational truth [that is, to recognize it as an obscurational truth], one definitely must have first found the view of the Middle Way. This is because if something is established as an obscurational truth, it must be established as a falsity, and actually to establish that something is a falsity, it is necessary first to refute with valid cognition that it is truly established. Therefore, with respect to [Chandrakīrti's saying that "The entity of the conventional, which is other than the ultimate, gains the existence of its own entity] through the force of the perceptions of falsities [by common beings]," although those ordinary persons see falsities, they do not necessarily establish them as falsities. This is just like the fact, for example, that when an audience at a magic show sees an illusory horse or elephant, although they see falsities, they do not necessarily establish that those appearances **are** falsities. Therefore, to be found by a perceiver of falsities that posits it as an obscurational truth means to be found by a conventional valid cognition that comprehends a false object of knowledge—a deceptive object [but does not necessarily realize that it is a falsity].

> Chandrakīrti's *Supplement to (Nāgārjuna's) "Treatise on the Middle"* continues (see also *Insight,* 114):[d]

---

[a] A conceptual cognition of emptiness while still a common being—that is to say, while on the path of accumulation and path of preparation or even prior to any of the five paths—is also a finding, or realization, of emptiness.

[b] *rang dga' ba.*

[c] This and the previous paragraph counter Dol-po-pa's statement (below, 277):

> The *Buddhāvataṃsaka Sūtra* says that those having and not having special insight have good and bad appearances [respectively] and that what appear to those without special insight do not appear to those with special insight...

[d] VI.23cd; Toh. 3861, vol. *'a,* 205a.6; La Vallée Poussin, *Madhyamakāvatāra,* 102.10-102.11; La Vallée Poussin, "*Introduction au traité du milieu,*" *Muséon* 11 (1910): 299.

Objects of perceptions of reality are suchnesses,
[And] objects of perceptions of falsities are obscurational truths.

Furthermore, from between those two natures, or entities, explained above, an object found by a rational consciousness perceiving, that is, comprehending, the meaning of reality is a suchness, an ultimate truth. This will be explained [below in stanza VI.29] at the point of "by the force of cataracts" and so forth. [An object] found by a conventional valid cognition perceiving a false object of knowledge is an obscurational truth. That is what the Teacher [Buddha] said; he spoke of an ultimate and a conventionality as two separate bases [that is, objects] that are found [by their respective valid cognitions]. It is not that there are two ways of finding a single [object].

Indicating other points about the two truths

[Basis of division]

Although there indeed are many different ways of asserting what the basis of division of the two truths is,[a] here it is taken to be objects of knowledge.[b] The *Meeting of Father and Son Sūtra*,[c] cited in Shāntideva's *Compendium of Instructions*, says (see also *Insight*, 104):[d]

> It is thus: Ones-Gone-Thus thoroughly understand the two, obscurationals and ultimates. Furthermore, objects of knowledge[e] are exhausted as these obscurational truths and ultimate truths. Moreover, because Ones-Gone-Thus have thoroughly perceived, known, and actualized well [these] as [having the aspect of][f] emptiness, they are called "omniscient."

[a] That is to say, what is being divided into the two truths. For Jam-yang-shay-pa's list of six incorrect assertions on the basis of division, see Hopkins, *Maps of the Profound*, 894.

[b] *shes bya, jñeya.*

[c] *yab dang sras mjal ba'i mdo, pitāputrasamāgamasūtra;* P760.16, vol. 23; Toh. 60, vol. *nga* (*dkon brtsegs*), 60b.4-60b.5.

[d] *bslab pa kun las btus pa, śikṣāsamuccaya;* Toh. 3940, vol. *khi*, 142b.3-142b.4; Sanskrit text, which leaves out the first sentence, in Bendall, *Çikshāsamuccaya*, 256: *etāvaccaitat jñeyam / yaduta saṃvṛtiḥ paramārthaśca / tacca bhagavatā śūnyataḥ sudṛṣṭaṃ suviditaṃ susākṣātkṛtaṃ / tena sa sarvajña ityucyate /*. English translation in Bendall and Rouse, *Śikṣā Samuccaya*, 236.

[e] *shes par bya ba;* or "those that are to be known."

[f] The bracketed addition is taken from Tsong-kha-pa's commentary below (223). Without the addition, the passage seems to say that a Buddha is called omniscient only because of having thoroughly realized emptiness; by taking the word emptiness as a

Because [the sūtra] says "Furthermore, objects of knowledge," objects of knowledge are the basis of division [into the two truths], and because it says "are exhausted as these," the number is limited to the two truths. Also, because Ones-Gone-Thus thoroughly understand both truths, they are indicated as being omniscient. Therefore, it is wrong to explain that the thought of Shāntideva's *Engaging in the Bodhisattva Deeds* is that ultimate truths are not objects of knowledge and that they are not realized by any mind.[a]

[The divisions]

The twofold division into obscurational truths and ultimate truths comprises the entities into which [objects of knowledge] are divided.[b]

[Relationship of the two divisions]

Although there are also many different [opinions] regarding the meaning of the division [that is, the relationship of the two divisions], here both [obscurational truths and ultimate truths] have entities, and since there is nothing that is not either one entity or different entities and since if phenomena[c] were different entities from [their respective] emptinesses of true existence, they would be truly established, [the two truths] are one entity but different isolates[d] [that is, one entity but conceptually isolatable], like product and impermanent thing. Nāgārjuna's *Essay on the Mind of Enlightenment* says (see also *Insight,* 107):[e]

> Suchness is not observed
> As a different [entity] from conventionalities,
>
> Conventionalities are described as emptiness [that is, as empty of inherent existence]
> And just emptiness is [posited with respect to] the conventional

bahuvṛhi compound meaning "those which have emptiness" or "those having the aspect of emptiness" the term comes to refer to all those that are empty and thus all obscurational truths and ultimate truths. The addition does indeed seem strained, but the sūtra itself, just above, speaks of both truths.

[a] See below, 222.

[b] For Jam-yang-shay-pa's explanation on how a third category is eliminated, see Hopkins, *Maps of the Profound,* 895.

[c] *chos can,* which literally is "those possessing the attribute [of emptiness]," that is to say, the substrata of emptiness, all phenomena.

[d] *ngo bo gcig la ldog pa tha dad pa.*

[e] Stanzas 67cd-68; Lindtner, *Master of Wisdom,* 54.

Because of the definiteness that [the one] would not occur
without [the other],
Like product and impermanent thing.

The meaning of the first four lines is that suchnesses do not exist as different entities from conventionalities because conventionalities are empty of true [existence] and because emptinesses of true [existence] also are posited with respect to conventionalities, which are [their] bases. The next two lines indicate that:

- it is thus, and the relationship that if the one does not exist, the other does not occur is definite
- and moreover since this is a relationship of one nature, [the two truths] are the same entity like product and impermanent thing.[a]

[Identifying the individual divisions]

The identifications of the individual divisions are, as set forth earlier in their individual definitions, that they are found by the two [types of] valid cognition.[b]

Question: If you are explaining this [work by Chandrakīrti] and Shāntideva's *Engaging in the Bodhisattva Deeds* as in agreement, then how do you explain this statement in Shāntideva's *Engaging in the Bodhisattva Deeds:*[c]

Conventionalities and ultimates,
These are asserted as the two truths.
The ultimate is not an object of activity of an awareness.
Awarenesses are said to be conventionalities.

Answer: In that, the first two lines indicate the divisions of the two truths, and [then] when identifying the entities of the individual divisions, [Shāntideva] indicates an identification of ultimate truths by one [line beginning with] "The ultimate," and an identification of obscurational truths by one [line having] "conventionalities" [in it]. The assertion[d] that [from between those two lines] the former ["The ultimate is

---

[a] For Jam-yang-shay-pa's and Nga-wang-pel-den's treatment of other assertions about the relationship of the two truths, see Hopkins, *Maps of the Profound,* 896-902.

[b] For refinements about the two definitions see Hopkins, *Maps of the Profound,* 902-903.

[c] Stanza IX.2; Toh. 3871, *dbu ma,* vol. *la,* 31a.1; Sanskrit in Swami Dwarika Das Shastri, *Bodhicaryāvatāra of Ārya Śāntideva with the Commentary Pañjikā of Shri Prajñākaramati* (Varanasi: Bauddha Bharati, 1988), 267: *saṃvṛttiḥ paramārthaśca satyadvayamidaṃ matam / buddheragocarastattvaṃ buddhiḥ saṃvṛtirucyate //.*

[d] Jam-yang-shay-pa's *Great Exposition of the Middle* (Newland, unpublished manuscript,

not an object of activity of an awareness"] sets the thesis that an ultimate truth is not an object of an awareness and that the latter line ["Awarenesses are said to be conventionalities"] proves this thesis does not at all appear to be the meaning of those passages.[a]

Therefore, with respect to this identification of the two truths, Shāntideva is stating in his *Engaging in the Bodhisattva Deeds* the meaning of a statement in the *Meeting of Father and Son Sūtra*[b] that he quoted in his *Compendium of Instructions:*[c]

> The One-Gone-Thus sees conventionalities as in the province of the world. That which is ultimate is inexpressible, is not an object of knowledge, is not an object of individual consciousness, is not an object of thorough knowledge, is undemonstrable....

Concerning that, the meaning of the explanation that the ultimate truth is not an object of knowledge is that it is not an object of an awareness in the manner of the meaning of a passage [that Chandrakīrti] cites from the *Introduction to the Two Truths Sūtra* which is explained below (260).[d]

If the meaning of [Shāntideva's statement that the ultimate is not an object of an awareness] is not posited that way but instead [is taken to mean that the ultimate] is not an object of any awareness, this would contradict the explanation [in the *Meeting of Father and Son Sūtra* cited above] that a Conqueror is posited as omniscient because of having actualized all that have the aspect of emptiness,[e] conventionalities and ultimates. This will also be explained more below.

40-43) identifies one such scholar as Tö-lung-gya-mar (*stod lung rgya dmar ba byang chub grags,* eleventh-twelfth century; he was one of Cha-pa Chö-kyi-seng-gay's (*phya pa chos kyi seng ge;* 1109-1169) teachers of the Middle Way School and of logic and epistemology.

[a] Rather, the first two lines of the stanza indicate the two truths in a general way, and then the last two lines identify what they are.

[b] *yab dang sras mjal ba'i mdo, pitāputrasamāgamasūtra,* P760.16, vol. 23; Toh. 60, vol. *nga* (*dkon brtsegs*), 60b.5.

[c] Toh. 3940, *dbu ma,* vol. *khi,* 142b.4-142b.5; Sanskrit in Bendall, *Çikshāsamuccaya,* 256.5: *tatra saṃvṛtirlokapracāratastathāgatena dṛṣṭā / yaḥ punaḥ paramārthaḥ so 'nabhilāpyaḥ / anājñeyo 'vijñeyo 'deśito 'prakāśito.* English translation in Bendall and Rouse, *Śikṣā Samuccaya,* 236.

[d] As Nga-wang-pel-den (*Explanation of the Obscurational and the Ultimate in the Four Systems of Tenets,* 111.6/56a.6) encapsulates this:

> [Shāntideva] is saying that an ultimate truth is a phenomenon that is not an object of activity of a directly perceiving awareness involving dualistic appearance and that a phenomenon that is an object of activity of directly perceiving awareness involving dualistic appearance is an obscurational truth.

[e] *stong pa nyid kyi rnam pa can thams cad.*

[Shāntideva's] identification of obscurational truths does not mean that only awarenesses are posited as obscurational truths; rather, they are **objects** of awarenesses. Moreover, since [the *Meeting of Father and Son Sūtra*] speaks of those [objects of awarenesses] as the province of the world, they are objects found within the province, that is, as objects of activity, of worldly, that is, conventional, consciousnesses comprehending falsities. Hence, the meaning of [Shāntideva's] assertion that objects of awarenesses are conventionalities is to be taken in that way.

[Definite enumeration as only two truths]

The division of objects of knowledge into the two truths indicates that objects of knowledge are limited to those two. Scriptural sources for this are the *Meeting of Father and Son Sūtra*, quoted earlier (220), and also the *Superior Sūtra of the Meditative Stabilization Definitely Revealing Suchness* which clearly says (see also *Insight*, 148):[a]

> The conventional and likewise the ultimate—
> There is not at all a third truth.

and Chandrakīrti's *Autocommentary on the "Supplement to (Nāgārjuna's) 'Treatise on the Middle'"* also says that all the many with the name "truth" that are mentioned in the *Sūtra on the Ten Grounds* are included in the two truths:[b]

> Similarly, any other truth that exists at all is also to be ascertained as only included within the two truths.

and he explains that the truth of differentiated realization mentioned there [in the *Sūtra on the Ten Grounds*] is the presentation of the aggregates, constituents, and sense-spheres. Therefore, this master [Chandrakīrti] also asserts that [objects of knowledge] are limited to the two truths.

The reasoning [why there are only two truths] is that if a certain base [that is, an object] is—on the positive side—distinguished as a falsity, a deceptive object, then on the exclusionary side it must be

---

[a] *de kho na nyid nges par bstan pa'i ting nge 'dzin, tattvanirdeśasamādhi.* Cited in Chandrakīrti's *Commentary on the "Supplement to (Nāgārjuna's) 'Treatise on the Middle,'"* commenting on stanza VI.80; Toh. 3682, *dbu ma,* vol. *'a,* 243a.4; La Vallée Poussin, *Madhyamakāvatāra,* 175.11-175.12; La Vallée Poussin, "*Introduction au traité du milieu,*" *Muséon* 11 (1910): 356.

[b] In his commentary on stanza V.1cd; Toh. 3862, *dbu ma,* vol. *'a,* 243b.1; La Vallée Poussin, *Madhyamakāvatāra,* 71.5-71.7; La Vallée Poussin, "*Introduction au traité du milieu,*" *Muséon* 8 (1907): 313.

eliminated that it is a non-deceptive suchness, due to which the deceptive and the non-deceptive are dichotomous explicit contradictories. Since whatever is [a dichotomous pair] covers all objects of knowledge, a further category that is both and a further category that is neither are eliminated. It is as Kamalashīla's *Illumination of the Middle* says:[a]

> Phenomena[b] that have the character of being a dichotomy are such that if something is refuted to be the one and it is not established to be the other, then it does not exist. Therefore, it also is not reasonable to think of it as in a class that is neither of those two.

and:

> Two that are such that something does not exist if it is neither [of them][c] have the character of being a dichotomy. Those that have the character of being a dichotomy cover all aspects [that is, whatever exists is either one or the other]. Those that cover all aspects eliminate other categories. Examples are, for instance, particular [pairs] such as the physical and the non-physical,[d] and so forth.

This is also to be understood with respect to all other explicit contradictories [that is, dichotomies].

If there were no such things as dichotomies that exclude a third category, there would be no way to make a refutation with analysis that limits the possibilities to two—[asking] whether it is asserted that something exists or does not exist, or is one or many, and so forth. If there are [dichotomies that exclude a third category], then when something is refuted as being one side of a dichotomy and it is not established as the other, it does not exist. Therefore, to say that there are no explicit contradictories in the Middle Way Consequence School is a case of not having formed [understanding of] the presentation of refutation and establishment[e] [in this system]. The Middle Way Autonomy School and the Middle Way Consequence School do not differ with respect to [asserting] that [within existents] if something is eliminated as being one side of a dichotomy, it must be established as the other and that if

[a] Toh. 3887, *dbu ma*, vol. *sa*, 191a.4-191a.5 and 219a.1-219a.2.

[b] *chos dag;* in this the *dag* ending could be dual since this is its strict usage, in which case the translation should read "two phenomena."

[c] *gang zhig yongs su gcod pa gang rnam par bcad pa med na med pa de gnyis;* the translation is loose.

[d] *lus can dang lus can ma yin pa.*

[e] *dgag gzhag gi rnam gzhag.*

one is refuted, the other is established.

Explaining the divisions of obscurational truths in relation to the world

Among conventionalities there are two [types], objects and subjects, and initially [Chandrakīrti] indicates that in relation to worldly consciousnesses,[a] subjects are twofold, right and wrong.[b]

> Chandrakīrti's *Supplement to (Nāgārjuna's) "Treatise on the Middle"* says:[c]
>
> > Also, those that perceive falsities are asserted to be of two types—
> > Those with clear sense powers and those having defective sense powers.
> > Consciousnesses of those having defective sense powers are asserted
> > To be wrong in relation to those having good sense powers.

Not only are objects of knowledge divided into the two truths, but also subjects perceiving falsities are asserted as twofold, right and wrong:

1. clear sense powers, that is to say, sense powers that are not polluted by superficial causes of mistake[d] and the consciousnesses that depend on them
2. defective sense powers, that is to say, subjects [consciousnesses] that are polluted by superficial causes of mistake.

Concerning those, polluted consciousnesses of those having defective sense powers are asserted to be wrong consciousnesses in relation to consciousnesses having good sense powers, that is, not polluted by superficial causes of mistake. The former [that is, those with clear sense powers] are asserted to apprehend non-erroneous objects. Moreover, those two distinctions are not the Middle Way system but are in

---

[a] *'jig rten pa'i shes pa la ltos nas.*

[b] *yang dag pa dang log pa.* With regard to subjects I translate these terms as "right and wrong," and with regard to objects, as "real and unreal." For interesting distinctions on these topics, see Hopkins, *Maps of the Profound*, 907-911.

[c] Stanza VI.24; Toh. 3861, *dbu ma,* vol. *'a,* 205a.6-205a.7; La Vallée Poussin, *Madhyamakāvatāra,* 103.11-103.14; La Vallée Poussin, "*Introduction au traité du milieu,*" *Muséon* 11 (1910): 300.

[d] See the note above, 191.

relation to worldly consciousnesses.

[Chandrakīrti] indicates that just as subjects are divided into two, erroneous and non-erroneous, so objects also are.

> Chandrakīrti's *Supplement to (Nāgārjuna's) "Treatise on the Middle"* (see also *Insight,* 119) says:[a]
>
> Objects realized by the world that are apprehended
> By [the consciousnesses of] the six sense powers unimpaired [by superficial causes of mistake]
> Are true [or real] just [relative] to the world [because of being phenomena that prior to realizing emptiness cannot be realized to be a combination of appearing to be inherently existent but being empty of such].
> The rest [that is, those apprehended by sense consciousnesses impaired by superficial causes of mistake such as reflections, echoes and so forth] are posited as unreal just [relative] to the world.

Objects realized by the world that are apprehended by the consciousnesses of the six sense powers unimpaired by superficial causes of mistake are true, that is, real, from just[b]—that is to say, only[c]—[the viewpoint of] the world. It is not that those objects are posited as true and real in relation to a Superior. Here "Superior" and "Middle Way system" [in the last sentence of the previous paragraph] have similar meanings.

The rest—that is to say, reflections and so forth—which appear as objects when sense powers are impaired are posited as being unreal in relation to just the world. The word "just"[d] indicates that just a conventional valid cognition is sufficient to posit those consciousnesses as mistaken; such does not rely on a rational consciousness [realizing emptiness].

About that, internal conditions that impair the sense powers are

---

[a] Stanza VI.25; Toh. 3861, *dbu ma,* vol. *'a,* 205a.7; La Vallée Poussin, *Madhyamakāvatāra,* 104.4-104.7; La Vallée Poussin, "*Introduction au traité du milieu,*" *Muséon* 11 (1910): 301. The Sanskrit, as cited from Prajñākaramati's *Commentary on the Difficult Points of (Shāntideva's) "Engaging in the Bodhisattva Deeds"* in Khangkar and Yorihito, 211 note 245, reads: *vinopaghātena yad indriyāṇāṃ saṇṇām api grāhyam avaiti lokaḥ/ satyaṃ hi tal loyata evaṃ śeṣaṃ vikalpitaṃ lokata eva mithyā//.* Brackets are from *Four Interwoven Annotations,* vol. 2, 314.5. Cited in *Great Treatise,* vol. 3, 167.

[b] *nyid.*

[c] *kho na.*

[d] *nyid.*

cataracts,[a] jaundice,[b] and so forth as well as having eaten *da du ra*[c] and so forth. *Da du ra* is thorn-apple;[d] when its fruit has been eaten, all appears to be golden. "And so forth" includes contagion and the like. External conditions that impair the sense powers are mirrors, sounds spoken from within caves, the rays of the summer[e] sun being proximate to white sand, and so forth; even though there might be no internal conditions impairing the sense powers, those serve as causes for apprehending, respectively, reflections, echoes, water in mirages, and so forth. Mantras and medicines[f] used by magicians and so forth also should be understood similarly [as cases of external causes of mistake].

Impairments to the mental sense power are those mantras, medicines, and so forth as well as wrong tenets, quasi-reasons,[g] sleep, and so forth. Since [Chandrakīrti] says that sleep impairs the mind[h] from among the six sense powers, it is hugely wrong to explain that this master asserts that sense consciousnesses exist in dreams. [Chandrakīrti describes the superficial causes of mistake that impair the mental consciousness this way, and] thus the impairment of being polluted by the ignorance consisting of the two apprehensions of self, which have operated beginninglessly, and so forth is not held to be a cause of impairment in this context. Rather, the superficial causes of mistake that impair sense powers as explained above are to be held [as the causes of impairment].

The positing of a conventional object—apprehended by [any of] the six consciousnesses without such impairment—as real and the positing of an object opposite to that as unreal is done in relation only to worldly consciousnesses because those [respectively] are not damaged and are damaged by worldly consciousnesses with respect to those existing as objects in accordance with how they appear. [Conventional

[a] *rab rib.*

[b] *mig ser.*

[c] La Vallée Poussin, "*Introduction au traité du milieu,*" *Muséon* 11 (1910): 301, n.3, questions the reading, saying that M. Max Walleser suggests *dardura*. Tsong-kha-pa glosses *da du ra* as *thang phrom,* which is also spelled *thang khrom*. The latter is identified as *dhūstūra* in Sarat Chandra Das's *Tibetan-English Dictionary*, 568.

[d] *thang phrom.*

[e] *sos ka;* this is variously translated as "spring" or "summer"; the reference is to the hot season before the summer rains descend.

[f] Kensur Lekden identified this medicine as a salve that a magician puts on a stick or pebble that serves as the basis of conjuring and which, upon the casting of a mantra, then appears to be an elephant, and so forth.

[g] *gtan tshigs ltar snang.*

[h] *yid.*

objects] are not [posited] as the two, real and unreal, in relation to Superiors because just as reflections and so forth do not exist as objects in accordance with how they appear, so although blue and so forth appear to be established by way of their own character to those who have ignorance, they do not exist as objects in accordance with how they appear. Therefore, these two consciousnesses [that is, a consciousness of a reflection and a consciousness to which blue appears to be established by way of its own character] cannot be divided even in terms of being mistaken or not mistaken [since both are mistaken with respect to their appearing objects].

Objection: Even an ordinary worldly awareness realizes that:

- due to the physical senses having superficial impairment objects appear wrongly, and
- due to the mental consciousness having superficial impairment by sleep and so forth
    - regarding appearances as humans and so forth in dreams there is erroneous apprehension of humans and so forth, and
    - when awake there is erroneous apprehension of horses and elephants in magical illusions of horses and elephants as well as erroneous apprehension of water in mirage-appearances as water.

However, an ordinary worldly awareness does not realize that objects—apprehended wrongly due to the mind having impairment by bad tenets—are erroneous. Therefore, how are these posited as wrong from just [the viewpoint of] the world [as Chandrakīrti says]?

Answer: Here the impairment that is analyzed as to whether or not there is impairment is not taken to be impairment by **innate** erroneous apprehension. Therefore, those that are imputed by bad tenets [and are realized to be wrong by a worldly consciousness do not include the inherent existence that is innately misapprehended but] are the principal[a] and so forth, which are wrongly imputed **only** by those whose awarenesses have been affected by tenets. Although those are not realized to be erroneous by an ordinary worldly awareness, they are realized to be so by conventional valid cognition that is not directed toward suchness, in which case they are realized to be wrong by a worldly consciousness.

The likes of objects that are apprehended by the two innate

[a] *gtso bo, pradhāna;* also called the fundamental nature (*rang bzhin, prakṛti*) in the Sāṃkhya system.

apprehensions of self are "objects apprehended by unimpaired sense powers" [since they are apprehended by a mind impaired not by superficial but by deep causes of mistake]. However, although these are real, or true, in relation to ordinary worldly thought, they do not exist even in conventional terms.

Objection: Since you do not assert real conventionalities, you do not divide [conventionalities] into real and unreal, but why do you not posit objects and subjects polluted by ignorance as unreal conventionalities?

Answer: It is because conventionalities must be posited by conventional valid cognition, and, therefore, if when unreal conventionalities are posited, they have to be posited in relation to those [conventional valid cognitions, objects and subjects] polluted by the predispositions of ignorance are not established by conventional valid cognitions to be mistaken.[a]

Showing that the conceived object, with respect to which [a wrong consciousness] is mistaken, does not exist even in conventional terms

[Chandrakīrti] has indicated in general that, due to impairment of the mind as just explained, [certain mental consciousnesses] are mistaken with respect to their conceived objects. Now, he indicates just that meaning in the manner of taking specific illustrations as examples.

> Chandrakīrti's *Supplement to (Nāgārjuna's) "Treatise on the Middle"* (see also *Insight,* 127) says:[b]
>
> Entities [such as a permanent self, principal, and so forth] as they are imputed by [the assertions of] Forders [driven by bad tenets and quasi-reasons],
> Strongly affected by the sleep of ignorance,

[a] Jam-yang-shay-pa explains this passage as meaning that objects and subjects affected by predispositions of ignorance and apprehended by consciousnesses that are not impaired by superficial causes of mistake "are not conventionalities that are unreal in relation to the perspective of the worldly consciousness **that is explicitly indicated in this context**" even though they are indeed unreal conventionalities, since all conventionalities are wrong in the sense that they appear one way and exist another. See Guy Newland, *The Two Truths* (Ithaca, N.Y.: Snow Lion Publications, 1992), 89-90.

[b] Stanza VI.26; Toh. 3861, *dbu ma,* vol. *'a,* 205b.1; La Vallée Poussin, *Madhyamakāvatāra,* 105.9-105.12; La Vallée Poussin, "*Introduction au traité du milieu,*" *Muséon* 11 (1910): 302. Brackets are from *Four Interwoven Annotations,* vol. 2, 343.1. Cited in *Great Treatise,* vol. 3, 178.

And [those horses and elephants, water, and so forth]
imputed to magical illusions, mirages, and so forth
Are just non-existent even in [the conventions of] the
world.

These [non-Buddhist] Forders, whose minds are strongly affected by the sleep of ignorance—their minds being impaired by erroneous bad tenets and quasi-reasons—want to enter into suchness. Hence, they do not hold onto the non-erroneous production, disintegration, and so forth that are renowned to untrained persons such as herders, women, and so forth on up but instead wish to rise above worldly beings. They thereby plunge into chasms of bad views with great pain like, for example, someone who, in climbing a tree, releases the lower branch without having grasped a higher one. Since they are bereft of good perception of the two truths, they will not attain the fruit, liberation. Therefore, entities such as the three qualities[a] as they are imputed by these Forders[b] in their respective texts do not exist even as worldly conventionalities. This refutes well the statement that what exists in the perspective of a mistaken awareness is posited as conventionally existing by this system.

Similarly, the horse or elephant that is imputed to a magical illusion, the water that is imputed to a mirage, the face that is imputed to a reflection, and so forth also just do not exist even from [the viewpoint of] worldly conventions. In that way, for something to exist in conventional terms, it must be established by valid cognition.

Although the conceived objects of such [wrong consciousnesses] do not exist even in conventional terms, such is not asserted with regard to their appearing objects. Since the appearance, in that way, of the five [sense objects]—forms, sounds, and so forth—to sense consciousnesses now as if they are established by way of their own character is polluted by ignorance, those consciousnesses and sense consciousnesses to which reflections, echoes, and the like appear, except for [a difference in] mere subtlety and coarseness, do not differ as to whether they are mistaken or non-mistaken with respect to their appearing objects [since both are mistaken]. Also, blue and so forth that are established by way of their own character and the existence of a reflection as a face do not occur, but just as a reflection, which does not exist as a face, exists, so although blue and so forth are not established by way of their

[a] *yon tan gsum, triguṇa.* These are mental potency (*snying stobs, sattva*), activity (*rdul, rajas*), and darkness (*mun pa, tamas*); for a brief exposition of the Sāṃkhya system see Hopkins, *Maps of the Profound,* chapter three.

[b] Such as in the Sāṃkhya system.

own character, they must exist. Furthermore, just as [blue and so forth] exist as external objects, so reflections also are asserted as form-sense spheres [that is, as forms that are objects of apprehension by an eye consciousness]. Below,[a] [Chandrakīrti] also says that a reflection generates the sense consciousness to which it appears. Those facts also should be understood with respect to magical illusions in which there is an appearance as a horse or an elephant to the eye as well as with respect to echoes, and so forth. These are uncommon presentations by this excellent system.

Applying this to the meaning at this point

> Chandrakīrti's *Supplement to (Nāgārjuna's) "Treatise on the Middle"* says:[b]
>
> Just as the observations of an eye with cataracts
> Do not invalidate a consciousness of one without cataracts,
> An undefiled awareness is not invalidated
> By an awareness of one who has forsaken the undefiled pristine wisdom.

Because the meaning of suchness is not posited by a conventional consciousness, the refutation of production from other is not done within abiding in only the world's views. Rather, it is refuted ultimately within having asserted the perception of suchness by Superiors. When it is the case that the qualification "ultimately" is affixed to this refutation of production from other, then just as the observations of falling hairs and so forth by a consciousness of one whose eyes have cataracts do not damage [that is, invalidate] the non-appearance of falling hairs and so forth to a consciousness that is not polluted with cataracts, so a common being's awareness, polluted by ignorance, that has forsaken—that is, is devoid of—undefiled uncontaminated pristine wisdom does not damage an undefiled uncontaminated awareness that is not polluted with ignorance. Therefore, even if it were allowed that [production from other] is established in the perspective of the world, [the world]

[a] *Supplement to (Nāgārjuna's) "Treatise on the Middle,"* stanza VI.37cd; Toh. 3861, *dbu ma,* vol. *'a,* 206a.1-206a.2; La Vallée Poussin, *Madhyamakāvatāra,* 123.13-123.14; La Vallée Poussin, "*Introduction au traité du milieu,*" *Muséon* 11 (1910): 315-316.

[b] Stanza VI.27; Toh. 3861, *dbu ma,* vol. *'a,* 205b.1-205b.2; La Vallée Poussin, *Madhyamakāvatāra,* 106.3-106.6; La Vallée Poussin, "*Introduction au traité du milieu,*" *Muséon* 11 (1910): 302-303.

would not damage [that production from other is refuted ultimately].[a] This being so, the other side [that is, the non-Buddhists who give up what is validly held in the world in order to rise above worldly beings but plunge into chasms of bad views][b] are fit to be laughed at by the excellent wise ones.

[a] Tsong-kha-pa says "even if it were allowed" because Chandrakīrti in fact does not assert that the world uses designations such as production from other.
[b] See above, 231.

2. Obscurational Truths

Explaining the individual natures of the two truths

This section has two parts: description of obscurational truths and description of ultimate truths.

Description of obscurational truths

This section has three parts: (1) the obscuring [consciousness] in the perspective of which these are truths and those [persons] in the perspective of whom these are not truths, (2) the ways in which mere conventionalities do and do not appear to the three types of persons, and (3) how there come to be ultimates and conventionalities relative to Superiors and common beings.

The obscuring [consciousness] in the perspective of which these are truths and those [persons] in the perspective of whom these are not truths

This section has two parts: the actual meaning and an explanation of [the Consequence School's] unique presentation of afflictive emotions.

Actual meaning of the obscuring [consciousness] in the perspective of which these are truths and those [persons] in whose perspective these are not truths

> Chandrakīrti's *Supplement to (Nāgārjuna's) "Treatise on the Middle"* (see also *Insight,* 110) says:[a]
>
> The Subduer said that because bewilderment [that is,
> the apprehension of inherent existence] obscures

---

[a] VI.28; Toh. 3861, *dbu ma,* vol. *'a,* 205b.2-205b.3; La Vallée Poussin, *Madhyamakāvatāra,* 107.1-107.4; La Vallée Poussin, "*Introduction au traité du milieu,*" *Muséon* 11 (1910): 303. The Sanskrit, as cited from Prajñākaramati's *Commentary on the Difficult Points of (Shāntideva's) "Engaging in the Bodhisattva Deeds"* in Khangkar and Yorihito, 211 note 245, reads: *mohaḥ svabhāvāvataṇād dhi saṃvṛtiḥ satyaṃ tayā khyāti yad eva kṛtrimam/ jagād tat saṃvṛtisatyam ity asau muniḥ padārthaṃ kṛtakaṃ ca saṃvṛtim//.* Brackets are from *Four Interwoven Annotations,* vol. 2, 356.5. The first three lines cited in *Great Treatise,* vol. 3, 182.

> [direct perception of] the nature [of the mode of subsistence of phenomena],
> [This ignorance] is all-obscuring (*kun rdzob*)[a] and he said that those fabrications appearing
> To be true due to this [ignorance] are obscurational truths (*kun rdzob bden*) [because of being true in the perspective of the obscurational apprehension of inherent existence].
> Things that are fabrications [exist] conventionally (*kun rdzob tu*).

Because, through it, sentient beings are obstructed, that is to say, beclouded, with respect to viewing the nature that is how things abide, it is [called] bewilderment.[b] Bewilderment, or ignorance,[c] which has an essence of obstructing[d] the perception of the nature that is the mode of being [of phenomena through] superimposing inherent existence on the entities of things that do not inherently exist, is the obscurer (*kun rdzob, saṃvṛti*). This is an identification of the obscuring [consciousness] (*kun rdzob / kun rdzob pa, saṃvṛti*) in the perspective of which truth in [the term] "obscurational truth" is posited; it is not an identification of *kun rdzob pa* (*saṃvṛti*) in general [which means "conventionality" or "conventional consciousness"].

Furthermore, that identification [in Chandrakīrti's *Supplement*] is the meaning of the statement in the *Descent into Laṅkā Sūtra* [above, 189] that an awareness making the mistake that what ultimately lacks inherent existence exists inherently is an obscurational (*kun rdzob pa*):[e]

> The production of things [exists] conventionally (*kun rdzob tu, saṃvṛtyā*);

---

[a] The *Four Interwoven Annotations* (357.1) gives an etymology of *kun rdzob:*

> *Kun* means "*all* of the nature of the mode of subsistence of phenomena" (*chos kyi gnas lugs kyi rang bzhin kun*), and *rdzob* means "obstructing" (*sgrib pa*) and "covering/veiling" (*'gebs pa*).

[b] *gti mug, moha.* Although Sanskrit dictionaries gloss *moha* by "delusion," this text does not describe it in these terms but as obstructing, or obscuring, and thus I translate the term as "bewilderment."

[c] *ma rig pa, avidyā.*

[d] *sgrib pa.*

[e] *lang kar gshegs pa'i mdo, laṅkāvatārasūtra,* stanza X.429; Sanskrit in Bunyiu Nanjio, *Laṅkāvatāra Sūtra,* 319: *bhāvā vidyanti saṃvṛtyā paramārthe na bhāvakāḥ / niḥsvabhāveṣu yā bhrāntistatsatyaṃ saṃvṛtirbhavet //.* This sūtra passage is given above (189), from Kamalashīla's citation of it, in elucidating the Autonomy School's understanding of true existence.

Ultimately it lacks inherent existence.
That [consciousness] mistaken with regard to the lack of inherent existence
Is asserted as the obscurer of reality (*yang dag kun rdzob, satyaṃ saṃvṛti*).

Since the Sanskrit original for "obscurer" (*kun rdzob, saṃvṛti*) [does not just mean "convention" but] is also used for "obstructor" (*sgrib byed*), this obscurer (*kun rdzob, saṃvṛti*) [in the final line] is an obstructor. What does it obstruct? Since [the sūtra] says that it is "the obscurer of reality (*yang dag kun rdzob, satyaṃ saṃvṛti*)," it says that since it obstructs [perception of] the meaning of reality, it is asserted as an obscurer, or obstructor. It is not indicating that it is a right conventionality (*yang dag kun rdzob, tathya-saṃvṛti*) from between the two [categories of conventionalities], right and wrong [conventionalities].[a]

The [*kun rdzob* (*saṃvṛti*) translated as] "conventionally" indicated in the first line and the [*kun rdzob* (*saṃvṛti*) translated as] "obscurer" indicated in the last line should not be construed to be identical. For, the first is the conventional way in which we ourselves assert things to be produced and so forth, whereas the latter is the obscurer—[a consciousness] apprehending true existence—in the perspective of which things are true [that is, a consciousness taking things to exist the way they appear to inherently exist].

Through the force of that obstructing [consciousness] apprehending true existence, fabricated phenomena such as blue and so forth—which, although lacking inherent establishment, are fabricated to appear to be inherently established and which appear to sentient beings to be true—are true in the perspective of the worldly, erroneous, obscuring [consciousness] described above. Hence, they are worldly obscurational truths. The Subduer said such; the way he said this is what is set forth in the above sūtra [that is, the *Descent into Laṅkā Sūtra*].

Those fabricated things—which [even though they do not inherently exist] are fabricated by thought [to appear to be inherently

[a] Conventionalities, or conventional phenomena, are of two types relative to worldly consciousnesses—right/real conventionalities (*yang dag kun rdzob*) and unreal/wrong conventionalities (*log pa'i kun rdzob*). Unable to find a single, evocative translation equivalent of *yang dag kun rdzob* that would apply to both consciousnesses and objects, I use "right conventionality" and "wrong conventionality" for consciousnesses and "real conventionality" and "unreal conventionality" for objects. Since the Tibetan for "right conventionality" or "real conventionality" is *yang dag kun rdzob* and the Tibetan for "obscurer of reality" is also *yang dag kun rdzob*, the two can be confused, and thus Tsong-kha-pa is pointing out that here in the *Descent into Laṅkā Sūtra* the term *yang dag kun rdzob* means "obscurer of reality."

existent] and which are not truths in the perspective of the three persons [that is, Hearer Foe Destroyers, Solitary Realizer Foe Destroyers, and Bodhisattvas on the eighth, ninth, and tenth grounds, called the three pure grounds]—are not truths in the perspective of **their own** obscuring [consciousnesses since they are beyond such ignorance], and hence those [phenomena] are called "mere conventionalities" (*kun rdzob tsam, saṃvṛtimātra*).

To explain the meaning [of Chandrakīrti's statement in his *Autocommentary* cited here in paraphrase]:[a]

> A few dependent-arisings such as reflections, echoes, and so forth appear to be false even to those who have ignorance, whereas a few [dependent-arisings] such as forms (blue and so forth), minds, feelings, and so forth appear to be true. The nature that is the mode of being of phenomena does not appear in any way to those having ignorance. Therefore, that nature and those that are false even conventionally are not obscurational truths.

In that, "a few" (*cung zad cig*) is rendered better in accordance with Nak-tso's[b] translation as "some" (*'ga' zhig*). That reflections and so forth, though false, appear is [the coarse form of] false appearance [to which Chandrakīrti is referring when he says, "Some dependent-arisings such as reflections, echoes, and so forth, appear to be false even to those who have ignorance."] Since [a reflection of a face] is a falsity that is a composite of the two—appearing to be a face and [being] empty of that [face]—its emptiness of truth [to which Chandrakīrti is referring] is its emptiness of truth as a face and does not have the meaning of a reflection's being empty of truth in the sense of its not being established by way of its own character. Therefore, a reflection is a thing such that although it is established as being empty of being a face, there is no contradiction at all in its being true in the perspective of an

[a] La Vallée Poussin, *Madhyamakāvatāra,* 107.11-107.17. For Chandrakīrti's *rang bzhin,* Tsong-kha-pa (101.2-101.3) reads *chos rnams kyi yin lugs kyi rang bzhin,* and for Chandrakīrti's *de* Tsong-kha-pa reads *rang bzhin de;* the changes make the passage easier to read, without distorting it. Tsong-kha-pa frequently does such with citations to improve on the reading of a translation.

[b] *nag tsho lo tsa ba tshul khrims rgyal ba* (b.1011) made the original translation of Chandrakīrti's *Supplement* from Sanskrit into Tibetan, working with the Indian Kṛṣhṇapaṇḍita. This translation, which survives in the Peking and Narthang Translation of the Treatises (*bstan 'gyur*), was gradually replaced by that of *pa tshab lo tsa ba nyi ma grags.* Nak-tso's translation was the basis for the commentary on Chandrakīrti's *Supplement* written by one of Tsong-kha-pa's teachers, Ren-da-wa Shön-nu-lo-drö (*red mda' ba gzhon nu blo gros,* 1349-1412).

obscuring (*kun rdzob, saṃvṛti*) [consciousness] apprehending it to be established by way of its own character. Hence, a reflection is an obscurational truth [despite Chandrakīrti's seeming to say that it is not, because his reference is to its not being a truth **as a face** for those who know about mirrors].

Therefore, [Chandrakīrti's] statement that a reflection is not an obscurational truth is in consideration that concerning a reflection of a face, for instance, its being a face is false in the perspective of a conventional (*kun rdzob, saṃvṛti*)[a] [consciousness] of worldly [persons] trained in language and hence is not an obscurational truth relative to that [that is, a reflection of a face is not a truth as a face in the perspective of that consciousness].[b] How could it be that [a reflection] is not posited as an obscurational truth described in "objects of perceptions of the false are obscurational truths"![c]

Otherwise, if it were contradictory for something to be an obscurational truth if it does not exist as a truth for a conventional (*kun rdzob, saṃvṛti*) [consciousness], this would contradict:

- [Chandrakīrti's] statement that establishment [of an object] by way of its own character does not exist even in conventional terms (*tha snyad du yang med pa*),[d] and
- all presentations done in conventional terms (*tha snyad du byed pa'i rnam gzhag thams cad*) [including] all refutations of true establishment and proofs of no true existence.[e]

---

[a] Tsong-kha-pa is unpacking the two meanings of *kun rdzob/ saṃvṛti*—as "obscuring consciousness" and as "conventional consciousness." See below.

[b] Those persons do not have the gross level of ignorance apprehending a reflection of a face to exist the way it appears to be a face.

[c] VI.23d. In the Dharmsala edition (101.8) and Varanasi edition (187.9), read *brdzun pa* for *brdzun pa'i* in accordance with La Vallée Poussin, *Madhyamakāvatāra*, (102.11).

[d] As Chandrakīrti's *Supplement to (Nāgārjuna's) "Treatise on the Middle"* (VI.36) says:

> Through that reasoning through which [it is seen] on the occasion of analyzing suchness
> That production from self and other are not reasonable,
> [It is seen] that [production] is not reasonable even in conventional terms.
> If so, through what [reasoning] would your production be [established]?

[e] If it were contradictory for something to be an obscurational truth if it does not exist as a truth for an obscuring consciousness, this would mean that all obscurational truths must be truths for an obscuring consciousness, and in the absence of any criterion for removing any of these that are truths for an obscuring consciousness from the class of obscurational truths this would amount to saying that whatever exists for an obscuring consciousness is an obscurational truth. Since ignorance, an obscuring consciousness, takes the establishment of objects by way of their own character to exist, such establishment would have to be an obscurational truth. Similarly, if inherent existence ex-

Therefore, [claims] stating that objects such as reflections, which even ordinary worldly consciousnesses understand to be mistaken, are not obscurational truths but are mere conventionalities [when in fact they are both] appear to be the talk of those who have not formed understanding concerning:

- the definite enumeration of two truths
- truth and falsity relative to the world and truth and falsity posited by Proponents of the Middle Way.

Also, [Chandrakīrti's] statement that "The nature [emptiness] does not appear in any way to those having ignorance" is in consideration that [emptiness] does not appear to **consciousnesses** polluted with ignorance [and is not in consideration of **persons** having ignorance], since he asserts that Superiors [on the first through seventh grounds] who have not [fully] abandoned ignorance directly realize suchness [emptiness]. Also, because a Learner Superior's pristine wisdom subsequent to meditative equipoise and a common being's viewing consciousness of suchness are polluted with ignorance and its predispositions, [emptiness] does not **directly**[a] appear [to those consciousnesses], but it must be asserted that, in general, ultimate truth [emptiness] does appear [to those consciousnesses].[b]

[Immediately after that, Chandrakīrti] says (see also *Insight,* 111):[c]

> In that way, respectively, obscurational truths are posited through the force of the afflictive ignorance that is included within the [twelve] links [of a dependent-arising] of cyclic existence.

Hence, he asserts that the ignorance apprehending phenomena to be truly [established]—renowned as [a consciousness] apprehending a self of persons and of phenomena—is the ignorance [that is the first] of the twelve links [of dependent-arising], and, therefore, he does not assert

---

isted conventionally, it would be impossible to say that the refutation of inherent existence and the proof of its opposite are done conventionally.

[a] *mngon sum du.*

[b] There are conceptual consciousnesses explicitly realizing emptiness among a Learner Superior's pristine wisdom subsequent to meditative equipoise; also, a common being's viewing consciousnesses of suchness is necessarily a conceptual consciousness explicitly realizing emptiness. The basic rule is that any object explicitly understood must appear to that consciousness.

[c] Commenting on VI.28; Toh. 3862, *dbu ma,* vol. *'a,* 255a.1; La Vallée Poussin, *Madhyamakāvatāra,* 107.17-107.19; La Vallée Poussin, "*Introduction au traité du milieu,*" *Muséon* 11 (1910): 304.

that it is an obstruction to omniscience [but is an afflictive obstruction. His] saying that obscurational truths are posited through the force of ignorance apprehending true existence indicates the mode of positing the obscuring [consciousness] in the perspective of which truth [that is, concordance between appearance and fact] is posited. He is not saying that pots, woolen cloth, and so forth, which are obscurational truths, are posited by that consciousness apprehending true existence because he asserts that what is posited by a consciousness apprehending true existence does not exist even in conventional terms. Therefore, it appears that, because of the similarity of name between the *saṃvṛti* [obscuring consciousness] in the perspective of which the truth that is part of *saṃvṛtisatya* [obscurational truth] is posited and the *saṃvṛti* [conventionality or conventional consciousness] in the positing of pots and so forth as existing conventionally, many cases of mistaking these even to have the same meaning have arisen; therefore, these should be differentiated well.

Question: Then, are these pots and so forth truths in the perspective of obscuring [consciousnesses] of all persons who have not become Buddhafied? Or, are there cases of these also not being truths in the perspective of some persons' obscuring [consciousnesses]?

Answer: Let us explain the meaning of [Chandrakīrti's] statement:[a]

> Moreover, for Hearers, Solitary Realizers, and Bodhisattvas who have abandoned afflictive ignorance and who see compositional phenomena as like reflections and so forth those forms, sounds, and so forth, which are posited as obscurational truths, have a fabricated nature and are not truths because they have no conceit of true existence.[b]

There are three types of persons in the perspective of whom these are not truths [that is, do not exist the way they appear—these being

[a] Commenting on stanza VI.28; Toh. 3862, *dbu ma*, vol. *'a*, 255a.2-255a.3; La Vallée Poussin, *Madhyamakāvatāra*, 107.19-108.3; La Vallée Poussin, "*Introduction au traité du milieu*," *Muséon* 11 (1910): 304.

[b] Again, Tsong-kha-pa is paraphrasing Chandrakīrti, not quoting the text exactly as it is. Though some contemporary Ge-luk-pa scholars explain this discrepancy by claiming that Tsong-kha-pa was quoting from memory, it strikes me that Tsong-kha-pa was deliberately trying to make the passage clearer by lifting it above mere literal translation into a more fluid rendering. Chandrakīrti actually says:

> Moreover, for Hearers, Solitary Realizers, and Bodhisattvas who have abandoned afflictive ignorance and who see compositional phenomena as just being like the existence of reflections and so forth, those [compositional phenomena] have a fabricated nature and are not truths because they have no conceit of true existence.

Hearers, Solitary Realizers, and Bodhisattvas]. Furthermore, because [Chandrakīrti] does not take these to be just any Hearers, Solitary Realizers, or Bodhisattvas, he mentions qualifications ["who have abandoned afflictive ignorance and who see compositional phenomena as like reflections and so forth"]. One qualification is the direct realization that all compounded phenomena are empty of inherent existence but appear to be inherently existent, like reflections. Since even Bodhisattvas on the seventh ground and below as well as Hearers and Solitary Realizers who are Learner Superiors [that is, who have reached the path of seeing but not the path of no more learning] have merely this [direct realization], in order to eliminate them [Chandrakīrti] says of the three persons that they "have abandoned ignorance." Hence, the three persons are to be taken as Bodhisattvas on the pure grounds [that is, on the eighth, ninth, and tenth grounds] and the two types of Foe Destroyers, Hearer and Solitary Realizer. [These pots and so forth] are not truths in the perspective of those three.

The reason why these are not truths [in their perspective] is that they have no conceit of true existence,[a] that is, they do not have the conception of true existence;[b] this is because they have extinguished the ignorance apprehending true existence.[c] Hence, it is proven that external and internal phenomena are not established as truths in the perspective of obscuring [consciousnesses] of those three types of persons [because they do not have such ignorance]. Through commenting in that way, [Chandrakīrti] has not at all proven that [external and internal phenomena] are not obscurational truths in their perspective but has proven that these are not truths [in their perspective]. Those who, despite this, hold that [Chandrakīrti's commentary] has proven that these are not obscurational truths [in the perspective of those three types of persons] have a bad mode of explanation, having contaminated the master [Chandrakīrti's] thought with the defilements of their own minds due to the very great coarseness of the operation of their minds.

[His] proving such also is not for the sake of those three types of persons. That [external and internal phenomena] are not truths in the perspective of those three is being proved for other persons such as ourselves.

Because lesser beings[d] who are not [included in] those three types

---

[a] *bden par rlom pa.*

[b] *bden par zhen pa.*

[c] *bden 'dzin gyi ma rig pa.*

[d] That is to say, Hearers, Solitary Realizers, and Bodhisattvas who have directly real-

of persons have innate [consciousnesses] apprehending true existence, it cannot be proven that in the perspective of all whatsoever of their conventional [consciousnesses] these [forms, sounds, and so forth] are not truly established [because such ignorance occurs among certain of their conventional consciousnesses even if they have directly realized emptiness].

If, in contrast to the above explanation, [Chandrakīrti] were proving that [external and internal phenomena] are not obscurational truths in the perspective of those [three types of persons, the reason that he stated, "because they have no conceit of true existence,"] would be an extremely unrelated proof because for a base [that is, an object] to be established as an obscurational truth in the perspective of a certain awareness, that base must be established as a falsity, and hence stating as the reason [why external and internal phenomena are not obscurational truths in the perspective of those three types of persons] that they do not have apprehension of true existence would be a source of laughter.[a] In order to establish for a certain awareness that a base [that is, an object] is an obscurational truth, [that object] must be established [for that awareness] as a falsity. The reason for this is by way of the essential that if it is seen that when positing the truth that is part of the term "obscurational truth" with respect to pots and so forth, it must be posited—from between an awareness and fact—as a truth in the perspective of just an obscuring [consciousness] that apprehends true existence and is not posited as a truth in fact, it must be seen that if that distinction [of being in the perspective of an obscuring consciousness] is not applied, it is not established as a truth and is a falsity.

Explanation of [the Consequence School's] unique presentation of afflictive emotions

This system [of the Consequence School] has a unique identification of afflictive emotions that does not accord with the upper and lower

ized emptiness but have not completed abandonment of afflictive ignorance. These are Hearers and Solitary Realizers on the paths of seeing and of meditation as well as Bodhisattvas on the first through seventh Bodhisattva grounds.

[a] That these beings do not have consciousnesses apprehending inherent existence indicates that they understand that external and internal phenomena are obscurational truths—objects that seem to exist the way they appear only for an ignorant consciousness. They can understand this because they no longer have such ignorance. Thus it would be ridiculous to indicate that these persons who understand that forms and so forth are falsities do not understand that these are obscurational truths.

Manifest Knowledges,[a] and since understanding it appears to be very important, let us explain it. Consciousnesses apprehending that things truly exist are of two types, those apprehending persons to truly exist and those apprehending [other] phenomena to truly exist. It has already been explained that just these are considered to be the two apprehensions of self. Both Chandrakīrti's *Autocommentary on the "Supplement to (Nāgārjuna's) 'Treatise on the Middle'"* and his *Commentary on (Āryadeva's) "Four Hundred"* explain that this consciousness apprehending true existence is an afflictive ignorance and explain that Hearer and Solitary Realizer Foe Destroyers have abandoned this ignorance,[b] and Chandrakīrti's *Commentary on (Āryadeva's) "Four Hundred"* explains that Bodhisattvas who have attained forbearance with respect to the doctrine of no production [this being at the beginning of the eighth Bodhisattva ground] have abandoned it. Therefore, afflictive ignorance is the faction discordant with knowledge of the suchness of selflessness, and, furthermore, afflictive ignorance is not to be taken as merely an absence of that knowledge [of selflessness] or as merely other than it but is the discordant faction that is the contrary [of knowledge of selflessness]—a superimposition that persons and [other] phenomena are inherently established.

Taken that way, [the Consequence School's] positing that a [consciousness] superimposing a self of phenomena is an afflictive ignorance and its positing that the two apprehensions—that "I" and "mine" are established by way of their own character—are views of the transitory collection[c] do not accord with the Proponents of Manifest Knowledge.[d] The systems of the Proponents of Manifest Knowledge, as is explained in the ninth chapter of Vasubandhu's *Autocommentary on the "Treasury of Manifest Knowledge,"*[e] posit a [consciousness] apprehending

---

[a] These are the *abhidharmas* that are primarily set forth, respectively, in Asaṅga's *Summary of Manifest Knowledge* (*chos mngon pa kun btus, abhidharmasamuccaya;* P5550, vol. 112) and in Vasubandhu's *Treasury of Manifest Knowledge* (*chos mngon pa'i mdzod, abhidharmakośa;* P5590, vol. 115).

[b] Chandrakīrti's *Autocommentary on the "Supplement to (Nāgārjuna's) 'Treatise on the Middle'"* explains that Hearers and Solitary Realizers know that all phenomena lack inherent existence; see Hopkins, *Compassion in Tibetan Buddhism,* 150-160; and La Vallée Poussin, *Madhyamakāvatāra,* 19.17ff; La Vallée Poussin, "*Introduction au traité du milieu,*" *Muséon* 8 (1907): 268.

[c] *'jig tshogs la lta ba, satkāyadṛṣṭi.*

[d] *mngon pa ba, *ābhidharmika.*

[e] *chos mngon pa'i mdzod kyi bshad pa, abhidharmakośabhāṣya;* P5591, vol. 115. The passage at the very beginning of the ninth chapter may be what Tsong-kha-pa refers to (Pruden trans., p. 1313): "There is no liberation outside of this teaching, because other doctrines are corrupted by a false conception of a soul. The word as other doctrines conceive it is

that a person substantially exists in the sense of being self-sufficient[a] to be a view of the transitory collection that is a [mis]apprehension of "I," and they posit a [consciousness] apprehending that the "mine" are objects controlled by that substantially existent person to be a view of the transitory collection that is a [mis]apprehension of "mine." These are greatly at variance [with the Consequence School's presentation].

Apprehension that persons substantially exist in the sense of being self-sufficient also exists among those whose awarenesses are not affected by tenets,[b] but [according to the Consequence School] apprehension that persons exist as other than the [mental and physical] aggregates in the sense of having a character discordant with them does not exist among those whose awarenesses are not affected by tenets. Thus, views holding to extremes also are of two types [innate and artificial].

Question: How does one prove to those whose position is that persons and phenomena are established by way of their own character that those apprehensions are afflictive ignorance and the two apprehensions of self?

Answer: The inherent establishment of persons and [other] phenomena is negated by the reasonings refuting this, and at that time it is established that a consciousness apprehending such is a consciousness apprehending true existence that is mistaken with respect to its conceived object. Also, when this is established, it is established that the apprehensions of the two, persons and [other] phenomena, as truly established are the two apprehensions of self. When those are established, it is established that this apprehension of true existence is the discordant faction that is the contrary of knowledge of suchness, whereby it is established that this is ignorance. Because it can be proven that until this is extinguished, the view of the transitory [as inherently existent "I" and "mine"] is also not extinguished, it is established that [these apprehensions of persons and other phenomena as truly existent] are afflictive ignorance. Hence, it is very important to know how to posit the [Consequentialists'] unique presentation of afflictive emotions.

With respect to how other afflictive emotions such as desire and so forth also operate from the bewilderment that is a consciousness apprehending true existence, let us explain this in accordance with

not a metaphoric expression for a series of skandhas. By the power of their belief in this soul as a substantial entity, there arises clinging to the soul, the defilements are generated, and liberation is impossible."

[a] *gang zag rang rkya thub pa'i rdzas su yod par 'dzin pa.*

[b] For more on this see Hopkins, *Maps of the Profound*, 650-654.

Chandrakīrti's commentary on the statement in Āryadeva's *Four Hundred* (see also *Insight* 45; *Illumination,* 212):[a]

> Just as the body sense power [pervades] the body,
> Bewilderment abides in all [afflictive emotions as their basis].

Chandrakīrti says (see also *Insight,* 51):[b]

> Bewilderment, due to being beclouded with respect to those [objects] from considering them to be true [that is, truly established], enters into the superimposition that things have their own true entities. Also, desire and so forth operate within the superimposition of features, such as beauty and ugliness, on just the inherent nature of things imputed by bewilderment. Hence, they operate non-separately from bewilderment and also depend on bewilderment, because bewilderment is just chief.

[The first sentence] "Bewilderment, due to being beclouded [with respect to things] from considering them to be true, enters into the superimposition that things have their own true entities" indicates that bewilderment is a [consciousness] apprehending true existence. That desire and so forth operate non-separately from bewilderment [means] that they operate in association with bewilderment; they do not operate separate from it. The reason for this is that they "operate within the superimposition of features, such as beauty and ugliness, on just the inherent nature of things imputed by bewilderment." Concerning this, [a consciousness] superimposing attractiveness or unattractiveness on objects is improper mental application, which is the cause producing the two, desire and hatred; therefore, [this passage] does not indicate the mode of apprehension of the two, desire and hatred.[c] Therefore,

[a] Stanza VI.10ab; stanzas VI.10-11; Toh. 3846, *dbu ma,* vol. *tsha,* 7b.2-7b.3; Lang, *Āryadeva's Catuḥśataka,* 66; Sonam Rinchen and Ruth Sonam, *Yogic Deeds of Bodhisattvas,* 156-157. Brackets are from *Four Interwoven Annotations,* vol. 2, 421.5. Cited in *Great Treatise,* vol. 3, 207.

[b] Toh. 3865, *dbu ma,* vol. *ya,* 112b.7-113a.2. Brackets are from *Four Interwoven Annotations,* vol. 2, 421.6. Cited in *Great Treatise,* vol. 3, 207.

[c] The Tibetan could wrongly be read as, "Also, desire and so forth **engage in superimposing** features, such as beauty and ugliness, on just the inherent nature of things imputed by bewilderment." Tsong-kha-pa is saying that the passage should not be read this way, for then the mode of apprehension of desire and hatred would be to superimpose a sense of inherently existent beauty and ugliness, whereas that is the mode of apprehension of improper mental application. First ignorance superimposes inherent existence on the object; then improper mental application superimposes inherently existent beauty or ugliness, after which desire and hatred are generated.

"desire and so forth operate within the superimposition of features, such as beauty and ugliness, on just the inherent nature of things imputed by bewilderment" says that the two, desire and hatred, operate in dependence upon the superimposition of only inherently established attractiveness or unattractiveness [superimposed by improper mental application].

[Chandrakīrti] is not indicating that just true establishment imputed by bewilderment is the object of observation [of desire and hatred] from between the two, the object of observation and the subjective aspect of desire and so forth. This is because—from between the two, the object of observation and the subjective aspect—the objects of observation of both innate [consciousnesses] apprehending self are established bases [that is, they are existent, whereas truly established objects do not exist at all], and desire and so forth have the same object of observation as bewilderment, since even they are in similar association with it.

[Consciousnesses] induced by those two improper mental applications [superimposing attractiveness or unattractiveness on the object] and that have the aspect of desiring the object or of not desiring—that is to say, turning away from—the object come to be desire and hatred. Hence, [in the Consequence School] mere [consciousnesses] that are induced by the apprehension of a person as substantially existent in the sense of being self-sufficient and that have the aspects of desiring or not desiring are not posited as [encompassing all] desire and hatred. Therefore, even the modes of positing the two, desire and hated, are different [in the Consequence School from how these are posited in the other schools.

That desire and hatred] "also depend on bewilderment" means that desire and so forth are induced by bewilderment that apprehends [objects] to be established by way of their own character and that precedes them.

The example [from the *Four Hundred* quoted above,] that "the body sense power [pervades] the body" means that just as the other four sense powers do not have a base posited separately from the body sense power, so all the other afflictive emotions operate in dependence upon bewilderment and operate without being separated from it. Therefore, all afflictive emotions are overcome through just overcoming bewilderment, and hence it is said that one should be intent on just discourse about its antidote—dependent-arising, the emptiness of inherent establishment.

Nāgārjuna's *Seventy Stanzas on Emptiness*[a] says that this apprehension of things as truly existent is the ignorance that is the root of cyclic existence. Also, Nāgārjuna's *Sixty Stanzas of Reasoning* says:[b]

> If any base [that is, an inherently existent object] is found,
> One is seized by the winding snake of the afflictive emotions.
> Whoever's mind is without [such] a base
> Is not seized [by the afflictive emotions].

He says that if one finds a base that is any focus of observation of [a consciousness] apprehending true existence, [one's mind] is seized by the snake of the afflictive emotions. Also, right after that [Nāgārjuna (see also *Insight,* 51) says]:[c]

> Why would the great poisonous afflictive emotions not arise
> In those whose minds have a basis [an inherently existent object]?

Therefore, this [tenet that the ignorance apprehending inherent existence is the root of cyclic existence] is the excellent assertion of the Superior [Nāgārjuna].

As transitional [commentary] before those latter two lines, [Chandrakīrti's *Commentary on (Nāgārjuna's) "Sixty Stanzas of Reasoning"*] says:[d]

> In order to indicate that an abandonment of afflictive emotions does not occur in those who although they apprehend an inherent nature [that is, inherent existence] of forms and so forth, want to abandon the afflictive emotions, [the text] says...

and his commentary following [those two lines] says:

> If one apprehends things to be truly existent,[e] myriad

[a] *stong pa nyid bdun cu pa'i tshig le'ur byas pa, śunyatāsaptatikārikā,* stanza 64:

> That which apprehends things produced
> From causes and conditions to be real
> Was said by the Teacher to be ignorance.
> From it the twelve links arise.

Toh. 3827, *dbu ma,* vol. *tsa,* 26b.3; Tibetan text edited and translated by Lindtner, *Master of Wisdom,* 114; Tibetan text, English translation, and contemporary commentary in Komito, *Seventy Stanzas,* 175.

[b] Stanza 51; Toh. 3825, *dbu ma,* vol. *tsa,* 22a.6-22a.7; Lindtner, *Master of Wisdom,* 88.

[c] Stanza 52; Toh. 3825, *dbu ma,* vol. *tsa,* 22a.7; Lindtner, *Master of Wisdom,* 88.

[d] Toh. 3864, *dbu ma,* vol. *ya,* 28a.5-28a.6; Scherrer-Schaub, *Yuktiṣaṣṭikāvṛtti,* 90-91.

[e] *dngos por dmigs pa yin na ni;* here *dngos po* is taken as meaning "true existence" and not just "thing."

> irreversible afflictive emotions, such as desire, definitely arise. How? Respectively, if the thing is agreeable to the mind, it is difficult to overcome desire for it. If it is disagreeable, it is difficult to overcome aggravation[a] and irritation[b] toward it.

[Chandrakīrti's] commentary says that even if the object is neither attractive nor unattractive, ignorance is generated. [Thus] it is asserted that when a consciousness apprehending an object as established by way of its own character is operating in [one's mental] continuum, either desire or hatred is generated, and even if those two are not, a similar type of bewilderment operates. Moreover, Shāntideva's *Engaging in the Bodhisattva Deeds* says:[c]

> [As long as] minds involved with apprehension [of inherent existence]
> Remain [manifestly] in some [persons' continuums, the manifest attachment induced by such minds will not be overcome].
> Though [manifest afflictive emotions] are [temporarily] halted in a mind lacking [realization of] emptiness,
> [Manifest afflictive emotions] are again produced,
> As in the case of [abiding in] the absorption of non-discrimination.

With respect to this position, the three—these two masters [Chandrakīrti and Shāntideva] as well as Buddhapālita—do not differ in how they comment on the thought of the Superior [Nāgārjuna].

---

[a] *khong khro ba;* I often translate this as "belligerence."

[b] *tshig pa za ba.*

[c] Stanza IX.48c-49c. The bracketed additions are from Gyel-tsap's *Explanation of (Shāntideva's) "Engaging in the Bodhisattva Deeds," Entrance for Conqueror Children* (*byang chub sems dpa'i spyod pa la 'jug pa'i rnam bshad rgyal sras 'jug ngog*) (Sarnath: Pleasure of Elegant Sayings Printing Press, 1973), 236.19-237.4. For further discussion of this topic from an earlier chapter of Tsong-kha-pa's *Illumination of the Thought,* see Hopkins, *Compassion in Tibetan Buddhism*, 150-171, and 157 in particular:

> If one lacks cognition of emptiness, then even though afflicted minds are temporarily halted through cultivating other paths, they cannot be totally overcome. Manifest afflictions are again produced, and thereby wandering in cyclic existence under the power of contaminated actions is not eliminated. That afflicted minds can be halted temporarily means, as was explained before, that manifest afflictions can be temporarily abandoned.

The Sanskrit is in Shastri, *Bodhicaryāvatāra of Ārya Śāntideva*, 319-320: *sālambanena cittena sthātavyaṃ yatra tatra vā // vinā śūnyatayā cittaṃ baddhamutpadyate punaḥ / yathāsaṃjñisamāpattau.*

Due to this essential, [Buddha's] explanation that one [can] pass away from sorrow merely through the paths of the sixteen [attributes of the four noble truths], impermanence and so forth,[a] has a thought behind it.[b] Furthermore, the identifications of afflictive emotions in terms of those paths [is incomplete and thus requires] more [in order to identify them on a subtler level].

In dependence upon those [points], pride and so forth also should be understood [as having coarse and subtle forms]. It should be known that the uncommon ignorance, the view of the transitory collection, and extreme views also have both artificial and innate forms. Fearing that such would take too many words, I will not write more.

Likewise, you should know that the treatment—of conceptual consciousnesses apprehending phenomena to be truly established—as nine levels of objects ([three sets each of] great, medium, and small) to be abandoned by the path of meditation and thereupon the association of these with nine levels of the path of meditation ([three sets each of] small, medium, and great) as antidotes [as is done in the Autonomy School] also requires interpretation, being something spoken with respect to certain trainees who temporarily are not able to realize fully both selflessnesses, coarse and subtle. This is like the fact that the [Mind-Only School's] treatment of conceptual consciousnesses apprehending apprehended object and apprehending subject as different substantial entities as nine levels of objects to be abandoned (great, medium, and small) by the path of meditation and thereupon the association of these with nine levels of the path of meditation [requires interpretation].

Ways in which mere conventionalities do and do not appear to the three types of persons

Furthermore, these things, whereas they do not inherently exist, appear to childish beings to inherently exist, thereby deceiving them.

---

[a] The sixteen aspects of the four noble truths are:

Suffering: impermanence, suffering, emptiness, and selflessness
Origins: cause, origin, strong production, condition
Cessation: cessation, pacification, auspiciousness, definite emergence
Path: path, suitability, achievement, and deliverance.

For Gung-tang's presentation of how to meditate on these, see Hopkins, *Meditation on Emptiness,* 285-296.

[b] Or "has an intention," meaning that when Buddha taught such, he had something else in mind but could not teach it due to the inadequacies of the listeners and thus taught something else that though literally unacceptable, was helpful to his listeners.

However, to the three types of persons, described earlier, who are other than them, these things become mere conventionalities due to being just dependent-arisings of fabricated things and do not become truths. Moreover, because [those three types of beings] partake of the mere non-afflictive ignorance that has the character of being an obstruction to omniscience, [these mere conventionalities] appear to Superiors abiding in subsequent realization [that is, outside of meditative equipoise directly realizing emptiness] which has objects of activity that are involved with appearances polluted by ignorance and its predispositions; they do not appear to Superiors abiding in meditative equipoise who have dominion over the object of activity [that is, emptiness] that has no appearance [polluted by ignorance and the predispositions of ignorance].

Question: What does this system take to be the obstructions to omniscience?

Answer: They are as Chandrakīrti says in his *Autocommentary on the "Supplement to (Nāgārjuna's) 'Treatise on the Middle'"*:[a]

> Concerning that, the predispositions of ignorance are obstacles to thoroughly distinguishing [all] objects of knowledge [simultaneously]. Existent predispositions of desire and so forth are also causes of such acts of body and speech. The predispositions of ignorance and also of desire and so forth are reversed only in knowledge-of-all-aspects[b] and Buddhahood, not for others.

The "acts of body and speech" [to which Chandrakīrti refers] are assumptions of bad states of body and speech that exist in Foe Destroyers, such as [uncontrollably] jumping like a monkey and calling another "bitch";[c] although the Teacher [Buddha] prohibited such, they have not been overcome.

[Chandrakīrti's saying] "also" [in "The existent predispositions of desire and so forth are **also** causes of such acts of body and speech"] indicates that the predispositions of desire and so forth are also obstacles to distinguishing [all] objects of knowledge [simultaneously]; therefore, predispositions [established by] afflictive emotions are obstructions to omniscience. Furthermore, all factors of mistaken dualistic appearance, which are fruits of those [predispositions], are included in those [obstructions to omniscience]. Among the seeds [established

---

[a] Commenting on XII.31; Toh. 3862, *dbu ma*, vol. *'a*, 342b.6-343a.1; La Vallée Poussin, *Madhyamakāvatāra*, 393.17-394.3.

[b] *rnam pa thams cad mkhyen pa, sarvākārajñāna.*

[c] *rmangs mo;* perhaps for *dmangs mo,* which means "woman of low caste."

by] afflictive emotions, there are two types, those deposited as predispositions [for afflictive emotions] and predispositions that are not seeds of afflictive emotions; from between these two, those assigned as obstructions to omniscience are the latter. Through extinguishing all seeds of afflictive emotions, consciousnesses apprehending true existence are not generated, but due to being polluted with predispositions, awarenesses mistaken with respect to their appearing objects [in that their appearing objects seem to inherently exist] are generated.

Since Superiors who have not been Buddhafied have not abandoned the ignorance that is an obstruction to omniscience, they have an alternation between conceptuality involving the appearance [of inherent existence and/or conventional phenomena] in states subsequent to meditative equipoise and the absence of [such] appearance in meditative equipoise. Buddhas, on the other hand, have completely, that is, entirely, become enlightened, that is, have realized actualization of the ultimate and conventional aspects of all phenomena; hence, all movements of conceptual minds and mental factors have utterly vanished, due to which they have no alternation between having or not having the conceptuality involving appearance [of inherent existence and/or conventional phenomena] in meditative equipoise and in states subsequent to meditative equipoise.

[Chandrakīrti's saying] "utterly" indicates that for other Superiors the vanishing [of the movement of conceptuality] in meditative equipoise is temporary; therefore, [for them] meditative equipoise and subsequent attainment [that is, states subsequent to meditative equipoise] alternate. Hence, [Chandrakīrti's saying] "because [those three types of beings] partake of the ignorance that is an obstruction to omniscience" is not a reason for their having appearance,[a] but is a proof for the alternating occurrence of the existence and non-existence of appearance in meditative equipoise and subsequent attainment.

The "movement of minds and mental factors" is asserted to be conceptuality, [since] Chandrakīrti's *Clear Words* (see also *Insight,* 132) explains:[b]

[a] If the reason for their perceiving mere appearances outside of meditative equipoise were that they had obstructions to omniscience, then when those obstructions were removed, they would no longer perceive appearances. To avoid saying this, Tsong-kha-pa explains Chandrakīrti's reason as being why they must **alternate** between meditative equipoise and a subsequent state in which they perceive appearances.

[b] Commenting on stanza XVIII.9; Toh. 3860, *dbu ma,* vol. *'a,* 120a.3-120a.4; La Vallée Poussin, *Mūlamadhyamakakārikās (Mādhyamikasūtras) de Nāgārjuna avec la Prasannapadā,* 374.1-374.2: *vikalpaścittapracāraḥ / tadrahitatvāttattattvaṃ nirvikalpaṃ // yathoktaṃ sūtre / paramārthasatyaṃ katamat / yatra jñānasyāpyapracāraḥ kaḥ punarvādo 'kṣarāṇāmiti /.*

> If conceptuality is the movement of the mind, due to being devoid of it suchness is non-conceptual. Sūtra says, "What is ultimate truth? If it is without even the movement of the mind, what need is there to mention letters?"

How there come to be ultimates and conventionalities relative to superiors and common beings

[Chandrakīrti says (see also *Insight,* 115):][a]

> Regarding this, those which are ultimates for common beings are mere conventionalities for Superiors acting on objects involving appearance [outside of meditative equipoise]. That which is the nature of those [objects]—emptiness—is the ultimate for them.

With respect to the meaning of the former [sentence], it indicates that just those pots and so forth that are held by common beings to be ultimately established are mere conventionalities for the three types of Superiors, described earlier, who, having risen from meditative equipoise, are in states of subsequent attainment that involve appearances. Therefore, Chandrakīrti is only eliminating that [pots and so forth] are truths in their perspective; he is not eliminating that these are obscurational truths [in their perspective. Also, he] is not indicating that the conceived objects of common beings' [mis]apprehensions of pots and so forth as being ultimately established are conventionalities for Superiors because such does not occur [that is, ultimately established pots and so forth do not exist].

With respect to the meaning of the latter sentence ["That which is their nature, emptiness, is the ultimate for them,"] it indicates that the nature, the noumenon,[b] of conventional dependent-arisings is the ultimate for Superiors. Hence, to propound opposite to [Chandrakīrti's] text that just one base, such as a pot, is an obscurational [truth] in relation to common beings and an ultimate [truth] in relation to Superiors is the talk of someone who does not know that in the perspective of an awareness for which something is an obscurational truth, it must be negated that [that object] is a truth.

Tibetan in de Jong, *Cinq chapitres de la Prasannapadā,* 104-105; his French translation is on p.30.

[a] Commenting on VI.28; Toh. 3862, *dbu ma,* vol. *'a,* 255a.5; La Vallée Poussin, *Madhyamakāvatāra,* 108.13-108.16; La Vallée Poussin, "*Introduction au traité du milieu,*" *Muséon* 11 (1910): 305.

[b] *chos nyid, dharmatā.*

[Chandrakīrti says:][a]

> The ultimate for Buddhas is just the nature, and it moreover is just non-deceptive, due to which it is the ultimate truth. It is that which is known by them by themselves individually.

The term "just" in "just the nature" is a delineator. With respect to what it eliminates, [the ultimate for Buddhas] is not the ultimate of other Superiors that alternates, for instance, between the nature that is without appearance in meditative equipoise and the nature that involves appearance in states subsequent to meditative equipoise; rather, it is the noumenon, the nature in which [a Buddha] is always set in meditative equipoise.

With respect to the meaning of "it moreover is just non-deceptive, due to which it is the ultimate truth," [Chandrakīrti] is explaining that abiding non-deceptively in the perspective of perceiving suchness is the meaning of "truth," asserting that the "truth" of "ultimate truth" does not indicate true establishment.

[a] Commenting on VI.28; Toh. 3862, *dbu ma,* vol. *'a,* 255a.5-255a.6; La Vallée Poussin, *Madhyamakāvatāra,* 108.16-108.19; La Vallée Poussin, "*Introduction au traité du milieu,*" *Muséon* 11 (1910): 305.

3. Ultimate Truth

Description of ultimate truth

This section has two parts: an explanation of the meaning of the root text and a dispelling of objections to that.

Explanation of the meaning of the root text

[Chandrakīrti's *Autocommentary on the "Supplement to (Nāgārjuna's) 'Treatise on the Middle'"*] says:[a]

> Due to wishing to teach ultimate truth and due to the fact that the ultimate truth cannot be taught directly because of being inexpressible by terms and because of just not being objects of consciousnesses that follow upon terms, [the root text] sets forth an example experienced by common beings[b] themselves for the sake of clarifying the nature of that [ultimate truth] for those wishing to listen.

In this, the meaning of [ultimate truth] not being an object of consciousness and verbalization is, as [Chandrakīrti] says, that it "cannot be taught directly"; moreover, Nak-tso's translation reads, "cannot be manifestly taught."[c] Regarding the meaning of that, Chandrakīrti's *Clear Words*, commenting on [Nāgārjuna's] statement that the meaning of suchness is not something known from another, says:[d]

> When those with cataracts see mistaken entities such as falling hairs and so forth, even though someone without cataracts has shown them, they cannot realize what is to be realized, exactly

---

[a] Introducing stanza VI.29; Toh. 3862, *dbu ma*, vol. *'a*, 255a.6-255a.7; La Vallée Poussin, *Madhyamakāvatāra*, 109.1-109.5; La Vallée Poussin, "*Introduction au traité du milieu*," *Muséon* 11 (1910): 305.

[b] Tsong-kha-pa adds the term "common beings" (*so skyes*) to Chandrakīrti's commentary (Poussin, 109.4) for the sake of clarity.

[c] Nak-tso's translation reads ***mngon sum du*** *bstan par mi nus* rather than ***dngos su*** *bstan par mi nus*. On Nak-tso, see 238 note b.

[d] Commenting on stanza XVIII.9; Toh. 3860, *dbu ma*, vol. *'a*, 119b.5; La Vallée Poussin, *Mūlamadhyamakakārikās (Mādhyamikasūtras) de Nāgārjuna avec la Prasannapadā*, 373.2-373.4: *yathā hi taimirikā vitathaṃ keśamaśakamakṣikādirūpaṃ paśyanto vitimiropadeśenāpi na śaknuvanti keśānāṃ yathāvadavasthitaṃ svarūpamadarśananyāyenādhigantavyamataimirikā ivādhigantuṃ /*. Tibetan in de Jong, *Cinq chapitres de la Prasannapadā*, 104; his French translation is on p. 29.

as it is, in the manner of not seeing the entities themselves of the falling hairs and so forth as those without cataracts do.

[Chandrakīrti] says that even though one without cataracts indicates to those with cataracts, "There are no falling hairs," they do not realize the non-existence of falling hairs in the way that such is seen by the one without cataracts. Hence, even though those listeners [having cataracts] do not realize such that way, it is not that they do not realize the non-existence of falling hairs.

Taking this as an example, [Chandrakīrti] is asserting that when suchness is taught, even though [listeners] do not realize it as it is seen by one who lacks the pollution of the cataracts of ignorance, it is not that in general they do not realize suchness. Therefore, it is not that ultimate truth cannot be expressed by definitive scriptures having the profound meaning [of emptiness] and by speech teaching such, and it is not that ultimate truth cannot be realized even by an awareness following upon those. You also should understand similarly all statements that the meaning of suchness is not an object of consciousness and verbalization.

> Chandrakīrti's *Supplement to (Nāgārjuna's) "Treatise on the Middle"* says (see also *Insight*, 124):[a]
>
> > Where just those unreal entities such as falling hairs
> >   and so forth
> > Are imputed through the force of cataracts,
> > What is seen by one with clear eyes is the suchness [of
> >   those falling hairs].
> > Understand it similarly here.

Though the force of his or her eyes being affected by cataracts, a person with cataracts sees falling hairs as well as bees and so on—which are [included] within [Chandrakīrti's] "and so forth"—inside a vessel for food and drink, such as rhinoceros horn and so forth, which is in the hand. Seeing these, the person wishes to clean away the erroneous entities that he or she has imputed to be falling hairs, bees, and so forth and thereupon gets the difficulties of again and again turning the vessel upside down. Someone without cataracts, whose eyes are clear, realizes this and approaches the person, whereupon even though the person without cataracts aims his or her sight to that place where the one with cataracts sees the entities of those falling hairs and so forth, he or

[a] Toh. 3861, vol. *'a*, 205b.3; La Vallée Poussin, *Madhyamakāvatāra*, 109.6-109.9; La Vallée Poussin, "*Introduction au traité du milieu*," *Muséon* 11 (1910): 305.

she does not observe those aspects of falling hairs and does not conceptualize anything having falling hairs as their substratum, that is to say, does not conceptualize any attributes of falling hairs.

Moreover, when the one with cataracts reveals his or her thought to the one without cataracts, saying, "[I] see falling hairs," the one without cataracts—wishing to clear up the idea of the one with cataracts—takes cognizance of his or her perspective and speaks words intent on negation, saying, "There are no falling hairs here," but the speaker has no deprecatory denial of falling hairs. The suchness of the falling hairs that are seen by the one with cataracts is what is seen by the one without cataracts; it is not what is seen by the one with cataracts. Understand the meaning at this point in accordance with these two examples.

With respect to how this is to be understood, the entities of the aggregates, constituents, sense spheres, and so forth observed by those who do not see suchness because their minds are damaged, that is, polluted, by the cataracts of ignorance are the conventional entities of those aggregates and so forth, like the hairs observed by those with cataracts. That object—which is observed by not seeing those very aggregates and so forth and which the Buddhas, being free from the predispositions of ignorance, the obstructions to omniscience, perceive as the nature of the aggregates and so forth in the way that the eyes of one without cataracts do not see falling hairs—is the ultimate truth of those Buddhas.

Dispelling objections to that

Objection: Just as the eyes of those without cataracts do not perceive even an appearance of falling hairs, so if a Buddha does not perceive conventionalities, such as aggregates and so forth, which appear to awarenesses polluted by ignorance, then those would not exist because if something exists, it must be perceived by a Buddha. If conventionalities such as aggregates do not exist, then even the attainment of Buddhahood would not exist because a person who initially generates a mind [of altruistic aspiration to Buddhahood] is one who is polluted by ignorance.

Answer: Let us explain how this fallacy does not occur. There are two ways that a Buddha's pristine wisdom knows objects of knowledge—a mode of knowing all objects of knowledge that are ultimate truths and a mode of knowing all objects of knowledge that are obscurational truths. Concerning those, the first is knowledge of the suchness of the aggregates and so forth in the manner of not perceiving their conventional appearances. The second is knowledge [of those aggregates and so forth] in the perspective of the pristine wisdom knowing the diversity [of phenomena] in the manner of dualistic appearance as object and subject; this is because it is not suitable to posit that a Buddha has implicit realization in which something is realized even though it does not appear and hence [everything] must be known upon its appearing.[a]

Although with respect to a Buddha's knowledge of the diversity the aggregates and so forth do not appear upon its being polluted by the predispositions of ignorance, what appears to the consciousnesses of other persons that are polluted with ignorance must appear to a Buddha. This is because it is not suitable for those appearances to be nonexistent, and if a conventionality exists, it must be observed by [a Buddha's] knowledge of the diversity. Although the falling hairs that appear to one with cataracts do not appear to the eye consciousness of one free from cataracts, those **appearances** do not need to be nonexistent; therefore, they are unlike [the situation with] a Buddha [wherein if a conventionality exists, it must appear to a Buddha, and if something does not appear to a Buddha, it must not exist].

Until the predispositions for mistaken dualistic appearance have been extinguished, the two direct comprehensions (1) of the mode of being [of phenomena] and (2) of the diversity [of phenomena] cannot be generated in one entity, due to which these must be comprehended within an alternation between meditative equipoise and states subsequent to meditative equipoise, and, therefore, comprehension of these two does not come within a single instant of pristine wisdom. When the predispositions for mistakenness have been completely abandoned, the generation of the two pristine wisdoms within each instant of pristine wisdom is continuous; hence, alternation between directly comprehending and not comprehending the two types of objects of knowledge at one time is not necessary. For this reason, [our presentation] also does not contradict the statement:

> A single instant of exalted knowledge
> Pervades the full circle of objects of knowledge.

That although the two pristine wisdoms are one entity, there is not even the slightest contradiction in there coming to be two different modes of knowledge in relation to two [types of] objects is an attribute

[a] This counters Dol-po-pa's notion that a Buddha only implicitly knows obscurational truths; see below, 275ff.

solely of a Buddha, a Supramundane Victor. Whereas that is the case, those who take only the mode of knowledge of suchness as the mode of a Buddha's mode of knowledge and thereupon say that knowledge of the diversity [of phenomena] does not exist in a Buddha's mental continuum but instead is included within the continuums of trainees are deprecating a Buddha's knowledge of the diversity. Also, some [other scholars] appear to deprecate both pristine wisdoms, saying that even knowledge of the mode [of being of phenomena] does not exist in a Buddha's mental continuum. Some remaining topics concerning this will be explained on the occasion of [explaining the eleventh ground,] the fruit.

Objection: Would a nature with such an aspect of the vanishing of dualistic appearance not be unseen? Therefore, how do those Buddhas perceive it?

Answer: Since dualistic appearance has vanished in the perspective of perceiving suchness, it is true that it is not perceived in a dualistic manner, but it is said that they perceive in the manner of non-perception.

How this serves as an answer to the objection is:

- because that knowledge of the mode [of being of phenomena] directly perceives the suchness of the aggregates and so forth, and
- because the non-establishment of the aggregates and so forth in the perspective of that perception is their suchness, and
- because the suchness of the aggregates and so forth must be perceived in the manner of not perceiving them.

Chandrakīrti's *Autocommentary on the "Supplement to (Nāgārjuna's) 'Treatise on the Middle'"* (see also *Insight,* 132) says:[a]

> Without contacting produced things, it actualizes solely the nature,[b] whereby suchness is understood; therefore, [a being who possesses such knowledge] is called "Buddha."

Thus, Chandrakīrti says that a Buddha's pristine wisdom knowing the ultimate realizes only the noumenon without contacting the substrata. This has the same meaning as the statement that the suchness of the aggregates and so forth is seen in the manner of not seeing them.

Also, with respect to the meaning of the statement (see also *Insight,*

[a] Commenting on VI.97; Toh. 3862, *dbu ma,* vol. *'a,* 283a.2; La Vallée Poussin, *Madhyamakāvatāra,* 201.17-201.19; La Vallée Poussin, "*Introduction au traité du milieu,*" *Muséon* 12 (1911): 255.

[b] *rang bzhin, svabhāva.* This is not the object of negation in emptiness, but the final nature of phenomena.

130) that "Non-seeing is the ultimate seeing," it is not being asserted that not seeing anything is to see. Rather, as explained earlier, not seeing the proliferations [of inherent existence and of conventionalities] is posited as seeing what is devoid of proliferations; therefore, the seen and the unseen do not refer to the same base. Moreover, in that way the *Verse Summary of the Perfection of Wisdom* (see also *Insight*, 130) says:[a]

> The One-Gone-Thus teaches that one who does not see forms,
> Does not see feelings, does not see discriminations,
> Does not see intentions, does not see
> Consciousness, mind, or sentience sees the *dharma*.[b]
>
> Analyze how space is seen as in the expression
> By sentient beings in words, "Space is seen."
> The One-Gone-Thus teaches that seeing the *dharma* is also like that.
> The seeing cannot be expressed by another example.

This says that the unseen is the aggregates, and the seen is the *dharma*,[c] which means suchness,[d] as in the statement, "Whoever sees dependent-arising sees the *dharma*."

Furthermore, it is like, for example, the fact that space is a mere elimination of the obstructive objects of touch, and that seeing it—or realizing it—is taken as not seeing the preventive obstruction that is the object of negation and is suitable to be observed if it were present. In that [example], the seen is space, and the unseen is preventive obstruction. The last [two] lines refute that suchness is seen while seeing blue [for instance], which would be not to see in accordance with the example [of seeing space].

As a source for seeing in the manner of not seeing, [Chandrakīrti] cites the *Introduction to the Two Truths Sūtra*:[e]

---

[a] *sañcayagāthāprajnāpāramitā, shes rab kyi pha rol tu phyin pa sdud pa*, stanzas XII.9-10; Toh. 13, vol. *ka* (*shes rab sna tshogs*); Sanskrit and Tibetan texts edited by Yuyama, *Saṃcaya-gāthā*, 52 and 171. For the Sanskrit, see the footnote on 260. English translation in Conze, *Perfection of Wisdom in Eight Thousand Lines*, 32.

[b] *chos*, which here means *chos nyid* (*dharmatā*), as Tsong-kha-pa says just below when he equates it with suchness.

[c] *chos*.

[d] *de kho na nyid, tathatā*.

[e] *bden pa gnyis la 'jug pa / bden pa po'i le'u, satyakaparivarta*; P813, vol. 32. This passage is cited by Chandrakīrti in his *Commentary on the "Supplement to (Nāgārjuna's) 'Treatise on the Middle,'"* commenting on VI.29; Toh. 3862, vol. *'a*, 256a.2; La Vallée Poussin, *Madhyamakāvatāra*, 111.1-111.4; La Vallée Poussin, "*Introduction au traité du milieu*," *Muséon* 11 (1910): 306-307.

> Devaputras, ultimately if the ultimate truth were of the nature of an object of body, of speech, or of mind, it would not be counted as an "ultimate truth"; it would be just an obscurational truth. However, Devaputras, ultimately the ultimate truth is passed beyond all conventions; it is not particularized, not produced, not ceasing, and devoid [of the duality] of object propounded and propounder as well as object known and consciousness.

The meaning of this first part of that sūtra passage is:

> If it were that the ultimate truth is not—in the perspective of seeing the ultimate—seen in the manner of not seeing conventionalities such as the aggregates and so forth, but is an object in the way that the aggregates and so forth become objects of body, of speech, and of mind, then since it would not be free from proliferations in the perspective of directly seeing suchness, it would not be the ultimate truth but would be a conventional proliferation.

Taken that way, [the first part of Chandrakīrti's citation] serves as a source for seeing in the manner of not seeing.

With respect to the meaning of the second part of that sūtra passage, that in the perspective of directly seeing the ultimate the ultimate truth "is not particularized," the meaning is that it is without many different features. The other three are easy to understand. That in the perspective of this perception it is devoid of the objects and agents of propositions is easy [to understand]. That it is not contradictory that although this pristine wisdom directly seeing suchness can be posited as a knower of the ultimate and ultimate truth can be posited as its object known, in the perspective of that pristine wisdom those two—agent and object—are absent is because agent and object are posited only in the perspective of conventional awarenesses. It is like the fact that, for example, although an inferential rational consciousness can be posited as a subject[a] and ultimate truth can be posited as [its] object, the two—the agentness and objectness of subject and object—are not posited in the perspective of the rational consciousness.

Then [Chandrakīrti's citation (see also *Insight,* 130 and 131) continues]:

[a] *yul can.*

> Devaputras, the ultimate truth is beyond [the objects of all consciousnesses] ranging right through the objects of omniscient pristine wisdoms endowed with the supreme of all aspects; it is not as expressed in the phrase "ultimate truth." All phenomena are false; they are deceptive phenomena.

The meaning of this citation is as follows:

- The first clause indicates that the ultimate truth is beyond the objects of omniscient pristine wisdoms.
- "It is not as expressed in the phrase 'ultimate truth'" indicates how it is beyond the objects of that [wisdom consciousness]. It is beyond the objects of the knowledge of the mode [of being of phenomena] by an omniscient consciousness in the sense of appearing in accordance with the individual dualistic appearance of separate subject and object to a conceptual consciousness induced by the expression "This is ultimate truth."
- Since all dualistically appearing phenomena are false, deceptive phenomena, those do not exist in the perspective of the perception of the solely non-delusive suchness.

All those [statements] are sources for the non-appearance of conventionalities, such as the aggregates, in the perspective of directly perceiving suchness.

Therefore, none of the proliferations of dualistic phenomena such as effective thing, non-effective thing, and so forth occur in the perspective of directly perceiving suchness because the entities of those proliferations are not observed in that [perspective]. In that case, in actuality only Superiors are valid with respect to contemplating[a] suchness; non-Superiors are not actually valid. Hence, the world does not damage [that is, invalidate] the refutation of production from other in the perspective of a Superior's perception of suchness.

[a] *bsam pa.*

Part Two:
Comparing Dol-po-pa's and Tsong-kha-pa's Views

Introduction

In some Buddhist systems, two conceptual poles are smashed against each other, thereby forcing movement to another level of consciousness in the resulting conceptual hiatus. However, in many Buddhist systems such as those of the Tibetan scholar-yogis Dol-po-pa Shay-rap-gyel-tsen[a] (the principal author of the Jo-nang-pa order), Tsong-kha-pa Lo-sang-drak-pa[b] (the founder of the Ge-luk-pa order), and Mi-pam-gya-tso[c] (the foremost twentieth-century exponent of the Nying-ma order) "complete" conceptual maps are laid out with the moves neatly delineated. In order to follow the map, one must undergo the battering and smashing of misbegotten conceptuality, gain the appropriate conceptual realization and then through becoming accustomed to it and gaining intense concentration, eventually arrive at non-conceptual realization.

It is a mistake to assume that these scholars are satisfied with a mere verbal lay-out of intricate philosophy. Rather, there is a basic recognition that we are controlled by our ideas, and thus re-formation of ideas in a harrowing process of analytical meditation—involving one's feelings in the most intimate sense—is of central importance. For instance, through not refuting phenomena themselves but qualifying that the object negated is inherent existence, Ge-luk-pa scholar-practitioners maintain the commonsense notion that one cannot say that something does not exist and then claim that it also is not non-existent. In this system the refutation of alternatives is not used to lift the mind to a non-conceptual level through shock but to penetrate the noumenon through a reasoned, conceptual process of refutation. When the negation of inherent existence is understood this way, realization during this phase is conceptual but not wandering among many conceptions; it is wholly focused on the absence of inherent existence. Subsequently, through combining that realization with the force of the stable meditative state of calm abiding, the ability to remain one-pointedly on emptiness is enhanced. Still, one needs to alternate stabilizing and analytical meditation on emptiness in order to induce special insight, which in turn is deepened over the path of preparation, resulting in a totally non-conceptual realization of emptiness on the path of seeing.

---

[a] *dol po pa shes rab rgyal mtshan,* 1292-1361.

[b] *tsong kha pa blo bzang grags pa;* 1357-1419.

[c] *mi pham 'jam dbyangs rnam rgyal rgya mtsho;* 1846-1912.

Thus, even though it is sometimes disappointing to encounter conceptual qualifications of scriptural passages that, without these qualifications, seem to lift the reader beyond conceptuality, it is a mistake to conclude that these systemizations are intended to intellectualize the profound to the point of stultifying and blocking non-conceptual meditation. Rather, they seek to put the intellect in its place, using it in a profound way in a process leading to non-conceptual direct perception. Such pursuit of conceptual intricacies stimulates thought to the point where topics can come alive, yielding profound insight.

What makes enlightenment possible?

It is incumbent upon systems of self-liberation to show what factors pre-exist in the mind or spirit that allow for transformation into a state of freedom from suffering. In Tibet in the fourteenth and fifteenth centuries there was great ferment about what makes enlightenment possible. This controversy about the nature of the mind, which persists to the present day, raises the questions:

- Is the reality of the mind already endowed with ultimate Buddha qualities, or is reality just the immaculate nature of the mind that allows for Buddha qualities to be developed?
- If conventional phenomena are empty of their ordinarily perceived status, is the reality of the mind empty of itself or is it empty only of conventional phenomena?
- Do conventional objects have so little status that they do not appear to a Buddha?
- Is the reality of the mind known only by pristine wisdom, or is it also known through inference?

In an earlier book[a] I presented a translation and analysis of a fourteenth-century Tibetan text, Dol-po-pa Shay-rap-gyel-tsen's *Mountain Doctrine, Ocean of Definitive Meaning: Final Unique Quintessential Instructions,*[b] which addressed these issues. Dol-po-pa's presentation prompted discussion among Tibetan and Mongolian scholars,[c] resounding to the

[a] Hopkins, *Mountain Doctrine,* 2006.

[b] *ri chos nges don rgya mtsho zhes bya ba mthar thug thun mong ma yin pa'i man ngag;* I primarily used two editions:

- Gangtok, Sikkim: Dodrup Sangyey Lama, 1976.
- Amdo, Tibet: 'Dzam thang bsam 'grub nor bu'i gling, n.d. This edition has few textual errors and includes much of Dol-po-pa Shay-rap-gyel-tsen's separate outline to the text, embedded within it.

[c] I will leave the many resonances with East Asian Buddhist traditions to the analysis of

present day. As Cyrus Stearns says:[a]

> Without question, the teachings and writing of Dol po pa, who was also known as "The Buddha from Dol po" (*Dol po sangs rgyas*), and "The Omniscient One from Dol po who Embodies the Buddhas of the Three Times" (*Dus gsum sangs rgyas kun mkhyen dol po pa*), contain the most controversial and stunning ideas ever presented by a great Tibetan Buddhist master. The controversies which stemmed from his teachings are still very much alive today among Tibetan Buddhists, more than 600 years after Dol po pa's death.

Dol-po-pa's work was of seminal importance in the Tibetan cultural region, stretching from Kalmyk Mongolian areas near the Volga River (in Europe where the Volga empties into the Caspian Sea), to Mongolia, to the Buriat Republic of Siberia, as well as to Bhutan, Sikkim, Ladakh, and parts of Nepal.

Dol-po-pa was born in 1292 in a family that practiced tantric rites of the Nying-ma order. After receiving tantric initiation at the age of five, he had a vision of Red Mañjushrī, after which his intelligence is said to have burgeoned. At twelve he was ordained and at seventeen fled, against his parents' wishes, to study in Mustang, where it is said that in a month he learned the doctrinal language of path-structure studies, epistemology and logic, and phenomenology. Dol-po-pa also received crucial teachings on the *Kālachakra Tantra* and related sūtras and commentaries that shaped his own practice and teachings.

At the age of twenty-two, while making a tour of western and Central Tibet to learn at other institutions, he was recognized as highly learned, even being called "Omniscient," an epithet that even his opponents still use. At twenty-nine in 1321, however, he was completely humbled when he visited the monastery of Jo-nang and saw that everyone who was seriously practicing meditation had realized the nature of reality. In 1322 he received in-depth instruction on the *Kālachakra Tantra* and entered into two retreats, during which he is said to have gained realization of the first four branches of the six-branched yoga of the Kālachakra system.

During the second retreat he realized the view of "other-emptiness" but did not speak about it for several years. In 1326 he was

other scholars.

[a] Cyrus R. Stearns, *The Buddha from Dol po: A Study of the Life and Thought of the Tibetan Master Dolpopa Sherab Gyaltsen* (Albany, N.Y.: State University of New York Press, 1999), 2. Stearns's excellent work (11-39) is the source of the short biography that follows, except for the parts drawn from my *Mountain Doctrine*.

installed as the head of the Jo-nang Monastery and in 1327 began work on a gigantic monument—the Glorious Stūpa of the Constellations—which was completed in 1333, to be restored in 1621 by Tāranātha and recently refurbished in 1990. Either during or after the building of the stūpa, for the first time he taught that conventional phenomena are self-empty, in the sense that they lack any self-nature, whereas the ultimate is other-empty, in the sense that it is empty of the relative but has its own self-nature. This realization Dol-po-pa himself stated to be previously unknown in Tibet. He completed his magnum opus, *Mountain Doctrine, Ocean of Definitive Meaning,* before the final consecration of the monument.

His view of "other-emptiness," based largely on his understanding of the *Kālachakra Tantra* and commentary by Kalkī Puṇḍarīka and bolstered by the *Aṅgulimāla Sūtra, Mahāparinirvāṇa Sūtra, Matrix of One-Gone-Thus Sūtra, Lion's Roar of Shrīmālādevī Sūtra,* and so forth, was received with amazement and shock. However, he was also highly lauded and received great offerings from exalted figures of the day. He gave teachings sometimes to thousands of persons and at other times to luminaries. Along with Bu-tön Rin-chen-drup[a]—another great master of Kālachakra—he was invited to China by the Yüan dynasty (Mongolian) Emperor Toghon Temür. Neither of them went, and to avoid the emperor's displeasure Dol-po-pa "stayed in different isolated areas for four years."[b]

In 1358, at the age of sixty-six, he departed from Jo-nang for a visit to Hla-sa. Along the way, he gave teachings to the Fifteenth Patriarch of Sa-kya, Sö-nam-gyel-tsen,[c] who requested that he compose *The Great Calculation of the Doctrine, which has the Significance of a Fourth Council,*[d] along with his own commentary. Dol-po-pa audaciously titled his work this way because he considered the doctrine of other-emptiness and its implications for the Buddha-nature to be like an addition to the famous three councils in India. After six months, when leaving Hla-sa to return to Jo-nang, he was thronged by believers, and again, along the way he taught huge crowds and received the praise of monastic leaders. When he stopped in Sha-lu[e] to debate with Bu-tön, the latter sought to avoid confrontation, but when Dol-po-pa nevertheless made "the opening exclamation for debate (*thal skad*), the force...produced a crack in the

[a] *bu ston rin chen grub,* 1290-1364.

[b] Stearns, *The Buddha from Dol po,* 29.

[c] *bsod nams rgyal mtshan.*

[d] *bka' bsdu bzhi pa'i don bstan rtsis chen po.*

[e] *zha lu.*

wall of Bu-ston's residence."[a]

Near the end of 1360, Dol-po-pa gave a teaching on his *Mountain Doctrine, Ocean of Definitive Meaning* and the next day passed away in deep meditation. Less than fifteen years after his death, the influential Sa-kya scholar Ren-da-wa Shön-nu-lo-drö[b] over three readings of the text first found it unappealing, then appealing, and then unappealing. Ren-da-wa's student, Tsong-kha-pa found it so provocative that he took Dol-po-pa's views as his chief opponent in his works on the view of emptiness.

Dol-po-pa developed a new doctrinal language through an amalgamation of the classical texts of the Mind-Only[c] and Middle Way[d] systems of India into a Great Middle Way,[e] and he also intertwined the particular vocabulary of the Kālachakra system. In what are typically considered the classical texts of separate systems, he saw presentations of multiple systems crowned by the Great Middle Way, which he declared to be concordant with Ultimate Mind-Only,[f] or Supramundane Mind-Only,[g] which is beyond consciousness.[h] Not just in sūtras and tantras but also in Indian treatises—usually taken to strictly present doctrines of the Mind-Only School—he found passages teaching Mind-Only and others teaching the Great Middle Way.

He also criticized the then (and still) popular notion that recognition of conceptions themselves as the body of attributes[i] of a Buddha would alone bring about enlightenment,[j] without requiring abandonment of any misconceptions.[k] Thus he was bucking two popular trends—(1) separation of the classical Indian texts of the Great Vehicle into isolated systems along with putting Sūtra and Tantra in isolated camps and (2) reduction of the final path to self-recognition of basic mind amidst conceptuality.

---

[a] Ibid., 34-35.

[b] *red mda' ba gzhon nu blo gros*, 1349-1412.

[c] *sems tsam pa, cittamātra.*

[d] *dbu ma pa, madhyamaka.*

[e] *dbu ma chen po, mahāmadhyamaka.*

[f] *don dam pa'i sems tsam*. Also, "Final Mind-Only" (*mthar thug gi sems tsam*).

[g] *'jig rten las 'das pa'i sems tsam.*

[h] *rnam shes las 'das pa.*

[i] *chos sku, dharmakāya.*

[j] For a clear and concise exposition of this position, see Stearns, *The Buddha from Dol po*, 98-105.

[k] For an excellent study of doctrines of enlightenment through seeing basic mind, see David Jackson, *Enlightenment by a Single Means* (Vienna: Verlag der Österreichischen Akademie der Wissenschaften, 1994).

Ren-da-wa's student Tsong-kha-pa (1357-1419), who became the founder of the Ge luk order, reacted to Dol-po-pa's dynamic synthesis with his own analysis of the classical texts, opposing such an amalgamation. Tsong-kha-pa emphasized philosophical controversies between schools that are evident in these same texts. Writing a book under the rubric not of intertwining texts but of distinguishing them, he titled it *Treatise Differentiating Interpretable and Definitive Meanings: The Essence of Eloquence*[a]—even the name of which can be seen to be in response to Dol-po-pa's *Mountain Doctrine, Ocean of Definitive Meaning*. Tsong-kha-pa's sense that the separateness of many texts[b] needed to be emphasized comes to life when we consider the context of his reaction to Dol-po-pa's synthesis. The vast amount of distinctions that Tsong-kha-pa had to make in order to construct his own grand overview of these systems indicates that his perspective is, in its own way, just as creative, synthetic, and syncretic. In order to undermine Dol-po-pa's view that the ultimate reality of the mind is endowed with ultimate Buddha qualities of body, speech, and mind, he attempted to show—through some of the very works that his predecessor cites as sources—that ultimate reality is a mere emptiness through concentration on which those qualities could be engendered.

In the following three chapters, I will highlight their points of divergence by considering central views found in Dol-po-pa's *Mountain Doctrine* and then Tsong-kha-pa's opposing opinions as found in his exposition of special insight in his *Medium-Length Exposition of the Stages of the Path* and in his descriptions of the object of negation and the two truths in his *Illumination of the Thought: Extensive Explanation of (Chandrakīrti's) "Supplement to (Nāgārjuna's) 'Treatise on the Middle.'"* The final chapter is an attempt at summarizing their core differences.

---

[a] *drang ba dang nges pa'i don rnam par phye ba'i bstan bcos legs bshad snying po;* P6142, vol. 153. For a translation of the complete text, see Thurman, *Tsong Khapa's Speech of Gold in the Essence of True Eloquence*. A Chinese translation was completed in Lhasa in 1916 by Venerable Fa Zun, "Bian Liao Yi Bu Liao Yi Shuo Cang Lun," in *Xi Zang Fo Jiao Jiao Yi Lun Ji* (Taipei: Da Sheng Wen Hua Chu Ban She, 1979), vol. 2, 159-276. For a translation of the introduction and section on the Mind-Only School, see Hopkins, *Emptiness in the Mind-Only School of Buddhism*.

[b] He did not do this for all texts. For instance, he considered Maitreya's *Ornament for Clear Realization* to contain passages that represent the opinions of the Consequence School subdivision of the Middle Way School and others that represent the views of the Autonomy School subdivision. See Tsong-kha-pa, Kensur Lekden, and Jeffrey Hopkins, *Compassion in Tibetan Buddhism*, 178-181.

1. Dol-po-pa Shay-rap-gyel-tsen's Views

Self-emptiness

For Dol-po-pa Shay-rap-gyel-tsen, there are two types of emptiness—self-emptiness and other-emptiness. He calls the first empty-emptiness, whereas he calls the second non-empty-emptiness,[a] because it is not self-empty. Self-emptiness means that conventional phenomena are empty of their own entities. Such phenomena cannot withstand analysis, for he says (*Mountain Doctrine,* 213), "subjects that cannot withstand analysis and finally disintegrate are empty of their own entities." Does this mean that an object is empty of itself? Is a table empty of a table, and a consciousness empty of a consciousness, and so forth? If so, would this mean that a table is not a table and that a consciousness is not a consciousness, and hence that tables and minds do not exist? In the *Mountain Doctrine* (214) Dol-po-pa quotes the *Mahāparinirvāṇa Sūtra,*[b] which clearly says that cows and horses exist:

> Child of lineage, as you propound, a horse does not exist in a cow, but it is not suitable to say that a cow does not exist, and a cow does not exist in a horse, but it is not suitable to say that even a horse does not exist.

From this, it seems that ordinary phenomena do indeed exist.

Also, some passages in the *Mountain Doctrine* limit the scope of the negation by qualifying that these phenomena do not appear to wisdom of reality, for Dol-po-pa speaks of their not existing **in the mode of subsistence** (*Mountain Doctrine,* 527-528):

> [Vasubandhu's] *Commentary on the Extensive and Middling Mothers* and so forth also say that because **in the mode of subsistence** these imputational three realms are utterly non-existent like the horns of a rabbit, they do not appear **to a consciousness of the mode of subsistence,** just as the horns of a rabbit do not appear to an unmistaken consciousness.

and (*Mountain Doctrine,* 535-536):

> That the noumenon exists **in the mode of subsistence** and that

[a] Hopkins, *Mountain Doctrine,* 213, 252, 301.

[b] *yongs su mya ngan las 'das pa chen po'i mdo, mahāparinirvāṇasūtra;* P787-789, vols. 30-31.

> phenomena do not exist **in the mode of subsistence** are set forth in many elevated, pure scriptural systems such as Maitreya's *Differentiation of the Phenomena and Noumenon* and so forth. If you are skilled in the thought of the similar, extensive statements of existing and not existing **in the mode of subsistence** such as:
>
> - the ultimate exists, but the conventional does not exist
> - nirvāṇa exists, but cyclic existence does not exist
> - true cessation exists, but the other three truths do not exist
> - the noumenal thoroughly established nature exists, but the other natures do not exist
> - thusness exists, but other phenomena do not exist
> - external and internal adventitious defilements do not exist, but the alternative supreme matrix-of-One-Gone-to-Bliss exists,
>
> you will know them within differentiating well existence and non-existence.

By qualifying non-existence with "in the mode of subsistence" he suggests that ordinary phenomena indeed exist but not ultimately.

However, at other points Dol-po-pa seems to indicate that not existing in the mode of subsistence means that conventional phenomena only provisionally exist in a way that is equivalent to not existing. He recognizes that this position has many consequences and carefully defends it against criticism:

1. He says that these phenomena exist only for consciousness,[a] which is necessarily mistaken, and thus what appears to pristine wisdom[b] does not appear to consciousness and what appears to consciousness does not appear to pristine wisdom (*Mountain Doctrine,* 527):

   > Also, the statement in Vasubandhu's *Principles of Explanation:*
   >
   > > Awakened from the sleep of ignorance
   > > And spread intelligence also to what is to be
   > > known,
   >
   > and so forth establishes that these three realms, which are appearances of ignorance, do not appear to the pristine wisdom of one awakened from the sleep of

[a] *rnam shes.*
[b] *yes shes.*

> ignorance because these three realms are appearances of consciousness and whatever is consciousness is ignorance. Vasubandhu's] *Extensive Commentary on the Perfection of Wisdom Sūtra in One Hundred Thousand Stanzas* also says that just as when awakened from sleep, dream appearances, which dawn in sleep, fade away, so these three realms, which are like dreams, do not appear to pristine wisdom for one awakened from the sleep of ignorance.

2. Dol-po-pa says that these phenomena appear "in the perspective of mistake," that is, only in the perspective of a mistaken consciousness (*Mountain Doctrine,* 537):

> Therefore, these mistaken karmic appearances of sentient beings are the private phenomena[a] just of sentient beings; they utterly do not occur in the mode of subsistence, like the horns of a rabbit, the child of a barren woman, a sky-flower, and so forth. Consequently, they are not established even as mere appearances to a cognition of the mode of subsistence, and appearing in the face of mistake does not fulfill the role of appearing in the mode of subsistence. In consideration of these [points], it is again and again said in many formats that all phenomena are not observed, non-appearing, unapprehendable, and so forth.

3. These mistaken phenomena do not even appear to a pristine wisdom that has extinguished mistakenness (*Mountain Doctrine,* 525-526):

> It is not reasonable for these to appear to a pristine wisdom in one for whom ignorance and imputation have been extinguished, just as falling hairs, a yellow conch, and so forth do not appear to those whose eyes are flawless. For Āryadeva's *Middle Way Conquest over Mistake* also says:
>
> > When the eye of intelligence is opened and the undefiled pristine wisdom of a One-Gone-to-Bliss dawns like awakening upon separating from the sleep of the predispositions of ignorance, nothing at all is perceived because an

[a] *sgos chos.*

entity of things is not observed.

and when, upon the dawning of the sun of the correct pristine wisdom knowing emptiness, signlessness, and wishlessness, all predispositions of non-knowledge and the afflictive emotions that make the connection [between lives] are cleared away, minds and mental factors as well as their objects of activity are not perceived and not observed as actualities and entities because, when the unsurpassed pristine wisdom dawns, the great rest is attained.

Having in that way indicated through reasoning that all phenomena conventionally are like dreams, falling hairs, and visual illusions and ultimately those are non-things, clear light, non-appearing, and devoid of proliferations, he also indicates such through scriptures. The holy master says that just as when one has awakened from sleep, dream appearances vanish and just as when the eyes become free from visual defect, appearances of hairs and so forth vanish, so to pristine wisdom—cleared of the sleep of ignorance and devoid of the visual cloudiness of consciousness—the phenomena of the three realms, minds and mental factors as well as their objects and so forth do not appear, because for pristine wisdom those as well as their seeds have stopped, been extinguished, and have vanished.

4. Dol-po-pa finds the perception of what exists in fact to be contradictory with perceiving what does not exist in fact, and thus if pristine wisdom, which has removed mistakenness, perceived the desire, form, and formless realms, which do not exist in fact, it would very absurdly follow that it does not perceive the noumenon, which abides in fact. Since these three realms have not passed beyond consciousness, if they did appear to such pristine wisdom, it would very absurdly follow that pristine wisdom would not have passed beyond consciousness, in which case it would not be a pristine wisdom perceiving the real. The headings for these sections (*Mountain Doctrine,* 528) make these points clearly:

    If such pristine wisdom perceived these three realms, which do not exist in fact, it would very absurdly follow that it does not perceive the noumenon, which abides in fact.

and (529):

> If these three realms, which have not passed beyond consciousness, did appear to such pristine wisdom, it would very absurdly follow that pristine wisdom would not have passed beyond consciousness.

and (530):

> If these unreal three realms did appear to such pristine wisdom, it would very absurdly follow that it would not be a pristine wisdom perceiving the real.

and (531):

> If sufferings and their origins did appear to such pristine wisdom, it would very absurdly follow that the seeds of cyclic existence and dualistic appearance would not have been stopped.

5. A consequence of the non-appearance of ordinary phenomena to pristine wisdom is that these phenomena do not appear to Buddhas. Dol-po-pa accepts this but holds that Buddhas are still omniscient, since they **implicitly** know these phenomena, in which case the phenomena themselves do not have to appear. He explains implicit realization in this context to mean that when Buddhas know the ultimate, they know that these phenomena do not exist and in this way know them (*Mountain Doctrine,* 532-534):

> *Objection:* In that case, a Buddha's pristine wisdom would not know the phenomena of the three realms, but this contradicts the statements even in the *Extensive* and *Medium-Length Mothers* and so forth that [a Buddha's pristine wisdom] knows—just as they are—minds involved with withdrawal, diffusion, and desire and so forth.
>
> *Answer:* There is no fault because, since there are innumerable cases of knowing within not appearing, knowing does not entail appearance [of the object], like knowing the past and the future, which are separated [from the present] by many eons, and knowing selflessness and so forth, even though those do not appear. Also, the thought of such statements in the *Mother* [scriptures] is said to be that knowing the diffusion, withdrawal, and so forth of the mind means to know

that the mind is not really established and hence to know that its diffusion, withdrawal, and so forth also are not really established and void.... Therefore, upon explicit appearance of the basis devoid of all phenomena—the noumenal thoroughly established nature—it is implicitly known that phenomena do not exist, whereby that is called "knowing all phenomena." Also, when such is seen, the real meaning of great significance is seen.

In consideration of these [statements] in that way of knowing but not appearing, it is said:

> Why? Because the Buddhas, knowing,
> Do not perceive phenomena.

This means that phenomena are known, although they do not appear. Similarly, [the *Verse Summary of the Perfection of Wisdom*] says:

> The One-Gone-Thus teaches that one who does not see forms,
> Does not see feelings, does not see discriminations,
> Does not see intentions, does not see consciousness,
> Mind, or mentality sees reality.
> Analyze how space is seen as in the expression
> By sentient beings in words, "Space is seen."
> The One-Gone-Thus teaches that seeing reality is also like that.
> The seeing cannot be expressed by another example.
> Whoever see thus see all phenomena....[a]

It is being said that the thought of the teachings that just not seeing is seeing is that—through just not seeing the phenomena that are the objects of negation—the basis of negation, the noumenon, is seen, and, through just knowing that all phenomena appearing in the face of mistake are not established in fact, all phenomena are known, this being inconceivable exalted knowledge....

[a] For Tsong-kha-pa's reading of this passage, see 260.

The *Buddhāvataṃsaka Sūtra* says that those having and not having special insight have good and bad appearances [respectively] and that what appear to those without special insight do not appear to those with special insight:

> What are seen by those without special insight
> Are the bad sights of phenomena.
> When special insight sees,
> All are not seen.

Because of this and because a conqueror's pristine wisdom is the finality of special insight, it is perforce established that these three realms do not appear to it because these appear to those without special insight.

6. A consequence is that a Buddha's pristine wisdom has both explicit and implicit realization (*Mountain Doctrine,* 535):

   Therefore, the final pristine wisdom perceiving the ultimate is a valid cognition of explicit realization with respect to knowing that the noumenon exists and is a valid cognition of implict realization with respect to knowing that phenomena do not exist.

7. Dol-po-pa faces an objection, based on scripture, that all phenomena whatsoever must **appear** to a Buddha's pristine wisdom by explaining away the passage as being metaphorical (*Mountain Doctrine,* 536):

   Objection: If these three realms do not appear to a Conqueror's pristine wisdom, it contradicts:

   > Just as the sun's emitting one ray
   > Illuminates transmigrating beings,
   > A conqueror's pristine wisdom simultaneously
   > Shines to all objects of knowledge.

   Answer: There is no fault:

   - because that was said considering [that is, meaning] that all objects of knowledge are known simultaneously
   - and because that passage says that a conqueror's pristine wisdom shines to all objects of knowledge

and does not indicate that all objects of knowledge appear to a conqueror's pristine wisdom

- and because here "shine" is just used metaphorically in relation to the example of the sun.

Moreover, it was proven above that knowledge of the non-existence of phenomena within their non-appearance is the meaning of knowing phenomena.

8. At the end of *Mountain Doctrine* Dol-po-pa makes it clear that these phenomena do not appear to a Buddha in any way at all, since a Buddha is always in meditative equipoise (538-539):

Objection: Although objects do not appear to the meditative equipoise of a conqueror's pristine wisdom, they appear to [a conqueror's] pristine wisdom subsequent [to meditative equipoise].

Answer: [A conqueror's] pristine wisdom is solely only meditative equipoise:

- because it is said that [a conqueror's pristine wisdom] is always just meditative equipoise, "Though an elephant rises, it is set in equipoise," and so forth
- and the holy Āryadeva also says:

Buddhas are always set
In equipoise on thusness.
Entry into and leaving
That inexpressible state does not exist.

How could the state subsequent to meditative equipoise
Be the way pristine wisdom is?
If this did occur in them,
How would they differ from those who have entered on grounds!

Hence, there is never non-equipoise in a Buddha's pristine wisdom.

Objection: That contradicts such statements as, "[Buddha] **rose** from being thoroughly set within," and "[Buddha] **rose** from the meditative stabilization."

Answer: Those are solely mere displays. Though [Buddhas] display rising from meditative stabilization, they do not have unequipoised minds because [their mind] is a pristine wisdom in which the mind-basis-of-all as well as the seeds are utterly extinguished, the continuum of all breaths has stopped, and the two obstructions as well as their seeds have been utterly extinguished. Therefore, you need to be skilled in the thought also of other such scriptural passages and need to be skilled also in the thought of other [scriptural passages speaking of] states subsequent [to meditative equipoise in a Buddha].

Self-emptiness is not the ultimate

For Dol-po-pa Shay-rap-gyel-tsen, self-emptiness is inadequate to being the ultimate truth. He carefully analyzes a sūtra passage that indicates that the ultimate is of a different order of being, beyond the temporary nature of compounded phenomena, which, like hail-stones, may appear solid but quickly disappear. In the *Aṅgulimāla Sūtra,*[a] Mañjushrī—the god of wisdom—pretends not to understand emptiness properly, holding that everything, even Buddha qualities, is empty. Aṅgulimāla, a sinner famed for having killed 999 persons and cut off a single finger (*aṅguli*) from each to make a rosary (*māla*) who then became a follower of Buddha, scathingly corrects the god of wisdom in what can be seen as a genre of comedy (*Mountain Doctrine,* 210-212):

Aṅgulimāla said to Mañjushrī:

> Mañjushrī, if you are the supreme of those seeing the great emptiness, then what is it to see emptiness? What is the meaning of "empty, empty"? O one endowed with great mind, speak quickly; cut off my doubts.

Then, the youthful Mañjushrī spoke in verse to Aṅgulimāla:

> The Buddha is like space;
> Space is signless.
> The Buddha is like space;
> Space is produced signlessly.
> The Buddha is like space;
> Space is formless.
> Attributes[b] are like space;

[a] *sor mo'i phreng ba la phan pa'i mdo, aṅgulimālīyasūtra;* P879, vol. 34.

[b] *chos, dharma.*

The One-Gone-Thus is the body of attributes.
Pristine wisdom is like space;
The One-Gone-Thus is the body of attributes.
Pristine wisdom unapprehendable, unfathomable,
Desireless is the One-Gone-Thus.
Liberation is like space;
Space also is signless.
Liberation is the Buddha, One-Gone-Thus.
How could you, Aṅgulimāla, understand
Empty nothingness!

Then, Aṅgulimāla further said this to the youthful Mañjushrī:

It is like this: For example, a rain-storm falls from a great cloud, and a person with a childish nature picks up a piece of hail. Thinking that it is a precious vaiḍūrya jewel, the person carries it home and, not daring to hold it due to its great coldness, thinks to treat it as a treasure and carefully puts it into a vase. Seeing that round piece of hail melt, the person thinks, "Empty," and turns speechless. Similarly, venerable Mañjushrī, one who meditates on extreme emptiness and considers emptiness to be profound uncomfortably sees all phenomena to be destroyed. Even non-empty liberation is seen and considered to be emptiness. It is like this: For example, having thought that a piece of hail is a jewel, the person meditates even on jewels as empty. Likewise, you also consider non-empty phenomena to be empty. Seeing phenomena as empty, you also destroy non-empty phenomena as empty. [However] empty phenomena are other; non-empty phenomena are other. The tens of millions of afflictive emotions, like hail-stones, are empty. The phenomena in the class of non-virtues, like hail-stones, quickly disintegrate. Buddha, like a vaiḍūrya jewel, is permanent. The scope of liberation also is like a vaiḍūrya jewel.

Space also is Buddha-form; there is no form of any Hearers and Solitary Realizers. The liberation of a Buddha also is form. Even if the liberations of Hearers and Solitary Realizers are formless, do not make a discrimination of non-division, saying, "The character of liberation is empty."

> Mañjushrī, an empty home in a built-up city is called empty due to the absence of humans. A pot is empty due to the absence of water. A river is empty due to water not flowing. Is a village that is without householders called "empty, empty?" Or are the households empty in all respects? They are not empty in all respects; they are called empty due to the absence of humans. Is a pot empty in all respects? It is not empty in all respects; it is called "empty" due to the absence of water. Is a river empty in all respects? It is not empty in all respects; it is called "empty" because water is not flowing. Similarly, liberation is not empty in all respects; it is called "empty" because of being devoid of all defects. A Buddha, a Supramundane Victor, is not empty but is called "empty" because of being devoid of defects and due to the absence of humanness and godhood that have ten of millions of afflictive emotions.
>
> Alas, venerable Mañjushrī, acting out the behavior of a bug, you do not know the real meaning of empty and non-empty. The naked ones[a] also meditate on all as empty. Do not say anything, you bug of the naked ones!

Dol-po-pa explains the meaning of the quotation as being that the mere finding that some phenomena are empty does not make all phenomena, such as the great liberation, also empty:

> The passage from "The Buddha is like space" through "How could you, Aṅgulimāla, understand/ Empty nothingness!" which indicates, in accordance with the assertions of some, that everything is a self-emptiness of nothingness, is an introduction by Mañjushrī. [It leads] to [Aṅgulimāla's] delineating the difference between self-emptiness and other-emptiness, despite the fact that [Mañjushrī actually] knows [the difference].
>
> Then, using the example of a hail-stone becoming non-existent upon melting, Aṅgulimāla teaches that all afflicted and non-virtuous phenomena are empty; this teaches that all that are included among mundane conventional truths are empty of themselves and of [their own] entities. Using the example of a *vaiḍūrya* jewel, which does not become non-existent upon melting, he teaches that the final liberation, Buddhahood, is not

[a] *gcer bu pa, nirgrantha;* the Jainas.

empty. This teaches that the ultimate supramundane truth, the body of attributes, is not empty of its own entity. Using the examples of an empty home, an empty vase, and an empty river, he teaches an emptiness of all defects; this teaches that the final liberation is other-emptiness. All descriptions of non-emptiness—"Liberation is not empty in all respects," "A Supramundane Victor is not empty," "Non-empty phenomena are other," and so forth—mean that the ultimate noumenon is not itself empty of itself. The very many statements in other sūtras and tantras of "is not empty" and "non-empty" also are similar.

The Superior Mañjushrī knows well both self-emptiness and other-emptiness. However:

- for the sake of teaching that those unskillful persons who assert that everything is only self-empty are like the naked ones
- and in order to indicate that the proposition that everything is self-emptiness is just bug[-like], relative to propositions made within good differentiation of what is and is not self-empty

[Aṅgulimāla] says:

> Venerable Mañjushrī, acting out the behavior of a bug, you do not know the real meaning of empty and non-empty. The naked ones also meditate on all as empty; do not say anything, you bug of the naked ones!

and:

> You also consider non-empty qualities to be empty. Seeing phenomena as empty, you also destroy non-empty qualities as empty

and so forth. These are advice and teachings for those who one-pointedly have decided that self-emptiness—which is that subjects[a] that cannot withstand analysis and finally disintegrate are empty of their own entities—is the final profundity.

Dol-po-pa describes self-emptiness as meaning that phenomena, which cannot withstand analysis and are subject to disintegration, are empty of their own entities. Self-emptiness is taught provisionally for those who take such to be the final reality. From this, it is clear that, for him, the actual ultimate truth, other-emptiness, is able to bear analysis and

[a] That is, phenomena.

is not impermanent.

Other-emptiness

Dol-po-pa faces the objection that, to the contrary, Āryadeva holds that realization and accustoming to self-emptiness is taught as an antidote to afflictive emotions (*Mountain Doctrine,* 394):

> *Objection:* Āryadeva's *Lamp Compendium for Practice* states:
>
>> All Ones-Gone-Thus possessing an essence of compassion—seeing all sentient beings fallen into a whirlpool of suffering, without refuge, and without defender—cause those beings to purify afflictive emotions through thorough knowledge of the nature of afflictive emotions in a conventional manner, and cause them to be thoroughly set in meditative stabilization having an essence of the mode of reality through having cleansed conventional truth also by means of ultimate truth.
>
> and so forth. Does this not say that the entities of afflictive emotions are purified through knowledge itself that they are self-empty?
>
> *Answer:* This is in consideration of temporarily suppressing or reducing the pointedness of coarse afflictive emotions because even this very passage says that, in the end, the conventional knowledge that afflictive emotions are self-empty must also be purified by non-conceptual pristine wisdom, meditative stabilization actualizing the ultimate.

Although self-emptiness does not fulfill the role of the actual ultimate, it has a place in the course of spiritual development as a means to temporarily reduce the force of coarse levels of afflictive emotions. Thoroughgoing release, however, is brought about through wisdom of other-emptiness (*Mountain Doctrine,* 394):

> Through merely knowing that things are self-empty one is not released; rather, when one is released from the stirrings of wind and mind, one is released from bondage; mistake as well as mistaken appearances having vanished, pristine wisdom manifests in self-appearance.

Dol-po-pa objects to the notion that the ultimate also could be self-empty, since then the ultimate would be empty of itself and thus would not exist at all (*Mountain Doctrine,* 213-214):

> Moreover, if everything were self-empty, then the body of attributes of release also would be self-empty, and if that is accepted, it also would be totally non-existent, whereby this would accord with the systems of the [non-Buddhist] Forder naked ones and so forth. The *Mahāparinirvāṇa Sūtra*... Also, that same sūtra, using the non-existence of a horse in a cow and the non-existence of a cow in a horse, pronounces that the ultimate noumenon, the great nirvāṇa, is other-empty in the sense of not being empty of itself. It extensively says:
>
> > Child of lineage, it is thus: Nirvāṇa is not formerly non-existent, like the non-existence of earthenware in clay. It is not non-existent upon ceasing, like earthenware's non-existence upon being destroyed. It is also not utterly non-existent, like the hairs of a turtle or the horns of a rabbit. Rather, it accords with the non-existence of the one in the other.
> >
> > Child of lineage, as you propound, a horse does not exist in a cow, but it is not suitable to say that a cow does not exist, and a cow does not exist in a horse, but it is not suitable to say that even a horse does not exist. Nirvāṇa also is like that; nirvāṇa does not exist in afflictive emotions, and afflictive emotions do not exist in nirvāṇa. Hence, it is said to be the non-existence of the one in the other.

Based on such passages, Dol-po-pa speaks of the thoroughly established nature not as empty of merely a non-existent object of negation, as Tsong-kha-pa does, but as empty of the other two natures—imputational natures and other-powered natures. If this rule for the ultimate—that if it is self-empty, it would be non-existent—is also to be applied to conventional phenomena, then since they are self-empty, they are decidedly non-existent. However, in the *Mountain Doctrine* Dol-po-pa does not explicitly extend this rule for the ultimate to the conventional.

In sum, the ultimate is empty of something other than itself and thus is other-empty. Just as a home is empty of humans, so the great liberation is empty of defects—which are other than itself and do not exist in reality—but it itself is not empty of itself. The great liberation does not melt under examination; it can bear analysis. In this way, other-emptiness, the thoroughly established nature, ultimately exists (*Mountain Doctrine*, 219-220):

> The imputational nature is empty in the sense of always not existing. Other-powered natures, although tentatively existent, are empty in the sense of not existing in reality; those two are fabricated and adventitious. It is said that the noumenal thoroughly established nature exists because the emptiness that is the [ultimate] nature of non-entities [that is, the emptiness that is the ultimate nature opposite from non-entities]—due to being just the fundamental nature—is not empty of its own entity, and it is also said that it does not exist because of being empty even of other-powered natures.

Thus, that other-emptiness ultimately exists means that it is able to withstand analysis.

Though Dol-po-pa himself does not explicitly say that the ultimate is truly established, or truly existent, the seventeenth-century Jo-nang savant Tāranātha, second only to Dol-po-pa Shay-rap-gyel-tsen in Jo-nang estimation, repeatedly uses this vocabulary in his short presentation of the schools of Buddhism, *The Essence of Other-Emptiness.* First let us cite his presentation of the ordinary, or inferior, Middle Way School:[a]

> In the country of Tibet, the Ordinary Middle Way is renowned as self-emptiness, and in both India and Tibet [this school] is renowned as the Proponents of Naturelessness.[b] This is the system of the masters Buddhapālita, Bhāvaviveka, Vimuktasena, and Shāntarakṣhita, as well as their followers.[c]
>
> Although among them there are many different divisions with respect to tenets, they all agree in asserting that:
>
> - All these phenomena—all compounded things (that is, the two, forms and minds, as well as non-associated composi-

[a] Tāranātha, *The Essence of Other-Emptiness,* translated and edited by Jeffrey Hopkins (Ithaca, N.Y.: Snow Lion Publications, 2007), 55-60. For the Tibetan, see *gzhan stong snying po,* Collected Works of Jo-naṅ rJe-btsun Tāranātha, vol. 4 (Leh, Ladakh: Smanrtsis Shesrig Dpemzod, 1985), 498.2.

[b] *ngo bo nyid med par smra ba, niḥsvabhāvavādin.*

[c] Tāranātha holds that all of these scholars are actually Proponents of the Great Middle Way, for as he says later (*The Essence of Other-Emptiness,* 92), "That Bhāvaviveka, Buddhapālita, and so forth are renowned as Proponents of Self-Emptiness and Proponents of Non-Nature is a case of mainly taking what is renowned to the ordinary world." In *Mountain Doctrine* Dol-po-pa cites these scholars (except for Shāntarakṣhita, whom he does not cite at all) in the context of the Great Middle Way. For Buddhapālita, see *Mountain Doctrine,* 343 and 530; Bhāvaviveka or Bhāvaviveka the Lesser (*legs ldan chung ba*), 307 and 469; Vimuktasena, 428.

tional factors) and all uncompounded phenomena and non-things, such as space—are conventionalities.[a]

- The mere absence of true existence, which is their nature, is the ultimate.
- Those two [that is, conventional truths and ultimate truths] are inexpressible as either one entity or different entities[b] and merely differ in the presentation of them. Since nothing at all exists in the entity of the ultimate basic element,[c] the voidness of proliferations[d] is taught through the example of space. Through the example of a magician's illusions, it is taught that although when conventionalities appear, they are empty of truth, their appearance is unimpeded.
- Both of these [that is, conventional truths and ultimate truths] are beyond all proliferations, such as existence and non-existence, is and is not, and so forth.

Moreover, this system of tenets is mistaken in:[e]

- asserting that the ultimate noumenon[f] is like space, a mere negation of proliferations[g]
- saying that a Buddha's pristine wisdom and so forth are conventionalities and do not truly exist[h]
- asserting that even ultimate truth does not truly exist[i]

---

[a] *kun rdzob.*

[b] Ge-luk-pa scholars uniformly assert that the two truths are one entity and different isolates (*ngo bo gcig la ldog pa tha dad*); for instance, see Jam-yang-shay-pa's presentation in Hopkins, *Maps of the Profound,* 896ff.

[c] *don dam dbyings.*

[d] *spros bral.*

[e] The first three of these are asserted in Ge-luk-pa presentations.

[f] *don dam chos nyid.*

[g] *spros pa bkag tsam.* According to the Ordinary Middle Way School, just as space is a mere negation of obstructive contact, so the ultimate noumenon is a mere negation of the proliferations of true existence. In the Great Middle Way, however, the ultimate noumenon is an affirming negative, not a mere absence or non-affirming negative, and includes positives, since ultimate Buddha-qualities of body, speech, and mind are integrally contained in the ultimate.

[h] In Ge-luk-pa presentations all types of mind, including a Buddha's pristine wisdom, are impermanent, even though at Buddhahood pristine wisdom is uninterruptedly continual. In the Great Middle Way, however, pristine wisdom itself is ultimate and, therefore, permanent and truly existent.

[i] In the Great Middle Way, ultimate truth itself ultimately exists and is truly established.

and in particular, mistaken also is the Consequentialists' non-assertion of anything—this being in order to avoid others' debates—despite positing a presentation of tenets. And mistaken are the Consequentialists' assertions that wrong conceptions are overcome even though an ascertaining consciousness is not generated, and so forth.

Tāranātha points out that it is indeed correct that apprehended object and apprehending subject lack true existence and that self-emptiness lacks true existence:[a]

> [This Consequentialist system of tenets] is not wrong [in asserting] that all phenomena included within apprehended object and apprehending subject do not truly exist and that even the mere absence of true existence is not truly established,[b] and so forth.
>
> These two, Proponents of Mind-Only and Middle Way Proponents of Self-Emptiness, do not assert in their own systems the mystery of the matrix-of-One-Gone-to-Bliss[c] and a self-cognizing and self-illuminating ultimate pristine wisdom.[d] Due to not having heard information[e] about these, earlier masters did not refute other-emptiness. However, later followers made refutations,[f] but not even a single one of them understood the essentials of the tenets of other-emptiness, and hence these are solely refutations in which the opposing position has not been apprehended.

For Tāranātha, the fact that Dol-po-pa repeatedly says that

[a] Tāranātha, *The Essence of Other-Emptiness,* 60-61.

[b] In the Great Middle Way also, self-emptiness—that is to say, the mere absence of true establishment—is not truly established. However, other-emptiness, the actual ultimate, is truly established.

[c] *bde gshegs snying po'i nges gsang.* Although Ge-luk-pas assert a matrix-of-One-Gone-to-Bliss that is the emptiness of inherent existence of a mind that is associated with defilement, they do not assert a matrix-of-One-Gone-to-Bliss endowed with ultimate Buddha-qualities of body, speech, and mind, whereas such is asserted in the Great Middle Way.

[d] *don dam ye shes rang rig rang gsal.*

[e] *gnas tshul ma go ba.*

[f] In his *Autocommentary on the "Supplement"* Chandrakīrti explains that the teaching of a matrix-of-One-Gone-to-Bliss endowed with ultimate Buddha-qualities of body, speech, and mind requires interpretation, and Tsong-kha-pa takes Dol-po-pa's presentation of other-emptiness as his main opponent in his *The Essence of Eloquence;* see Jeffrey Hopkins, *Reflections on Reality: The Three Natures and Non-Natures in the Mind-Only School* (Berkeley: University of California Press, 2002), Part Four.

other-emptiness ultimately exists and is ultimately established and does not use the vocabulary of "true existence" and "true establishment" is of no significance. The two sets of terminology are equivalent.

In his exposition of the Great Middle Way in *The Essence of Other-Emptiness,* Tāranātha describes the meaning of true existence/establishment the same way that Dol-po-pa describes the meaning of ultimate existence or ultimate establishment—being able to bear analysis:[a]

> The Great Middle Way is the Middle Way School of Cognition, renowned in Tibet as Other-Emptiness. It is illuminated by the texts of the foremost holy Maitreya, by the Superior Asaṅga, and by the supreme scholar Vasubandhu and is greatly illuminated also in the Superior Nāgārjuna's *Praise of the Element of Attributes.* Therefore, the assertion of both of the supreme Superiors [that is, Asaṅga and Nāgārjuna] is other-emptiness.
>
> In this system, the truthless [that is, those lacking true existence] are in brief:
>
> 1. all *basal* phenomena of cyclic existence—non-things[b] (that is, imputed uncompounded phenomena,[c] such as the three uncompounded phenomena[d] asserted in the Mind-Only School and below), forms and so forth that are renowned to be external objects, the eight collections of consciousness, the fifty-one mental factors, and so forth
> 2. all temporary phenomena included within *paths*
> 3. from among those included within the *fruit,* Buddhahood, newly arisen factors[e] and those [phenomena] included within the other-appearance[f] of trainees

[a] Tāranātha, *The Essence of Other-Emptiness,* 63-72.

[b] *dngos med, abhāva.*

[c] *'dus ma byas btags pa ba.* These are called "imputed" because the actual uncompounded is the ultimate truth according to the Great Middle Way, as Tāranātha explicitly says in the *Twenty-one Differences Regarding the Profound Meaning;* see Tāranātha, *The Essence of Other-Emptiness,* 127.

[d] The three renowned uncompounded phenomena are uncompounded space, analytical cessations, and non-analytical cessations. The latter two are to be distinguished from ultimate true cessations.

[e] *gsar du byung ba'i cha.* These are produced fruits (*bskyed pa'i 'bras bu*), that is to say, effects produced by the spiritual path as opposed to separative fruits (*bral ba'i 'bras bu*), which are merely uncovered by the path and thus already existent factors that need only to be separated from defilement.

[f] *gzhan snang.* These are displays by Buddhas in accordance with the dispositions and

> that is to say, all appearing and renowned phenomena, or phenomena in the division of phenomena and noumenon,[a] or all phenomena included within apprehended object and apprehending subject, or—on this occasion of delineating the ultimate—all effective things and non-things, namely, all that are compounded and adventitiously posited.[b]
>
> Self-cognizing, self-illuminating pristine wisdom[c] that is non-dual with the basic element is called the ultimate truth, the uncompounded noumenon. It is only truly established, able to bear analysis by reasoning.[d] They assert that because, when analyzed, the space-like [absence of true establishment] asserted by the Proponents of Self-Emptiness is a non-thing,[e] it is not the ultimate truth.[f] These tenets are flawless and endowed with all good qualities.

Tāranātha describes the type of analysis that the ultimate can withstand is the reasonings of dependent-arising, the lack of being one or many, and so forth, which are the typical reasonings of the Middle Way School:[g]

> Therefore, the glorious great Jo-nang-pa, knowing such, understood through rational analysis that:
>
> - Because of being partless and because of being all-pervasive the noumenon is only one in the individual environments and beings therein, in the threefold basis, path, and fruit, and in all Buddhas and sentient beings.

---

needs of trainees and thus are compounded, impermanent, and conventional. See especially the quotes from Maitreya's *Sublime Continuum of the Great Vehicle* in the fruit section of Dol-po-pa's *Mountain Doctrine;* see Hopkins, *Mountain Doctrine,* 492-511.

[a] *chos dang chos nyid.*

[b] *glo bur bar gzhag pa.* Even non-things are compounded, since only the ultimate is actually uncompounded.

[c] *ye shes rang rig rang gsal.*

[d] In his *Twenty-one Differences Regarding the Profound Meaning* Tāranātha specifies this as "the reasoning of dependent-arising, the lack of being one or many, and so forth."

[e] *dngos med.*

[f] See Dol-po-pa's long exposition that self-emptiness is not the ultimate in *Mountain Doctrine* in a section titled "Extensive explanation of damage to the assertion that self-emptiness, the ultimate, and so forth are synonyms," 254-315.

[g] The following is quoted from Tāranātha's *Twenty-one Differences Regarding the Profound Meaning,* which I have included as a supplemental text in Tāranātha, *The Essence of Other-Emptiness,* 133.

- And for that reason the matrix-of-One-Gone-to-Bliss is endowed with all [ultimate Buddha-]qualities.
- And for that reason [the noumenon] is not damaged by the reasoning of dependent-arising, the lack of being one or many, and so forth, and hence withstands analysis.
- And since that is the case, the uncommon tenets of the Autonomists and Consequentialists, who assert that [the noumenon] falls apart under analysis, are in error, and hence the views of the Autonomy School and the Consequence School are incorrect and therefore do not accord with the thought of the middle wheel of doctrine.
- and so forth.

Due to being partless, the ultimate is not damaged by the reasoning examining whether it is one or many, since it is one. Due to not being a dependent-arising (see below, 301ff.), it is not damaged by the reasoning of dependent-arising.

Other-emptiness is an affirming negative, not a non-affirming negative

Since the ultimate, although without the phenomena of cyclic existence, is replete with beneficial qualities, it is not a mere absence. In the *Mountain Doctrine,* Dol-po-pa identifies the ultimate as an affirming negative (nine times), something that implies a positive in place of the negation. For instance (132-133):

> Earlier statements due to the perspective of trainees that all—liberation and so forth—do not exist, are empty, selfless, and so forth are in consideration of the non-existence of whatsoever [object of negation] in something, whereas later statements of non-emptiness, existence of self, and so forth are in consideration of the remainder after the negation. Therefore, the fact that, although earlier and later scriptures seem to be contradictory but are, when analyzed well, non-contradictory is because an affirming negative exists as the basis of a non-affirming negative and because a pristine wisdom in which all fundamental qualities are contained abides—in the manner of thorough establishment pervading space—in the basis which from the start is naturally pure and devoid of all defects.

and (205-206):

> When, through having yogically made endeavor at the perfection of wisdom, a meditative stabilization that is a union of calm abiding and special insight has been generated, you need to be taught within differentiating existence and non-existence, emptiness and non-emptiness, and so forth, and you need to identify these in accordance with how they abide and how they are:
>
> - because all do not abide as non-existent and non-established, and so on, and there exists an affirming negative as the basis of non-affirming negatives—such as non-existence and emptiness and the basis of them
> - and because an inclusionary elimination abides as the basis of an exclusionary elimination
> - and because realization that contains all final qualities spontaneously abides in the basis that naturally has abandoned all defects.
>
> Therefore, the third wheel of doctrine is said to be "possessed of good differentiation."

Other-emptiness and the middle wheel of doctrine

Although Dol-po-pa recognizes that the middle wheel of doctrine teaches that even the ultimate does not ultimately exist, he explains this away as a technique for developing non-conceptual meditation at a certain level of practice. Dol-po-pa depicts the middle wheel of doctrine and Nāgārjuna's Collection of Reasonings as presenting the view that phenomena are as unfounded as a flower of the sky, the horns of a rabbit, and the child of a barren woman **in the perspective of their final nature** (*Mountain Doctrine,* 199):

> About that, in order to realize well the commonly renowned correct view [of self-emptiness], it is necessary to conclude that all phenomena are like a sky-flower because in the mode of abiding they are not anything and are not established as anything, like the horns of a rabbit and the child of a barren woman. Since sources for this are well renowned in the middle wheel of Buddha's word and in Nāgārjuna's Collection of Reasonings and so forth, and since here an exposition on this topic would be too much, I will not write on it.

The second wheel of doctrine is seen as providing a means for entry into meditative equipoise beyond conceptuality (*Mountain Doctrine,* 205):

> When yogically performing the perfection of wisdom, it is necessary to be devoid of all conceptuality, and hence all objects are refuted for the sake of stopping all apprehending subjects. Therefore [in the second wheel of doctrine, Buddha] was intent on teaching everything as emptiness through many aspects such as everything's non-existence, non-establishment, voidness, and so forth but was not intent on differentiating existence, non-existence, and so forth, due to which the second wheel of doctrine is said to be "through the aspect of speaking on emptiness."

However, the middle wheel's blanket teaching of emptiness and non-existence does not take into account that the ultimate ultimately exists (*Mountain Doctrine,* 206):

> In this fashion, the second wheel out of purposeful intent teaches that even what are not self-empty are self-empty, and so on, and is not possessed of good differentiation, that is to say, is not without internal contradictions, and for such reasons [the *Sūtra Unraveling the Thought*] says that [the second wheel] "is surpassable, affords an occasion [for refutation], requires interpretation, and serves as a basis for controversy." About the third wheel by reason that, opposite from those, it differentiates meanings well just as they are, and so forth, [the *Sūtra Unraveling the Thought*] says that it "is unsurpassable, does not afford an occasion [for refutation], is of definitive meaning, and does not serve as a basis for controversy."

The third wheel, however, clearly differentiates what does and does not truly exist (*Mountain Doctrine,* 202):

> The first wheel of doctrine concords with a precursor to meditating on the profound definitive meaning of the Great Vehicle; the second wheel of doctrine concords with practicing a special meditative stabilization of equipoise on the profound meaning; and the third wheel concords with profound Secret Mantra identifying—within good differentiation—existence, non-existence, and so forth.

Seeing an underlying harmony in the three wheels of doctrine, he indicates that the third wheel of doctrine makes clear that the ultimate truly exists and thus is distinctively superior. From this viewpoint, he sees the middle and final wheels as differing primarily in terms of clarity, not in terms of meaning:

> Absence of production, absence of cessation, quiescence from the start, and naturally passed beyond sorrow are taught even in the third wheel and are taught in the vajra vehicle. By reason of teaching unclearly [in the middle wheel], clearly [in the third wheel], and very clearly [in tantra], there are great and also very great differences of being obscured, not obscured, and so forth with respect to the meaning of those. Therefore, even the statements of being surpassable or unsurpassable, affording an opportunity [for refutation] or not affording an opportunity, and so forth are due to differences in those texts with respect to whether the final profound meaning is unclear and incomplete or clear and complete, and so forth, and are not due to the entity of the meaning.[a]

Dol-po-pa sees—as the meaning of a great many pronouncements in Great Vehicle scriptures about non-existence and existence—that the non-existent are conventionalities and the existent is the noumenon (*Mountain Doctrine*, 222):

> Here, in accordance with the statement in that way of the meaning of not existing and not not existing, Maitreya's *Differentiation of the Middle and the Extremes* says, "Not existent, and also not non-existent," and moreover the thought of all the statements—in a great many stainless texts of the middle way—of being devoid of the extremes of existence and non-existence is that:
>
> - Since all dependently arisen conventionalities do not really exist, when one realizes this, one does not fall to an extreme of existence and is released from the extreme of superimposition.
> - Since the ultimate noumenon that is beyond dependent-arising is never non-existent, when one realizes this, one does not fall to an extreme of non-existence and is released from the extreme of deprecation.

[a] He does not explain how the middle wheel could teach what is opposite to the ultimate—by proclaiming that the ultimate which is actually not self-empty is self-empty—and yet be unclear and incomplete with respect to the ultimate. Nowadays, some Jonang-pas explain that these statements in the middle wheel of doctrine that the ultimate also is self-empty merely refer to a conceptualized ultimate.

The middle wheel of doctrine requires interpretation both because of its lack of clarity on what does and does not ultimately exist and because it over-extends statements of non-existence to include the ultimate. For Dol-po-pa, the final wheel of doctrine **clearly** teaches a truly established "other-emptiness"—that is, a thoroughly established nature that is empty of imputational natures and other-powered natures—and hence is definitive, whereas the middle wheel does not clearly teach the actual mode of subsistence of phenomena and hence requires interpretation. He refers to the third wheel as teaching directly and clearly and to the other two wheels as teaching obliquely by way of intentional speech (*Mountain Doctrine,* 394-395):

> Consequently, the noumenal ultimate truth—the basis of the emptiness of all phenomena abiding as empty—is the final definitive meaning of the profound scriptures, be they those that directly teach clearly or those that teach by way of oblique intention.

In this way, he is able to frame the three wheels of doctrine as a harmonious whole. Still, he does not obliterate any difference between the teachings of the middle and final wheels. For he holds that the middle wheel of doctrine teaches what is non-empty to be empty—that is, that the ultimate is empty of true establishment—and he says that the middle wheel is even internally contradictory. He repeats this point later (*Mountain Doctrine,* 364):

> Similarly, it should be understood that all statements—in these and those texts of the middle wheel of doctrine—of the non-self-empty as self-empty are just of interpretable meaning with a thought behind them. [Understanding] this depends on the lamp of unique quintessential instructions of good differentiation [found in the three cycles of Bodhisattva commentaries].

The "purposeful intent of," or "thought behind," the second wheel is to draw practitioners into a state of non-conceptual meditative equipoise (*Mountain Doctrine,* 209-210):

> Therefore, although the meaning of the last two wheels of doctrine and of the vajra vehicle is one, when they are practiced, you set in equipoise in the conclusive profound noumenon devoid of proliferation in accordance with the middle wheel, and then when making distinctions in subsequent attainment [after meditative equipoise], you individually discriminate phenomena in a correct way, at which time you make identifications

> upon good differentiation in accordance with what is said in the final wheel and in the vajra vehicle. When [this procedure is followed], practice of the meaning of all the scriptures of the Great Vehicle becomes complete, unmistaken, and just thoroughly pure. Hence, here I will teach within making good differentiation of:
>
> - existing and not existing in the mode of subsistence
> - emptiness and non-emptiness of its own entity
> - exclusionary elimination and inclusionary elimination
> - non-affirming negation and affirming negation
> - abandonment and realization
>
> and so forth in accordance with how these are in the basic disposition of things.

Dol-po-pa's opinion is that the middle wheel overstates the doctrine of self-emptiness when it extends this to the ultimate, declaring it to be without true existence.

Two truths

In Dol-po-pa's system the ultimate is true ultimately, and obscurational truths are true obscurationally, or conventionally (*Mountain Doctrine,* 342-344):

> *Objection:* Since truth does not exist in any phenomenon, the ultimately true does not occur.
>
> *Answer:* That is not so. If something is not true conventionally, it is not suitable as a conventional truth, and hence that which is a conventional truth is conventionally true and is not ultimately true. Just so, if something is not ultimately true, it is not suitable as an ultimate truth, and hence that which is an ultimate truth is ultimately true and is not conventionally true. Furthermore, that which is the ultimate truth is ultimately true because:
>
> - the honorable Superior Nāgārjuna's autocommentary,[a] the *Akutobhayā* says:
>
>   > Since the ultimate truth is realized by Superiors to be non-erroneous, that which is perceived as the non-production of all phenomena is itself

[a] Ge-luk-pa scholars do not accept that this is Nāgārjuna's autocommentary, since it cites Nāgārjuna's own student, Āryadeva, in it.

ultimately true for them themselves, whereby it is the ultimate truth.

- and [a sūtra cited therein] says, "Monastics, it is thus: this non-deceptive phenomenon, nirvāṇa, is the supreme of truths."
- and the master Avalokitavrata, in his *Commentary on (Bhāvaviveka's) "Lamp for (Nāgārjuna's) 'Wisdom',"* also quotes those same words
- and Buddhapālita's *Commentary on (Nāgārjuna's) "Treatise on the Middle"* also quotes those same words and says, "Furthermore, truth is one; there is no second."
- and Nāgārjuna's *Sixty Stanzas of Reasoning* also says:

  When the conqueror said
  That only nirvāṇa is a truth,
  What wise person would think,
  "The rest are not unreal"?...

- and the *Shrīmālādevī Sūtra* also says, "The truth of the cessation of suffering itself is—in reality—true, permanent, and a refuge."
- and Chandrakīrti's middle way *Clear Words* also says, "The Supramundane Victor said, 'Monastics, this is the ultimate truth—nirvāṇa having the attribute of non-deceptiveness.'"
- and profound Secret Mantra texts also have extensive statements as in:

  Endowed with the truth
  And abiding in the manner of the two truths.

  and so forth.

Similarly, conventional truths are not really true, and if, though unproduced, it is refuted that they are produced conventionally, it would incur fault, because Jñānagarbha's *Two Truths* refutes such:

> Some who are renowned for bad arguments
> Say that things that are not produced in reality
> Also are not produced conventionally,
> Like the child of a barren woman and so forth.

as do other passages.

Here Dol-po-pa clearly indicates that conventional objects are produced conventionally and that they are not non-existent like the child of a barren woman.

Furthermore, despite suggestions that conventional phenomena are only diseased phenomena to be transcended, there are conventional types of four of the five pristine wisdoms of a Buddha (*Mountain Doctrine,* 456-457):

> Similarly, the pristine wisdom of the pure element of attributes is only ultimate, whereas there are compounded and uncompounded [types] with regard to the four—the mirror-like wisdom and so forth—whereby it should be known that there are conventional [ones] and there are also ultimate [ones].

Conventional form bodies, unlike ultimate form bodies, are impermanent (*Mountain Doctrine,* 448):

> Conventional form bodies are endowed with correct pristine wisdom, the non-perverse thoroughly established nature; they are endowed with the Great Vehicle pristine wisdom of a non-learner that is not beyond momentariness.

Tāranātha gives a brief summary of which Buddha qualities are ultimate and which are conventional:[a]

> Therefore, the pristine wisdom of the element of attributes necessarily is only an ultimate truth; although the other four pristine wisdoms are mainly the primordially abiding ultimate, each in a minor way has conventional portions that are newly attained through having cultivated the path. The ten powers, four fearlessnesses, and so forth also are similar to those [four pristine wisdoms in mainly being the primordially abiding ultimate, but each in a minor way has conventional parts that are newly attained through having cultivated the path]. The qualities of exalted body (the marks, the beauties, and so forth) and the qualities of exalted speech (the sixty branches [of vocalization] and so forth) each equally has conventional and ultimate portions. Likewise, the nature body is only ultimate; the body of attributes is mostly ultimate; the two, the complete enjoyment body and emanation bodies, have equal portions when a division of actual and imputed types is not made; moreover, the appearances of exalted activities in others' perspectives are conventional, whereas the pristine wisdom of capable power is ultimate.

---

[a] Tāranātha, *The Essence of Other-Emptiness,* 95-96.

> Hence, all exalted body, pristine wisdom, qualities, and activities that are included within the ultimate abide primordially in the matrix-of-One-Gone-Thus. When a person is Buddhafied, those are not newly attained and are merely separated from defilements obscuring them, but those that are conventional are newly attained. In past Buddhas and in future Buddhas those that are ultimate are one entity, and even those that are conventional are indivisible in nature upon attaining Buddhahood and thereafter but at the point of attainment are different; hence, they are unpredicable as either the same or different.[a]

In this way, Tāranātha shows the multiple viewpoints in which these two types of qualities are the same and/or are different.

Relationship of the two truths

Dol-po-pa clearly holds that the ultimate exists and is an object of knowledge (*Mountain Doctrine,* 241):

> Likewise, the *Tantra of the Supreme Original Buddha* also speaks of it as being the ultimate object of knowledge and also the ultimate mind with:
>
>> That object of knowledge seen here,
>> Unproduced and unceasing,
>> Is none other than one's own mind.

The two truths, obscurational/conventional and ultimate, are different and are not the same entity (*Mountain Doctrine,* 404-405):

> An emptiness of all[b] does not occur because an emptiness of the noumenon does not occur. A basis of the emptiness of all phenomena[c] occurs; it is the noumenon. A basis empty of the noumenon[d] does not occur because that is damaged by immeasurable, great, absurd consequences. Therefore, empty of all and empty of all phenomena are extremely different because the mode of subsistence is empty of phenomena but is not empty of the noumenon.[e] This also clears away the

[a] They are the same from one perspective and different from another perspective and thus inexpressible as either.

[b] *thams cad kyi stong pa.*

[c] *chos thams cad kyi stong pa'i gzhi.*

[d] *chos nyid kyi stong pa'i gzhi.*

[e] *des na thams cad kyis stong pa dang chos thams cad kyi stong pa ni khyad par shin tu che ste/* ***gnas lugs la*** *chos kyis stong yang chos nyid kyis mi stong:* 384.5/207b.7. The usage of *la* in *gnas*

assertion that phenomena and noumenon are one entity and different isolates[a] and the assertion that they are not at all different because those two are different in the sense of negating that they are the same entity.[b]

Objection: Well then, this contradicts the *Sūtra Unraveling the Thought,* which says that the two truths are not either one or different:

> The character of the compounded realm and of the ultimate
> Is a character devoid of sameness and difference.
> Those who consider that they are the same or different
> Are improperly oriented.

Answer: That passage refutes that the two truths are the same entity or different entities because although ultimate entities are established in the mode of subsistence, conventional entities are not established [in the mode of subsistence].

Hence, the two truths are neither one nor one entity. They are different, though not different entities. Hence, an ultimate truth is not an obscurational truth, and an obscurational truth is not an ultimate truth. Their difference means simply that they are not the same entity.

The ultimate is other than lowly conventionalities (*Mountain Doctrine,* 389-391):

> Similarly, without the flaws of a combination of contradictions many scriptural statements—speaking of body without body, existence without existence, wondrous form without form, the aspectless endowed with all aspects, and so forth—again and again teach the profound ultimate other-emptiness, the basis of emptiness, beyond worldly examples....The *Revelation of the Thought Tantra...* and *Glorious Union of All Buddhas...* extensively speak of natural, fundamental, noumenal, naturally pure aggregates, constituents, and so forth—which primordially are bases of emptiness of fabricated, adventitious aggregates, constituents, and so forth—alternative, supreme, transcendent, and ultimate. In this way, ultimate truths are other than these lowly external and internal conventionalities; they are transcendent, ultimate, and supreme. Moreover, in elevated tantras

lugs la is unclear to me.

[a] *ngo bo gcig la ldog pa tha dad.*

[b] *ngo bo gcig pa bkag pa'i tha dad.*

it is said:

> As is the external, so is the internal.
> As is the internal, so is the alternative.

It is said that just as although the external husk of a grain, the internal part, and the essence of the grain are not the same entity, but abide similarly in terms of aspect, so although this external world of the container-environment, the internal sentient beings who are contents, and the alternative matrix-of-One-Gone-to-Bliss, thusness, are indeed not the same entity, they are similar in aspect. This mode abides as equivalent also to the statement in other texts of the great middle:

> Just this as it appears is conventional.
> The counterpart is other.

"Just this as it appears" [means that] these externals and internals appearing to consciousness are conventionalities. That which is "other" than these is the ultimate noumenal, which is other than these conventional phenomena—transcendent or the ultimate of the supreme. From between the two truths, ultimate truth is the counterpart to conventional truths; therefore, it is called "the counterpart." Thus this statement that whatever are ultimates are other than conventionalities also clears away the assertion by some that the two truths are undifferentiable.

The otherness of the two truths eliminates the possibility that somehow they are undifferentiable.

Though the two truths are different, their difference is not that conventionalities are appearances and their emptinesses are ultimate truths, since the ultimate also appears to pristine wisdom and since conventionalities are self-empty (*Mountain Doctrine,* 391):

Furthermore, those who assert that these things appearing to consciousness are conventionalities and the factors of their emptiness of themselves are ultimate truths are extremely mistaken:

- because it is impossible for those that are self-empty to be ultimate truths and it is impossible for those that are ultimate truths to be self-empty
- and because many pure sources for those have been set forth and will be set forth.

Similarly, the assertion that all whatsoever appearances are conventionalities and all whatsoever emptinesses are ultimates also is babble because since both appearance and emptiness are contained in conventionalities and both appearance and emptiness are contained in ultimates, this [assertion] is harmed by the absurd consequence that even the appearance of the noumenon would be a conventionality and by the extreme absurdity that conventional emptiness [that is, self-emptiness] would be ultimate.

The ultimate is not a dependent-arising

For Dol-po-pa, dependent-arisings are limited to impermanent phenomena produced from causes and conditions, and, therefore, the ultimate cannot be a dependent-arising. This seems to contradict Nāgārjuna's statement that all phenomena are dependent-arisings, but Dol-po-pa explains that it does not, first by showing that the ultimate is necessarily not impermanent and deceptive through citing a Perfection of Wisdom Sūtra, the *Sūtra Unraveling the Thought*, the *Shrīmālādevī Sūtra*, and Nāgārjuna's *Fundamental Treatise on the Middle, Called "Wisdom"* and then by indicating that Nāgārjuna's reference about the mutuality of dependent-arising and emptiness both here and in his *Essay on the Mind of Enlightenment* has to be to self-emptiness, not other-emptiness (*Mountain Doctrine*, 398-400):

Objection: Nāgārjuna's *Fundamental Treatise on the Middle, Called "Wisdom"* says:

> Because there are not any phenomena
> That are not dependent-arisings,
> There are not any phenomena
> That are not empty.

Hence, just as whatever are dependent-arisings are emptinesses, whatever are emptinesses must also be dependent-arisings, and since dependent-arisings are self-empty, all emptinesses are only self-empty.

Answer: Since some think this, let me explain. That passage says that whatever are dependent-arisings are emptinesses, but it does not say that whatever are emptinesses are dependent-arisings. If it is asserted that all whatsoever emptinesses are dependent-arisings, then since all synonyms of the basis of emptiness—ultimate, noumenon, limit of reality, and so forth—

are emptinesses, they would be dependent-arisings, and it would have to be asserted that they are also compounded, impermanent, false, deceptive, and so forth. However, that is not reasonable because there would be the great fallacy of contradicting extensive statements in the *Mother of the Conquerors:*

> Subhūti, it is taught that conventional truths, taken as valid, create effects. It cannot be taught that ultimate truths create effects.

and so forth and also in the *Sūtra Unraveling the Thought:*

> Subhūti, it is like this: Thusness, the ultimate, selflessness in phenomena does not arise related to causes; it is not compounded; it also does not become non-ultimate. An ultimate other than that ultimate is not to be sought. In permanent, permanent time and in everlasting, everlasting time, whether Ones-Gone-Thus arise or do not arise, the noumenon of phenomena, the basic element that is the abode of attributes only abides; it is not otherwise.

and so forth. Moreover, if ultimate truths were not beyond dependent-arisings, even final true cessations would not be beyond dependent-arisings. And if that is asserted, they would not be beyond compounded phenomena, in which case they would most absurdly have the attributes of impermanence, falsity, and deceptiveness and would not be final sources of refuge. This is because the *Shrīmālādevī Sūtra* says:

> Supramundane Victor, among these four noble truths, three truths are impermanent, and one truth is permanent. Why? Supramundane Victor, it is because the three truths are included in what have the characteristic of being compounded, and, Supramundane Victor, those included in what have the characteristic of being compounded are impermanent. Those that are impermanent have the attribute of falsity, deceptiveness. Supramundane Victor, those that are impermanent have the attribute of falsity—deceptiveness—and are untrue, impermanent; they are not a refuge. Supramundane Victor, consequently, the noble truths of suffering, source of suffering, and path going to the cessation of suffering are, in reality, untrue and impermanent; they

> are not a refuge. Supramundane Victor, among those [four truths], one truth, [the cessation of suffering,] is beyond the realm of the character of the compounded. Supramundane Victor, that which is beyond the realm of the character of the compounded is permanent. Whatever is permanent has the attribute of non-deceptiveness. Supramundane Victor, that which has the attribute of non-deceptiveness is true, permanent, and a refuge. Supramundane Victor, consequently, among these the truth of the cessation of suffering itself is—in reality—true, permanent, and a refuge. Supramundane Victor, the truth of the cessation of suffering, which is beyond the objects of consciousness of all sentient beings, is inconceivable; it is not the domain of knowledge of Hearers and Solitary Realizers.

and Nāgārjuna's *Fundamental Treatise on the Middle, Called "Wisdom"* also says:

> The bhagavān said that whatsoever phenomena
> Are deceptive are falsities.
> All compounded things are deceptive phenomena.
> Therefore, those are falsities.

and a passage cited in the commentaries on that also says, "All compositional things have the attributes of falsity and deceptiveness," and so forth, at length. Consequently, although whatever are compounded dependent-arisings are necessarily empty, those who assert that all whatsoever emptinesses are dependent-arisings are mistaken because although the ultimate emptiness is beyond dependent-arising, it is the profound very final emptiness.

Dol-po-pa openly faces an objection that this would contradict the frequently made statement that conventionalities and emptinesses are mutually pervasive by answering that in such a context "emptiness" refers to self-emptiness, not other-emptiness (*Mountain Doctrine,* 400-401):

Objection: Well then, this contradicts [Nāgārjuna's statement in the *Essay on the Mind of Enlightenment*]:

> Conventionalities are described as emptinesses,
> And just emptinesses are conventionalities

> Because it is definite that without the one, the other does not occur,
> Like product and impermanent thing.
>
> *Answer:* There is no fault because emptiness on this occasion is dependently arisen self-emptiness, and he is indicating that it is a mutually pervasive single entity with dependent-arising, and we also assert this in that way.

For Dol-po-pa also, all conventionalities are self-empty, or self-emptinesses—the two terms being used interchangeably—and thus self-emptiness is a conventionality, not the ultimate.

Third category

Dol-po-pa holds that the ultimate—since it is an object of pristine wisdom—is an object of knowledge, and thus he does not resort to a third category with regard to whether it is or is not an object of knowledge. Also, as detailed above, he holds that the two truths are different, and whatever exists must be either an ultimate truth or an obscurational truth. However, he uses the notion of a third category in other contexts, for he holds that the ultimate is not a wing of a dichotomy between existing as an effective thing and not existing as an effective thing, since it is neither (*Mountain Doctrine,* 338):

> Hence, those who propound that all objects of knowledge are limited to the two, existing as an effective thing and not existing as an effective thing, are reduced to only not having realized the ultimate mode of subsistence, since although it is an object of knowledge, it does not either exist as an effective thing or not exist as an effective thing. Consequently, it is also established as just a third category and the center or middle.

and (346):

> Similarly, that:
>
> - a non-fallacious combination of contradictions does not occur
> - a third category does not occur with regard to direct contradictories [that is, with respect to dichotomies]
> - objects of knowledge are limited to the two, effective thing and non-effective thing
>
> and so forth are in terms of conventionalities, but ultimate

truths are not included in any of those.

The matrix-of-One-Gone-Thus ultimately exists

Dol-po-pa's opinion is that the body of the basic element of attributes exists in the dispositional mode of subsistence, but nothing else does. "Existing in the dispositional mode of subsistence" is the meaning of ultimately existing, and he finds support for this position in the statement in Nāgārjuna's *Sixty Stanzas of Reasoning*[a] that "only nirvāṇa is a truth" (*Mountain Doctrine,* 425):

> If you know the division of the two truths also with respect to the statements that the bodies of a Buddha bhagavān are one, two, three, four, and so forth, you will not be obscured about the word of the Subduer. Concerning this, the body of the final mode of subsistence, reduced to one, is the ultimate body. It is said that, except for the body of the element of attributes, no phenomenon exists in the dispositional mode of subsistence; [Nāgārjuna's *Sixty Stanzas of Reasoning*] says, "Only nirvāṇa is a truth,"[b] and, "There are no phenomena that are not enlightenment," and:
>
> > Except for the element of attributes
> > Phenomena do not exist.
>
> and:
>
> > There are no phenomena
> > Except for the element of attributes.
>
> and it is said that in the final mode of subsistence there is one truth, the ultimate truth, the noumenal exalted body—without example or parallel, sole, noumenal, manifold within one taste, the exalted body in which knower and known are the same: "The one, having the nature of a vajra—hard, indivisible," and

[a] *rigs pa drug cu pa, yuktiṣaṣṭikā,* stanza 35; Toh. 3825, *dbu ma,* vol. *tsa,* 21b.5; Lindtner, *Master of Wisdom,* 84.

[b] Stanza 35; Toh. 3825, vol. 68, 21b.5; Lindtner, *Master of Wisdom,* 84. The complete stanza is:

> When the conqueror said
> That only nirvāṇa is a truth,
> What wise person would think,
> "The rest are not unreal"?

Dol-po-pa takes this quote as supporting the notion that the mode of subsistence ultimately or truly exists.

"The truth is one, there is no second," and "The true is single; there are not two; it is the truth of cessation," and so forth.

Dol-po-pa's focuses on demonstrating that the final object of meditation for purifying obstructions is the matrix-of-One-Gone-Thus, endowed with ultimate Buddha qualities and ultimately existent:

- the uncontaminated primordial wisdom empty of all the phenomena of cyclic existence
- permanent, stable, eternal, everlasting, uncompounded by causes and conditions, and intrinsically possessing the ultimate qualities of a Buddha such as the ten powers.

He shows that Nāgārjuna in his Collections of Praises asserts such a matrix-of-One-Gone-Thus (*Mountain Doctrine,* 102-105):

> *Objection:* Although others assert the matrix-of-One-Gone-to-Bliss as of definitive meaning, it is not so asserted in the Middle Way School.
>
> *Answer:* The honorable Superior Nāgārjuna, [the foremost proponent of the Middle Way School,] asserts it. His *Praise of the Element of Attributes* says:[a]
>
> Homage and obeisance to [the sole jewel,] the element of attributes,
> Definitely dwelling [pervasively] in all sentient beings,
> Which if one does not thoroughly know [with pristine wisdom],
> One wanders in the three existences.
>
> From having purified [by means of the path the defilements of] just that [element of attributes]
> Which serves as the cause of cyclic existence [due to being together with adventitious defilements],
> That very [element of attributes] purified [of defilement] is nirvāṇa.
> The body of attributes also is just that.
>
> [Due to being mixed with limitless defilement, the element of attributes is not seen;
> For example,] just as due to being mixed with milk,
> The essence of butter is not seen,

[a] *chos kyi dbyings su bstod pa, dharmadhātustotra;* P2010, vol. 46, 31.3.7-31.4.6; brackets are from Dol-po-pa Shay-rap-gyel-tsen's *[Interlinear Commentary on Nāgārjuna's] Praise of the Element of Attributes,* 1b.2ff.

So due to being mixed with afflictive emotions
The element of attributes also is not seen.

[From purifying defilement, it is seen;
For example,] just as due to having purified milk
The essence of butter [is seen] without [obstructive] defilement,
So due to having purified [and extinguished] the afflictive emotions [through the path]
The very undefiled element of attributes [is manifestly seen].

[During the basal state of a sentient being, for example,]
Just as a butter-lamp dwelling inside a pot
Is not in the least perceived,
So the element of attributes also
Is not perceived inside the pot of afflictive emotions.

[During the path] from whatsoever directions [of proceeding on the grounds and paths]
Holes in the pot [of afflictive emotions] emerge,
From just those directions
A nature of [clear] light arises.

[Finally] when by the vajra meditative stabilization
The [obstructive] pot has [entirely] been broken,
[The element of attributes] illuminates
[And is seen] to the ends of space.

[Would the element of attributes which has ceased while one is a sentient being and is produced at the time of the path and fruit not be compounded?]
The element of attributes is not [newly] produced,
[And its entity] never ceases [while one is a sentient being].
At all times [during the basal state, the path, and the fruit] it is without afflictive emotions [in its nature]—
In the beginning [in the basal state], the middle [during the path], and the end [during the fruit primordially] free from defilement [in its nature].

[If the element of attributes exists luminously without ever being produced or ceasing, then why is it that all sentient beings, Bodhisattvas, and Buddhas without

distinction do not see it as luminous?]
Just as a vaiḍūrya[a] gem
At all times is luminous
But dwelling inside an [obstructive] stone
Its light is not manifest [to anyone],

So the element of attributes obscured
By afflictive emotions is very undefiled [in its nature],
But its light is not manifest in the cyclic existence [of afflictive emotions],
Becoming [manifestly] luminous in nirvāṇa.

and:

[Although the element of attributes is naturally pure, it is obstructed by obstructing factors;
For example,] even the undefiled sun and moon
Are obscured by five obstructions—
Clouds, mist, smoke,
The face of rāhu, dust,[b] and so forth.

Similarly, the mind of clear light [which is the nature of all sentient beings]
Is obscured by five obstructions—
Desire, harmful intent, laziness,
Excitement, and doubt.

[Therefore, although a Buddha in which all qualities such as the powers and so forth are integrally complete exists primordially in all sentient beings, the defilements are extinguished through striving at the path clearing away obstructions, but the clear light is not consumed; for example,]
When a garment [made from a hard mineral[c]] that is stained
With various defilements and to be cleansed [of defilement] by fire
Is put in fire, its stains
Are burned but it is not.

---

[a] Cat's-eye gem.

[b] Dol-po-pa aligns these five respectively with the five obstructors mentioned in the next stanza.

[c] This is likely asbestos, a naturally occurring mineral; I have read about asbestos garments from ancient times but have lost the reference.

So, similarly, with regard to the mind of clear light
Which has the stains of desire and so forth,
Its stains are burned by the fire of wisdom [on the path]
But [since it does not burn the clear light, the qualities of the clear light do not become non-existent the way iron is consumed or worn away, and hence] that [path] does not [burn away] the clear light.

[Well then, since the sūtras teaching emptiness spoken by the conqueror indicate that all are emptiness, do they not refute that even the clear light is in the mode of being?]
All the sūtras [such as the Mother Sūtras and so forth]
Spoken by the conqueror that teach emptiness
Overcome the afflictive emotions [of conceiving self]
But do not diminish [and refute] the essential constituent.

[Ultimately the element of attributes cannot be refuted;
For example,] just as water existing on the sphere of earth
Resides [in its nature] without defilement,
So the pristine wisdom inside afflictive emotions
Similarly [always] abides without defilement [never suitable to be non-existent].

and:

[Though it exists, it is not seen if the obstructions are not purified;
For example,] just as a child exists in the belly
Of the womb but is not seen,
So the element of attributes covered
With afflictive emotions also is not seen [though always resident].

and:

[A single river has different states due to relation with other causes and conditions;]
Just as a river in summer
Is said to be "warm"
But that [same river] itself in cold season
Is said to be "cold,"

> So when [the element of attributes is] covered with the nets of afflictive emotions,
> It is called "sentient being,"
> But when that [element of attributes] itself is separated from afflictive emotions,
> It is called "Buddha."

and so forth. Hence, by way of many examples Nāgārjuna speaks at length of the matrix-of-One-Gone-to-Bliss that is equivalent to the element of attributes, body of attributes, mind of natural clear light, self-arisen pristine wisdom, and so forth.

At the beginning of the *Mountain Doctrine,* Dol-po-pa inspiringly speaks of the matrix-of-One-Gone-Thus as the basic reality and pristine wisdom (61):

> Just that final Buddha, the matrix-of-One-Gone-Thus, the ultimate clear light, element of attributes, self-arisen pristine wisdom, great bliss, and partless pervader of all is said to be the basis and source of all phenomena and also is said in reality to be the basis that is empty of all phenomena, the void basis, and the basis pure of all defilements. It also is said to be endowed with the qualities of the body of attributes beyond the count of the sands of the Ganges River, within an indivisible nature.

These ultimate Buddha qualities inherently exist (*Mountain Doctrine,* 100):

> The *Aṅgulimāla Sūtra,* rare as an udaṃvāra flower, also extensively says that faulty factors such as production and cessation do not exist inherently[a] and that the Buddha-element or elemental Buddha[b]—endowed with multitudes of qualities established inherently, the endless signs and beauties of the noumenon—exists in all sentient beings.

Thus, although Dol-po-pa himself uses the vocabulary of inherent existence and ultimate existence, Tāranātha, as mentioned above, appears to be justified in extending the set of vocabulary to include "true existence."

[a] *rang bzhin gyis med pa;* that is, they do not exist in the basic disposition.

[b] *sangs rgyas kyi dbyings sam dbyings kyis sangs rgyas.*

Two types of effects: separative and produced

Although ultimate Buddha qualities pre-exist in the matrix-of-One-Gone-Thus, effort at the spiritual path is nevertheless required because there are two types of effects, separative and produced, and the latter have to be generated through practice. In this way, although Dol-po-pa holds that the basis and the fruit are undifferentiable, he makes the distinction that while a person is still a sentient being, the basis is obstructed by defilements, and when a person has become a Buddha, the basis has separated from defilements (*Mountain Doctrine,* 148-151):

> That all sentient beings nevertheless do not perceive [ultimate qualities] is due to being obstructed by adventitious defilements, since those [ultimate qualities] are not objects of consciousness and since they are objects of activity just of self-cognizing pristine wisdom. Moreover, the *Mahāparinirvāṇa Sūtra* says:
>
> > Then, the Bodhisattva mahāsattva Lion's Roar asked:
> >
> > > Supramundane Victor, if all sentient beings possess the Buddha-nature which is like a powerful vajra, why is it that all sentient beings do not see it?
> >
> > Buddha said:
> >
> > > Child of lineage, for example, although there are different forms—blue, yellow, red, white, long, and short—a blind person does not see them. Such are not seen, but it is not suitable to say that the differences of blue, yellow, red, and white do not exist and that long and short shapes do not exist. Why? Even though a blind person does not see them, it is not that one with eyes does not see them. The Buddha-nature is like this.
> > >
> > > Even though all beings do not see it, Bodhisattvas on the ten grounds see a portion, and a One-Gone-Thus sees it entirely. Bodhisattvas on the ten grounds see the Buddha-nature like a form seen at night. The One-Gone-Thus sees it like a form in daytime. Child of lineage, the semi-blind do not see a form clearly, but when a doctor skilled in medicine cures them, through the power of the medicine it is clearly seen. Bodhisattvas on the ten

> grounds are like this; they see the Buddha-nature, but it is not clear. Through the power of the meditative stabilization [called] proceeding like a hero, they will see it very clearly.

and:

> There are cases in which it is known but not seen. When it is known that all sentient beings have the Buddha-nature, but, overwhelmed and obstructed by afflictive emotions, it is not seen, this is called "known but not seen." Also, there are cases in which it is known and seen a little. Bodhisattva mahāsattvas on the ten grounds know that all beings have the Buddha-nature, but cannot see it clearly; this is like the moon being unclear during the day. Moreover, there are cases in which it is both seen and known—by Buddhas, Ones-Gone-Thus—this is called "perceived and known."

and:

> It is not that nirvāṇa did not exist in the beginning but presently exists. If nirvāṇa did not exist in the beginning but presently exists, it would not be a phenomenon that always abides. Whether Buddhas arise or do not arise, the nature and character [of nirvāṇa] always abides. Because sentient beings are obstructed by afflictive emotions, they do not see nirvāṇa, and hence think, "It does not exist." Bodhisattva mahāsattvas who have familiarized with ethics, meditative stabilization, and wisdom excise the afflictive emotions and thereupon see it. Hence, nirvāṇa has the quality of always abiding. Since it is known that it is not formerly nonexistent and presently existent, it is therefore called "permanent."

and:

> All sentient beings have the Buddha-nature. Due to being thoroughly veiled by afflictive emotions it is not seen.

and so forth, and the *Great Drum Sūtra* also says:

Kāshyapa, these four are examples of causes of obstructions to the basic constituent of sentient beings and examples of reasons [for its existence]. What are the four? Like eyes darkened by yellow and blue eye film; like the moon covered by clouds; like digging a well; like a lamp inside a pot. Kāshyapa, these four are causes and reasons for saying, "The matrix exists." By way of these causes and reasons all sentient beings and all living beings have the Buddha-constituent; its adornment, the endless good signs and beauties, will be perceived, and due to that basic constituent sentient beings will attain nirvāṇa.

With respect to "one whose eyes are [afflicted] with cataracts," the eyes, darkened from being covered with yellow and blue film, are suitable to be cured but will be blind until a physician is found, and when a physician is found, will speedily see again. About this basic constituent, covered by a sheath of millions of afflictive emotions, like being darkened upon being covered with blue film: as long as one takes a liking to Hearers and Solitary Realizers, the self will not be the self; it will be the self's self. When one takes a liking to the Buddha Supramundane Victors, [the self] becomes the self, and after this, one becomes a human fit for advancement. The afflictive emotions are to be viewed as like that human's eye disease—the darkness of yellow and blue film. The matrix-of-One-Gone-Thus definitely exists, like the eye.

With respect to "like the moon covered by clouds," just as the sphere of the moon covered by awful clouds is not perceived, the basic constituent covered by a sheath of afflictive emotions is not perceived. When it is separated from the collections of afflictive emotions, like clouds, then the basic constituent, like the full moon, is perceived.

With respect to "like digging a well," when, for example, a person digs and digs a well, as long as the ground comes up dry, this sign makes the person think, "Water is a long ways from here." When mud comes up, this sign causes the knowledge, "Water is near here." When water is arrived at, that is the end of digging.

> Similarly, Hearers and Solitary Realizers please the Ones-Gone-Thus and partake of good practices, whereby they dig out the afflictive emotions. Having dug them out, the matrix-of-One-Gone-Thus, like water, is found.
>
> With respect to "like a lamp inside a pot," just as the light of a lamp inside a pot is not bright and vivid and does not do anything for sentient beings, so the matrix-of-One-Gone-Thus, said to possess limitless good marks and beauties, does not bring about the welfare of sentient beings. Just as when the pot is broken, then the lamp brings about the welfare of living beings through its own illumination, so when the afflictive emotions of cyclic existence are consumed due to the intense burning, like a lamp, of the matrix-of-One-Gone-Thus abiding in the pot of cyclic existence, which has the covering of millions of afflictive emotions, the matrix-of-One-Gone-Thus—like the lamp of a broken pot—brings about the welfare of sentient beings.
>
> Through these four reasons it should be understood that just as I have the basic constituent of a sentient being, so all sentient beings also have it.

and so forth and:

> Some, wanting to view the self, asked, "If one looks into the self's afflictive emotions and the self's beginning and end, will they be found?"
>
> The Supramundane Victor said, "They will not. Upon having purified the afflictive emotions, then the self will be found."

and so forth. Thereby, many very profound sūtras set forth many examples for and reasons why although the pure nature, the matrix-of-One-Gone-to-Bliss, always dwells in all sentient beings, it is not seen and is not attained if not separated from adventitious defilements.

Thus, there is no question that a process of purification must take place before Buddhahood can be attained.

Although sentient beings already possess Buddha qualities, Dol-po-pa avoids having to hold that ordinary sentient beings are already Buddhas by making distinctions between ultimate and conventional

Buddha and between ultimate and conventional qualities, as indicated above. Ultimate Buddha and Buddha qualities are already present in the noumenon, whereas conventional Buddha and conventional Buddha qualities must be attained.

Great Middle Way

Dol-po-pa Shay-rap-gyel-tsen developed a new doctrinal language through an amalgamation of the classical texts of the Mind-Only and Middle Way systems into a Great Middle Way,[a] and he also intertwined the particular vocabulary of the Kālachakra system. As he says:[b]

> Tantras should be understood by means of other tantras.
> Sūtras should be understood by means of other sūtras.
> Sūtras should also be understood by means of the tantras.
> Tantras should also be understood by means of the sūtras.
> Both should be understood by means of both.

In what are usually considered the classical texts of separate systems, he saw presentations of multiple systems crowned by the Great Middle Way. For instance, he considered separate passages of the *Sūtra Unraveling the Thought,* usually considered to be Mind-Only, to present the views of Mind-Only and the Great Middle Way, the latter being concordant with Ultimate Mind-Only,[c] or Supramundane Mind-Only,[d] which is beyond consciousness.[e] In his *Mountain Doctrine,* he takes the following passage from the ninth chapter of the *Sūtra Unraveling the Thought* to evince the view of the Great Middle Way (235):

> That which brings about definite emergence [from obstructions] by means of the middle path upon having abandoned the extreme of superimposition and the extreme of deprecation is their wisdom. Also, by way of that wisdom, they also thoroughly and correctly know, just as it is, the meaning of the doors of liberation with respect to the three doors of liberation—emptiness, wishlessness, and signlessness. They also thoroughly and correctly know, just as it is, the meaning of the natures with respect to the three natures: imputational natures, other-powered natures, and thoroughly established

[a] *dbu ma chen po.*

[b] Stearns, *The Buddha from Dol po*, 98.

[c] *don dam pa'i sems tsam;* also "Final Mind-Only" (*mthar thug gi sems tsam*).

[d] *'jig rten las 'das pa'i sems tsam.*

[e] *rnam shes las 'das pa.*

> natures. They also thoroughly and correctly know, just as it is, the meaning of non-nature with respect to the three non-natures: character-non-natures, production-non-natures, and the ultimate-non-nature.

Not just in sūtras and tantras but also in Indian treatises that are usually taken to be strictly Mind-Only he finds passages teaching Mind-Only but others teaching the Great Middle Way.

Thus Dol-po-pa Shay-rap-gyel-tsen's synthesis is by no means a collage drawing a little from here and a little from there and disregarding the rest. Rather, he had a comprehensive, thorough, and overarching perspective born from careful analysis. For him, others had just not seen what the texts themselves were saying and, instead of that, read into the classical texts the views of single systems. For instance, he says that the mere fact that the three natures and the eight collections of consciousness are taught in Maitreya's *Differentiation of the Middle and the Extremes* does not make it a Mind-Only text, since these are also taught in sūtras and tantras of the Great Middle Way. He adds (*Mountain Doctrine,* 235):

> Furthermore, the meaning of the statement in Maitreya's *Differentiation of the Middle and the Extremes,* "All are just name-only," contradicts the view of the Mind-Only School.

He quotes many sūtras to the same end (*Mountain Doctrine,* 236-237):

> Similarly, the *Descent into Laṅkā Sūtra* also says that, for the time being, one is taught mind-only, but finally having thoroughly passed beyond that, one is taught the middle without appearance, and that, having also passed beyond this, one is taught the middle with appearance, and it says that if one does not arrive at that, one has not seen the profound meaning of the Great Vehicle:
>
> Relying on mind-only,
> One does not imagine external objects.
> Relying on non-appearance,
> One passes beyond mind-only.
>
> Relying on observing reality,
> One passes beyond non-appearance.
> If yogis dwell in non-appearance,
> They do not perceive the Great Vehicle.

In this way, Dol-po-pa's perspective is syncretic in that he draws from a great variety of sūtras, tantras, and treatises. It is synthetic perhaps only in the sense that he finds within these an exposition of a view beyond the traditional schools. It is not a mere putting together of pieces from here and there. Since he breaks boundaries between set systems, it is no wonder that his grand, overarching, iconoclastic perspective shocked many Tibetan scholars and attracted others from his own day to the present. It offers so much provocative food for thought that it has to be taken into account.

2. Tsong-kha-pa Lo-sang-drak-pa's Rebuttal

Tsong-kha-pa's writings on the view of emptiness deliberately differ markedly from those by Dol-po-pa. Both implicitly and explicitly he rebuts his predecessor's opinions, even though he never mentions Dol-po-pa Shay-rap-gyel-tsen by name. Making distinctions in basic terminology, he reveals his own overarching perspective on the Middle Way view.

Not all ordinary consciousnesses are wrong

Dol-po-pa's perspective is that the phenomena of the three realms exist only for consciousness,[a] which is necessarily mistaken, as when he says (above, 273), "these three realms are appearances of consciousness and whatever is consciousness is ignorance." To counter this and to establish that conventional consciousnesses can be valid, Tsong-kha-pa distinguishes between three types of awarenesses with regard to the apprehension of true, or inherent, existence (above, *Insight,* 57):

> In brief, when the many supreme scholars who commented on the meaning of the scriptures on the profound [emptiness] delineated the meaning of suchness, they analyzed by way of scripture and reasoning. They did this from having perceived that selflessness and emptiness cannot be realized without seeing that the self as apprehended by erroneous apprehension does not exist and without seeing the emptiness of that self. It is important to gain ascertainment with respect to this.
>
> For if you do not meditate on the meaning of the negation of the erroneous object that is the root of being bound in cyclic existence, even though you meditate on the meaning of something else that you consider to be profound, it will not harm the apprehension of self at all:
>
> - because unless the mind becomes absorbed in the suchness of selflessness and emptiness, conquest of the apprehension of self cannot occur, and
> - because without rejecting the object of the apprehension of self, although you perform the mere withdrawal of the mind that moves there to its object, this cannot constitute being absorbed in selflessness.

---

[a] *rnam shes.*

> The reason for this is that there are three modes of the mind's operating on an object—(1) apprehending the object of observation to truly exist, (2) apprehending it to not truly exist, and (3) apprehending it without qualifying it with either of those. Hence, just as although one is not apprehending [an object] as not truly existent, one is not necessarily apprehending it as truly existent, so, although one is not involved in the two selves, it is not necessary that one is involved in the two selflessnesses. For there are limitless minds abiding in the third category.

Tsong-kha-pa's opinion is that when the "I," for instance, is apprehended, there are basically three possibilities with respect to how it is being apprehended in relation to true, or inherent, existence:

1. One may be apprehending the "I" to be inherently existent.
2. Or, if one has understood the view of the Middle Way School, one may apprehend the "I" as only being nominally existent.
3. Or, whether one has understood the view of the Middle Way School or not, one may apprehend the "I" without qualifying it with either inherent existence or an absence of inherent existence.

In this vein, the Fifth Dalai Lama's *Sacred Word of Mañjushrī* says:[a]

> Furthermore, consciousnesses innately apprehending "I"—which conceive an "I," or self, based on the [nominally existent] person—are of three types:
>
> 1. A conceptual consciousness [correctly] apprehending "I" that exists in a person who has generated the Middle Way view in his/her mental continuum. This consciousness [correctly] apprehends "I" taken to be qualified as being only designated in the context of its basis of designation [the mental and physical aggregates].
> 2. An actual innate [consciousness mis]apprehending "I" taken to be qualified as being inherently existent. It is to be overcome through its antidote here on this occasion [of the path of wisdom].

[a] Nga-wang-lo-sang-gya-tso (*ngag dbang blo bzang rgya mtsho*, 1617-1682), Dalai Lama V, *Instruction on the Stages of the Path to Enlightenment, Sacred Word of Mañjushrī* (*byang chub lam gyi rim pa'i khrid yig 'jam pa'i dbyangs kyi zhal lung*) (Thimphu: kun-bzang-stobs-rgyal, 1976), 182.5-210.6. For an English translation, see Jeffrey Hopkins, "Practice of Emptiness" (Dharamsala: Library of Tibetan Works and Archives, 1974).

3. A conventional validly cognizing consciousness that establishes [the existence of] "I." This consciousness exists [for example] in the continuums of those common beings whose mental continuums have not been affected by systems of tenets and who thus do not differentiate between nominal imputation and inherent existence. In this case, the "I" is not taken to be qualified as being either nominally imputed or inherently existent.

In Tsong-kha-pa's system, though uneducated common beings do not *propound* either inherent existence or nominal imputation, the "I" appears to them to be inherently existent, and because they sometimes assent to that appearance—though without reasoning—they also have a consciousness apprehending an inherently existent "I." Moreover, they, like all other beings, even including those who have been educated in wrong systems of tenets, have consciousnesses that do not engage in apprehensions of inherent existence, such as when just apprehending themselves without any particular attention.

Thus, in the continuum of uneducated persons some consciousnesses apprehending "I" or other phenomena of the three realms are right, and some are wrong. Moreover, even in the continuum of a falsely educated person some consciousnesses apprehending "I" or other phenomena are right. In Tsong-kha-pa's system, both the uneducated and the falsely educated have misapprehensions of an inherently existent "I" and other phenomena as well as consciousnesses apprehending these without qualifying them as being either nominally imputed or inherently existent. In this way, Tsong-kha-pa makes room for correct consciousnesses that can certify the existence of common phenomena, and on this platform he holds that common phenomena are established by valid cognition.

Nevertheless, for Tsong-kha-pa, since the objects of all three types of consciousness mentioned above *appear* to exist inherently, all three are mistaken with respect to their appearing object[a] but not necessarily mistaken with respect to their object of operation[b] because they do not necessarily apprehend that the object inherently exists. This distinction allows him to hold that in the continuum of anyone but a Buddha a validly cognizing consciousness, such as an eye consciousness apprehending blue—while valid and hence not a wrong consciousness[c]—is

[a] *snang yul.*

[b] *'jug yul.* In the case of conceptual consciousnesses the object of operation is also called the conceived object (*zhen yul*).

[c] *log shes.*

mistaken with respect to its appearing object. An eye consciousness apprehending blue as blue is non-deceived about its main object and, therefore, is a valid cognition, and even though the patch of blue appears to it to exist inherently, the eye consciousness itself does not mistakenly *apprehend,* or conceive, blue to be inherently existent; it does not affirm the false appearance of inherent existence. From the viewpoint of its object of operation, which is just the patch of blue, it is non-mistaken, even if it is mistaken with respect to its appearing object.

This is how Tsong-kha-pa can have validity and mistake in the same consciousness. Thus, for both Dol-po-pa and Tsong-kha-pa all ordinary consciousnesses are mistaken, but Tsong-kha-pa, by making a distinction between the appearing object and the object of operation, holds that the mistaken can be valid.

Despite his emphasis on valid cognition in the continuums of ordinary beings, Tsong-kha-pa asserts that neither the falsely educated nor the uneducated can distinguish between imputedly existent objects and inherently existent objects. Both must become educated in the Middle Way view of the absence of inherent existence and the presence of imputed existence in order to overcome the innate tendency to assent to the false appearance of the "I" and other phenomena as if inherently existent, that is to say, existing from their own side and existing under their own power. This is the immediate purpose of meditation on selflessness.

Saṃvṛti does not just mean obscurer

Dol-po-pa considers conventional objects to exist only in the perspective of mistaken consciousness (above, 273):[a]

> Therefore, these mistaken karmic appearances of sentient beings are the private phenomena[b] just of sentient beings; they utterly do not occur in the mode of subsistence, like the horns of a rabbit, the child of a barren woman, a sky-flower, and so forth. Consequently, they are not established even as mere appearances to a cognition of the mode of subsistence, and appearing in the face of mistake does not fulfill the role of appearing in the mode of subsistence. In consideration of these [points], it is again and again said in many formats that all phenomena are not observed, non-appearing, unapprehendable, and so forth.

[a] I have lengthened the citation here; see Hopkins, *Mountain Doctrine,* 537-538.

[b] *sgos chos.*

Objection: In that case, this contradicts Shāntideva's explanation that these appearances of apprehended object and apprehending subject are not objects of negation. His *Engaging in the Bodhisattva Deeds* says:

> Here these which are seen, heard,
> And known are not what are negated.
> Here the conceptualization of truth
> That is the cause of suffering is just what is to be overcome.

Answer: There is no fault:

- because [Shāntideva's] meaning is that "Since it is not contradictory for those to be untrue in the mode of subsistence but to appear in the face of mistake, do not deprecate the appearance of those conventionally"; he is not indicating that those appear to a consciousness of the mode of subsistence
- and because we also do not assert that as long as mistake has not been stopped, mistaken appearances stop.

He associates appearing "in the face of mistake"—that is, appearing to a mistaken consciousness—with existing conventionally. It is likely that he takes "existing conventionally" (*kun rdzob tu yod pa, saṃvṛtisat*) to mean existing for ignorance, since it is generally agreed that in the term "obscurational truth" (*kun rdzob bden pa, saṃvṛtisatya*), *kun rdzob* (*saṃvṛti*) means that which obscures, or conceals, reality, and thus *kun rdzob bden pa* (*saṃvṛtisatya*) means "that which is a truth for ignorance," that is to say, something that an ignorant consciousness takes to exist the way it appears, to have a concordance between the way it appears and the way it is in fact.

For Tsong-kha-pa to make the case that conventional objects can be obscurational truths but be validly established, he must distinguish between the *saṃvṛti* of obscurational truths (*kun rdzob bden pa, saṃvṛtisatya*) and the *saṃvṛti* of conventionally existent (*kun rdzob tu yod pa, saṃvṛtisat*). He justifies the distinction by citing Chandrakīrti and the *Descent into Laṅkā Sūtra* (above, *Insight,* 109):

> Chandrakīrti's *Clear Words* describes three [meanings] for *saṃvṛti*—(1) obstructing suchness,[a] (2) mutually dependent objects,[b] and (3) worldly conventions.[a] Since he explains the last

[a] *de kho na nyid la sgrib pa, tattvāvacchādana.*

[b] *phan tshun brten pa, parasparasaṃbhavana.*

as having the character of object of expression and means of expression, knower and object of knowledge, and so forth, it is not just subjective conventions—consciousnesses and expressions—[but also objects of knowledge and objects of expression]. Nevertheless, [this is not a definition since] not all whatsoever objects of knowledge and objects of expression should be held to be obscurational truths [because an emptiness is an object of knowledge and object of expression but is an ultimate truth].

The *saṃvṛti* that is the obscuring consciousness with respect to which forms and so forth are posited as truths [in the sense that ignorance takes them to exist the way they appear to be inherently existent] is the first among the three [meanings]. It is the ignorance superimposing on phenomena the existence of their own inherently established entity, whereas they do not have such. This is because:

- true establishment does not occur in objects, and therefore the positing of [objects that appear to be truly existent] as truths is in the perspective of an awareness, and
- there is no positing [of objects that appear to be truly existent] as truths in the perspective of a mind that is not an apprehender of true existence.

In that way moreover, Chandrakīrti's *Supplement to (Nāgārjuna's) "Treatise on the Middle"* says:

> The Subduer said that because bewilderment [that is, the apprehension of inherent existence] obscures [direct perception of] the nature [of the mode of subsistence of phenomena],
> [This ignorance] is all-obscuring (*kun rdzob*) and he said that those fabrications appearing
> To be true due to this [ignorance] are obscurational truths (*kun rdzob bden*) [because of being true in the perspective of the obscurational apprehension of inherent existence].
> Things that are fabrications [exist] conventionally (*kun rdzob tu*).

Concerning this, Chandrakīrti's *Commentary on the "Supplement to (Nāgārjuna's) 'Treatise on the Middle'"* says (see also *Illumination,*

[a] *'jig rten gyi tha snyad, lokavyavahāra.*

240):

> In that way, respectively, obscurational truths are posited through the force of the afflictive ignorance that is included within the [twelve] links [of the dependent-arising] of cyclic existence. Moreover, for Hearer [Foe Destroyers], Solitary Realizer [Foe Destroyers], and [eighth ground] Bodhisattvas, who have [entirely] abandoned afflictive ignorance and who see that [although] compositional phenomena [are thoroughly empty of being established by way of their own character but appear to be established by way of their own character] like the existence of reflections and so forth, these have [only] a fabricated [false] nature and are not truths, because they do not exaggerate [forms and so forth] into being truly [established]. To childish [common beings] these are deceptive, but to the others [that is, to the Hearers, Solitary Realizers, and Bodhisattvas described above] they are mere conventionalities[a] due to being dependent-arisings, like a magician's illusions and so forth [appearing to truly exist while not truly existing the way they appear].

This passage does not indicate that (1) the positing of obscurational truths as existent is a positing of their **existence** by ignorance or (2) that obscurational truths are not posited in the perspective of Hearers, Solitary Realizers, and Bodhisattvas who have abandoned afflictive ignorance. The reasons for the first point are:

> because, as explained before, afflictive ignorance is a consciousness apprehending true existence, due to which the object apprehended by it does not exist even in conventional terms, and because whatever is an obscurational truth necessarily exists in conventional terms.

Therefore, whatever is the conventionality (*kun rdzob, saṃvṛti*) that is the ground from which phenomena are posited as existing conventionally (*kun rdzob tu yod pa, saṃvṛtisat*) must be something that is not the afflictive ignorance that is taken as the obscurer (*kun rdzob, saṃvṛti*) [in "obscurational truth" (*kun*

[a] Or, "mere fraudulences" (*kun rdzob tsam, saṃvṛtimātra*).

rdzob bden pa, saṃvṛtisatya)].

The reason for the second point is:

> Chandrakīrti is establishing that because those who have abandoned the obscurer, afflictive ignorance, do not have the obscurer—a consciousness adhering to true existence—in the perspective of which [objects appearing to exist inherently] are posited as truths, compositional phenomena are not truths for them; he is not establishing that compositional phenomena are not obscurational truths.[a]

Consequently, Chandrakīrti's statement that compositional phenomena are mere conventionalities for them means that, between conventionality and truth, those are not positable as truths for them, and therefore the term "mere" [in "mere conventionalities"] eliminates truth, not obscurational truth. Hence, Chandrakīrti's thought in speaking of the two—mere conventionality and obscurational truth—should be understood in that way.

Tsong-kha-pa affirms that *kun rdzob bden pa (saṃvṛtisatya)* means "obscurational truth" because here *kun rdzob (saṃvṛti)* means the ignorance in the perspective of which objects are mistakenly posited to be true, that is, to exist the way they appear. However, he insists that the consciousness in the perspective of which objects are posited as *existing* is not ignorance, despite the fact that objects are said to be *kun rdzob tu yod pa (saṃvṛtisat)*. He finds support for this in the first line of a passage in the *Descent into Laṅkā Sūtra,* which he cites in his *Extensive Explanation of (Chandrakīrti's) "Supplement to (Nāgārjuna's) 'Treatise on the Middle'": Illumination of the Thought*. He takes the sūtra as using both meanings of *kun rdzob (saṃvṛti)* (above, 236):

> Because, through it, sentient beings are obstructed, that is to say, beclouded, with respect to viewing the nature that is how things abide, it is [called] bewilderment. Bewilderment, or ignorance, which has an essence of obstructing the perception of the nature that is the mode of being [of phenomena through] superimposing inherent existence on the entities of things that do not inherently exist, is the obscurer (*kun rdzob, saṃvṛti*).

[a] Even for Hearers, Solitary Realizers, and Bodhisattvas who have abandoned afflictive ignorance and who see compositional phenomena as like the existence of reflections and so forth, compositional phenomena are obscurational truths, since they know that others take them to be truths and since these exist but are not ultimate truths.

This is an identification of the obscuring [consciousness] (*kun rdzob / kun rdzob pa, saṃvṛti*) in the perspective of which truth in [the term] "obscurational truth" is posited; it is not an identification of *kun rdzob pa* (*saṃvṛti*) in general [which means "conventionality" or "conventional consciousness"].

Furthermore, that identification [in Chandrakīrti's *Supplement*] is the meaning of the statement in the *Descent into Laṅkā Sūtra* [above, 189] that an awareness making the mistake that what ultimately lacks inherent existence exists inherently is an obscurational (*kun rdzob pa*):

> The production of things [exists] conventionally (*kun rdzob tu, saṃvṛtyā*);
> Ultimately it lacks inherent existence.
> That [consciousness] which is mistaken regarding the lack of inherent existence
> Is asserted as the obscurer of reality (*yang dag kun rdzob, satyaṃ saṃvṛti*).

Since the Sanskrit original for "obscurer" (*kun rdzob, saṃvṛti*) [does not just mean "convention" but] is also used for "obstructor" (*sgrib byed*), this obscurer (*kun rdzob, saṃvṛti*) [in the final line] is an obstructor. What does it obstruct? Since [the sūtra] says that it is "the obscurer of reality (*yang dag kun rdzob, satyaṃ saṃvṛti*)," it says that since it obstructs [perception of] the meaning of reality, it is asserted as an obscurer, or obstructor. It is not indicating that it is a right conventionality (*yang dag kun rdzob, tathya-saṃvṛti*) from between the two [categories of conventionalities], right and wrong [conventionalities].

The [*kun rdzob* (*saṃvṛti*) translated as] "conventionally" indicated in the first line and the [*kun rdzob* (*saṃvṛti*) translated as] "obscurer" indicated in the last line should not be construed to be identical. For, the first is the conventional way in which we ourselves assert things to be produced and so forth, whereas the latter is the obscurer—[a consciousness] apprehending true existence—in the perspective of which things are true [that is, a consciousness taking things to exist the way they appear to inherently exist].

Through the force of that obstructing [consciousness] apprehending true existence, fabricated phenomena such as blue and so forth—which, although lacking inherent establishment, are fabricated to appear to be inherently established and which

> appear to sentient beings to be true—are true in the perspective of the worldly, erroneous, obscuring [consciousness] described above. Hence, they are worldly obscurational truths. The Subduer said such; the way he said this is what is set forth in the above sūtra [that is, the *Descent into Laṅkā Sūtra*].

If everything that exists for ignorance did exist conventionally, then even absurdities such as the offspring of a barren woman or of a sterile man, a permanent creator, and so forth, would have to exist conventionally. By holding that *kun rdzob tu yod pa* (*saṃvṛtisat*) means conventionally existent with *kun rdzob* (*saṃvṛti*) in this phrase referring to a conventional valid cognition, Tsong-kha-pa is able to allow for refuting objects that are only imagined to exist. Without mentioning Dol-po-pa by name, Tsong-kha-pa concludes in his *Illumination* that these distinctions refute the opinion that existing for a mistaken consciousness is the meaning of existing conventionally (above, 231):

> Therefore, entities such as the three qualities as they are imputed by these Forders[a] in their respective texts do not exist even as worldly conventionalities. This refutes well the statement that what exists in the perspective of a mistaken awareness is posited as conventionally existing by this system.
>
> Similarly, the horse or elephant that is imputed to a magical illusion, the water that is imputed to a mirage, the face that is imputed to a reflection, and so forth also just do not exist even from [the viewpoint of] worldly conventions. In that way, for something to exist conventionally, it must be established by valid cognition.

Self-emptiness does not mean an object is empty of itself

Dol-po-pa explains that other-emptiness eliminates and is beyond the extremes of non-existence, whereas self-emptiness, despite avoiding the extreme of existence, does not eliminate the extreme of non-existence (*Mountain Doctrine*, 328-329):

> This emptiness, which is thus equivalent to the element of attributes and so forth, is the meaning of the emptiness of non-entities, other-entity emptiness, and non-empty emptiness mentioned again and again in stainless scriptures. Mere self-emptiness does not fulfill its role. Why? It is because that which

[a] Such as in the Sāṃkhya system.

> is the ultimate emptiness not only clears away the extreme of existence but also clears away the extreme of non-existence—"not existent and not non-existent"—but self-emptiness does not clear away the extreme of non-existence. Concerning this, whereas conventional phenomena do not at all exist in the mode of subsistence, the extreme of existence is the superimposition that they do. Whereas the partless, omnipresent pristine wisdom of the element of attributes always abides pervading all, the extreme of non-existence is the deprecation that it does not exist and is not established and is empty of its own entity. That which is the middle devoid of those extremes is the basis devoid of all extremes such as existence and non-existence, superimposition, and deprecation, permanence and annihilation, and so forth, due to which it is the final great middle. It is non-material emptiness, emptiness far from an annihilatory emptiness, great emptiness that is the ultimate pristine wisdom of Superiors, five immutable great emptinesses, six immutable empty drops, *a* which is the supreme of all letters, Buddha earlier than all Buddhas, primordially released One-Gone-Thus, causeless original Buddha, aspectlessness endowed with all aspects—insuperable and not fit to be abandoned. Not to be deprecated, it is the inconceivable element of attributes beyond phenomena of consciousness and not in the sphere of argument; it is to be realized in individual self-cognition by yogis.
>
> Consequently, those who come to the conclusion that:
>
> - the "middle" is solely designated to the mere voidness of all extremes
> - "even the middle is empty of the middle"
> - "even the ultimate is empty of the ultimate"
>
> and so forth do not accord with the thought of the conqueror because, for the character of the emptiness that is the final mode of subsistence, the mere emptiness of non-entities is not sufficient. Rather, the emptiness that is the [ultimate] nature of non-entities [that is, emptiness that is the ultimate nature opposite from non-entities] is required.

Tsong-kha-pa responds that Dol-po-pa has not understood the meaning of self-emptiness; first he states his predecessor's opinion (see *Insight*, 97):

> *Objection:* The meaning of the statement that compounded phenomena are empty of their own inherently existent entity is that those phenomena do not have their own entities, whereby this is an annihilatory emptiness. However, since thusness has its own entity, it truly exists.

Then Tsong-kha-pa proceeds to make the case that Dol-po-pa has completely misunderstood what is negated in self-emptiness. Whereas Dol-po-pa holds that it is the entities of phenomena themselves that are negated, Tsong-kha-pa holds that it is the inherent existence of those entities:

> *Answer:* [The first part of that assertion] is the final place of going wrong with respect to delineating compounded phenomena as empty of inherent establishment, a view deprecating the dependent-arising of compounded phenomena. The latter [part of that assertion] is an awful view of permanence superimposing true existence on whatever has its own entity. Therefore, [the proponents of this] are wrongly perspected with respect to the correct meaning of emptiness.
>
> If [an object's] emptiness of its own inherently established entity [meant that] it did not exist in itself, then since not existing in itself [means] that existence would not occur anywhere, holders of the thesis that some phenomena truly exist as well as the scriptures and reasonings proving this, and so forth, would not be established bases [that is, would not exist] due to being empty of their own inherently established entity. Therefore, the positing of a tenet that some phenomena truly exist[a] is an unexamined propounding of whatever appears to mind.

In the previous chapter we saw that there is some question as to just how far Dol-po-pa takes the negation in self-emptiness; Tsong-kha-pa, however, indicates that he reads his predecessor as denying the very existence of compounded phenomena. This is hard to square with Dol-po-pa's assertion that persons do not become Buddhas until the compounded qualities of Buddhahood are attained and does not include his frequent statements that conventionalities do not exist **in the mode of subsistence**, but Tsong-kha-pa's estimation does reflect tendencies in other parts of Dol-po-pa's presentation like that given at the head of

[a] Dol-po-pa Shay-rap-gyel-tsen holds that suchness, the matrix-of-One-Gone-Thus, and all of the ultimate Buddha attributes associated with the matrix-of-One-Gone-Thus ultimately, or truly, exist, whereas all conventional phenomena are empty of themselves.

this section. Tsong-kha-pa concludes that (see *Insight,* 98):

> Also, with respect to those here [in Tibet] who propound two discordant [positions] regarding suchness, you should through the above explanation, understand well the status of their modes of debate—as to whether the ultimate is ultimately established or not—in the context of their affinity for the former mode of conventionalities being empty of their own inherently established entity [mistaking this to mean that self-emptiness means that phenomena are empty of themselves and wanting to avoid holding that the ultimate is empty of itself and hence non-existent, which would be a view of deprecatory nihilism]. For the two—(1) [correctly] not asserting true existence with respect to all things and all phenomena, having [properly] refuted with reasoning true existence in phenomena, and (2) propounding that all things and all phenomena do not truly exist based on an annihilatory emptiness in which the way of understanding emptiness is faulty—are dissimilar in all respects.

Tsong-kha-pa attributes Dol-po-pa's assertion that the ultimate truly exists to his misunderstanding of self-emptiness.

Tsong-kha-pa's position that what is negated in self-emptiness is not the object itself but the inherent existence of the object allows him to hold that self-emptiness is not annihilatory, whereby the ultimate can be a non-affirming negative.

The ultimate does not truly exist: "ultimate" in "ultimate truth" and in "ultimately existent" are not the same

Contrary to Dol-po-pa's view that other-emptiness is ultimately established in the sense that it can withstand analysis, Tsong-kha-pa holds that everything, including the ultimate, is not ultimately established because of not being able to withstand analysis (see *Insight,* 82):

> When sought with reasoning analyzing suchness, persons—who are born and transmigrate—and so forth, able to withstand analysis, are not found, not even a particle.

and (see *Insight,* 99):

> Therefore, when [an ultimate truth] is analyzed with the reasoning investigating whether it is truly established or not, it is

not truly established in the sense of being able to withstand analysis.

To establish that emptiness is the ultimate truth but is not ultimately existent, Tsong-kha-pa distinguishes between the meanings of "ultimate" in these two usages. For Dol-po-pa the ultimate truth has to be ultimately existent, for if it were not, it would not exist as the ultimate. Dol-po-pa (for more context see 295 above) holds that:

> If something is not true conventionally, it is not suitable as a conventional truth, and hence that which is a conventional truth is conventionally true and is not ultimately true. Just so, if something is not ultimately true, it is not suitable as an ultimate truth, and hence that which is an ultimate truth is ultimately true and is not conventionally true.

Tsong-kha-pa responds that Dol-po-pa has failed to make a distinction between:

- truly, or ultimately, established in the sense of being able to withstand analysis, and
- ultimately true in the sense of being true for a rational consciousness.[a]

Tsong-kha-pa re-explains one of Dol-po-pa's sources and then openly refutes Dol-po-pa's opinion by drawing an absurd conclusion (see *Insight*, 126):

> Moreover, with respect to the master Jñānagarbha's statement [in his *Commentary on the "Differentiation of the Two Truths"*], "Because of being a truth ultimately, it is an ultimate truth," since he also describes a rational consciousness as the ultimate, he is saying that what is non-deceptive in its perspective is a truth. His thought is not that [an ultimate truth] is **truly established** in the sense of being able to withstand analysis because in his text the true establishment of all phenomena is refuted. Therefore:
>
> - we accept the proposition that "If an ultimate is not true ultimately [that is, in the perspective of a rational consciousness called the ultimate], then a conventionality is not a truth conventionally [that is, in the perspective of a

[a] *rigs shes.* This term specifically refers to an inference realizing emptiness or to a consciousness of meditative equipoise directly realizing emptiness; it does not refer to a consciousness engaged in reasoning in general.

conventional valid cognition],"

- but to propound [as Dol-po-pa does] that "If the ultimate is not ultimately established, then a conventionality is not conventionally established," is to [absurdly] say that if a negative of truth [that is, a negative of true establishment] is not truly established, then the subjects that are the bases of the negation would be truly established.

This is because an ultimate truth is posited as just a negative of truth [that is, an absence of true establishment] in the subject that is the basis of negation and because the suggestion that subjects are not established conventionally suggests that they are not falsely established. Thus, [to propound such] would be even extremely senseless because the bases of negation must be established as false due to the very fact that the subjects—appearances—do not exist as truly established, that is to say, are not truly established.

In the process of discussing the reasoning probing the relationship between the person and the mental and physical aggregates, Tsong-kha-pa makes the point that whatever is truly established must always appear within the context of its mode of appearance being concordant with how it actually is (see *Insight,* 67):

> Concerning that, if the two—the self and the aggregates—are one inherently established entity, from among three fallacies the first damage to this position is that the assertion of a self [or person] would be senseless. If the sameness of entity of those two were inherently established, then they would become an utterly indivisible one. This is because if a sameness of entity were ultimately established, then to whatever awareness those two appeared, they would necessarily not appear to be different. The reason for this is that although among falsities—conventionalities—it is not contradictory for the mode of appearance and mode of being to be in disagreement, **such is necessarily contradictory in what is truly established because the mode of being of what truly exists must appear just as it is to any mind to which it appears.**

Let us take this a step further. For Tsong-kha-pa, since the ultimate is not truly established and is falsely established, it can appear falsely to an inferential consciousness as if it inherently existed but appear to a wisdom directly realizing it without any falsity whatsoever, that is, within the context of its mode of appearance being concordant with how it actually is. For Dol-po-pa, the ultimate, other-emptiness, appears only to pristine wisdom, never to consciousness; thus, there is always a concordance between how it appears and how it actually is. It could be said that in this sense he agrees with Tsong-kha-pa about one of the implications of true establishment; however, they disagree on the fundamental point—whether utterly everything is unable to bear analysis.

For Tsong-kha-pa, that Dol-po-pa makes an exception for other-emptiness is just foolish (see *Insight,* 98):

> Seeing well the implications of the reasoning of this situation, all our own [Buddhist] sects in the country of Superiors [India] who propound that phenomena truly exist are called proponents of [truly existent] things since they definitely propound that things truly exist. Once things are propounded as not truly existent, not to assert any phenomenon [as truly existent] appears to be a sign of greatly surpassing those who propound the foolishness of this position [that thusness truly exists].

He finds it pointless and counterproductive to assert that the ultimate truly exists (see *Insight,* 96):

> With regard to how it is easy to establish [uncompounded phenomena as not truly existent], when the inherent establishment of compounded phenomena is refuted as before, it is established that even though [phenomena] do not inherently exist, it is permissible to posit agents, activities, and objects—bondage and liberation, cause and effect, object comprehended and comprehender, and so forth—with respect to them. When that is established, even though uncompounded phenomena such as the noumenon and analytical cessations also do not truly exist, it is permissible to posit well the presentations of them as the objects of attainment and objects of comprehension of the path, as well as the doctrine jewel that is a source of refuge for trainees, and so forth. Hence, when those are not asserted to truly exist, there is no way to say that these presentations of the necessity for positing them as these are not feasible. Consequently, there is no point in asserting them to truly exist.
>
> Even those who assert that [the noumenon, cessations, and so forth] truly exist must indeed assert and do indeed assert—with respect to those—presentations of definiendum and

> definition, separative cause and separative effect, comprehension by such-and-such valid cognition, and so forth. Then, if [it is claimed that the noumenon, cessations, and so forth] are not related with one's object of attainment, definition, means of comprehension, and so forth, it could not be refuted that all unrelated [phenomena] would be [in the relationship of] definition and definiendum, and so forth. If a relation is asserted, then since dependence on another is not suitable in what truly exists, that is to say, is inherently established, a relationship cannot be posited [since it is being claimed that the noumenon, cessations, and so forth truly exist].

Positing the ultimate as truly existent undermines the assertion that other phenomena do not truly exist (see *Insight,* 97):

> Similarly, [the inherent existence of an uncompounded phenomenon] should also be refuted through analyzing whether [it and its basis of imputation] are one or different. If the assertion of these as truly existent could not be refuted by this reasoned analysis, then since it would also be the same in all respects with regard to compounded phenomena, true existence could not even in the least be refuted.

As we saw earlier (301), Dol-po-pa holds that the ultimate is not a dependent-arising and thus there is no way that dependent-arising could be used to prove that the ultimate does not truly exist. Tsong-kha-pa, however, sees just the opposite (see *Insight,* 95):

> Thinking that when in this way compounded things—persons and other phenomena—have been established as not truly existent by way of the reasonings described earlier, it can be established with little difficulty that uncompounded phenomena such as space, analytical cessations, non-analytical cessations, thusness, and so forth are not truly existent, Nāgārjuna says in the *Fundamental Treatise on the Middle, Called "Wisdom":*
>
> > Since compounded phenomena are thoroughly not established,
> > How could the uncompounded be established?

Whereas for Dol-po-pa dependent-arising necessarily means arising in dependence on causes and conditions, Tsong-kha-pa posits two types of dependent-arising (1) from the viewpoint of reliance on causes and conditions and (2) from the viewpoint of reliance of the object's own parts (see *Insight*, 91):

> Therefore, external things such as sprouts and internal things such as compositional activity arise in dependence, respectively, on seeds and so forth, and on ignorance and so forth. This being so, that those [sprouts, compositional activity, and so forth] are established by way of their own character is not feasible because whatever is established by way of its own nature must be inherently established—that is, be able to set itself up under its own power—due to which it is contradictory for it to rely on causes and conditions. Āryadeva's *Four Hundred* says:
>
> > That which has a dependent arising
> > Is not under its own power.
> > All these are not under their own power;
> > Therefore, self [inherent existence] does not exist.
>
> Through this you should understand that persons, pots, and so forth also are without inherent establishment because of being imputed in dependence on their own collection [of parts]. Those are two presentations of the reasoning of dependent-arising.[a]

Jam-yang-shay-pa's *Great Exposition of Tenets* shows that *samutpāda* does not just mean arising in the sense of being produced but also includes "existing" and "being established":[b]

> Hence, *pratītyasamutpāda* means the dependent-arising of products—their arising in reliance on their own causes and conditions.
>
> It also means the dependent-arising [of all phenomena, products and non-products]—their existence meeting to or in reliance on their own parts, their own bases of imputation, or their own components because:
>
> - with regard to the Sanskrit original of "arising" (*samutpāda*), Vasubandhu's *Commentary on the "Sūtra on Dependent-Arising"* explains *sam* as "coming together," "aggregating," and so forth, and
> - Rājaputra Yashomitra explains *pāda* as "existing" and so forth.

[a] The two are (1) arising in dependence upon causes and conditions and (2) being imputed in dependence on their own collection of parts.

[b] Hopkins, *Meditation on Emptiness*, 673-674, and Hopkins, *Maps of the Profound*, 863.

> Also, because all phenomena are just established in dependence upon, in reliance upon, or meeting to [causes and conditions, their parts, and their basis of imputation], they are not self-instituting and do not exist through their own power.

From Tsong-kha-pa's viewpoint, Dol-po-pa's limitation of dependent-arising to what is arisen from causes and conditions reflects non-comprehension of the basic Middle Way tenet of the compatibility of dependent-arising and emptiness and has not risen above the explanation of dependent-arising in the Great Exposition School, Sūtra School, and Mind-Only School.

However, it is not that Dol-po-pa is without sources for his assertion that the ultimate truly exists, and thus Tsong-kha-pa must explain away quotes from Nāgārjuna that Dol-po-pa uses to buttress his argument. Specifically, Dol-po-pa takes the statement in Nāgārjuna's *Sixty Stanzas of Reasoning* that "only nirvāṇa is a truth" (above, 305) and statements in Nāgārjuna's *Praise of the Element of Attributes* as supporting his notion that the mode of subsistence ultimately or truly exists. Tsong-kha-pa accurately re-states Dol-po-pa's argument but re-frames Nāgārjuna's statements so that they support the opposite opinion (see *Insight*, 98):

> *Objection:* If the meaning of the statement [in Nāgārjuna's *Treatise on the Middle*]:
>
> > Since compounded phenomena are thoroughly not established,
> > How could the uncompounded be established?
>
> is as you have explained above (96), does it not contradict (1) the statement in his *Sixty Stanzas of Reasoning* that only nirvāṇa is true and that the others are not:
>
> > When the Conqueror said
> > That only nirvāṇa is a truth,
> > What wise person would think,
> > "The rest are not unreal"?
>
> and (2) the statement also in his *Praise of the Element of Attributes* that the sūtras teaching emptiness—the absence of inherent existence—are for the sake of abandoning the afflictive emotions and do not teach the non-existence of the naturally pure basic constituent:
>
> > All the sūtras teaching emptiness

Set forth by the Conqueror
Overcome the afflictive emotions.
[These sūtras] do not diminish this basic constituent.

Answer: Those [who say such] are wrongly perspected with respect to the meaning of the scriptures as follows. The meaning of the former scripture is expressed [in sūtra]:

> The Supramundane Victor said, "Monastics, this ultimate truth is one—non-deceptive nirvāṇa. All compositional things have the attribute of falsity, deceptiveness."

This sūtra passage also says that nirvāṇa is a truth and all compositional things are false. The early part of the passage very clearly explains that truth means non-deceptive, and the latter part very clearly explains that falsity means deceptive. Furthermore, nirvāṇa [here refers] to ultimate truth [that is to say, the natural nirvāṇa, which is the emptiness of inherent existence, and not the nirvāṇa that is the cessation of obstructions attained through practice of the path], as is explained in Chandrakīrti's *Commentary on (Nāgārjuna's) "Sixty Stanzas of Reasoning."* ... Moreover, Nāgārjuna's *Sixty Stanzas of Reasoning* says:

> These two, cyclic existence and nirvāṇa,
> Do not [inherently] exist.
> The thorough knowledge itself of cyclic existence
> Is called "nirvāṇa."

He explains that **both** cyclic existence and nirvāṇa are not inherently existent and that [the emptiness which is] just the object of the knowledge that cyclic existence is not inherently established is posited as nirvāṇa. Therefore, how could this be a position asserting that the emptiness that is the absence of true existence of cyclic existence is an annihilatory emptiness!

Moreover, the passage from Nāgārjuna's *Praise of the Element of Attributes* (above, 99) means:

> For the sake of overcoming the apprehension of things as truly existent—the root of all other afflictive emotions—the sūtras teaching emptiness, the absence of inherent establishment, teach that the conceived object of the apprehension of true existence does not exist. They do not teach that emptiness—the naturally pure

> basic constituent, the negative of the two selves that are the objects of the apprehension of true existence—does not exist.

Since although this emptiness exists, it is not truly established, that passage serves as a source refuting the proposition that the emptiness that is a negative of true existence—its object of negation—does not exist. It also refutes the proposition that it is not necessary to realize emptiness, the ultimate suchness, in order exhaustively to abandon the afflictive emotions. Hence, Nāgārjuna's *Praise of the Element of Attributes* itself says:

> Through the three called impermanence, [coarse] emptiness,
> And suffering, the mind is purified.
> The doctrine supremely purifying the mind
> Is naturelessness [that is, the absence of inherent existence].

and:

> The naturelessness of phenomena
> Should be meditated upon as the element of attributes.

He says that the absence of an inherently established nature in these phenomena is the element of attributes that is the object of meditation, and he says that just meditation on it is the supreme purifier of the mind. Therefore, how could it be suitable to cite this [*Praise of the Element of Attributes*] for the position that the emptiness that is the absence of inherent establishment of phenomena appearing in this way is an annihilatory emptiness and that, therefore, a truly existent emptiness separate from it is to be posited as the emptiness that is the object of meditation!

This is like propounding that in order to remove the suffering of fright upon apprehending a snake in the east despite there being none there, the demonstration that there is no snake in the east will not serve as an antidote to it, but rather one should indicate, "There is a tree in the west." For, one is propounding that in order to remove the suffering upon adhering to the true existence of what appears in this way to sentient beings, realization that those bases [that is, objects]—which are apprehended to truly exist—do not truly exist will not serve as an antidote, but that rather one must indicate that some other senseless base truly exists.

From this viewpoint Tsong-kha-pa repeatedly criticizes Dol-po-pa for turning to a truly existent ultimate as the principal object of meditation. Tsong-kha-pa emphasizes that because suffering is caused by misapprehending the nature of persons and phenomena, reflective and meditative attention must be paid to the **absence** of such a status. Otherwise, it is impossible to overcome the afflictive emotions driving the very process of cyclic existence.

The fundamental principle is that because beings misapprehend the status of phenomena, they must concentrate on understanding the **lack** of such a status in order to overcome the tendency to this basic error and all the ills built on it. Otherwise, meditation would be unrelated to the problem sought to be overcome (see *Insight*, 57):

> ...it is like searching for a robber on the plain after the robber has gone to the woods.

and in the context of the Mind-Only School:[a]

> ...since ordinary sentient beings conceive just these other-powered internal and external things—eyes, forms, and so forth which are objects seen, heard, and so forth—as self [that is, as objects and subjects that are different entities or as established by way of their own character as the referents of conceptual consciousnesses and of words], emptiness must be delineated within taking just these as the bases of emptiness. The error does not come through holding that the other two natures [that is, other-powered natures and imputational natures] exist as other factualities in the thoroughly established nature. Therefore, how could selflessness be delineated within thinking [as the Jo-nang-pas do] that the thoroughly established nature is empty because of existing as factually other than the other two natures! ...Therefore, Sthiramati's *Explanation of (Vasubandhu's) Commentary on (Maitreya's) "Differentiation of the Middle and the Extremes"* also says that it is not like a temple's being empty of monastics and so forth but like a rope's being empty of a snake... Therefore, without letting it become like the worldly [example] of putting a scapegoat effigy at the western door when a demon is bringing harm at the eastern door, one should meditate on an emptiness that is such that the

[a] Hopkins, *Emptiness in the Mind-Only School of Buddhism*, 226-228. For Dol-po-pa's position, see Hopkins, *Reflections on Reality*, 273-293, 328-351.

emptiness of the imputational self as it is apprehended in just those other-powered natures—these being the bases apprehended as self—is the thoroughly established nature. If this is done, it will serve as an antidote to the apprehension of self. If, on the other hand, one meditates on an emptiness the mode of which is other than this style, it will not harm the apprehension of self at all.

Tsong-kha-pa makes the cogent case that innate misapprehension of the self of phenomena must be countered by taking those same phenomena—which are misperceived so as to lead beings into suffering and finitude—and by seeing that they do not have the falsely superimposed quality of the imputational nature. He indicts Dol-po-pa for putting forth a system that is inadequate to the task of opposing the basic ignorance drawing beings into suffering and finitude:[a]

> With respect to that, when the thoroughly established nature that is the selflessness of phenomena is delineated in either the Yogic Practice School or the Middle Way School, the bases of emptiness with respect to which [the thoroughly established nature] is delineated are relative to those bases with respect to which a self of phenomena is apprehended by a consciousness apprehending a self of phenomena. It is like, for example, the fact that if you wish to remove the suffering of fright from someone upon that person's apprehending a rope as a snake, you must show—upon taking the rope as the basis of emptiness—that it is empty of a snake. However, it is not suitable to take the rope's **emptiness** of a snake as the basis of emptiness and say that it is empty [of being a rope and a snake] because of existing as factually other [than them].
>
> Furthermore, with respect to the apprehension of a self of phenomena, such apprehensions as that directionally partless minute particles exist and that objects of apprehension composed of them exist or that a moment of consciousness that has no earlier and later temporal parts exists or that a consciousness that is a continuum composed of those exists—these being imputed only by those whose awarenesses have been affected by [mistaken] tenets—occur only among those proponents of tenets and do not exist among other sentient beings. Therefore, though an emptiness that is no more than merely an absence of those [objects of negation] is taught, it does not at all harm the

[a] Hopkins, *Emptiness in the Mind-Only School of Buddhism*, 226-227.

> innate apprehension of self that has resided [in the mental continuum] beginninglessly. Therefore, it must be taught that those bases—that the innate apprehension of self apprehends as self—are empty of self in the way that such is apprehended. It must be understood that the refutation of imputational factors that are constructed by tenet systems is a branch [of the process] of refuting that [innate apprehension of self].
>
> This being the case, since ordinary sentient beings apprehend just these other-powered internal and external things—eyes, forms, and so forth which are objects seen, heard, and so forth—as self [that is, as objects and subjects that are different entities or as established by way of their own character as the referents of conceptual consciousnesses and of words], emptiness must be delineated within taking just these as the bases of emptiness. The error does not come through holding that the other two natures [that is, other-powered natures and imputational natures] exist as other factualities in the thoroughly established nature. Therefore, how could selflessness be delineated within thinking [as the Jo-nang-pas do] that the thoroughly established nature is empty because of existing as factually other than the other two natures! ...
>
> Therefore, without letting it become like the worldly [example] of putting a scapegoat effigy at the western door when a demon is bringing harm at the eastern door, one should meditate on an emptiness that is such that the emptiness of the imputational self as it is apprehended in just those other-powered natures—these being the bases apprehended as self—is the thoroughly established nature. If this is done, it will serve as an antidote to the apprehension of self.[a] If, on the other hand, one meditates on an emptiness the mode of which is other than this style, it will not harm the apprehension of self at all.[b]

In sum, Tsong-kha-pa's indictment is that Dol-po-pa's reliance on other-emptiness makes his system bereft of an adequate means of undermining afflictive emotions, since it does not directly address the way objects are misapprehended. In this way, he shows that it is both feasible and necessary for the object of meditation for overcoming

[a] "Self" here does not mean "person" but (1) the establishment of objects by way of their own character as the referents of conceptual consciousnesses and of words and (2) the establishment of subject and object as different entities.

[b] For a thorough explanation of this quotation, see the Synopsis in Hopkins, *Emptiness in the Mind-Only School of Buddhism*, 335-341.

obstructions to be a mere elimination of an object of negation, specifically, inherent existence.

The two truths are one entity

As we saw earlier (298), Dol-po-pa holds that:

1. the ultimate exists and is an object of knowledge
2. the two truths are neither one, nor the same entity, nor one but different isolates[a]
3. the two truths are different but not different entities
4. the two truths are different in the sense of negating that they are the same entity.[b]

Tsong-kha-pa agrees that:

1. the ultimate exists and is an object of knowledge
2. the two truths are not one
3. the two truths are different but not different entities.

However, he holds that the two truths are the same entity, but different isolates.[c] He presents his opinion in the context of refuting that a oneness of entity is not feasible when one of the elements (ultimate truth) is permanent (see *Insight,* 105):

> *Question:* Since the two of the division into two must be different, what kind of difference is this?
>
> *Answer:* With respect to this, many earlier [scholars] propounded:
>
>> Pot and woolen cloth, for instance, are different entities.[d] Product and impermanent thing, for instance, are one entity and different isolates.[e] In these two cases, the two that are different are both effective things; however, in cases of difference when either is a non-effective thing [that is, a permanent phenomenon] they have a difference that [merely] negates sameness.[f] Among these three [modes of] difference, the two truths are different in the sense of negating sameness.

[a] *gcig la ldog pa tha dad;* 384.6.

[b] *ngo bo gcig pa bkag pa'i tha dad;* 384.6.

[c] *ngo bo gcig la ldog pa tha dad.*

[d] *ngo bo tha dad.*

[e] *ngo bo gcig la ldog pa tha dad.*

[f] *gcig pa dkag pa'i tha dad.*

> However, some [correctly] asserted that the two truths are one entity and different isolates.

Despite their difference about the relationship of the two truths, Dol-po-pa and Tsong-kha-pa agree that the ultimate is an object of knowledge and a wing of a dichotomy: whatever exists must be either an ultimate truth or an obscurational truth. Dol-po-pa (above, 304) holds that the ultimate—since it is an object of pristine wisdom—is an object of knowledge and that the two truths are different, and Tsong-kha-pa similarly says (see *Illumination,* 224):

> The reasoning [why there are only two truths] is that if a certain base [that is, an object] is—on the positive side—distinguished as a falsity, a deceptive object, then on the exclusionary side it must be eliminated that it is a non-deceptive suchness, due to which the deceptive and the non-deceptive are dichotomous explicit contradictories. Since whatever is [a dichotomous pair] covers all objects of knowledge, a further category that is both and a further category that is neither are eliminated. It is as Kamalashīla's *Illumination of the Middle* says:
>
> > Phenomena that have the character of being a dichotomy are such that if something is refuted to be the one and it is not established to be the other, then it does not exist. Therefore, it also is not reasonable to think of it as in a class that is neither of those two.
>
> and:
>
> > Two that are such that something does not exist if it is neither [of them] have the character of being a dichotomy. Those that have the character of being a dichotomy cover all aspects [that is, whatever exists is either one or the other]. Those that cover all aspects eliminate other categories. Examples are, for instance, particular [pairs] such as the physical and the non-physical, and so forth.
>
> This is also to be understood with respect to all other explicit contradictories [that is, dichotomies].
>
> If there were no such things as dichotomies that exclude a third category, there would be no way to make a refutation with analysis that limits the possibilities to two—[asking] whether it is asserted that something exists or does not exist,

> or is one or many, and so forth. If there are [dichotomies that exclude a third category], then when something is refuted as being one side of a dichotomy and it is not established as the other, it does not exist. Therefore, to say that there are no explicit contradictories in the Middle Way Consequence School is a case of not having formed [understanding of] the presentation of refutation and establishment [in this system]. The Middle Way Autonomy School and the Middle Way Consequence School do not differ with respect to [asserting] that [within existents] if something is eliminated as being one side of a dichotomy, it must be established as the other and that if one is refuted, the other is established.

Still, as we saw above (304) Dol-po-pa does not hold that the ultimate is a wing of a dichotomy between existing as an effective thing and not existing as an effective thing, since it is neither, and thus is "a third category and the center or middle." Tsong-kha-pa, on the other hand, holds that the ultimate is a non-effective thing; he does not opt for a third category here.

A pristine wisdom is not an ultimate

To establish that a pristine wisdom is not an ultimate, as opposed to Dol-po-pa's fundamental assertion (above, 306) that self-arisen pristine wisdom is an ultimate truth and a thoroughly established nature, Tsong-kha-pa distinguishes between many different usages of the term "ultimate" in the literature of the Middle Way School (see *Insight,* 141):

> Though indeed the object, the noumenon, is to be taken as the ultimate, there are also many descriptions of the subject—the rational consciousness—as an ultimate, as is set forth in:
>
> - Jñānagarbha's *Differentiation of the Two Truths:*
>
>   Because of being undeceiving, a rational [consciousness] is an ultimate.
>
> - and moreover in Kamalashīla's *Illumination of the Middle:*
>
>   The statements also that production and so forth do not **ultimately** exist are asserted to mean the following: All consciousnesses arisen from correct hearing, thinking, and meditating are non-erroneous subjects; hence, they are called "ultimates" because of being the ultimate among these [consciousnesses.

> Production and so forth do not exist for such consciousnesses and in this sense do not exist ultimately.]

There are two types of rational consciousnesses:

1. non-conceptual: a Superior's non-conceptual pristine wisdom of meditative equipoise
2. conceptual: a rational consciousness comprehending suchness in dependence on a reason, and so forth.

The thought of Bhāvaviveka's *Blaze of Reasoning* in describing the ultimate as twofold—a non-conceptual pristine wisdom and a wisdom concordant with that—and the thought of Kamalashīla's *Illumination of the Middle* in describing two ultimates are the same. Therefore, it is not the meaning of those texts that the explanation of two ultimates should be taken as ultimates only in terms of objects and not in terms of subjects.

Concerning this, when the first [that is, a Superior's non-conceptual pristine wisdom of non-conceptual meditative equipoise] understands suchness, it is able simultaneously to eliminate with respect to its object the proliferations of [the apprehension of] true [existence] and the proliferations of dualistic appearance; hence, [a Superior's non-conceptual pristine wisdom of non-conceptual meditative equipoise] is an actual ultimate; also, that is the meaning of being "beyond all proliferations" (in the quote above on 139). Although the second [that is, a conceptual rational consciousness comprehending suchness in dependence on a sign, and so forth] is able to cease the proliferations [of the apprehension] of true [existence] with respect to its own object [that is, emptiness], it cannot eliminate the proliferations of dualistic appearance; hence, it is an ultimate that accords in aspect with the supramundane ultimate.

It is necessary to set forth two modes also with respect to the object-ultimate[a] that is the negative of ultimately [existent] production—and so forth—of forms and so on. Concerning this:

- In the perspective of a non-conceptual rational consciousness, the object-emptiness is the actual ultimate free from both proliferations.
- In the perspective of a conceptual rational consciousness,

[a] *yul gyi don dam;* 483.6. This is the ultimate that is the object of the wisdom consciousness, not the wisdom consciousness that is called an ultimate.

> the object-emptiness is not the actual ultimate free from both proliferations, since it is free from only one class of proliferations. However, this is not to say that **in general** it is not an actual ultimate truth.
>
> Therefore, except for the case of being free from all proliferations of dualistic appearance **in the perspective of certain awarenesses**, an emptiness of true existence free from all proliferations of appearance does not occur, and hence the meaning of those texts is not that whatever is an ultimate truth is necessarily free from all proliferations of dualistic appearance.

Nga-wang-pel-den's *Annotations for (Jam-yang-shay-pa's) "Great Exposition of Tenets"*[a] draws out the meaning of this passage within emphasizing that the distinction of actual and concordant emptinesses is made relative to the perspectives of different types of realizational consciousnesses and that emptiness itself, whether realized by a conceptual consciousness or a non-conceptual consciousness, is always the actual ultimate:

> This says that a Superior's uncontaminated pristine wisdom is an actual **subject**-ultimate, not that it is an actual ultimate. In general, an ultimate truth is an actual ultimate free from both proliferations in the perspective of a non-conceptual rational consciousness and is the ultimate free from only one class of proliferations in the perspective of a conceptual rational consciousness. It is utterly not the case that the emptiness that is the object comprehended by a non-conceptual rational consciousness is the ultimate free from both proliferations and that the emptiness that is the object comprehended by a conceptual rational consciousness is the ultimate free from only one class of proliferations because both an ultimate free from both proliferations and an ultimate free from only one class of proliferations do not occur [that is, they are impossible], since whatever is an ultimate truth necessarily is involved with proliferations.

For elucidation of the last clause—"whatever is an ultimate truth necessarily is involved with proliferations"—Nga-wang-pel-den refers readers to his *Explanation of the Obscurational and the Ultimate in the Four Systems*[b] where he emphasizes that the frequent description of the

a *dngos, la,* 188.4.

b 194.2, 195.1, 199.1.

ultimate as free from the proliferations of conceptuality is in terms of certain consciousnesses, for if the ultimate were free from proliferations in general, it could not be either existent or non-existent or either one or different.[a]

These distinctions, beyond trying to have fun with Dol-po-pa's and others' emphasis on reality as free from conceptual proliferations, explain away the many descriptions of wisdom as the ultimate by consigning such a designation to the realm of the metaphoric, since, according to this explanation, the only actual ultimate is emptiness even if in direct realization of emptiness there is not the least recognition of difference between the wisdom consciousness and emptiness. Whereas Dol-po-pa's system and many others start from equating pristine wisdom and emptiness, Tsong-kha-pa starts from their difference, despite his own description of the state of non-conceptual realization as undifferentiated.

A Buddha's omniscient wisdom perceives the conventional explicitly, not implicitly

For Tsong-kha-pa an omniscient mind must know all phenomena, including the ordinary (see *Insight,* 135):

> If a Buddha did not perceive the aggregates and so forth, it would deprecate the exalted knowledge of the diversity and all the diverse objects because the existent and what is not known by a Buddha are mutually exclusive.

Dol-po-pa (above, 275) similarly holds that an omniscient mind must know all phenomena, but he makes the distinction that it only **implicitly** knows ordinary phenomena, which, therefore, do not appear to it. Tsong-kha-pa, to the contrary, asserts that an omniscient mind must **explicitly** know all phenomena, which, therefore, must appear to it. He continues:

> Consequently, the diverse objects must appear to an exalted knower of the diversity [of phenomena]. Since exalted knowledge without the aspect [of the object appearing] is not this [Consequentialist] system, [objects are known by an omniscient consciousness] upon the appearance of their aspect.

[a] This is the type of initially mind-boggling but eventually cogent, in-your-face distinction that Tibetan (not just Ge-luk-pa) scholars love to make: there is non-conceptual realization of emptiness, but this does not necessitate that emptiness itself has to be free from the proliferations of conceptuality.

To establish that an omniscient mind explicitly knows all phenomena, including the ordinary, and yet does not itself become mistaken, Tsong-kha-pa distinguishes between what an omniscient mind knows from its own perspective and what it knows from others' perspectives:

> With respect to the mode of appearance, when the marks and beauties of a Buddha appear to persons who have not abandoned ignorance, their appearance as established by way of their own character—despite not being so established—is not by reason of those objects' having arisen through the force of the latencies of ignorance but is an appearance due to the [perceiving] subject's being polluted by the latencies of ignorance. For those [marks and beauties of a Buddha] do not appear to that subject [that is, a Buddha's consciousness] from the viewpoint of merely appearing thus[a] to other persons but appear thus from [a Buddha's] own viewpoint.
>
> The appearance of objects such as forms and sounds[b]—which appear in the perspective of those who have not abandoned ignorance as established by way of their own character whereas they are not so established—to a Buddha's pristine wisdom knowing the diversity is an appearance to a Buddha only from the viewpoint of [these phenomena] appearing to persons who have the pollutions of ignorance. Without depending on their appearing thus to others, they do not appear from a Buddha's own viewpoint. Therefore, a Buddha's knowing forms and so forth—which appear to be inherently established whereas they are not so established—is also from the viewpoint of their appearing thus to those who possess ignorance. Without depending on the appearance of them to those persons, Buddhas from their own viewpoint do not know them in the manner of their appearing this way; hence, there is no sense in which [a Buddha's consciousness] could become mistaken through their appearing. This is because, although they do not appear within the context of the pristine wisdom's having pollution, they appear by way of the essential that the pristine

[a] That is, as the marks and beauties of a Buddha.

[b] The false appearance of objects such as forms and sounds as if they inherently exist is itself something that exists, and thus it must be known by an omniscient Buddha and hence must appear to a Buddha. However, this appearance occurs to a Buddha not because of a fault in that Buddha, but only because it occurs this way for beings who have the pollutions of ignorance. From a Buddha's own viewpoint, only endless purity is perceived.

> wisdom must know all objects of knowledge.
>
> From the viewpoint of an exalted knower of the diversity itself, all things appear in the perspective of selflessness and the absence of inherent existence, whereby they appear as falsities, like illusions; they do not appear as truths. When [phenomena] appear to that pristine wisdom from the factor of appearing to those who have ignorance, this is a mere becoming visible of the appearance [of those] as true to other persons.

To maintain that a Buddha actually perceives all phenomena, Dol-po-pa holds that Buddhas know obscurational truths only implicitly in the sense that by explicitly knowing the truth they know that these other phenomena do not exist. Tsong-kha-pa, to uphold a Buddha's omniscience, makes an entirely different distinction that allows for explicit realization of everything.

As a reason why conventional phenomena do not appear to a Buddha, Dol-po-pa cites several sources clearly indicating that Buddhas are always in meditative equipoise (above, 278). Tsong-kha-pa counters that an omniscient mind has two types of knowledge simultaneously. First he gives sources for his own position and then explains away Dol-po-pa's sources as referring only to a Buddha's knowledge of suchness (see *Insight*, 137):

> In that way Jñānagarbha's *Differentiation of the Two Truths* explains that [this pristine wisdom] vividly perceives directly all the diversity:
>
> > An omniscient knower directly perceives
> > All the dependently produced
> > Just as they appear
> > Devoid of the superimposed entity.
>
> and he explains that [Buddhas] never rise from the meditative stabilization in which dualistic appearance has been pacified:
>
> > Because that which does not see knowers,
> > Objects known, and selfhood has a stable abiding
> > Due to the non-arising of signs,
> > [Buddhas] do not rise [from meditative stabilization].
>
> Although to those who do not properly understand those two explanations it seems to be contradictory to assert both—rather than just one of the two—there is no contradiction. This is because although the two pristine wisdoms perceiving

suchness and perceiving the diversity are one entity, there is not the slightest contradiction that in relation to individual objects [that is, the ultimate and the conventional] there come to be two—a rational consciousness and a conventional consciousness.

Tsong-kha-pa makes the distinction that the two types of a Buddha's pristine wisdom—dualistically knowing the diversity of phenomena and knowing suchness non-dualistically—are determined relative to particular objects. In this way, each of the two types of pristine wisdom realizes both the diversity and suchness, but in relation to those objects they are called knowing the diversity and knowing suchness.

Tsong-kha-pa stresses that all phenomena must **appear** to a Buddha (see *Illumination*, 257):

> There are two ways that a Buddha's pristine wisdom knows objects of knowledge—a mode of knowing all objects of knowledge that are ultimate truths and a mode of knowing all objects of knowledge that are obscurational truths. Concerning those, the first is knowledge of the suchness of the aggregates and so forth in the manner of not perceiving their conventional appearances. The second is knowledge [of those aggregates and so forth] in the perspective of the pristine wisdom knowing the diversity [of phenomena] in the manner of dualistic appearance as object and subject; this is because it is not suitable to posit that a Buddha has implicit realization in which something is realized even though it does not appear and hence [everything] must be known upon its appearing.[a]
>
> Although with respect to a Buddha's knowledge of the diversity the aggregates and so forth do not appear upon its being polluted by the predispositions of ignorance, what appears to the consciousnesses of other persons that are polluted with ignorance must appear to a Buddha. This is because it is not suitable for those appearances to be non-existent, and if a conventionality exists, it must be observed by [a Buddha's] knowledge of the diversity. Although the falling hairs that appear to one with cataracts do not appear to the eye consciousness of one free from cataracts, those **appearances** do not need to be non-existent; therefore, they are unlike [the situation with] a Buddha [wherein if a conventionality exists, it must appear to a

[a] This counters Dol-po-pa's notion that a Buddha only implicitly knows obscurational truths; see above, 275ff.

> Buddha, and if something does not appear to a Buddha, it must not exist].

He goes on to accept at face value the quote (or one similar to it) that Dol-po-pa (above, 277) had to explain away:

> Just as the sun's emitting one ray
> Illuminates transmigrating beings,
> A conqueror's pristine wisdom simultaneously
> Shines to all objects of knowledge.

Tsong-kha-pa takes the passage literally:

> Until the predispositions for mistaken dualistic appearance have been extinguished, the two direct comprehensions (1) of the mode of being [of phenomena] and (2) of the diversity [of phenomena] cannot be generated in one entity, due to which these must be comprehended within an alternation between meditative equipoise and states subsequent to meditative equipoise, and, therefore, comprehension of these two does not come within a single instant of pristine wisdom. When the predispositions for mistakenness have been completely abandoned, the generation of the two pristine wisdoms within each instant of pristine wisdom is continuous; hence, alternation between directly comprehending and not comprehending the two types of objects of knowledge at one time is not necessary. For this reason, [our presentation] also does not contradict the statement:
>
> > A single instant of exalted knowledge
> > Pervades the full circle of objects of knowledge.
>
> That although the two pristine wisdoms are one entity, there is not even the slightest contradiction in there coming to be two different modes of knowledge in relation to two [types of] objects is an attribute solely of a Buddha, a Supramundane Victor. Whereas that is the case, those who take only the mode of knowledge of suchness as the mode of a Buddha's mode of knowledge and thereupon say that knowledge of the diversity [of phenomena] does not exist in a Buddha's mental continuum but instead is included within the continuums of trainees are deprecating a Buddha's knowledge of the diversity.

Dol-po-pa's opinion, as documented earlier (275), is that a Buddha explicitly knows only the mode of being, including all ultimate qualities subsisting in it, but only implicitly knows the diversity of ordinary phenomena through knowing them to be non-existent.

Tsong-kha-pa explains away Dol-po-pa's evidence for his position in sūtra passages saying that the non-seeing of phenomena is seeing the noumenon (see *Insight,* 130):

> "They see it in the manner of non-seeing" does not refer to not seeing any and all objects but indicates that if these that are observed through the power of the cataracts of ignorance existed as [their own] suchness, they would have to be observed by the pristine wisdom of uncontaminated meditative equipoise of Superiors, whereas they are not, and thus their seeing suchness is by way of not seeing any of those. For due to not observing the object of negation—despite the fact that if it did exist, it would be suitable to be observed—it is posited that the negative of the object of negation is realized [and hence emptiness is seen and it is not that nothing at all is seen]. The meaning of "Non-seeing is the excellent seeing" (see *Illumination,* 259) is to be understood similarly.
>
> Moreover, in that way the *Verse Summary of the Perfection of Wisdom* (see also *Illumination,* 260) says:
>
> > The One-Gone-Thus teaches that one who does not see forms,
> > Does not see feelings, does not see discriminations,
> > Does not see intentions, does not see
> > Consciousness, mind, or sentience sees the *dharma.*[a]
> >
> > Analyze how space is seen as in the expression
> > By sentient beings in words, "Space is seen."
> > The One-Gone-Thus teaches that seeing the *dharma* is also like that.
> > The seeing cannot be expressed by another example.
>
> This says that the unseen is the aggregates, and the seen is the *dharma,* which means suchness, as in the statement, "Whoever sees dependent-arising sees the *dharma.*"
>
> Furthermore, it is like, for example, the fact that space is a mere elimination of obstructive objects of touch, and that seeing—or realizing—it is taken as not seeing the preventive obstruction that is the object of negation and is suitable to be

[a] *chos,* which here means *chos nyid* (*dharmatā*), as Tsong-kha-pa says just below when he equates it with suchness.

> observed if it were present. In that [example], the seen is space, and the unseen is preventive obstruction. The last two lines refute that suchness is seen while seeing blue [for instance], which would be not to see in accordance with the example [of seeing space]. The statement that the five aggregates are not seen indicates that the substrata [that is, these phenomena,] are not seen in the perspective of perception of suchness by uncontaminated meditative equipoise.

In this way, Tsong-kha-pa limits the scope of the many statements that conventional phenomena do not appear to the pristine wisdom non-dualistically realizing suchness (see *Illumination*, 262):

> All those [statements] are sources for the non-appearance of conventionalities, such as the aggregates, **in the perspective of directly perceiving suchness.**
>
> Therefore, none of the proliferations of dualistic phenomena such as effective thing, non-effective thing, and so forth occur **in the perspective of directly perceiving suchness** because the entities of those proliferations are not observed **in that [perspective].**

3. Summary

Twenty-four major points highlight Dol-po-pa's and Tsong-kha-pa's systems.

1.

Dol-po-pa: Self-emptiness is empty emptiness in that compounded phenomena are empty of themselves.

Tsong-kha-pa: Self-emptiness is empty emptiness in that both compounded and uncompounded phenomena are empty of inherent existence, but they are not empty of themselves.

2.

Dol-po-pa: Other-emptiness is non-empty emptiness in that the ultimate is the basis of emptiness, which is empty of the other, that is to say, conventionalities, and is not empty of itself.

Tsong-kha-pa: It can be said that the ultimate is other-empty in that the ultimate is not the conventional, but it is empty of inherent existence, and thus the ultimate is a self-emptiness and thus an empty emptiness.

3.

Dol-po-pa: Self-emptiness is not the ultimate.

Tsong-kha-pa: Self-emptiness is the ultimate.

4.

Dol-po-pa: The ultimate is able to bear analysis.

Tsong-kha-pa: Even the ultimate is not able to bear analysis.

5.

Dol-po-pa: The middle wheel of doctrine teaches that the ultimate is self-empty only out of a purposeful intent and thus requires interpretation.

Tsong-kha-pa: The teaching in the middle wheel of doctrine that the ultimate is self-empty is literally acceptable because the ultimate also is empty of inherent existence.

6.

Dol-po-pa: Realizing and accustoming to self-emptiness just temporarily suppresses or reduces the pointedness of only coarse afflictive emotions.

Tsong-kha-pa: Realizing and accustoming to self-emptiness totally removes all coarse and subtle afflictive emotions.

7.

Dol-po-pa: The third wheel of doctrine is definitive because it clearly teaches that the ultimate ultimately exists but conventionalities do not ultimately exist.

Tsong-kha-pa: The third wheel requires interpretation because it teaches that all phenomena, ultimate and conventional, are established by way of their own character.

8.

Dol-po-pa: The ultimate exists and is an object of knowledge.

Tsong-kha-pa: Agreed.

9.

Dol-po-pa: The ultimate is not a dependent-arising, since dependent-arisings are necessarily impermanent and deceptive.

Tsong-kha-pa: Even the ultimate is a dependent-arising, since dependent-arising means (1) arising in dependence on causes and conditions, (2) existing in dependence on parts, and (3) existing in dependence on a basis of imputation and in dependence upon conceptuality that imputes it, due to which even the permanent are dependent-arisings.

10.

Dol-po-pa: The two truths, obscurational and ultimate, are neither one nor one entity since they are different, though not different entities. Their difference simply means that they are not the same entity. Hence, an ultimate truth is not an obscurational truth, and an obscurational truth is not an ultimate truth.

Tsong-kha-pa: The two truths are not one but are one entity. They are different isolates but not different entities. Hence, an ultimate truth is not an obscurational truth, and an obscurational truth is not an ultimate truth.

11.

Dol-po-pa: Whatever exists is either an ultimate truth or an obscurational truth.

Tsong-kha-pa: Agreed.

12.

Dol-po-pa: Although there is no third category between ultimate truth and obscurational truth since whatever exists must be either an ultimate truth or an obscurational truth, there is a third category between existing as an effective thing and not existing as an effective thing.

Tsong-kha-pa: There is no third category between existing as an effective thing and not existing as an effective thing. The ultimate is the latter.

13.

Dol-po-pa: The ultimate is true ultimately, and obscurational truths are true conventionally.

Tsong-kha-pa: The ultimate truth could not ultimately exist without contradicting that it is the absence of inherent existence of all phenomena.

14.

Dol-po-pa: "Ultimately existent" means "existing as able to bear analysis by a rational consciousness," and ultimate truth is able to bear analysis by a rational consciousness and is, therefore, ultimately existent.

Tsong-kha-pa: "Ultimately existent" means "existing from its own side," a consequence of which is that any object that ultimately exists must be able to bear analysis by a rational consciousness, and nothing can bear such analysis.

15.

Dol-po-pa: If the ultimate were self-empty, it would be empty of itself and thus would not exist at all.

Tsong-kha-pa: The object of negation of self-emptiness is not the object that is the substratum of self-emptiness but its inherent existence, due to which even though the ultimate is self-empty, it exists.

16.

Dol-po-pa: The ultimate is an affirming negative, not a non-affirming negative.

Tsong-kha-pa: The ultimate is non-affirming negative, not an affirming negative.

17.

Dol-po-pa: Conventionalities do not exist in the mode of subsistence, but the ultimate (including ultimate Buddha qualities of body, speech, and mind) exist in the mode of subsistence.

Tsong-kha-pa: Nothing exists in the mode of subsistence in that nothing exists as its own mode of subsistence, since then it would inherently exist. Thus, the mode of subsistence, that is, emptiness, is not its own mode of subsistence, but the mode of subsistence exists, and the mode of subsistence is the mode of subsistence.

18.

Dol-po-pa: Karmic appearances of sentient beings exist in the perspective of mistaken consciousness and do not exist in the perspective of pristine wisdom. Nothing is both a valid cognition and a mistaken consciousness.

Tsong-kha-pa: Karmic appearances of sentient beings exist in the perspective of valid cognitions that are mistaken consciousness only in the sense that their objects *appear* to inherently exist whereas they do not. They also are directly perceived by a pristine wisdom knowing the diversity of phenomena.

19.

Dol-po-pa: Pristine wisdom and the ultimate are equivalent.

Tsong-kha-pa: Pristine wisdom and the ultimate are mutually exclusive, even though there is no sensing of their difference in direct realization of the ultimate.

20.

Dol-po-pa: The matrix-of-One-Gone-Thus, endowed with ultimate Buddha qualities of body, speech, and mind, is the basic reality and pristine wisdom.

Tsong-kha-pa: The matrix-of-One-Gone-Thus is not endowed with ultimate Buddha qualities of body, speech, and mind; the matrix-of-One-Gone-Thus is the emptiness of inherent existence of a defiled mind and thus is not endowed with Buddha qualities of body, speech, and mind, which are generated through observing and meditating on emptiness.

21.

Dol-po-pa: The Great Middle Way is presented in texts by Great Vehicle masters such as Nāgārjuna, Asaṅga, Āryadeva, Buddhapālita, Bhāvaviveka, Vasubandhu, and so forth up to but not always including Chandrakīrti, who is self-contradictory in both refuting and propounding a matrix-of-One-Gone-Thus endowed with ultimate Buddha qualities.

Tsong-kha-pa: The Great Middle Way is the view of the Consequence School itself, as presented by Nāgārjuna, Āryadeva, Buddhapālita, Chandrakīrti, and Shāntideva.

22.

Dol-po-pa: Pristine wisdom is simply permanent and not in the sense that its continuum goes on forever.

Tsong-kha-pa: Pristine wisdom even at the stage of Buddhahood is impermanent, though at Buddhahood its continuum goes on forever, and in this sense is called permanent.

23.

Dol-po-pa: Buddhas are omniscient in that they know the phenomena of the desire, form, and formless realms implicitly. Through knowing the ultimate explicitly, they know that the phenomena of the desire, form, and formless realms do not exist and thus implicitly know them.

Tsong-kha-pa: Buddhas know both the ultimate and the conventional explicitly, that is, through the appearance of everything to their omniscient wisdom. They perceive only endless purity from their own perspective, but they explicitly and directly perceive other phenomena by way of these phenomena appearing to sentient beings.

24.

Dol-po-pa: Buddhas are always in meditative equipoise directly realizing the ultimate.

Tsong-kha-pa: Buddhas have a state of wisdom in which meditative equipoise directly realizing the ultimate and the state subsequent to meditative equipoise are fused in one mind without having to alternate between them.

Five quintessential perspectives

I see these marked differences as stemming from five basic perspectives:

- Both Dol-po-pa and Tsong-kha-pa agree that there is totally non-dual non-conceptual realization of the ultimate, in which from the viewpoint of experience wisdom and emptiness are undifferentiable. Dol-po-pa takes this to mean that reality and pristine wisdom are identical and bases his system on this identity, resulting in such tenets as holding that wisdom is permanent. Tsong-kha-pa, on the other hand, does not build his system stemming from this experience, although it is one of its aims; rather, he conceptually separates wisdom and emptiness, allowing pristine wisdom to be impermanent, though continuous at Buddhahood.
- Both agree that ordinary phenomena do not appear to a wisdom of meditative equipoise realizing the ultimate, and both agree that such phenomena do not exist in the mode of subsistence or as their own mode of subsistence. From this viewpoint Dol-po-pa posits conventional phenomena as self-empty, that is, empty of

themselves, whereas Tsong-kha-pa considers this an over-extension of the import of profound meditative equipoise.

- Both agree that a yogi's perspective is crucially important. Dol-po-pa makes this the center of his presentation of even ordinary phenomena, whereas Tsong-kha-pa argues that a yogi's perspective wreaks havoc with a presentation of the world and centers his presentation of ordinary phenomena around ordinary perception, even though he relegates ordinary phenomena to a realm of coarse conventions. He considers a yogi's perspective to be an exception, whereas for Dol-po-pa an experienced and highly developed yogi's perspective is the norm. When their respective systems work well with certain trainees, Dol-po-pa's presentation pulls his followers into the higher level, whereas Tsong-kha-pa's presentation fits ordinary perception and provides a way pushing his followers toward the higher state. (When their systems do not work well for certain practitioners, Dol-po-pa's presentation seems too other-worldly, beyond reach, whereas Tsong-kha-pa's seems too this-worldly. Both of these are cases of mistaking the intention of the respective systems.)
- Both agree that conventional phenomena are posited by mistaken consciousness. Dol-po-pa holds that these consciousnesses are just mistaken, whereas Tsong-kha-pa posits that a consciousness mistaken with respect to its appearing object can be valid with respect to its object of operation. Taken to their respective extreme, Dol-po-pa's emphasis on the mistakenness of ordinary consciousness seems to leave no room for any sort of valid progression of thought, possibly resulting in a quandary of how to posit spiritual progress, whereas Tsong-kha-pa's emphasis on the validity of a great deal of ordinary thought might seem to sanctify the ordinary outlook, leading to mistakenly undermining the need for spiritual progress.
- Both agree that a Buddha is omniscient and explicitly knows the ultimate. Dol-po-pa holds that a Buddha knows ordinary phenomena only implicitly in that through explicitly knowing the ultimate a Buddha implicitly knows that ordinary phenomena do not exist. Tsong-kha-pa holds that a Buddha also knows ordinary phenomena explicitly, but relegates this knowledge to occurring by way of such phenomena appearing to sentient beings, not from the Buddha's own perspective. Dol-po-pa's opinion might seem to undercut his own claim that a Buddha brings about immeasurable benefit for sentient beings, whereas Tsong-kha-pa's opinion might seem to devalue his own claims of the validity of most ordinary perceptions,

since Buddhas do not perceive ordinary phenomena from their own perspective.
- Both agree that spiritual progress is wrought through intense effort at merit and wisdom.

One root difference

It seems to me that the fundamental distinction is that Dol-po-pa holds that whatever is explicitly realized by pristine wisdom must be ultimately established,[a] whereas Tsong-kha-pa holds that although the ultimate is realized by pristine wisdom, it is not ultimately established. Tsong-kha-pa is able to do this by making a distinction between being realized (or found) by a rational consciousness (*rigs shes kyis rtogs sam rnyed pa*) and being able to bear analysis by a rational consciousness (*rigs shes kyis dpyad bzod du grub pa*), whereas Dol-po-pa does not. They agree that if something is able to bear analysis by a rational consciousness, it must be ultimately existent, and thus Dol-po-pa asserts that the ultimate is ultimately existent, but Tsong-kha-pa does not.

Dol-po-pa holds that the ultimate can bear analysis by the reasoning of dependent-arising simply because the ultimate is not a dependent-arising, a category which he limits to the impermanent and conventional. Also, he holds that the ultimate can bear analysis by reasoning into whether it is one or many because the ultimate is partless and thus one.

By extending the scope of ultimate existence to whatever a Buddha's pristine wisdom explicitly realizes, Dol-po-pa asserts that ultimate qualities of body, speech, and mind must also be ultimately established and permanent. This, in turn, requires that ordinary body, speech, and mind and so forth cannot appear to an omniscient mind, which then must know them only implicitly, for otherwise the ordinary would be ultimately established and permanent and hence not subject to removal. Correspondingly, once ultimate qualities of body, speech, and mind are permanent, they must pre-exist in the continuums of sentient beings, a position requiring that the matrix-of-One-Gone-Thus is endowed with ultimate qualities of body, speech, and mind and is not just the emptiness of the mind in the continuum of a defiled mind, as it is for Tsong-kha-pa.

[a] Tsong-kha-pa (*Illumination,* 123) accurately describes Dol-po-pa's stance as "the proposition that if there is anything found by uncontaminated meditative equipoise, it is truly established." See also *Illumination,* 194, and Nga-wang-pel-den's summation of other scholars' reactions to the same issue in the accompanying footnote, which is drawn from Hopkins, *Maps of the Profound,* 745, where there is more context.

For the latter, the ultimate is a dependent-arising and has parts, due to which it cannot bear analysis by a rational consciousness and hence is not ultimately established. Also, Tsong-kha-pa makes distinctions with regard to how an omniscient mind knows the ultimate and the conventional, such that the conventional can manifestly appear to an omniscient mind and all phenomena can be explicitly realized.

Both systems are illustrations of the magnificent flowering of Buddhist thought in Tibet, where many savants presented overarching perspectives incorporating not just a few texts but the entire range of major Indian expositions.

Appendix: Mode of Analysis of Grossness/Peacefulness

From Gedün Lodrö, *Calm Abiding and Special Insight*, trans. and ed. by Jeffrey Hopkins (Ithaca, N.Y.: Snow Lion Publications, 1998), 260-267.

The lower level, such as the Desire Realm, is seen as faulty or disadvantageous, and the upper, such as the First Concentration, as advantageous.[a] Many different faults are perceived with regard to the Desire Realm. Asaṅga's *Grounds of Hearers,* however, speaks mainly of five faults related to the Desire Realm.

The Five Faults Related to the Desire Realm[b]

First fault
- *a.* Desire Realm beings are of little import.[c]
- *b.* They have many sufferings.[d]
- *c.* They have many faulty objects of observation.[e]

Second fault
- *a.* When one depends on phenomena of the Desire Realm, one does not experience auspiciousness.[f]
- *b.* When one depends on phenomena of the Desire Realm, one does not know satisfaction.[g]
  - (1) not knowing satisfaction [h]
  - (2) having great desire [i]
- *c.* With respect to Desire Realm phenomena, there is no end that satisfies the heart.[j]

Third fault
- *a.* Excellent ones,[k]

[a] See also the description of these in Lati Rinbochay, Denma Lochö Rinbochay, Leah Zahler, and Jeffrey Hopkins, *Meditative States in Tibetan Buddhism: The Concentrations and Formless Absorptions* (London: Wisdom Publications, 1983), 93-96.
[b] *'dod pa la brten pa'i nye dmigs lnga.*
[c] *'dod pa rnams ni gnog chung ba.*
[d] *sdug bsngal mang ba.*
[e] *nyes dmigs mang ba.*
[f] *'dod pa rnams la brten pa na ngoms mi myong.*
[g] *'dod pa rnams la chog mi shes.*
[h] *chog mi shes.*
[i] *'dod chen can.*
[j] *'dod pa rnams la snying tshim pa'i mtha' med pa.*
[k] *dam pa rnams.*

b. those who have become elevated,[a] and

c. excellent beings deride the Desire Realm on many counts.[b]

Fourth fault

a. When one depends on [phenomena of] the Desire Realm, one will accumulate [one of the nine] thorough enwrapments.[c]

Fifth fault

a. When one depends on [phenomena of] the Desire Realm, there is not the least sinful non-virtue that one will not do.[d]

The first fault has three categories. The first is that beings of the Desire Realm are of little import. Even if they achieve some virtue, it brings little profit. This is because the mental basis is a mind of the Desire Realm. Until one arrives at a high Bodhisattva ground, one cannot use a mind of the Desire Realm with great profit.

The second category is that there are many sufferings. This means that no matter what conditions or circumstances one meets with, they mostly generate suffering. It is obvious that the feeling of pain is a case of suffering; feelings of pleasure and neutral feelings also induce suffering.

The third category means that there are many objects of observation which generate faulty states—that is, there are many objects capable of generating afflictive emotions, such as desire and hatred, in the perceiver. Usually, in texts, the word *nyes dmigs*,[e] which we often translate merely as "fault," applies to the afflictive emotions themselves. Here, however, the object of observation is designated with the name of the afflictive emotion. Usually, *nyes dmigs* refers to the internal, but here it refers to external objects of observation that serve as causes for generating afflictive emotions.

The second of the five faults related to the Desire Realm also has three categories. The first is that when one depends on phenomena of the Desire Realm—virtuous, non-virtuous, or neutral—one does not experience auspiciousness. There is no discussion of the first category in either Indian or Tibetan commentaries; however, there are phrases in other books in dependence on which it can be understood. The word *ngoms* is interpreted to mean *gya noms pa*, "auspiciousness,"[f] although it usually means "satisfaction." For instance, when one speaks of eating

[a] *yang dag par song ba.*

[b] *skyes bu dam pa rnams kyis rnam grangs du ma'i sgo nas smad pa.*

[c] *'dod pa rnams la brten pa na kun tu sbyor ba rnams nye bar gsog par 'gyur ba.*

[d] *'dod pa la brten pa na sdig pa mi dge ba mi bya ba cung zad kyang med pa.*

[e] *ādīnava.*

[f] *praṇīta.*

ordinary gross foods, one does not include the experiencing of the food of meditative stabilization, an experience of auspiciousness that is more elevated than just nourishing the body. Probably, the food of meditative stabilization is being contrasted to the gross food of the Desire Realm.

The second category is that when one depends on phenomena of the Desire Realm one does not know satisfaction. No matter what one gets in terms of place, food, clothing, and so forth, more attachment is generated; something further is desired. This second category is divided into two parts: itself—that is, not knowing satisfaction—and another, having great desire. This latter means that within knowing you cannot get something, you are impelled to keep thinking about getting it. This fact is used as a reason for stopping afflictive emotions—because there is no end to them. The occurrence of this condition serves as a proof that they will increase limitlessly.

The third category is that with respect to Desire Realm phenomena there is no end that satisfies the heart. All three of these are basically similar; however, the afflictive emotions of sentient beings have many different forms. Even one afflictive emotion can occur in many different types. What is indicated here is that there would be no end which would fulfill the heart. I think there is probably a difference in strength among these three, the third being the worst. The first, that there is no auspiciousness in the Desire Realm, is general. The third, although much the same as the second, is a little stronger.

The third of the five faults of the Desire Realm, that great beings have derided the Desire Realm on many counts, also has three categories corresponding to three types of great beings who have done so. There are no clear Tibetan commentaries on this; thus, we cannot come to a very definite decision on these three categories.

In the first category, the word *dam pa*, which we generally translate as "excellent," can be posited in two ways, one in terms of good qualities and the other in terms of persons. For instance, Chandrakīrti's *Supplement to (Nāgārjuna's) "Treatise on the Middle"*[a] refers to engagement in the ten excellent paths of action, which are good qualities. Persons who have all ten of these excellent paths of action are known as excellent persons. Thus, the first of the three categories related to the third fault of the Desire Realm concerns these excellent ones.

The second category, people who have become elevated, refers to people up to the point of being just about to attain a path. In the

[a] *dbu ma la 'jug pa, madhyamkāvatāra;* P5261, P5262, vol. 98.

Sitātapatrā Tantra,[a] the term *yang dag par song ba* is applied to a person who is about to enter a path but has not yet done so; however, there are also cases in which this term refers to people on the paths of accumulation and preparation. Thus, this category is more elevated than the first one.

The last category is an excellent being. This is almost the same as a valid person.[b] Such a person is one who, at the very least, has directly realized the four truths. Therefore, these excellent beings would be posited in terms of a Superior path, from the path of seeing on up. These three categories of people deride the Desire Realm. The latter part of the phrase, "deride on many counts,"[c] goes with all three categories.

Another text refers to seven transmigrators[d] who are excellent beings. They are all identified as Never Returners—seven types of Never Returners who will take rebirth in the Form Realm, become enlightened in the intermediate state, and so forth. These are special types of excellent beings, not the general type to which the above term refers. It is clear in sūtra that an excellent being is one who has attained the path of seeing, and so forth.

The fourth fault of the Desire Realm is that, when one depends on the phenomena of the Desire Realm, one will accumulate one of the nine thorough enwrapments.[e]

The Nine Thorough Enwrapments

1 thorough enwrapment of desire[f]
2 thorough enwrapment of anger[g]
3 thorough enwrapment of pride[h]
4 thorough enwrapment of doubt[i]
5 thorough enwrapment of ignorance[j]
6 thorough enwrapment of [bad] view:[k] view of the transitory collec-

[a] *gdugs dkar.*
[b] *tshad ma'i skyes bu.*
[c] *rnam grangs du ma'i sgo nas smad pa.*
[d] *'gro ba, gati.*
[e] *kun tu sbyor ba, saṃyojana.*
[f] *'dod chags kyi kun sbyor, *rāgasaṃyojana.*
[g] *khong khro'i kun sbyor, *pratighasaṃyojana.*
[h] *nga rgyal gyi kun sbyor, *mānasaṃyojana.*
[i] *the tshom gyi kun sbyor, *vicikitsāsaṃyojana.*
[j] *ma rig pa'i kun sbyor, *avidyāsaṃyojana.*
[k] *lta ba'i kun sbyor, *dṛṣṭisaṃyojana.*

tion [as real I and mine],[a] view holding to an extreme,[b] and wrong view[c]

7 thorough enwrapment of misapprehension of the supreme:[d] conception of a [bad] view as supreme[e] and conception of ethics and systems of behavior as supreme[f]

8 thorough enwrapment of jealousy[g]

9 thorough enwrapment of miserliness[h]

The eighth and ninth, jealousy and miserliness, are chosen out of the long list of twenty secondary afflictive emotions because they are the two chief factors opposing altruism; helping others may be damaged through either jealousy or miserliness. Miserliness here does not refer only to resources; it means not using anything one might have—education, good qualities, and so forth—to help others.

The five [bad] views are separated into two groups as divisions of the sixth and seventh thorough enwrapments because the first three, the divisions of thorough enwrapments of [bad] views, are like objects and the divisions of thorough enwrapment of misapprehension of the supreme are like subjects, or apprehenders. The first three [bad] views are the objects of the two consciousnesses that misapprehend the supreme. It is these three that are viewed as marvelous.

What distinguishes the various misconceptions of being supreme? The misconception of [bad] views as supreme involves only the conceptions of the above three [bad] views as supreme; the conception of these as highly auspicious is the misconception that one has completely abandoned all afflictive emotions and that they will not return again.

How could one have this view with respect to ethics? The term "ethics" or "mode of conduct" here does not refer only to our usual modes of behavior. It refers to the abandonment of the afflictive emotions and not only to the abandonment of bad activities such as killing. If one conceived that the abandonment of the ten non-virtues was highly auspicious in the sense of considering it to be a complete abandonment of cyclic existence, then that would be a case of conceiving ethics and modes of conduct to be supreme, or better than they

[a] *'jig tshogs la lta ba, satkāyadṛṣṭi.*

[b] *mthar 'dzing pa'i lta ba, antagrāhadṛṣṭi.*

[c] *log lta, mithyādṛṣṭi.*

[d] *lta ba mchog 'dzin gyi kun sbyor, *dṛṣṭiparāmarśasaṃyojana.*

[e] *lta ba mchog 'dzin, dṛṣṭiparāmarśa.*

[f] *tshul khrims dang brdul zhugs mchog 'dzin, śīlavrataparāmarśa.*

[g] *phrag dog gi kun sbyor, *irṣyāsaṃyojana.*

[h] *ser sna'i kun sbyor, *mātsaryasaṃyojana.*

actually are. This thorough enwrapment could exist only up to the path of seeing because someone who has attained a Superior path actually has something that is highly auspicious inasmuch as some afflictive emotions have been utterly abandoned. Before that, on the paths of accumulation and preparation, if one conceived one's attainments as some type of final abandonment, they would actually not be as auspicious as one conceived them to be.

The illustrations often used in texts for this are, for instance, the asceticisms of non-Buddhists which are mistakenly conceived to be sufficient cause for attaining liberation. Some non-Buddhists believe that, as a result of their engaging in severe asceticism, the body dries up and becomes thin, and one's sins diminish; thus, severe asceticism is included in this category. Buddhists might also have such a misapprehension of the supreme, however, if, for example, they felt that abandonment of the ten non-virtues was sufficient for liberation. This would also be a case of exaggerating their value. Some people say that a person who conceives the supreme mistakenly must be a non-Buddhist, but this is not the case. The ethics which are the object of this view do not necessarily have to be bad. They may be bad only in the sense that they are not highly auspicious and one is wrongly satisfied with them alone.

An illustration of a bad mode of conduct would be severe asceticism conceived as highly auspicious. A case of misconceiving ethics as highly auspicious would be to separate temporarily from attachment to afflictive emotions and to consider this as liberation. This does not mean whoever has any of these qualities is, as in the illustrations, a non-Buddhist.

The fifth fault of the Desire Realm is that, when one depends on phenomena of the Desire Realm, there is not the least sinful non-virtue that one would not do. Those who have attained actual concentrations and actual formless absorptions are able to take good measure of themselves, recognizing when their afflictive emotions are excessive. However, when one is engaged in the afflictive emotions of the Desire Realm, it is difficult to take one's own measure independently and to know what the limit should be.

Asaṅga's *Grounds of Hearers* makes many references to thorough entanglements,[a] such as the eight thorough entanglements:

1 non-shame[b]
2 non-embarrassment[a]

[a] *kun dkris, paryavasthāna.*
[b] *ngo tsha med pa, āhrīkya.*

3 excitement[b]
4 contrition[c]
5 sleep[d]
6 lethargy[e]
7 jealousy[f]
8 miserliness[g]

The first, non-shame, means not avoiding ill deeds from one's own point of view—one's own estimation of what one should be doing. It would be, for instance, not thinking about the future and not reflecting on what will happen if one engages in a certain ill deed. Non-embarrassment is a case of not avoiding ill deeds from the viewpoint of considering others. It means that no matter what one does, there is no concern for others' estimation of oneself. The other thorough entanglements have already been explained.

These eight thorough entanglements are factors opposing the three trainings.[h] The first two are factors opposing proper ethics.[i] Excitement and contrition are factors opposing wisdom; sleep and lethargy are factors opposing meditative stabilization. Jealousy and miserliness are factors opposing all three trainings—ethics, wisdom, and meditative stabilization. This is because they are factors opposing altruism. Therefore, among these eight, the last two—jealousy and miserliness—are considered in the Mahāyāna to be very strong and very bad...The sleep and contrition included within the eight thorough entanglements are only the non-virtuous forms, not the general ones. "Sleep" here is not merely sleepiness, but it could not include deep sleep. It is by way of motivation that sleep becomes non-virtuous.

[a] *khrel med, anapatrāpya.*
[b] *rgod pa, auddhatya.*
[c] *'gyod pa, kaukṛtya.*
[d] *gnyid, middha.*
[e] *rmug pa, styāna.*
[f] *phrag dog, irṣyā.*
[g] *ser sna, mātsarya.*
[h] *bslab pa, śikṣā.*
[i] *tshul krims, śīla.*

List of Abbreviations

"Dharma" refers to the *sde dge* edition of the Tibetan canon published by Dharma Press: the *Nying-ma Edition of the sDe-dge bKa'-'gyur and bsTan-'gyur* (Oakland, Calif.: Dharma, 1980).

"Golden Reprint" refers to the *gser bris bstan 'gyur* (Sichuan, China: krung go'i mtho rim nang bstan slob gling gi bod brgyud nang bstan zhib 'jug khang, 1989).

"*Illumination*" refers to the translation in this book of Tsong-kha-pa's *Illumination of the Thought: Extensive Explanation of (Chandrakīrti's) "Supplement to (Nāgārjuna's) 'Treatise on the Middle'"*

"*Insight*" refers to the translation in this book of the special insight section of Tsong-kha-pa's *Medium-Length Exposition of the Stages of the Path to Enlightenment*

"Karmapa *sde dge*" refers to the *sde dge mtshal par bka' 'gyur: A Facsimile Edition of the 18th Century Redaction of Si tu chos kyi 'byung gnas Prepared under the Direction of H.H. the 16th rGyal dbang Karma pa* (Delhi: Delhi Karmapae Chodhey Gyalwae Sungrab Partun Khang, 1977).

"Khangkar and Yorihito" refers to Tsultrim Kelsang Khangkar and Takada Yorihito, *A Study of Tsong khapa's Mādhyamika Philosophy 1: Annotated Japanese translation of the Vipaśyanā Section of Medium Exposition of the Stages of the Path (Lam rim).* Tsong kha pa chuugan tetsugaku no kenkyuu 1, Bodaidousidairon chuuhen, kan no shou: wayaku, Tsultrim Kelsang Khangkar and Takada Yorihito, Kyoto: Buneido, 1996.

"P," standing for "Peking edition," refers to the *Tibetan Tripiṭaka* (Tokyo-Kyoto: Tibetan Tripiṭaka Research Foundation, 1955-1962).

"Toh." refers to the *Complete Catalogue of the Tibetan Buddhist Canons,* edited by Prof. Hukuji Ui (Sendai, Japan: Tohoku University, 1934), and *A Catalogue of the Tohuku University Collection of Tibetan Works on Buddhism,* edited by Prof. Yensho Kanakura (Sendai, Japan: Tohoku University, 1953).

"Tokyo *sde dge*" refers to the *sDe dge Tibetan Tripiṭaka—bsTan ḥgyur preserved at the Faculty of Letters, University of Tokyo,* edited by Z. Yamaguchi, et al. (Tokyo: Tokyo University Press, 1977-1984).

Bibliography

Sūtras and tantras are listed alphabetically by English title in the first section; the terms "glorious" and "supreme" at the beginning of titles are often dropped in the Bibliography. Indian and Tibetan treatises are listed alphabetically by author in the second section; other works are listed alphabetically by author in the third section. Works mentioned in the first or second sections are not repeated in the third section.

1. Sūtras and Tantras

Aṅgulimāla Sūtra
aṅgulimālīyasūtra
sor mo'i phreng ba la phan pa'i mdo
P879, vol. 34
English translation of chap. 1: Nathan S. Cutler. *The Sutra of Sor-mo'i Phreng-ba (from the Lhasa, Peking, and Derge editions of the bKa'-'gyur).* MA thesis, Indiana University, 1981.

Brief Explication of Initiations
sekhoddeśa
dbang mdor bstan
P3, vol. 1
Sanskrit and Tibetan: Giacomella Orofino. *Sekoddeśa: A Critical Edition of the Tibetan Translations.* Rome: Istituto Italiano per il Medio ed Estremo Oriente, 1994. The Sanskrit is found in the appendix, edited by Raniero Gnoli.
Commentary: Mario E. Carelli, ed., *Sekoddeśaṭīkā of Nāḍapāda (Nāropā) being a commentary of the Sekoddeśa section of the Kālacakra tantra.* Baroda: Oriental Institute, 1941. Italian translation: Raniero Gnoli and Giacomella Orofino. *Nāropā. L'iniziazione, Traduzione e commento della Sekoddeśaṭīkā di Nāropā.* Milano: Adelphi, 1994.

Buddhāvataṃsaka Sūtra
buddhāvataṃsakanāma-mahāvaipulyasūtra
sangs rgyas phal po che zhes bya ba shin tu rgyas pa chen po'i mdo
P761, vols. 25-26.

Cloud of Jewels Sūtra
ratnameghasūtra
dkon mchog spring gyi mdo
P879, vol. 35; Toh. 231, vol. wa

Descent into Laṅkā Sūtra
laṅkāvatārasūtra
lang kar gshegs pa'i mdo
P775, vol. 29; Toh. 107, vol. ca
Sanskrit: Bunyiu Nanjio. *Bibl. Otaniensis,* vol. 1. Kyoto: Otani University Press, 1923. Also: P. L. Vaidya. *Saddharmalaṅkāvatārasūtram.* Buddhist Sanskrit Texts, 3. Darbhanga, India: Mithila Institute, 1963.
English translation: D. T. Suzuki. *The Lankavatara Sutra.* London: Routledge and Kegan Paul, 1932.

Great Drum Sūtra
mahābherīharakaparivarta
rnga bo che chen po'i mdo
P888, vol. 35

Guhyasamāja Tantra (a root Highest Yoga Tantra)
sarvatathāgatakāyavākcittarahasyaguhyasamājanāmamahākalparāja
de bzhin gshegs pa thams cad kyi sku gsung thugs kyi gsang chen gsang ba 'dus pa zhes bya ba brtag pa'i rgyal po chen po
P81, vol. 3; Toh. 442, vol. ca; Dharma vol. 29

Heart Sūtra / Heart of Wisdom Sūtra
prajñāhṛdaya / bhagavatīprajñāpāramitāhṛdayasūtra
shes rab snying po / bcom ldan 'das ma shes rab kyi pha rol tu phyin pa'i snying po'i mdo
P160, vol. 6; Toh. 21, vol. ka (*shes rab sna tshogs*)
Sanskrit: in E. Conze. *Thirty Years of Buddhist Studies*, 148-153. Oxford: Cassirer, 1967.
English translation: E. Conze. *Buddhist Texts Through the Ages*, 152-153. rpt. New York: Harper, 1964. Also in Geshe Rabten. *Echoes of Voidness*, 18-19. Stephen Batchelor, ed. and trans. London: Wisdom Publications, 1983. English translation with explanation and Sanskrit text: E. Conze. *Buddhist Wisdom Books*, 77-107. London: George Allen & Unwin, 1958.

Introduction to the Two Truths Sūtra
satyakaparivarta / āryabodhisattvagocara-upāyaviṣaya-vikurvāṇa-nirdeśa-nāma mahāyānasūtra
bden pa gnyis la 'jug pa / bden pa po'i le'u / 'phags pa byang chub sems dpa'i spyod yul gyi thabs kyi yul la rnam par 'phrul pa bstan pa zhes bya ba theg pa chen po'i mdo
P813, vol. 32
English translation: Lozang Jamspal. *The Range of the Bodhisattva: A Study of an early Mahāyānasūtra, "Āryasatyakaparivarta," Discourse of Truth Teller.* Ph.D. diss, Columbia University, 1991.

Kāshyapa Chapter Sūtra
kāśyapaparivartasūtra
'od srung gi le'u'i mdo
P760.43, vol. 24; Toh. 87, vol. cha
Sanskrit: Alexander von Staël-Holstein. *Kāçyapaparivarta: A Mahāyanasūtra of the Ratnakūṭa Class.* Shanghai: Commercial Press, 1926; reprint, Tokyo: Meicho-fukyū-kai, 1977.
English translation: Garma C. C. Chang, ed. *A Treasury of Mahāyāna Sūtras.* University Park: Pennsylvania State University Press, 1983.

King of Meditative Stabilizations Sūtra
samādhirājasūtra sarvadharmasvabhāvasamatāvipañcatasamādhirājasūtra
ting nge 'dzin rgyal po'i mdo / chos thams cad kyi rang bzhin mnyam pa nyid rnam par spros pa ting nge 'dzin gyi rgyal po'i mdo
P795, vols. 31-32; Toh. 127, vol. da; Dharma, vol. 20
Sanskrit: P. L. Vaidya. *Samādhirājasūtram.* Buddhist Sanskrit Texts, 2. Darbhanga, India: Mithila Institute, 1961.
Sanskrit, Tibetan, Chinese and English translation (of chap. 9): Cristoph Cüppers. *The IXth Chapter of the Samādhirājasūtra: A Text-critical Contribution to the Study of Mahāyāna Sūtras.* Alt- und Neu-Indische Studien, 41. Stuttgart: Franz Steiner Verlag, 1990.
Partial English translation (of chaps. 8, 19, and 22): K. Regamey. *Three Chapters from the Samādhirājasūtra.* Warsaw: Publications of the Oriental Commission, 1938.
Partial English translation (of chaps. 1-4): Translation Committee of the University of Michigan's Collegiate Institute for the Study of Buddhist Literature. "The Sūtra of the *King of Samādhis*: Chapters I-IV" in *Studies in the Literature of the Great Vehicle.* Michigan Studies in Buddhist Literature No. 1, edited by Luis O. Gómez and Jonathan A. Silk, 1-88. Ann Arbor: Collegiate Institute for the Study of Buddhist Literature and Center for South and Southeast Asian Studies, University of Michigan, 1989.

Mahāparinirvāṇa Sūtra
mahāparinirvāṇasūtra
yongs su mya ngan las 'das pa chen po'i mdo
P787-789, vols. 30-31

English translation: K. Yamamoto. *The Mahayana Mahaparinirvana-Sutra.* Ube City, Japan: Karin-bunko, 1974.

Meeting of Father and Son Sūtra
pitāputrasamāgamasūtra
yab dang sras mjal ba'i mdo
P760.16, vol. 23; Toh. 60, vol. nga (*dkon brtsegs*)

Non-Conceptual Retention Sūtra
avikalpapraveśanāmadhāraṇī
rnam par mi rtog par 'jug pa'i gsungs
Toh. 142, vol. pa

Perfection of Wisdom Sūtra in One Hundred Thousand Stanzas
śatasāhasrikāprajñāpāramitā
shes rab kyi pha rol tu phyin pa stong phrag brgya pa
P730, vols. 12-18
Condensed English translation: Edward Conze. *The Large Sūtra on Perfect Wisdom.* Berkeley: University of California Press, 1975

Questions of Anavatapta, the King of Nāgas, Sūtra
anavataptanāgarājaparipṛcchāsūtra
klu'i rgyal po ma dros pas zhus pa'i mdo
P823, vol. 33; Toh. 156, vol. pha

Questions of Sāgaramati Sūtra
sāgaramatiparipṛcchāsūtra
blo gros rgya mtshos zhus pa'i mdo
P819, vol. 33; Toh. 152, vol. pha

Questions of Upāli Sūtra
upāliparipṛcchā
nye bar 'khor gyis zhus pa
Toh. 68, vol. ca (*dkon brtsegs*); Dharma, vol. 16
Tibetan and Chinese texts and Sanskrit fragments: Pierre Python. *Vinaya-Viniścaya-Upāli-Paripṛcchā.* Collection Jean Przyluski, Tome V. Paris: Adrien-Maisonneuve, 1973.

Śrīmālādevī Sūtra
śrīmālādevīsiṃhanādasūtra
lha mo dpal 'phreng gi seng ge'i sgra'i mdo
P760.48, vol. 24
English translation: Alex Wayman and Hideko Wayman. *The Lion's Roar of Queen Śrīmālā: A Buddhist Scripture on the Tathāgatagarbha Theory.* New York: Columbia University Press, 1974.

Superior Sūtra of the Meditative Stabilization Definitely Revealing Suchness
tattvanirdeśasamādhi
de kho na nyid nges par bstan pa'i ting nge 'dzin

Sūtra on the Secrecies of the One-Gone-Thus
tathāgatācintyaguhyanirdeśasūtra
de bzhin gshegs pa'i gsang ba bsam gyis mi khyab pa bstan pa'i mdo
Toh. 47, vol. ka (*dkon brtsegs*)

Sūtra on the Ten Grounds
daśabhūmikasūtra
mdo sde sa bcu pa
P761.31, vol. 25
Sanskrit: *Daśabhūmikasūtram.* P. L. Vaidya, ed. Buddhist Sanskrit Texts 7. Darbhanga: Mithila Institute, 1967.
English translation: M. Honda. "An Annotated Translation of the 'Daśabhūmika.'" In D. Sinor, ed, *Studies in South, East and Central Asia,* Śatapitaka Series 74. New Delhi: International Academy of Indian Culture, 1968, 115-276.

Sūtra Unraveling the Thought
saṃdhinirmocanasūtra
dgongs pa nges par 'grel pa'i mdo
P774, vol. 29; Toh. 106, vol. ca; Dharma, vol. 18
Tibetan text and French translation: Étienne Lamotte. *Saṃdhinirmocanasūtra: L'Explication des mystères*. Louvain: Université de Louvain, 1935.
English translation: John C. Powers. *Wisdom of Buddha: Saṃdhinirmocana Sūtra*. Berkeley, Calif.: Dharma, 1995. Also: Thomas Cleary. *Buddhist Yoga: A Comprehensive Course*. Boston: Shambhala, 1995.

Verse Summary of the Perfection of Wisdom
prajñāpāramitāsañcayagāthā
shes rab kyi pha rol tu phyin pa sdud pa tshigs su bcad pa
P735, vol. 21; Toh. 13, vol. ka (*shes rab sna tshogs*)
Sanskrit and Tibetan: Akira Yuyama. *Prajñā-pāramitā-ratna-guṇa-saṃcaya-gāthā (Sanskrit Recension A): Edited with an Introduction, Bibliographical Notes and a Tibetan Version from Tunhuang*. London: Cambridge University Press, 1976.
Sanskrit: E. E. Obermiller. *Prajñāpāramitā-ratnaguṇa-sañcayagāthā*. Osnabrück, Germany: Biblio Verlag, 1970. Also: P. L. Vaidya. *Mahāyāna-sūtra-saṃgraha*. Part I. Buddhist Sanskrit Texts, 17. Darbhanga, India: Mithila Institute, 1961.
English translation: Edward Conze. *The Perfection of Wisdom in Eight Thousand Lines & Its Verse Summary*. Bolinas, Calif.: Four Seasons Foundation, 1973.

2. Other Sanskrit and Tibetan Works

Ajitamitra
Commentary on [Nāgārjuna's] Precious Garland
ratnāvalīṭīkā
rin po che'i phreng ba'i 'grel ba
P5659, vol. 129

Āryadeva (*'phags pa lha*, second to third century C.E.)
Four Hundred / Treatise of Four Hundred Stanzas
catuḥśatakaśāstrakārikā
bstan bcos bzhi brgya pa zhes bya ba'i tshig le'ur byas pa
P5246, vol. 95; Toh. 3846, vol. tsha
Edited Tibetan and Sanskrit fragments along with English translation: Karen Lang. *Āryadeva's Catuḥśataka: On the Bodhisattva's Cultivation of Merit and Knowledge*. Indiske Studier, 7. Copenhagen: Akademisk Forlag, 1986.
English translation: Geshe Sonam Rinchen and Ruth Sonam. *Yogic Deeds of Bodhisattvas: Gyeltsap on Āryadeva's Four Hundred*. Ithaca, N.Y.: Snow Lion Publications, 1994.
Italian translation of the last half from the Chinese: Giuseppe Tucci. "Study Mahāyānici: La versione cinese del Catuḥśataka di Āryadeva, confronta col testo sanscrito e la traduzione tibetana." *Rivista degli Studi Orientali* 10 (1925): 521-567.
Lamp Compendium for Practice
caryāmelāpakapradīpa
spyod bsdus sgron ma
P2668, vol. 61

Asaṅga (*thogs med*, fourth century)
Grounds of Bodhisattvas
bodhisattvabhūmi
byang chub sems pa'i sa
P5538, vol. 110; Toh. 4037, vol. dzi
Sanskrit: Unrai Wogihara. *Bodhisattvabhūmi: A Statement of the Whole Course of the Bodhisattva*

(Being the Fifteenth Section of Yogācārabhūmi). Leipzig: 1908; Tokyo: Seigo Kenyūkai, 1930-1936. Also: Nalinaksha Dutt. *Bodhisattvabhumi (Being the XVth Section of Asangapada's Yogacarabhumi).* Tibetan Sanskrit Works Series, 7. Patna, India: K. P. Jayaswal Research Institute, 1966.

English translation of the Chapter on Suchness, the fourth chapter of Part I which is the fifteenth volume of the Grounds of Yogic Practice: Janice D. Willis. *On Knowing Reality.* New York: Columbia University Press, 1979; reprint, Delhi: Motilal Banarsidass, 1979.

Grounds of Hearers

śrāvakabhūmi

nyan sa

P5537, vol. 110; Toh. 4036, vol. dzi

Sanskrit: Karunesha Shukla. *Śrāvakabhūmi.* Tibetan Sanskrit Works Series, 14. Patna, India: K. P. Jayaswal Research Institute, 1973.

Atisha (982-1054)

Introduction to the Two Truths

satyadvayāvatāra

bden pa gnyis la 'jug pa

P5298, vol. 101; P5380, vol. 103; Toh. 3902, vol. a

Edited Tibetan and English translation: Christian Lindtner. "Atiśa's Introduction to the Two Truths, and Its Sources." *Journal of Indian Philosophy* 9 (1981): 161-214.

Edited Tibetan and English translation: Richard Sherburne. *The Complete Works of Atīśa.* New Delhi: Aditya Prakashan, 2000

Bhāvaviveka (*legs ldan 'byed,* c. 500-570?)

Blaze of Reasoning / Commentary on the "Heart of the Middle Way": Blaze of Reasoning

madhyamakahṛdayavṛttitarkajvālā

dbu ma'i snying po'i 'grel pa rtog ge 'bar ba

P5256, vol. 96; Toh. 3856, vol. dza

Partial English translation (chap. 3, 1-136): Shotaro Iida. *Reason and Emptiness.* Tokyo: Hokuseido, 1980.

Heart of the Middle Way

madhyamakahṛdayakārikā

dbu ma'i snying po'i tshig le'ur byas pa

P5255, vol. 96; Toh. 3855, vol. dza

Partial English translation (chap. 3. 1-136): Shōtarō Iida. *Reason and Emptiness.* Tokyo: Hokuseido, 1980.

Partial Sanskrit and Tibetan edition (chaps. 1-3): Annette L. Heitmann. *Textkritischer Beitrag zu Bhavyas Madhyamakahṛdayakārikā Kapitel 1-3.* Copenhagen: Videnskabsbutikkens Forlag, Kobenhavns Universitet, 1998.

Buddhapālita (*sangs rgyas bskyangs,* c. 470-540?)

Buddhapālita Commentary on (Nāgārjuna's) "Treatise on the Middle"

buddhapālitamūlamadhyamakavṛtti

dbu ma rtsa ba'i 'grel pa buddha pā li ta

P5254, vol. 95; Toh. 3842, vol. tsha; Tokyo *sde dge* vol. 1

Edited Tibetan (Ch.1-12): Max Walleser. Bibliotheca Buddhica 16. Osnabrück: Biblio Verlag, 1970.

English translation of Ch.1: Judit Fehér. "Buddhapālita's *Mūlamadhyamakavṛtti*—Arrival and Spread of Prāsaṇgika-Mādhyamika Literature in Tibet." In *Tibetan and Buddhist Studies Commemorating the 200th Anniversary of the Birth of Alexander Csoma de Kūros,* vol. 1, edited by Louis Ligeti, 211-240. Budapest: Akadmiai Kiado, 1984.

Tibetan edition and English translation of Ch.18: Christian Lindtner. "Buddhapālita on Emptiness." *Indo-Iranian Journal* 23 (1981): 187-217.

Chandrakīrti (*zla ba grags pa,* seventh century)

[Auto]commentary on the "Supplement to (Nāgārjuna's) 'Treatise on the Middle'"

madhaymakāvatārabhāṣya
dbu ma la 'jug pa'i bshad pa / dbu ma la 'jug pa'i rang 'grel
P5263, vol. 98; Toh. 3862, vol. 'a. Also: Dharmsala, India: Council of Religious and Cultural Affairs, 1968.
Tibetan: Louis de La Vallée Poussin. *Madhyamakāvatāra par Candrakīrti*. Bibliotheca Buddhica 9. Osnabrück, Germany: Biblio Verlag, 1970.
French translation (up to chap. 6, stanza 165): Louis de La Vallée Poussin. *Muséon* 8 (1907): 249-317; *Muséon* 11 (1910): 271-358; *Muséon* 12 (1911): 235-328.
German translation (chap. 6, stanzas 166-226): Helmut Tauscher. *Candrakīrti-Madhyamakāvatāraḥ und Madhyamakāvatārabhāṣyam*. Wiener Studien zur Tibetologie und Buddhismuskunde, 5. Vienna: Arbeitskreis für Tibetische und Buddhistische Studien Universität Wien, 1981.

Clear Words, Commentary on (Nāgārjuna's) "Treatise on the Middle"
mūlamadhyamakavṛttiprasannapadā
dbu ma rtsa ba'i 'grel pa tshig gsal ba
P5260, vol. 98; Toh. 3860, vol. 'a. Also: Dharmsala, India: Tibetan Cultural Printing Press, 1968.
Sanskrit: Louis de La Vallée Poussin. *Mūlamadhyamakakārikās de Nāgārjuna avec la Prasannapadā commentaire de Candrakīrti*. Bibliotheca Buddhica 4. Osnabrück, Germany: Biblio Verlag, 1970. Also, J.W. de Jong. "Text-critical Notes on the Prasannapadā." *Indo-Iranian Journal* 20, nos. 1/2 (1978): 25-59 and nos. 3/4 (1978): 217-252. Also, Sanskrit, Tibetan, and French translation of the *Madhyamakaśāstrastuti* that concludes *Clear Words:* J.W. de Jong. "La Madhyamakaśāstrastuti de Candrakīrti." *Oriens Extremus* 9 (1962): 47-56.
English translation (chaps. 1 and 25): T. Stcherbatsky. *Conception of Buddhist Nirvāṇa, 77-222.* Leningrad: Office of the Academy of Sciences of the USSR, 1927; rev. reprint, Delhi: Motilal Banarsidass, 1978.
English translation (chap. 2): Jeffrey Hopkins. "Analysis of Coming and Going." Dharmsala, India: Library of Tibetan Works and Archives, 1974.
Partial English translation: Mervyn Sprung. *Lucid Exposition of the Middle Way: The Essential Chapters from the Prasannapadā of Candrakīrti translated from the Sanskrit*. London: Routledge, 1979; Boulder: Prajñā Press, 1979.
French translation (chaps. 2-4, 6-9, 11, 23, 24, 26, 28): Jacques May. *Prasannapadā Madhyamakavṛtti, douze chapitres traduits du sanscrit et du tibétain*. Paris: Adrien-Maisonneuve, 1959.
French translation (chaps. 18-22): J. W. de Jong. *Cinq chapitres de la Prasannapadā*. Paris: Geuthner, 1949.
French translation (chap. 17): É. Lamotte. "Le Traité de l'acte de Vasubandhu, Karmasiddhiprakaraṇa." *Mélanges chinois et bouddhiques* 4 (1936): 265-288.
German translation (chaps. 5, 12-26): Stanislaw Schayer. *Ausgewählte Kapitel aus der Prasannapadā*. Krakow: Naktadem Polskiej Akademji Umiejetnosci, 1931.
German translation (chap. 10): Stanislaw Schayer. "Feuer und Brennstoff." *Rocznik Orjentalistyczny* 7 (1931): 26-52.

Commentary on (Āryadeva's) "Four Hundred Stanzas on the Yogic Deeds of Bodhisattvas"
bodhisattvayogacaryācatuḥśatakaṭīkā
byang chub sems dpa'i rnal 'byor spyod pa gzhi brgya pa'i rgya cher 'grel pa
P5266, vol. 98; Toh. 3865, vol. ya; Tokyo *sde dge* vol. 8
Edited Tibetan text and Sanskrit fragments and English translation: Karen Lang. *Āryadeva's Catuḥśataka: On the Bodhisattva's Cultivation of Merit and Knowledge*. Indiske Studier 7. Copenhagen: Akademisk Forlag, 1986. Also: Karen Lang. *Four Illusions: Candrakīrti's Advice to Travelers on the Bodhisattva Path*. New York: Oxford University Press, 2003.
Edited Sanskrit fragments: Haraprasād Shāstri, "Catuḥśataka of Ārya Deva." Memoirs of the Asiatic Society of Bengal, III no. 8 (1914), 449-514. Also (chaps. 8-16): Vidhusekhara Bhattacarya, ed. *The Catuḥśataka of Āryadeva: Sanskrit and Tibetan texts with copious extracts from the commentary of Candrakīrti*, Part II. Calcutta: Visva-Bharati Bookshop, 1931.
Edited Sanskrit fragments and Tibetan: *Sanskrit fragments and Tibetan translation of Candrakīrti's*

Bodhisattvayogacaryācatuḥśatakaṭīkā. Tokyo: 1994.
Commentary on (Nāgārjuna's) "Sixty Stanzas of Reasoning"
yuktiṣaṣṭikāvṛtti
rigs pa drug cu pa'i 'grel pa
P5265, vol. 98; Toh. 3864, vol. ya
Edited Tibetan and French translation: Cristina Anna Scherrer-Schaub. *Yuktiṣaṣṭikāvṛtti. Commentaire à la soixantaine sur le raisonnement ou Du vrai enseignement de la causalité par le Maitre indien Candrakīrti.* Mélanges chinois et bouddhiques 25. Brussels: Institut belge des hautes etudes chinoises, 1991.
Supplement to (Nāgārjuna's) "Treatise on the Middle"
madhyamakāvatāra
dbu ma la 'jug pa
P5261, P5262, vol. 98; Toh. 3861, Toh. 3862, vol. 'a
Tibetan: Louis de La Vallée Poussin. *Madhyamakāvatāra par Candrakīrti.* Bibliotheca Buddhica 9. Osnabrück, Germany: Biblio Verlag, 1970.
English translation: C. W. Huntington, Jr. *The Emptiness of Emptiness: An Introduction to Early Indian Mādhyamika,* 147-195. Honolulu, Hawaii: University of Hawaii Press, 1989.
English translation (chaps. 1-5): Jeffrey Hopkins. *Compassion in Tibetan Buddhism.* London: Rider, 1980; reprint, Ithaca, N.Y.: Snow Lion Publications, 1980.
English translation (chap. 6): Stephen Batchelor. *Echoes of Voidness* by Geshé Rabten, 47-92. London: Wisdom Publications, 1983.
See also references under Chandrakīrti's *[Auto]commentary on the "Supplement."*
Dharmakīrti (*chos kyi grags pa,* seventh century)
Commentary on (Dignāga's) "Compilation of Prime Cognition"
pramāṇavārttikakārikā
tshad ma rnam 'grel gyi tshig le'ur byas pa
P5709, vol. 130; Toh. 4210, vol. ce. Also: Sarnath, India: Pleasure of Elegant Sayings Press, 1974.
Sanskrit: Dwarikadas Shastri. *Pramāṇavārttika of Āchārya Dharmakīrtti.* Varanasi, India: Bauddha Bharati, 1968.
Sanskrit and Tibetan: Yūsho Miyasaka. "*Pramāṇavarttika-kārikā:* Sanskrit and Tibetan." *Indo Koten Kenkyu (Acta Indologica)* 2 (1971-72): 1-206.
English translation (chap. 2): Masatoshi Nagatomi. "A Study of Dharmakīrti's Pramāṇavarttika: An English Translation and Annotation of the Pramāṇavarttika, Book I." Ph. D. diss., Harvard University, 1957.
English translation (chap. 4): Tom J.F. Tillemans. *Dharmakīrti's Pramāṇavārttika: An Annotated Translation of the Fourth Chapter (parārthānumāna),* vol. 1 (k. 1-148). Vienna: Österreichischen Akademie der Wissenschaften, 2000.
Dol-po-pa Shay-rap-gyel-tsen (*dol po pa shes rab rgyal mtshan;* 1292-1361)
The Great Calculation of the Doctrine, Which Has the Significance of a Fourth Council
bka' bsdu bzhi pa'i don bstan rtsis chen po
Matthew Kapstein. *The 'Dzam-thang Edition of the Collected Works of Kun-mkhyen Dol-po-pa Shes-rab-rgyal-mtshan: Introduction and Catalogue,* vol. 5, 207-252. Delhi: Shedrup Books, 1992.
English translation: Cyrus R. Stearns. *The Buddha from Dol po: A Study of the Life and Thought of the Tibetan Master Dolpopa Sherab Gyaltsen,* 127-173. Albany, N.Y.: State University of New York Press, 1999.
Mountain Doctrine, Ocean of Definitive Meaning: Final Unique Quintessential Instructions
ri chos nges don rgya mtsho zhes bya ba mthar thug thun mong ma yin pa'i man ngag
Gangtok, India: Dodrup Sangyey Lama, 1976.
Also: 'dzam thang bsam 'grub nor bu'i gling, n.d.
Also: Matthew Kapstein. *The 'Dzam-thang Edition of the Collected Works of Kun-mkhyen Dol-po-pa Shes-rab-rgyal-mtshan: Introduction and Catalogue,* 25-707. Delhi: Shedrup Books, 1992.
Also: Beijing: mi rigs dpe skrun khang, 1998.

English translation: Jeffrey Hopkins. *Mountain Doctrine: Tibet's Fundamental Treatise on Other-Emptiness and the Buddha Matrix.* Ithaca, N.Y.: Snow Lion Publications, 2006.

Gung-tang (*gung thang dkon mchog bstan pa'i sgron me*)

Difficult Points / Beginnings of a Commentary on the Difficult Points of (Tsong-kha-pa's) "Differentiating the Interpretable and the Definitive": Quintessence of "The Essence of Eloquence"

drang nges rnam 'byed kyi dka' 'grel rtsom 'phro legs bshad snying po'i yang snying

New Delhi: Ngawang Gelek Demo, 1975

Gyel-tsap-dar-ma-rin-chen (*rgyal tshab dar ma rin chen*, 1364-1432)

Explanation of (Āryadeva's) "Four Hundred": Essence of Eloquence

bzhi brgya pa'i rnam bshad legs bshad snying po

Sarnath, India: Pleasure of Elegant Sayings Printing Press, 1971; also, n.d., blockprint in library of HH the Dalai Lama

English translation: *Yogic Deeds of Bodhisattvas: Gyel-tsap on Āryadeva's Four Hundred.* Commentary by Geshe Sonam Rinchen, translated and edited by Ruth Sonam. Ithaca, N.Y.: Snow Lion Publications, 1994.

Explanation of (Shāntideva's) "Engaging in the Bodhisattva Deeds," Entrance For Conqueror Children

byang chub sems dpa'i spyod pa la 'jug pa'i rnam bshad rgyal sras 'jug ngog

Sarnath: Pleasure of Elegant Sayings Printing Press, 1973

Illumination of the Essential Meanings of (Nāgārjuna's) "Precious Garland of the Middle Way"

dbu ma rin chen 'phreng ba'i snying po'i don gsal bar byed pa

Collected Works, *ka.* Lhasa: zhol par khang, 15th rab 'byung in the fire rooster year, that is, 1897 (78 folios); also, Collected Works, *ka.* New Delhi: Guru Deva, 1982 (349-503, 78 folios), "reproduced from a set of prints from the 1897 lha-sa old zhol (*dga' ldan phun tshogs gling*) blocks." [These are two separate editions.]

Jam-yang-shay-pa (*'jam dbyangs bzhad pa*, 1648-1721)

Great Exposition of the Middle / Analysis of (Chandrakīrti's) 'Supplement to (Nāgārjuna's) "Treatise on the Middle"', Treasury of Scripture and Reasoning, Thoroughly Illuminating the Profound Meaning [of Emptiness], Entrance for the Fortunate

dbu ma chen mo / dbu ma 'jug pa'i mtha' dpyod lung rigs gter mdzod zab don kun gsal skal bzang 'jug ngogs

Buxaduor, India: Gomang, 1967

Jang-kya (*lcang skya*, 1717-1786)

Presentations of Tenets / Clear Exposition of the Presentation of Tenets, Beautiful Ornament for the Meru of the Subduer's Teaching

grub pa'i mtha'i rnam par bzhag pa gsal bar bshad pa thub bstan lhun po'i mdzes rgyan

Varanasi, India: Pleasure of Elegant Sayings Printing Press, 1970

Jñānagarbha (*ye shes snying po*, c. 700)

Commentary on the "Differentiation of the Two Truths"

satyadvayavibhaṅgavṛtti

bden pa gnyis rnam par 'byed pa'i 'grel pa

Toh. 3882, vol. sa

Edited Tibetan text and English translation: Malcolm David Eckel. *Jñānagarbha's Commentary on the Distinction between the Two Truths: An Eighth Century Handbook of Madhyamaka Philosophy.* Albany, N.Y.: State University of New York Press, 1987.

Differentiation of the Two Truths

satyadvayavibhaṅga

bden pa gnyis rnam par 'byed

Toh. 3881, vol. sa

Edited Tibetan text and English translation: Malcolm David Eckel. *Jñānagarbha's Commentary.*

Kalkī Puṇḍarīka (*rigs ldan pad ma dkar po*)

Great Commentary on the "Kālachakra Tantra": Stainless Light

vimālaprabhānāmamūlatantrānusāriṇīdvādaśasāhasrikālaghukālacakra-tantrarājaṭīkā

bsdus pa'i rgyud kyi rgyal po dus kyi 'khor lo'i 'grel bshad rtsa ba'i rgyud kyi rjes su 'jug pa stong

phrag bcu gnyis pa dri ma med pa'i 'od ces bya ba / 'grel chen dri med 'od
P2064, vol. 46
Kamalashīla
Illumination of the Middle
madhyamakāloka
dbu ma snang ba
P5287, vol. 101; Toh. 3887, vol. sa
Stages of Meditation
bhāvanākrama
sgom pa'i rim pa
P5310-5312, vol. 102; Toh. 3915-17, vol. ki; Dharma vol. 73, Tokyo *sde dge* vol. 15
Sanskrit: *First Bhāvanākrama.* G. Tucci, ed. *Minor Buddhist texts, II.* Serie Orientale Roma 9. Rome: Istituto Italiano per il Medio ed Estremo Oriente, 1958. Pp.185-229. *Third Bhāvanākrama.* G. Tucci, ed. *Minor Buddhist texts, III.* Serie Orientale Roma 43. Rome: Istituto Italiano per il Medio ed Estremo Oriente, 1971.
English translation (Second *Bhāvanākrama*): Geshe Lhundup Sopa, Elvin W. Jones, and John Newman. *The Stages of Meditation: Bhāvanākrama II.* Madison, Wisconsin: Deer Park Books, 1998. Also: Geshe Lobsang Jordhen, Lobsang Choephel Ganchenpa, and Jeremy Russell. *Stages of Meditation.* Ithaca, N.Y.: Snow Lion Publications, 2001.
Contemporary commentary: Dalai Lama. *An Open Heart: Practicing Compassion in Everyday Life.* New York: Little Brown, 2001.
Lo-den-shay-rap (*blo ldan shes rab, rngog lo chen po;* 1059-1109)
Epistolary Essay, Drop of Ambrosia
spring yig bdud rtsi'i thigs pa
Incompletely cited in Ser-dok Paṇ-chen Shākya-chok-den's (*gser mdog paṇ chen shākya mchog ldan,* 1428-1507) *Explanation of the "Epistolary Essay, Drop of Ambrosia," Magical Rosary Fulfilling All Wishes* (*spring yig bdud rtsi'i thigs pa'i rnam bshad dpag bsam yong 'du'i ljon phreng*). The Collected works of Gser-mdog Paṇ-chen, vol. 24, 320.6-348.6. Thimphu, Bhutan: Kunzang Topgey, 1978.
Lo-sang-dor-jay (*blo bzang rdo rje;* fl. nineteenth century)
Decisive Analysis of (Tsong-kha-pa's) "Stages of the Path to Enlightenment": Ship for Entering into the Ocean of Textual Systems
byang chub lam gyi rim pa'i mtha' dpyod gzhung lugs rgya mtshor 'jug pa'i gru gzings
New Delhi: Mongolian Lama Gurudeva, 1980
Maitreya (*byams pa*)
Five Doctrines of Maitreya
1. *Great Vehicle Treatise on the Sublime Continuum / Treatise on the Later Scriptures of the Great Vehicle*
mahāyānottaratantraśāstra
theg pa chen po rgyud bla ma'i bstan bcos
P5525, vol. 108; Toh. 4024, Dharma vol. 77
Sanskrit: E. H. Johnston (and T. Chowdhury). *The Ratnagotravibhāga Mahāyānottaratantraśāstra.* Patna, India: Bihar Research Society, 1950.
English translation: E. Obermiller. "Sublime Science of the Great Vehicle to Salvation." *Acta Orientalia* 9 (1931): 81-306. Also: J. Takasaki. *A Study on the Ratnagotravibhāga.* Rome: Istituto Italiano per il Medio ed Estremo Oriente, 1966.
2. *Differentiation of Phenomena and Noumenon*
dharmadharmatāvibhaṅga
chos dang chos nyid rnam par 'byed pa
P5523, vol. 108; Toh. 4022, Dharma vol. 77
Edited Tibetan: Jōshō Nozawa. "The *Dharmadharmatāvibhaṅga* and the *Dharmadharmatāvibhaṅgavṛtti,* Tibetan Texts, Edited and Collated, Based upon the Peking and Derge Editions." In *Studies in Indology and Buddhology: Presented in Honour of Professor Susumu Yamaguchi on the Occasion of his Sixtieth Birthday,* edited by Gadjin M. Nagao and Jōshō Nozawa.

Kyoto: Hozokan, 1955.

English translation: John Younghan Cha. *A Study of the* Dharmadharmatāvibhāga*: An Analysis of the Religious Philosophy of the Yogācāra, Together with an Annotated Translation of Vasubandhu's Commentary.* PhD diss., Northwestern University, 1996.

English translation: Jim Scott. *Maitreya's Distinguishing Phenomena and Pure Being with Commentary by Mipham.* Ithaca, N.Y.: Snow Lion Publications, 2004.

3. *Differentiation of the Middle and the Extremes*
   madhyāntavibhaṅga
   dbus dang mtha' rnam par 'byed pa
   P5522, vol. 108; Toh. 4021, Dharma vol. 77
   Sanskrit: Gadjin M. Nagao. *Madhyāntavibhāga-bhāṣya.* Tokyo: Suzuki Research Foundation, 1964. Also: Ramchandra Pandeya. *Madhyānta-vibhāga-śāstra.* Delhi: Motilal Banarsidass, 1971.
   English translation: Stefan Anacker. *Seven Works of Vasubandhu.* Delhi: Motilal Banarsidass, 1984.
   Also, of chapter 1: Thomas A. Kochumuttom. *A Buddhist Doctrine of Experience.* Delhi: Motilal Banarsidass, 1982. Also, of chapter 1: F. Th. Stcherbatsky. *Madhyāntavibhāga, Discourse on Discrimination between Middle and Extremes ascribed to Bodhisattva Maitreya and Commented by Vasubandhu and Sthiramati.* Bibliotheca Buddhica 30 (1936). Osnabrück, Germany: Biblio Verlag, 1970; reprint, Calcutta: Indian Studies Past and Present, 1971. Also, of chapter 1: David Lasar Friedmann. *Sthiramati, Madhyāntavibhāgaṭīkā: Analysis of the Middle Path and the Extremes.* Utrecht, Netherlands: Rijksuniversiteit te Leiden, 1937. Also, of chapter 3: Paul Wilfred O'Brien, S.J. "A Chapter on Reality from the Madhyāntavibhāgaçāstra." *Monumenta Nipponica* 9, nos. 1-2 (1953): 277-303 and *Monumenta Nipponica* 10, nos. 1-2 (1954): 227-269.
4. *Ornament for Clear Realization*
   abhisamayālaṃkāra
   mngon par rtogs pa'i rgyan
   P5184, vol. 88; Toh. 3786, vol. ka; Dharma vol. 63
   Sanskrit: Th. Stcherbatsky and E. Obermiller, eds. *Abhisamayālaṃkāra-Prajñāpāramitā-Upadeśa-Śāstra.* Bibliotheca Buddhica 23. Osnabrück, Germany: Biblio Verlag, 1970.
   English translation: Edward Conze. *Abhisamayālaṃkāra.* Serie Orientale Roma. Rome: Istituto Italiano per il Medio ed Estremo Oriente, 1954.
5. *Ornament for the Great Vehicle Sūtras*
   mahāyānasūtrālaṃkāra
   theg pa chen po'i mdo sde rgyan gyi tshig le'ur byas pa
   P5521, vol. 108; Dharma vol. 77
   Sanskrit: Sitansusekhar Bagchi. *Mahāyāna-Sūtrālaṃkāraḥ of Asaṅga* [with Vasubandhu's commentary]. Buddhist Sanskrit Texts 13. Darbhanga, India: Mithila Institute, 1970.
   Sanskrit text and translation into French: Sylvain Lévi. *Mahāyānasūtrālaṃkāra, exposé de la doctrine du grand véhicule selon le système Yogācāra.* 2 vols. Paris: Bibliothèque de l'École des Hautes Études, 1907, 1911.

Mön-lam-pel-lek-pay-lo-drö (*smon lam dpal legs pa'i blo gros;* born 1414)

Instructions on the Profound View of the Middle Way: Clearing Away All Extremes
zab mo dbu ma'i lta khrid mthar 'dzin kun sel
In *Stoṅ thun chen mo of Mkhas-grub Dge-legs-dpal-bzaṅ: and other texts on Madhyamika Philosophy,* 525-579; Madhyamika text series, v. 1
New Delhi: Lha-mkhar yoṅs-'dzin bstan-pa-rgyal-mtshan, 1972

Nāgārjuna (*klu sgrub,* first to second century, C.E.)

Essay on the Mind of Enlightenment
bodhicittavivaraṇa
byang chub sems kyi 'grel pa
P2665 and 2666, vol. 61; Toh. 1800 and 1801, vol. ngi
Edited Tibetan and Sanskrit fragments along with English translation: Christian Lindtner.

Master of Wisdom: Writings of the Buddhist Master Nāgārjuna. Oakland: Dharma Publishing, 1986.

Praise of the Element of Attributes
dharmadhātustotra
chos kyi dbyings su bstod pa
P2010, vol. 46; Toh. 1118, vol. ka

Praise of the Supramundane [Buddha]
lokātītastava
'jig rten las 'das par bstod pa
P2012, vol. 46; Toh. 1120, vol. ka
Edited Tibetan and Sanskrit along with English translation: Christian Lindtner. *Master of Wisdom.* Oakland: Dharma Publishing, 1986.

Six Collections of Reasoning

1. *Precious Garland of Advice for the King*
rājaparikathāratnāvalī
rgyal po la gtam bya ba rin po che'i phreng ba
P5658, vol. 129; Dharma vol. 93
Sanskrit, Tibetan, and Chinese: Michael Hahn. *Nāgārjuna's Ratnāvalī.* vol. 1. *The Basic Texts (Sanskrit, Tibetan, and Chinese).* Bonn: Indica et Tibetica Verlag, 1982.
English translation: Jeffrey Hopkins. *Buddhist Advice for Living and Liberation: Nāgārjuna's Precious Garland,* 94-164. Ithaca, New York: Snow Lion Publications, 1998. Supersedes that in: Nāgārjuna and the Seventh Dalai Lama. *The Precious Garland and the Song of the Four Mindfulnesses,* translated by Jeffrey Hopkins, 17-93. London: George Allen and Unwin, 1975; New York: Harper and Row, 1975; reprint, in H.H. the Dalai Lama, Tenzin Gyatso. *The Buddhism of Tibet.* London: George Allen and Unwin, 1983; reprint, Ithaca, New York: Snow Lion Publications, 1987.
English translation: John Dunne and Sara McClintock. *The Precious Garland: An Epistle to a King.* Boston: Wisdom Publications, 1997.
English translation of 223 stanzas (chap. 1, 1-77; chap. 2, 1-46; chap. 4, 1-100): Giuseppe Tucci. "The *Ratnāvalī* of Nāgārjuna." *Journal of the Royal Asiatic Society* (1934): 307-325; (1936): 237-52, 423-35.
Japanese translation: Uryūzu Ryushin. *Butten II, Sekai Koten Bungaku Zenshu,* 7 (July, 1965): 349-72. Edited by Nakamura Hajime. Tokyo: Chikuma Shobō. Also: Uryūzu Ryushin. *Daijō Butten,* 14 (1974): 231-316. *Ryūju Ronshū.* Edited by Kajiyama Yuichi and Uryūzu Ryushin. Tokyo: Chūōkōronsha.
Danish translation: Christian Lindtner. *Nagarjuna, Juvelkaeden og andre skrifter.* Copenhagen: 1980.

2. *Refutation of Objections*
vigrahavyāvartanīkārikā
rtsod pa bzlog pa'i tshig le'ur byas pa
P5228, vol. 95; Toh. 3828, vol. tsa
Edited Tibetan and Sanskrit and English translation: Christian Lindtner. *Master of Wisdom.* Oakland: Dharma Publishing, 1986.
English translation: K. Bhattacharya, E. H. Johnston, and A. Kunst. *The Dialectical Method of Nāgārjuna.* New Delhi: Motilal Banarsidass, 1978.
English translation from the Chinese: G. Tucci. *Pre-Diṅnāga Buddhist Texts on Logic from Chinese Sources.* Gaekwad's Oriental Series, 49. Baroda, India: Oriental Institute, 1929.
French translation: S. Yamaguchi. "Traité de Nāgārjuna pour écarter les vaines discussion (Vigrahavyāvartanī) traduit et annoté." *Journal Asiatique* 215 (1929): 1-86.

3. *Seventy Stanzas on Emptiness*
śūnyatāsaptatikārikā
stong pa nyid bdun cu pa'i tshig le'ur byas pa
P5227, vol. 95; Toh. 3827, vol. tsa

Edited Tibetan and English translation: Christian Lindtner. *Master of Wisdom*. Oakland: Dharma Publishing, 1986.

English translation: David Ross Komito. *Nāgārjuna's "Seventy Stanzas": A Buddhist Psychology of Emptiness*. Ithaca, N.Y.: Snow Lion Publications, 1987.

4. *Sixty Stanzas of Reasoning*

yuktiṣaṣṭikākārikā

rigs pa drug cu pa'i tshig le'ur byas pa

P5225, vol. 95; Toh. 3825, vol. tsa

Edited Tibetan with Sanskrit fragments and English translation: Christian Lindtner. *Master of Wisdom*. Oakland: Dharma Publishing, 1986.

5. *Treatise Called the Finely Woven*

vaidalyasūtranāma

zhib mo rnam par 'thag pa zhes bya ba'i mdo

P5226, vol. 95; Toh. 3826, vol. tsa

Tibetan text and English translation: Fermando Tola and Carmen Dragonetti. *Nāgārjuna's Refutation of Logic (Nyāya) Vaidalyaprakaraṇa*. Delhi: Motilal Banarsidass, 1995.

6. *Treatise on the Middle / Fundamental Treatise on the Middle, Called "Wisdom"*

madhyamakaśāstra / prajñānāmamūlamadhyamakakārikā

dbu ma'i bstan bcos / dbu ma rtsa ba'i tshig le'ur byas pa shes rab ces bya ba

P5224, vol. 95; Toh. 3824, vol. tsa

Edited Sanskrit: J. W. de Jong. *Nāgārjuna, Mūlamadhyamakakārikāḥ*. Madras, India: Adyar Library and Research Centre, 1977; reprint, Wheaton, Ill.: Agents, Theosophical Publishing House, c1977. Also: Christian Lindtner. *Nāgārjuna's Filosofiske Vaerker*, 177-215. Indiske Studier 2. Copenhagen: Akademisk Forlag, 1982.

English translation: Frederick Streng. *Emptiness: A Study in Religious Meaning*. Nashville, Tenn.: Abingdon Press, 1967. Also: Kenneth Inada. *Nāgārjuna: A Translation of His Mūlamadhyamakakārikā*. Tokyo: Hokuseido Press, 1970. Also: David J. Kalupahana. *Nāgārjuna: The Philosophy of the Middle Way*. Albany, N.Y.: State University Press of New York, 1986. Also: Jay L. Garfield. *The Fundamental Wisdom of the Middle Way*. New York: Oxford University Press, 1995. Also: Stephen Batchelor. *Verses from the Center: A Buddhist Vision of the Sublime*. New York: Riverhead Books, 2000.

Italian translation: R. Gnoli. *Nāgārjuna: Madhyamaka Kārikā, Le stanze del cammino di mezzo*. Enciclopedia di autori classici 61. Turin, Italy: P. Boringhieri, 1961.

Danish translation: Christian Lindtner. *Nāgārjuna's Filosofiske Vaerker*, 67-135. Indiske Studier 2. Copenhagen: Akademisk Forlag, 1982.

Nga-wang-pel-den (*ngag dbang dpal ldan*, b. 1797), also known as Pel-den-chö-jay (*dpal ldan chos rje*)

Annotations for (Jam-yang-shay-pa's) "Great Exposition of Tenets": Freeing the Knots of the Difficult Points, Precious Jewel of Clear Thought

grub mtha' chen mo'i mchan 'grel dka' gnad mdud grol blo gsal gces nor

Sarnath, India: Pleasure of Elegant Sayings Press, 1964. Also: Collected Works of Chos-rje ṅag-dbaṅ Dpal-ldan of Urga, vols. 4 (entire)-5, 1-401. Delhi: Guru Deva, 1983.

Explanation of the Obscurational and the Ultimate in the Four Systems of Tenets

grub mtha' bzhi'i lugs kyi kun rdzob dang don dam pa'i don rnam par bshad pa legs bshad dpyid kyi dpal mo'i glu dbyangs

New Delhi: Guru Deva, 1972. Also: Collected Works of Chos-rje ṅag-dbaṅ Dpal-ldan of Urga, vol. 1, 3-273. Delhi: Mongolian Lama Gurudeva, 1983.

Po-to-wa (*po to ba rin chen gsal*, 1027/31-1105)

Small Vessel

be'u bum

dge bshes po to ba sogs. *bka gdams be'u bum sngon po'i rtsa 'grel*, gangs can rig brgya'i sgo 'byed lde mig 16. Kokonor: mi rigs dpe skrun khang, 1991

Prajñākaramati (*shes rab 'byung gnas blo gros*, 950-1030)

Commentary on the Difficult Points of (Shāntideva's) "Engaging in the Bodhisattva Deeds"

bodhicaryāvatārapañjikā
byang chub kyi spyod pa la 'jug pa'i dka' 'grel
P5139, vol. 91
Sanskrit edition: Louis de La Vallée Poussin. *Prajñākaramati's Commentary to the Bodhicaryāvatāra of Śāntideva.* Bibliotheca Indica. Calcutta: Asiatic Society of Bengal, 1902-1914.

Ratnākarashānti (*rin chen 'byung gnas zhi ba*)
Quintessential Instructions on the Perfection of Wisdom
prajñāpāramitopadeśa
shes rab kyi pha rol tu phyin pa'i man ngag
P5579, vol. 114; Toh. 4079, vol. hi

Ren-da-wa Shön-nu-lo-drö's (*red mda' ba gzhon nu blo gros,* 1349-1412)
Commentary on (Āryadeva's) Four Hundred
dbu ma bzhi brgya pa'i 'grel pa
Sarnath: Sakya Students' Union, 1974

Sha-mar Gen-dün-ten-dzin-gya-tso (*zhwa dmar dge bdun btsan 'dzin rgya mtsho,* 1852-1910)
Lamp Illuminating the Profound Thought, Set Forth to Purify Forgetfulness of the Difficult Points of (Tsong-kha-pa's) "Great Exposition of Special Insight"
lhag mthong chen mo'i dka' gnad rnams brjed byang du bkod pa dgongs zab snang ba'i sgron me
Delhi: Mongolian Lama Guru Deva, 1972

Shāntarakṣhita (*zhi ba 'tsho,* eighth century)
Ornament for the Middle
madhyamakālaṃkāra
dbu ma rgyan
Toh. 3884, vol. sa
Edited Tibetan and English translation: Masamichi Ichigō. "Śāntarakṣita's Madhyamakālaṃkāra." In *Studies in the Literature of the Great Vehicle.* Michigan Studies in Buddhist Literature No. 1, edited by Luis O. Gómez and Jonathan A. Silk, 141-240. Ann Arbor: Collegiate Institute for the Study of Buddhist Literature and Center for South and Southeast Asian Studies, The University of Michigan, 1989.

Shāntideva (*zhi ba lha,* eighth century)
Compendium of Instructions
śikṣāsamuccaya
bslab pa kun las btus pa
P5272, vol. 102; Toh. 3940, vol. khi
English Translation: C. Bendall and W.H.D. Rouse. *Śikṣā Samuccaya.* Delhi: Motilal, 1971.
Edited Sanskrit: Cecil Bendall. *Çikshāsamuccaya: A Compendium of Buddhistic Teaching.* Bibliotheca Buddhica 1. Osnabrück, Germany: Biblio Verlag, 1970.
Engaging in the Bodhisattva Deeds
bodhi[sattva]caryāvatāra
byang chub sems dpa'i spyod pa la 'jug pa
Toh. 3871, dbu ma, vol. *la*
Sanskrit: P. L. Vaidya. *Bodhicaryāvatāra.* Buddhist Sanskrit Texts 12. Darbhanga, India: Mithila Institute, 1988.
Sanskrit and Tibetan: Vidhushekara Bhattacharya. *Bodhicaryāvatāra.* Bibliotheca Indica, 280. Calcutta: Asiatic Society, 1960.
Sanskrit and Tibetan with Hindi translation: Rāmaśaṃkara Tripāthī, ed. *Bodhicaryāvatāra.* Bauddha-Himālaya-Granthamālā, 8. Leh, Ladākh: Central Institute of Buddhist Studies, 1989.
English translation: Stephen Batchelor. *A Guide to the Bodhisattva's Way of Life.* Dharmsala, India: Library of Tibetan Works and Archives, 1979. Also: Marion Matics. *Entering the Path of Enlightenment.* New York: Macmillan, 1970. Also: Kate Crosby and Andrew Skilton. *The Bodhicaryāvatāra.* Oxford: Oxford University Press, 1996. Also: Padmakara Translation Group.

The Way of the Bodhisattva. Boston: Shambhala, 1997. Also: Vesna A. Wallace and B. Alan Wallace. *A Guide to the Bodhisattva Way of Life*. Ithaca, N.Y.: Snow Lion Publications, 1997.

Contemporary commentary by H.H. the Dalai Lama, Tenzin Gyatso. *Transcendent Wisdom*. Ithaca, N.Y.: Snow Lion Publications, 1988. Also: H.H. the Dalai Lama, Tenzin Gyatso. *A Flash of Lightning in the Dark of the Night*. Boston: Shambhala, 1994.

Shūra (*dpa' bo*)

Cultivation of the Ultimate Mind of Enlightenment

paramārthabodhicittabhāvanā

don dam byang chub sems sgom

P5431, vol. 103

Tāranātha

The Essence of Other-Emptiness

gzhan stong snying po

Collected Works of Jo-naṅ rJe-btsun Tāranātha, vol. 4

Leh, Ladakh: Smanrtsis Shesrig Dpemzod, 1985; 491-514.

English translation: Tāranātha, *The Essence of Other-Emptiness*, translated and edited by Jeffrey Hopkins. Ithaca, N.Y.: Snow Lion Publications, 2007.

Tak-tsang Shay-rap-rin-chen (*stag tshang lo tsā ba shes rab rin chen*, b.1405)

Explanation of "Freedom from Extremes through Understanding All Tenets": Ocean of Good Explanations

grub mtha' kun shes nas mtha' bral grub pa zhes bya ba'i bstan bcos rnam par bshad pa legs bshad kyi rgya mtsho

photographic reprint in the possession of Khetsun Sangpo, no other data, and Thimphu, Bhutan: Kun-bzang-stobs rgyal, 1976

Tsong-kha-pa Lo-sang-drak-pa (*tsong kha pa blo bzang grags pa*, 1357-1419)

Explanation of (Nāgārjuna's) "Treatise on the Middle": Ocean of Reasoning / Great Commentary on (Nāgārjuna's) "Treatise on the Middle"

dbu ma rtsa ba'i tshig le'ur byas pa shes rab ces bya ba'i rnam bshad rigs pa'i rgya mtsho / rtsa shes ṭik chen

P6153, vol. 156. Also: Sarnath, India: Pleasure of Elegant Sayings Printing Press, n.d. Also: *rJe tsong kha pa'i gsung dbu ma'i lta ba'i skor*, vols. 1-2. Sarnath, India: Pleasure of Elegant Sayings Press, 1975. Also: Delhi: Ngawang Gelek, 1975. Also: Delhi: Guru Deva, 1979.

English translation: Geshe Ngawang Samten and Jay L. Garfield. *Ocean of Reasoning: A Great Commentary on Nāgārjuna's* Mūlamadhyamakakārikā. Oxford: Oxford University Press, 2006.

English translation (chap. 2): Jeffrey Hopkins. *Ocean of Reasoning*. Dharmsala, India: Library of Tibetan Works and Archives, 1974.

Extensive Explanation of (Chandrakīrti's) "Supplement to (Nāgārjuna's) 'Treatise on the Middle'": Illumination of the Thought

dbu ma la 'jug pa'i rgya cher bshad pa dgongs pa rab gsal

P6143, vol. 154. Also: Dharmsala, India: Tibetan Cultural Printing Press, n.d. Also: Sarnath, India: Pleasure of Elegant Sayings Press, 1973. Also: Delhi: Ngawang Gelek, 1975. Also: Delhi: Guru Deva, 1979.

English translation (chaps. 1-5): Jeffrey Hopkins. *Compassion in Tibetan Buddhism*, 93-230. Ithaca, N.Y.: Snow Lion Publications, 1980.

English translation (chap. 6, stanzas 1-7): Jeffrey Hopkins and Anne C. Klein. *Path to the Middle: Madhyamaka Philosophy in Tibet: The Oral Scholarship of Kensur Yeshay Tupden*, by Anne C. Klein, 147-183, 252-271. Albany, N.Y.: State University of New York Press, 1994.

Four Interwoven Annotations on (Tsong-kha-pa's) "Great Exposition of the Stages of the Path" / The Lam rim chen mo of the incomparable Tsong-kha-pa, with the interlineal notes of Ba-so Chos-kyi-rgyal-mtshan, Sde-drug Mkhan-chen Ngag-dbang-rab-rtan, 'Jam-dbyangs-bshad-pa'i-rdo-rje, and Bra-sti Dge-bshes Rin-chen-don-grub

lam rim mchan bzhi sbrags ma/ mnyam med rje btsun tsong kha pa chen pos mdzad pa'i byang chub lam rim chen mo'i dka' ba'i gnad rnams mchan bu bzhi'i sgo nas legs par bshad pa theg chen lam gyi gsal sgron

New Delhi: Chos-'phel-legs-ldan, 1972

Great Exposition of Secret Mantra / The Stages of the Path to a Conqueror and Pervasive Master, a Great Vajradhara: Revealing All Secret Topics

sngags rim chen mo / rgyal ba khyab bdag rdo rje 'chang chen po'i lam gyi rim pa gsang ba kun gyi gnad rnam par phye ba

P6210, vol. 161. Also: Delhi: Ngawang Gelek, 1975. Also: Delhi: Guru Deva, 1979.

English translation (chap. 1): H.H. the Dalai Lama, Tsong-kha-pa, and Jeffrey Hopkins. *Tantra in Tibet.* London: George Allen and Unwin, 1977; reprint, with minor corrections, Ithaca, N.Y.: Snow Lion Publications, 1987.

English translation (chaps. 2-3): H.H. the Dalai Lama, Tsong-kha-pa, and Jeffrey Hopkins. *The Yoga of Tibet.* London: George Allen and Unwin, 1981; reprinted as *Deity Yoga.* Ithaca, N.Y.: Snow Lion Publications, 1987.

English translation (chap. 4): H.H. the Dalai Lama, Dzong-ka-ba, and Jeffrey Hopkins. *Yoga Tantra: Paths to Magical Feats.* Ithaca, N.Y.: Snow Lion Publications, 2005.

Great Exposition of the Stages of the Path / Stages of the Path to Enlightenment Thoroughly Teaching All the Stages of Practice of the Three Types of Beings

lam rim chen mo / skyes bu gsum gyi nyams su blang ba'i rim pa thams cad tshang bar ston pa'i byang chub lam gyi rim pa

P6001, vol. 152. Also: Dharmsala, India: Tibetan Cultural Printing Press, 1964. Also: Delhi: Ngawang Gelek, 1975. Also: Delhi: Guru Deva, 1979.

Edited Tibetan: Tsultrim Kelsang Khangkar. *The Great Treatise on the Stages of the Path to Enlightenment (Lam Rim Chen Mo).* Japanese and Tibetan Buddhist Culture Series, 6. Kyoto: Tibetan Buddhist Culture Association, 2001.

English translation: Lamrim Chenmo Translation Committee. *The Great Treatise on the Stages of the Path to Enlightenment.* 3 vols. Joshua W.C. Cutler, editor-in-chief, Guy Newland, editor. Ithaca, N.Y.: Snow Lion Publications, 2000-2004.

English translation of the part on the excessively broad object of negation: Elizabeth Napper. *Dependent-Arising and Emptiness,* 153-215. London: Wisdom Publications, 1989.

English translation of the part on the excessively narrow object of negation: William Magee. *The Nature of Things: Emptiness and Essence in the Geluk World,* 179-192. Ithaca, N.Y.: Snow Lion Publications, 1999.

English translation of the parts on calm abiding and special insight: Alex Wayman. *Calming the Mind and Discerning the Real,* 81-431. New York: Columbia University Press, 1978; reprint, New Delhi, Motilal Banarsidass, 1979.

Medium-Length Exposition of the Stages of the Path to Enlightenment to be Practiced by Beings of the Three Capacities / Medium-Length Exposition of the Stages of the Path to Enlightenment to be Practiced by Beings of the Three Capacities together with an Outline / Short Exposition of the Stages of the Path to Enlightenment

skyes bu gsum gyis nyams su blang ba'i byang chub lam gyi rim pa / skyes bu gsum gyi nyams su blang ba'i byang chub lam gyi rim pa bring po sa bcad kha skong dang bcas pa / lam rim 'bring / lam rim chung ngu

Mundgod, India: dga' ldan shar rtse, n.d. (includes outline of topics by Trijang Rinbochay). Also: Bylakuppe, India: Sera Je Library, 1999 (includes outline of topics by Trijang Rinbochay). Also: P6002, vol. 152-153. Also: Dharmsala, India: Tibetan Cultural Printing Press, 1968. Also: Delhi: Ngawang Gelek, 1975. Also: Delhi: Guru Deva, 1979.

English translation of the section on special insight in this book. Also, Robert Thurman. "The Middle Transcendent Insight." *Life and Teachings of Tsong Khapa,* 108-185. Dharmsala, India: Library of Tibetan Works and Archives, 1982.

Edited Tibetan text and Japanese translation of the section on special insight: Tsultrim Kelsang Khangkar and Takada Yorihito. *A Study of Tsong khapa's Mādhyamika Philosophy 1: Annotated Japanese translation of the Vipaśyanā Section of Medium Exposition of the Stages of the Path (Lam rim).* Tsong kha pa chuugan tetsugaku no kenkyuu 1, Bodaidousidairon chuuhen, kan no shou: wayaku, Tsultrim Kelsang Khangkar and Takada Yorihito, Kyoto: Buneido, 1996.

Japanese translation: Tsultrim Kelsang Khangkar and Takashi Rujinaka. *The Treatise on the Stages of the Path to Enlightenment by rJe Tsong kha pa: An Annotated Japanese Translation of Byang chub Lam rim chung ba.* Kyoto: Unio Corporation, 2005.

Treatise Differentiating Interpretable and Definitive Meanings: The Essence of Eloquence
drang ba dang nges pa'i don rnam par phye ba'i bstan bcos legs bshad snying po
P6142, vol. 153.
English translation of the Prologue and Mind-Only section: Jeffrey Hopkins. *Emptiness in the Mind-Only School of Buddhism. Dynamic Responses to Dzong-ka-ba's* The Essence of Eloquence, Volume 1. Berkeley: University of California Press, 1999.
English translation of the entire text: Robert A. F. Thurman. *Tsong Khapa's Speech of Gold in the Essence of True Eloquence,* 185-385. Princeton, N.J.: Princeton University Press, 1984

Vajragarbha (*rdo rje snying po*)
Commentary on the Condensation of the Hevajra Tantra
hevajrapiṇḍārthaṭīkā
kye'i rdo rje bsdus pa'i don gyi rgya cher 'grel pa
P2310, vol. 53

Vajrapāṇi (*phyag na rdo rje*)
Meaning Commentary on the Chakrasaṃvara Tantra
lakṣābhidhānāduddhṛtalaghutantrapiṇḍārthavivaraṇa
phyag rdor don 'grel: mngon par brjod pa 'bum pa las phyung ba nyung ngu'i rgyud kyi bsdus pa'i don rnam par bshad pa
P2117, vol. 48

Vasubandhu (*dbyig gnyen,* fl. 360)
Commentary on the Extensive and Medium Length Mothers / Conquest Over Objections about the Three Mother Scriptures
āryaśatasāhasrikāpañcaviṃsatisāhasrikā-aṣṭadaśasāhasrikāprajñāpāramitābṛhaṭṭīkā
'phags pa shes rab kyi pha rol tu phyin pa 'bum pa dang nyi khri lnga stong pa dang khri brgyad stong pa'i rgya cher bshad pa / yum gsum gnod 'joms
P5206, vol. 93

Commentary on the "Sūtra on the Ten Grounds"
daśabhūmivyākhyāna
sa bcu'i rnam par bshad pa
P5494, vol. 104

Principles of Explanation
vyākyhayukti
rnam par bshad pa'i rigs pa
P5562, vol. 113; Toh. 4061, vol. shi

Treasury of Manifest Knowledge
abhidharmakośa
chos mngon pa'i mdzod
P5590, vol. 115
Sanskrit: Swami Dwarikadas Shastri. *Abhidharmakośa and Bhāṣya of Ācārya Vasubandhu with Sphuṭārtha Commentary of Ācārya Yaśomitra.* Bauddha Bharati Series, 5. Banaras: Bauddha Bharati, 1970. Also: P. Pradhan. *Abhidharmakośabhāṣyam of Vasubandhu.* Patna, India: Jayaswal Research Institute, 1975.
French translation: Louis de La Vallée Poussin. *L'Abhidharmakośa de Vasubandhu.* 6 vols. Brussels: Institut Belge des Hautes Études Chinoises, 1971.
English translation of the French: Leo M. Pruden. *Abhidharmakośabhāṣyam.* 4 vols. Berkeley, Calif.: Asian Humanities Press, 1988.

Ye-shay-day (*ye shes sde,* fl. c. 800)
Distinctions in the Views
lta ba'i khyad par
P5847; Toh. 4360

3. Other Works

Apte, Vaman Shivaram. *Sanskrit-English Dictionary.* Poona, India: Prasad Prakashan, 1957.

Das, Sarat Chandra. *A Tibetan-English Dictionary.* Calcutta: 1902; reprint, Delhi: Motilal Banarsidass, 1969, 1970; compact reprint, Kyoto, Japan: Rinsen Book Company, 1981.

Edgerton, Franklin. *Buddhist Hybrid Sanskrit Grammar and Dictionary.* New Haven: Yale University Press, 1953; reprint, Delhi: Motilal, 1972.

H.H. the Dalai Lama. *How to Practice: The Way to a Meaningful Life.* Edited and translated by Jeffrey Hopkins. New York: Pocket Books, 2002.

———. *How to See Yourself As You Really Are.* Edited and translated by Jeffrey Hopkins. New York: Atria Books, 2006.

Hopkins, Jeffrey. "A Tibetan Delineation of Different Views of Emptiness in the Indian Middle Way School: Dzong-ka-ba's Two Interpretations of the *Locus Classicus* in Chandrakīrti's *Clear Words* Showing Bhāvaviveka's Assertion of Commonly Appearing Subjects and Inherent Existence." *Tibet Journal* 14, no. 1 (1989): 10-43.

———. *Absorption In No External World: 170 Issues in Mind-Only Buddhism. Dynamic Responses to Dzong-ka-ba's* The Essence of Eloquence, Volume 3. Ithaca, N.Y.: Snow Lion Publications, 2005.

———. *Cultivating Compassion.* New York: Broadway Books, 2001.

———. *Emptiness in the Mind-Only School of Buddhism. Dynamic Responses to Dzong-ka-ba's* The Essence of Eloquence, Volume 1. Berkeley: University of California Press, 1999.

———. *Emptiness Yoga.* Ithaca, N.Y.: Snow Lion Publications, 1987.

———. *Maps of the Profound: Jam-yang-shay-ba's Great Exposition of Buddhist and Non-Buddhist Views on the Nature of Reality.* Ithaca, N.Y.: Snow Lion Publications, 2003.

———. *Meditation on Emptiness.* London: Wisdom Publications, 1983; rev. ed., Boston, Ma.: Wisdom Publications, 1996.

———. *Reflections on Reality: The Three Natures and Non-Natures in the Mind-Only School. Dynamic Responses to Dzong-ka-ba's* The Essence of Eloquence, Volume 2. Berkeley: University of California Press, 2002.

Van der Kuijp, Leonard W. J. "Apropos of a Recent Contribution to the History of Central Way Philosophy in Tibet: *Tsong Khapa's Speech of Gold.*" *Berliner Indologische Studien* 1 (1985): 47-74.

Lodrö, Gedün. *Calm Abiding and Special Insight.* Edited and translated by Jeffrey Hopkins. Ithaca, N.Y.: Snow Lion Publications, 1998.

Lopez, Donald S. Jr. *The Heart Sūtra Explained.* Albany, N.Y.: State University of New York Press, 1988.

Mimaki, Katsumi. *Blo gsal grub mtha'.* Kyoto: Université de Kyoto, 1982.

———. "The *Blo gsal grub mtha'*, and the Mādhyamika Classification in Tibetan *grub mtha'* Literature." In *Contributions on Tibetan and Buddhist Religion and Philosophy,* edited by Ernst Steinkellner and Helmut Tauscher, 161-167. Vienna: Arbeitskreis für tibetische und buddhistische Studien, 1983.

Napper, Elizabeth. *Dependent-Arising and Emptiness.* London: Wisdom Publications, 1989.

Newland, Guy. *The Two Truths.* Ithaca, N.Y.: Snow Lion Publications, 1992.

Ruegg, David Seyfort. *The Literature of the Madhyamaka School of Philosophy in India.* Wiesbaden: Otto Harrasowitz, 1981.

della Santina, Peter. *Madhyamaka Schools in India.* Delhi: Motilal Banarsidass, 1986.

Sopa, Geshe Lhundup and Jeffrey Hopkins. *Cutting Through Appearances: The Practice and Theory of Tibetan Buddhism.* Ithaca, N.Y.: Snow Lion Publications, 1989.

Stearns, Cyrus R. *The Buddha from Dol po: A Study of the Life and Thought of the Tibetan Master Dolpopa Sherab Gyaltsen.* Albany, N.Y.: State University of New York Press, 1999.

Yotsuya, Kodo. *The Critique of Svatantra Reasoning by Candrakīrti and Tsong-kha-pa: A Study of Philosophical Proof According to Two Prāsaṅgika Madhyamaka Traditions of India and Tibet.* Tibetan and Indo-Tibetan Studies, 8. Stuttgart: Franz Steiner Verlag, 1999.

Index